MW00573908

# HENRI DE LUBAC AND THE SHAPING OF MODERN THEOLOGY

# Henri de Lubac and the Shaping of Modern Theology

*A Reader*

EDITED BY
DAVID GRUMETT

IGNATIUS PRESS SAN FRANCISCO

Except in previously published excerpts, Scripture quotations are from Revised Standard Version of the Bible—Second Catholic Edition (Ignatius Edition) copyright © 2006 National Council of the Churches of Christ in the United States of America. All rights reserved worldwide.

Except in texts quoted from other sources or unless otherwise indicated, translations of Vatican and papal documents have been taken from the Vatican website.

All excerpted texts used with the express permission of the copyright holders.

Cover design by Riz Boncan Marsella

© 2020 by Ignatius Press, San Francisco
All rights reserved
ISBN 978-1-62164-342-5
Library of Congress Control Number 2019947849
Printed in the United States of America ∞

# Contents

# Introduction

Henri de Lubac was born into a Roman Catholic family in 1896, in the industrial town of Cambrai in the far northeast of France. His father, Maurice, who was a bank official, and his mother, Gabrielle, had six children, of whom he was the third. During the First World War, Henri fought with the French army in the trenches, rising to the rank of sub-lieutenant. However, because the religious orders had been banned from teaching in France by the state authorities, he undertook most of his Jesuit formation in exile on Jersey, one of the Channel Islands, and at Hastings, on the south coast of England, relocating to the Jesuit scholasticate at Fourvière in Lyon in 1926, when it reopened. In Lyon, he later had a key role in launching the *Sources chrétiennes* series of patristic and early medieval theological texts. Then, during the Second World War, he contributed to the city's spiritual witness against Nazism. During the 1950s, he was prohibited by the Church authorities from publishing theology, being regarded as too liberal by the conservative standards of his superiors. Nevertheless, close to the decade's end, he was rehabilitated, and his theology informed several of the decrees of the Second Vatican Council (1962–1965), which he served as a theological expert. In 1983, he was made a cardinal, although due to age was excused episcopal consecration. De Lubac's theology was rooted in an exceptionally long and varied life during which he directly experienced multiple upheavals in Church life and secular politics, culminating in the fall of communism in Eastern Europe, before his death in 1991.

## The Method of *Ressourcement*

De Lubac was a leading proponent of *ressourcement*. This approach to theology aimed to re-source, and thereby to revivify, theology by recovering forgotten and underused sources from the patristic and early medieval Christian periods and deploying them in constructive theology. In France, interest in these sources was nothing new. During the middle third of the nineteenth century, the Abbé Jacques-Paul Migne had, in collaboration with the later Jean-Baptiste-François Cardinal Pitra, employed 300 people to produce collections including the massive *Patrologia Latina* (1844–1855), which comprised 217 volumes, and the *Patrologia Graeca* (1857–1866), which contained 166 volumes. These sold well and augmented the learning of the new generation of post-Revolutionary clergy, and de Lubac used them extensively in his own research.[1]

As a commercial enterprise, Migne and Pitra's project was impressive. Nevertheless, their editions, produced at speed, lacked any critical apparatus and did not include a French translation. Moreover, it seemed to de Lubac and other Jesuits that the systematized neo-Thomist Scholasticism that was the norm within Roman Catholic seminaries—often with a Suárezian inflection in Jesuit philosophates—had failed to assimilate the variety of theological sources that were by then available. This was both a matter of content and a question of expository style. The textbook mode of teaching presented a unified, coherent position on a topic, rather than acknowledging the validity of competing historical perspectives. When historical sources were directly engaged, they tended to be treated either as proof texts or as erroneous. Also, Latin sources such as Ambrose, Augustine, and Jerome, tended to be preferred to Greek sources, not least because Latin was the language of the Roman Catholic Church.

During the late nineteenth century, Modernism had emerged in France as an alternative to Scholasticism. Its leading figure was Alfred Loisy (1857–1940), with other names including Joseph Turmel (1859–1943), Marcel Hébert (1851–1916), and Prosper Al-

[1] David Grumett, "The Concordat Era in France: From Jansenism to Neo-Thomism", in *The Oxford Handbook to the Reception History of Christian Theology*, ed. Sarah Coakley and Richard Cross (Oxford: Oxford University Press, forthcoming).

faric (1876–1955), as well as, at the movement's margins, Lucien Laberthonnière (1860–1932) and Édouard Le Roy (1870–1954).[2] Several marks of Modernism may be identified, even if not all of these were actively promoted by all of the figures just listed. Modernists embraced biblical criticism, which called into question the literal historicity of some of the events recorded in Scripture. They contested the suppositions that doctrine could be directly extracted from Scripture and that the institutional Church had been founded by Christ. They accepted the philosophical and cognitive approach to religion associated with Immanuel Kant (1724–1804). Modernism was vigorously suppressed by Pope Pius X (in office 1903–1914) in his 1907 encyclical *Pascendi dominici gregis* as well as by means of his anti-Modernist oath, to which all clergy were required to subscribe from 1910 until 1967.

Despite his dislike of the Scholastic method, de Lubac was skeptical that Modernist theology would be sufficiently substantive for the formation of clergy, for building up the Church, or for combatting secularism. He rightly saw the necessity of combining the constructive doctrinal project of Scholasticism with the attention to sources that was characteristic of Modernism. This task assumed added urgency because, during the first half of the twentieth century, there was no recent council with a coherent body of work to which reference could be made. The First Vatican Council (1869–1870) had promulgated just two constitutions and was suspended after less than a year, following the annexation of Rome by the Kingdom of Italy, with most of its projected work never finished. Reconvening in another location was considered but did not happen. The last council that had concluded its business had been convoked as many as four centuries earlier at Trent (1545–1563). As will be seen in the course of this introduction, de Lubac had tremendous respect for the historic teaching of councils and the Magisterium, and his ecclesiology and his doctrine of the supernatural were each given impetus by it. Nevertheless, to promote Church engagement with historical theological sources, he needed to look beyond formal documents and teaching.

[2] Alec Vidler, *A Variety of Catholic Modernists* (Cambridge: Cambridge University Press, 1970).

Patristic and medieval sources permeate de Lubac's oeuvre. However, in addition to his own constructive theology, de Lubac made a major contribution to *ressourcement* by founding and editing, with the later Cardinal Jean Daniélou (1905–1974), the *Sources chrétiennes*.[3] This project was conceived by Victor Fontoynont, the prefect of the Jesuit scholasticate at Fourvière in Lyon, with a view to developing ecumenical links with the Orthodox Churches by disseminating Greek texts among Roman Catholics. During the 1940s, relations between the two Churches were hostile: the historic mutual excommunications of 1054 would not be revoked until 1965, and any ecumenical gatherings that took place were few and in secret. For the *Sources*, a parallel text format was quickly established, with the Greek or Latin original on the left-hand page facing a French translation on the right-hand page. Their other key feature was an extended critical introduction, which situated the text in its wider setting. Early volumes included Gregory of Nyssa's *Life of Moses*, Clement of Alexandria's *Exhortation to the Heathen*, Nicholas Cabasilas' *Commentary on the Divine Liturgy*, and Origen's *Homilies on Genesis*. The collection now runs to six hundred volumes.

In summary, de Lubac's theology was motivated by several concerns. He wished to make the Christian theological heritage more widely available. He hoped to nurture ecumenical links between the Roman Catholic and Orthodox Churches in an era when these were virtually nonexistent. He also had the apologetic aim of articulating the Christian faith in a way that was entirely faithful to theological tradition but that addressed people in their modern secular context.

## Overview of de Lubac's Work

De Lubac's oeuvre was voluminous, encompassing theological anthropology, doctrine, ecclesiology, fundamental theology, eucharistic theology, scriptural exegesis, and religion. In this book, only a small portion may be presented. Priority is given to those texts that contribute an understanding of the method and content of de

[3] David Grumett, "Henri de Lubac", in *Theologies of Retrieval: An Exploration and Appraisal*, ed. Darren Sarisky (London: T&T Clark, 2017), 135–52.

Lubac's constructive Christian theology. The texts are presented in the order adopted by his French publisher, Cerf, which is in the process of publishing his complete works in a single series. This ordering was established by the Italian publisher Jaca for its translation of de Lubac's complete works, which commenced during his lifetime and about which he was consulted, and is theologically significant.[4]

For de Lubac, the starting point for constructive theology is the human before God. Because people are created by God, their minds are naturally oriented to God. Although they often fail to recognize God, due to the weakness of their cognitive powers, which are misdirected by their sinful wills, an obscure spark remains within them that impels them to seek their creator. De Lubac views the human before God both individually and collectively, and he spent much time trying to understand how the atheist ideologies of Marxism and Nazism could arise and be accepted by so many millions of people across the historically Christian continent of Europe. His Christian view of mankind standing collectively before God brings him to doctrine: the historic credal formulations about the Christian faith as these have been defined, developed, and assented to through history. By giving doctrine this priority in his theology, de Lubac sets clear boundaries to what he regards as Christian. He nevertheless draws these boundaries widely, positively appraising a figure such as Origen (184/185–253/254), who has often been wrongly regarded as a heretic. De Lubac's considerations of man before God, and of basic Christian doctrine, lead him to the theology of the Church. Being the collective body of believers in Christ, the Church is, for him, the social reality of shared Christian belief that has continued from the New Testament to the present day. In order to be truly social and concretely expressed, this reality requires order and institutions. De Lubac does not believe that the Roman Catholic Church is perfect. Nevertheless, he justly recognizes the Church's tremendous significance as the universal yet concrete manifestation of belief in Christ in the world. Bishops, for de Lubac, serve and

---

[4] Henri de Lubac, *Oeuvres complètes*, 50 vols. (Paris: Cerf, 1999–); de Lubac, *Opera Omnia*, 32 vols. (Milan: Jaca, 1975–2009); de Lubac, *At the Service of the Church: Henri de Lubac Reflects on the Circumstances that Occasioned His Writings*, trans. Anne Elizabeth Englund (San Francisco: Ignatius Press, 1993), 157.

preserve the universality of local churches, performing this essential function more effectively and personally than conferences or committees.

The next topic in de Lubac's collected works is the supernatural, which concerns the relation between grace and nature. He contests the interpretation of Augustine (354–430), which had been developed by the Jansenists of the 1640s, that men, because of their corruption by the sin of Adam, are incapable of freely willing any good action. Against this, he recovers an Augustinian theology of created grace, which alone makes possible all good actions. In so doing, he calls into question Scholastic readings of Thomas Aquinas (1225–1274), which, under the influence of Aristotle (385–323 B.C.), posit a class of human actions that are naturally good without grace. In particular, de Lubac sees the idea of "pure nature" as leaving an ungraced territory open to occupation by modern secularism, which is not merely neutral with regard to the Christian faith but actively hostile to it. In his works on the Eucharist and on Scripture, de Lubac continues to address the theme of how the spiritual and the natural are related. He presents the Eucharist as Christ's spiritual and mystical body that sustains his real body, the Church, questioning the view, which originated in the thirteenth century, that the Church is a mystical institution sustained by sacred political power. In his studies of scriptural exegesis, de Lubac holds in balance the literal sense and the spiritual sense, distinguishing within the latter allegorical, moral, and eschatological senses and contending that none of these senses is ultimately in competition with any other. He draws on a rich tradition of interpretation extending back to patristic writers in which Scripture's literal sense, which recounts historical events and other narratives, receives close attention. Some portions of Scripture, such as the Passion narratives and the Pauline letters, refer to Christ directly. Others, such as the Old Testament and the Lukan parables, make indirect reference to Christ by presenting histories or stories that may be interpreted by means of typology. In any case, Christ is the abridged word of the whole of Scripture, being both its subject and the key that unlocks its meaning.

De Lubac's theological interests extend beyond Christianity. In his studies of the Church and of Scripture, he inevitably engages historic Judaism. However, from the early 1930s, he lectured in Lyon on the wider history of religions. He returned to these interests in the 1950s, when he developed a deep interest in Pure Land Buddhism, which is the dominant Buddhist school in Japan. For de Lubac, the study of religions is valuable because it demonstrates that, across many cultures and time periods, people have been naturally disposed to monotheism. He chose to focus on Pure Land Buddhism rather than on Zen, which is better known in the West, because he viewed it as having greater affinity with Christian belief in general and with Roman Catholicism in particular. Points of convergence between Pure Land Buddhism and Roman Catholicism include the divine personhood of Amida Buddha and of Jesus Christ. Moreover, in the True Pure Land (Shin) school, belief in a heavenly place and reliance for liberation on the "other power" of Amida Buddha's infinite compassion may be viewed as corresponding with Christian understandings of heaven and of grace.

In addition to these elements of his constructive theology, de Lubac produced studies of three individual figures. The first was his Jesuit confrère, the controversial philosophical theologian and paleontologist Pierre Teilhard de Chardin (1881–1955). The other two figures were historical, and his works on them remain untranslated. The first is on the spiritual Franciscan Joachim of Flora (ca. 1132–1202), whose theology of history and personal belief was that he was living in an eschatological third age of the Spirit, prefiguring modern views of history as linear and developmental. The second figure is Giovanni Pico della Mirandola (1463–1494), the Renaissance humanist and defender of Origen.

There now follows a detailed overview of the contours of de Lubac's theology in sections corresponding to those in which the source texts are arranged.

## Man before God

Following the French Revolution, it was widely assumed that reason had dethroned faith and provided the only reliable source of knowledge. The stridently secularist philosophy of French universities in the early twentieth century reflected this assumption. The vitalism of the Jewish philosopher Henri Bergson (1859–1941) was exciting the more open-minded, replacing the traditional static categories with a new alliance of thought and morality, with movement and change. But Bergsonian philosophy was immanentist, locating the source of reason's dynamism wholly within nature. It reflected the spiritualism of the era, conceiving the spiritual as a function of nature.

Although Bergson's ideas seemed radical to many, they were really another iteration of philosophical secularism. De Lubac was inspired by a very different philosophy, which informed his project just as much as the retrieval of historic theological texts. In his 1893 study of action, Bergson's contemporary Maurice Blondel (1861–1949) had argued that, although willing and motivation are properly understood philosophically, they are not purely natural in either their origin or their end. Rather, philosophy exposes the incommensurability of what I will in my actions and the real object of my willing. The latter always exceeds the object of an action and is satisfied only by an absolute spiritual principle. Even an ordinary, everyday action is situated within a far larger context of motivation and purpose whose final end is God. For Blondel, every person is continually confronted with the "option" either to embrace or to deny this higher meaning and value. Every person is continually faced with the divine and has the option of responding yes or no.

De Lubac's response is yes. When using reason to reflect inwardly on their existence and motivations, rather than to construct deductive arguments for or against particular doctrinal or moral positions, people are brought to recognize a power working within them that is not itself a part of them. De Lubac draws on a rich tradition of patristic and medieval thought in which faith is proven by the reflective use of reason. Many different names may be given to this commerce of faith and reason: encounter, contact, apperception, illumination, vision, or hearing. The common point, however, is that faith and reason each play a role in the discovery of truth, even if one or the other assumes a greater importance in particular cases. De Lubac writes: "The idea of the one God springs up spontaneously at the heart of consciousness, whether as a result of the exigencies of reason or of some supernatural illumination, and imposes itself upon the mind of itself, of its own necessity."[5]

This understanding of faith as assent to a single, absolute truth indicates that de Lubac identifies religion with monotheism. However, he acknowledges that this category encompasses a range of faith manifestations that are not limited to Christianity, Judaism, and Islam. In a lecture course first delivered in 1935, de Lubac embraces the "primitive monotheism" thesis of the Roman Catholic priest and ethnographer Wilhelm Schmidt (1868–1954). He accepts that a variety of native peoples exhibit a "few flashes of the belief in a clearly superior Being".[6] This applies, he argues, even to those lacking what have commonly been regarded as prerequisites for religious belief, such as figurative art for religious representation and settled agriculture to supply a sacrificial system. Examples of how this belief might be revealed include intentional burial practices and creation myths. However, de Lubac sharply distinguishes a "monotheism of accommodation" from an "exclusivist monotheism".[7] Gods may be formed in the image of earthly realities, such as by an imperial or social religion grounded in secular reason. However, in such cases, the result is either an abstract deity or a divinized nature, often accompanied by an acceptance of polytheism. An exclusivist monotheism, in contrast, admits no such limitation to divine power or the possibility of competing sources of divine power, positing a unique and transcendent being who is nevertheless all-powerful in the world. It must be to this kind of deity, de Lubac argues, that any true assent of faith is made.

De Lubac contests two views of the faith–reason relation that are opposed to his own. The first competing view is atheistic, and he regards the use of reason to rebut faith claims as the great spiritual crisis of modern times. Yet in so doing, he realizes that it is no

---

[5] Henri de Lubac, *The Discovery of God*, trans. Alexander Dru with Marc Sebanc and Cassian Fulsom (Edinburgh: T&T Clark, 1996), 32.

[6] Henri de Lubac, *Theological Fragments*, trans. Rebecca Howell Balinski (San Francisco: Ignatius Press, 1989), 309–32 (322).

[7] De Lubac, *Discovery*, 26–29. For further discussion, David Grumett, "On Religion", in *T&T Clark Companion to Henri de Lubac*, ed. Jordan Hillebert (London: T&T Clark, 2017), 247–68.

longer sufficient for Christians to establish and defend their own position. They now need to take the intellectual argument to the opposition, demonstrating its internal inconsistencies, and to fashion the spirit of the new generation in such a way that they will resist falling back into a liberalism and democracy that may again succumb to fascist corruption. What is needed in politics, he believes, is a post-liberal communitarian personalism that reconnects with the nation's Christian roots. De Lubac began this work during the Second World War, giving addresses to groups in venues such as the Uriage Officer School, which sought to form a new generation of postwar leaders.[8] His principal objective was to combat atheism.

In *The Drama of Atheist Humanism*, de Lubac pursues this project, engaging Auguste Comte (1798–1857), Ludwig Feuerbach (1804–1872), Pierre-Joseph Proudhon (1809–1865), Karl Marx (1818–1883), and Friedrich Nietzsche (1844–1900). His strategy is to argue that, despite their protestations to the contrary, atheists implicitly and unavoidably affirm theistic claims, albeit in a corrupted form, whenever attempting to refute theism. Comte believed that theology had been inevitably displaced by rational positivism, in which reason was worshipped as an idol and the human collectivity was exalted as a Great Being, yet also thought that not everyone could be assimilated into this religion of humanity.[9] Feuerbach treated God as merely a myth expressing the aspirations of alienated human consciousness and as the sum of the attributes of human greatness, yet, in so doing, remained in thrall to the ancient spiritual commandment to "know yourself."[10] Proudhon affirmed the existence of human conscience and its demand for justice, although by refusing that its inwardness and immanence imply "in the final reckoning, the active presence of a transcendent being" failed to escape

---

[8] Bernard Comte, *Une utopie combattante: l'École des cadres d'Uriage: 1940–1942* (Paris: Fayard, 1991), 188–89, 237. For an account in English: John Hellman, *The Knight-Monks of Vichy France: Uriage, 1940–1945*, 2nd ed. (Liverpool: Liverpool University Press, 1997), although the school's radical agenda is not here articulated.

[9] Henri de Lubac, *The Drama of Atheist Humanism*, trans. Edith Riley, Anne Englund Nash, and Mark Sebanc (San Francisco: Ignatius Press, 1995), 131–267.

[10] Ibid., 26–33.

theism.[11] Marx claimed that religion was the delusion of materially alienated humanity, yet his view of history as developing toward a social utopia was indebted to Christian conceptions of providence and liberation.[12] Nietzsche, while raging against what he saw as the Christian herd mentality and its pathology of weakness, which he believed had brought about the death of God, remained captivated by the power of Christian mysticism and haunted by the person of Christ, even as he strove to surpass him.[13] Despite what atheists may claim, de Lubac contends, these examples cumulatively suggest that there is no secular reason capable of conclusively rebutting faith claims.

Neither, however, may reason be deployed to establish the fundamentals of belief unaided by faith. Yet Neo-Scholasticism, which had been ascendant in France since the 1850s, appeared to be founded on just this supposition and embodied the second view of the faith–reason relation that de Lubac calls into question. The Neo-Scholastic method was grounded in a view of humans as primarily rational creatures with the capacity to gain knowledge by the autonomous exercise of their own rational powers. This knowledge includes not only the causes and essences of ordinary things in the world, but extends to their first cause and final end. From 1920 to 1923, while de Lubac was a student at the Jesuit philosophate on the island of Jersey, he had been instructed by the Suárezian Neo-Scholastic theologian Pedro Descoqs (1877–1946). He regarded the propositional approach of this "modern" and "new" theology, which was taught using textbooks, as arid and hubristic.[14] In reaction, he cautions: "Our intelligence does not grasp the Absolute . . . without first of all having been grasped by it."[15] God is the uncreated light shining

[11] Henri de Lubac, *The Un-Marxian Socialist: A Study of Proudhon*, trans. R. E. Scantlebury (London: Sheed & Ward, 1948), 258.

[12] De Lubac, *Drama*, 36–42, 431–43.

[13] Ibid., 42–58, 73–95, 114–22, 469–509.

[14] In Henri de Lubac, *Augustinianism and Modern Theology*, trans. Lancelot Sheppard (New York: Crossroad, 2000), see 106, 115, 179, and 207 ("modern theology" and "modern theologians"), and 182 and 215 ("new theology"). In de Lubac, *The Mystery of the Supernatural*, trans. Rosemary Sheed with John M. Pepino (New York: Crossroad, 1998), see 37, 80, and 207 ("modern theologian" and "modern theology").

[15] De Lubac, *Discovery*, 134.

at the heart of human reason, illuminating the mind at a deep, preconceptual level. Yet de Lubac does not suggest that sources of theological authority such as Scripture, Church teaching, or tradition by themselves provide full knowledge of God. An act of faith is also required. De Lubac does not portray revelation, whether scriptural, ecclesial, or historical, as reigning victoriously over vanquished reason. Rather, every act of faith interior to every individual is prepared and completed by reason.

De Lubac's theological method is primarily affirmative. God, who is infinitely intelligible but also absolutely transcendent, permits to reason a degree of understanding of the divine mystery by penetrating reason and revealing this mystery. Nevertheless, de Lubac sees an important role for negative theology, because the light of truth radiating from God has, at the same time, the effect of obscuring the mystery.[16] This is not because of a distance between God and human beings, but because God is revealed precisely as incommensurable with human beings and as inapprehensible by them. Rejecting the notions that gaining knowledge of God is like amassing and coveting wealth or like gradually improving upon a sketch until the representation may be enjoyed in its fullness, de Lubac compares the mind with a swimmer, who "can only keep afloat by moving and who cleaves a new wave at each stroke. He is forever brushing aside the representations which are continually reforming, knowing full well that they support him, but that if he were to rest for a single moment he would sink and perish."[17] This image neatly illustrates how de Lubac sees affirmation and negation as two aspects of a single movement. Negative theology, of the kind that accumulates a multiplicity of negations, is based on the supposition that nothing can ultimately be known. However, negations are always relative to particular affirmations. An extreme negative theology is no more justified than the kind of Scholastic theology that supposes the possibility of the full comprehension of absolute truth. In contrast with both, de Lubac favors the language of a "theology of negation". This suggests a method of transcending any specific affirmation rather than of simply denying it, and,

---

[16] Ibid., 117–43.

[17] Ibid., 119.

with Pseudo-Dionysius, de Lubac describes that which is said of God with truth as being "subsequently denied with more truth".[18] Negation is thereby doubly positive, obliging affirmation but, in so doing, preventing unworthy representations.

For de Lubac, the faith–reason relation was more than an academic debate confined to seminaries. It was clearly evident in the rise and fall of the two political evils that overshadowed his adult life. Nazism, by discriminating against Jews and other minorities and then trying to annihilate them, denied the equal value of all people before God, which is grounded in the common reflective capacity by which they all bear the divine image. During the Second World War, the whole of France was under Nazi rule, whether by occupation in the northern zone or by governmental cooperation in the southern zone. At the end of the war, Communism became the reigning political ideology in Eastern Europe. By accepting Marx' dialectical materialism and a class analysis of society, its adherents conceived history to be driven by inevitable conflicts over the distribution of economic resources and sought to eradicate the cultural and spiritual expressions of human life, which, according to Marxist analysis, were at best superfluous and at worst harmful. In so doing, Communism denied any space to individual Christian faith.

In sharp contrast with each of these political ideologies, de Lubac's theological anthropology is founded on the conviction that the divine image is imprinted upon every person. For this reason, the natural revelation of God that reason brings is, in principle, sufficient grounding for Christian belief. De Lubac writes: "The divine image in the soul is at the center and principle of all rational activity."[19] Knowledge of the world leads to the affirmation of God, just as progressively unfolding self-knowledge by means of interior reflection leads the soul to recognize itself as an image of the divine. In practice, the positive revelation provided by Scripture and Church teaching are needed because the soul's natural knowledge is impaired by sin. Nevertheless, de Lubac insists, sin does not entirely destroy the possibility of natural revelation. Neither does it

---

[18] Ibid., 124.

[19] Ibid., 13; also de Lubac, *Mystery*, 104–5. See Gen 1:26–27, 9:6; Rom 8:29, 1 Cor 15:49, Col 3:10.

strip any person or group of persons of their dignity before God or of their entitlement to the social and political recognition and protection of this dignity.

In Christian theology, the notion that people bear the divine image has frequently been associated with a bipartite and even oppositional theological anthropology, such as the Pauline distinction between flesh and spirit. When related to such an anthropology, the divine image is frequently identified with the spirit. However, de Lubac promotes a tripartite anthropology, inspired also by Paul. In his bold prayer for the Thessalonians that concludes his first letter to them, the apostle asks that their "spirit [*pneuma*] and soul [*psyche*] and body [*soma*] be kept sound and blameless at the coming of our Lord Jesus Christ."[20] This triadic language is echoed in the words spoken by God to Moses on Mount Sinai: "Love the Lord your God with all your heart, and with all your soul, and with all your might."[21] De Lubac understands the spirit, soul, and body, not as three separate faculties. but trinitarianly, with the soul identified with the Father, the body with the incarnate Son, and the spirit with the Holy Spirit.[22] This is not, however, simply a matter of analogical correspondence. The Spirit unifies the three related aspects of the single person and thereby becomes, in them, the principle of a higher life. Breathed into Adam at his creation and bestowed anew at Pentecost, this Spirit is both of humanity and of Christ. Because people are created to share God's existence, their lives are not purely natural. Nonetheless, they are called to a moral life, with their spiritual contemplation grounded in corporeal activity.

It was his deep conviction about universal human dignity that motivated de Lubac's resistance to the Nazi persecution of Jews. In June 1940, France and Germany had signed an armistice. However, by the following spring, it had become clear to him that Roman Catholic Church leaders in France had been seduced and corrupted by Nazism and were failing to bear witness against it. Since

---

[20] 1 Thess 5:23.

[21] Deut 6:5.

[22] Henri de Lubac, *Theology in History*, trans. Anne Englund Nash (San Francisco: Ignatius Press, 1996), 117–200 (146).

the French Revolution, the Roman Catholic Church in France had been understandably more concerned to defend its own interests in an uncompromisingly secular state than to defend the political rights of any other religious group. This approach had brought some success, as in September 1940 the new Vichy government had passed a law that once again formally permitted the religious orders to teach. This encouraged the acquiescence of many of their members in the growing persecution. In a lengthy letter to his superiors of April 25, 1941, de Lubac presented his concerns. Opening by identifying the war being prosecuted by Nazi Germany as in essence an anti-Christian revolution, he reminds them that Germany had already experienced eight years of religious persecution and that ecclesial acquiescence in this had benefitted no one.[23] Citing Pope Pius XI (in office 1922–1939), as well as the German and Austrian bishops, de Lubac enumerates the closure of religious schools, the dissolution of Roman Catholic associations, the suppression of the university theological faculties, the continued undermining of religious orders, and the silencing of the Roman Catholic press. Alongside these anti-Christian measures were concentration camps, a developing cult of the state, and the dissemination of anti-Semitic propaganda.

Many clergy were justifying their silence by claiming that the Church's proper concerns were spiritual and that "political Catholicism" was to be avoided. However, de Lubac saw that, because charity and justice had been undermined, the Christian faith was now itself under attack. Close to the end of his letter, he sums up his protest as follows:

> The anti-Semitism of today was unknown to our fathers; besides its degrading effect on those who abandon themselves to it, it is anti-Christian. It is against the Bible, against the Gospel as well as the Old Testament, against the universalism of the Church, against what is called the "Roman International"; it is against all that Pius XI, following Saint Paul, claimed as ours the day he cried out: "Spiritually we are Semites!" It is all the more important to be on guard, for this anti-Semitism is already gaining ground among the Catholic

[23] Ibid., 428–39.

> elite, even in our religious houses. There we have a danger that is only all too real.[24]

The natural solidarity that de Lubac identifies between Christians and Jews became an increasingly prominent strand of his theology. In the chapter on scriptural interpretation in *Catholicism*, which was first published in 1938, he already recognizes the profound indebtedness of Christianity to its Jewish heritage: patristic writers built upon the historical and social aspects of the Jewish religion, and numerous Old Testament figures and episodes may be identified with Christ and the Church.[25] Importantly, de Lubac stresses that the New Testament does not communicate a plenitude of spiritual truth that may be contrasted with an incomplete, legalistic, and literalist Old Testament faith. The New Testament is similarly lacking in the fullness of truth, pointing beyond itself to the mystery of Christ, which not even it can contain.

During the summer of 1941, the persecution of Jews increased, with a law enacted requiring them to register. This would later facilitate their identification, internment, and deportation. Immediately, de Lubac and three colleagues convened under the direction of Father Joseph Chaine to prepare a "Draft of a Declaration of the Catholic Theology Faculty of Lyon", which they intended would state, in unambiguous terms, their Faculty's opposition to the escalating persecution.[26] The text affirms that, in the context of French secularism, Roman Catholics are entitled to freedom from harassment on grounds of religion only if they defend this for other religions. Its key paragraph, which immediately follows, merits full quotation:

> The Church cannot forget that the Israelites are the descendants of the people who were the object of the divine election of which she is

[24] Ibid., 437–38. Pope Pius XI proclaimed "Spiritually we are Semites" to a group of Belgian pilgrims on September 6, 1938. His unscripted words were inspired by the reference in the Canon of the Mass to the sacrifices of Abel, Abraham, and Melchizedek.

[25] Henri de Lubac, *Catholicism: Christ and the Common Destiny of Man*, trans. Lancelot C. Sheppard and Sister Elizabeth Englund, O.C.D. (San Francisco: Ignatius Press, 1988), 165–216.

[26] Henri de Lubac, *Christian Resistance to Anti-Semitism: Memories from 1940–1944*, trans. Sister Elizabeth Englund, O.C.D. (San Francisco: Ignatius Press, 1990), 66–70.

> the culmination, of those people from whom Christ, our Savior, the Virgin Mary and the apostles sprang; that they have in common with us the books of the Old Testament, the inspired pages of which we read in our liturgy, the psalms from which we sing to praise God and to express our hope for his Kingdom; that, according to the words of Pius XI, we, like they, are sons of Abraham, the father of believers, and that the blessing promised to his descendants is still upon them, to call them to recognize in Jesus the Christ who was promised to them.[27]

This document, known as the "Chaine Declaration", had been conceived as a formal public statement of the Catholic Theological Faculty of Lyon. However, clandestine circulation was deemed the best mode of dissemination, being less likely to incriminate a publisher and possibly allowing a more extensive dissemination.[28] This provided a model for the underground *Cahiers* and *Courriers du Témoignage chrétien*. These popular journals enabled reliable information about Nazi domination and atrocities to be shared, exhorted citizens to resist this tyranny by whatever peaceful means they could, and provided accurate versions of papal pronouncements. Risking his life, de Lubac wrote for both the *Cahiers* and the *Courriers*, helped to edit them, and assisted in their distribution. His contributions included articles on: anti-Semitism and the Christian conscience; two pronouncements by Pope Pius XII; justice and the fight against evil; collaboration and the *service obligatoire du travail*; the scandal of truth; and the critique of Aryan "Christianity" in thrall to fascism.[29] De Lubac thereby made a leading contribution to disseminating reliable information about the Nazi genocide, and about French cooperation with it, and to exhorting the French people to spiritual resistance. On at least one occasion, he narrowly escaped arrest by the Gestapo, being tipped off about an imminent raid. Despite its increasingly determined efforts to destroy the journals' editorial and distribution networks, the Gestapo never decisively

---

[27] Ibid., 67–68.

[28] Ibid., 61, 71.

[29] *Résistance chrétienne au nazisme*, ed. Jacques Prévotat and Renée Bédarida (Paris: Cerf, 2006), 351–455. Under the *service obligatoire du travail* (compulsory work service), French students were required to spend two years in Germany in support of the Nazi war effort.

breached them, thanks to the courage and mutual trust of de Lubac and his colleagues.[30]

## The Christian Faith

From 1930, de Lubac held a professorship at the Catholic Theological Faculty in Lyon in fundamental theology. This is the theological subdiscipline concerned with understanding the relation between faith and reason and with the possibility and character of revelation. In the opening lecture of his course in fundamental theology, de Lubac presents it as a form of apologetics, in which the natural grounding and rationality of faith are established and the arguments of skeptics are refuted.[31] For de Lubac, fundamental theology is thereby an essential preparation for doctrinal theology. It predisposes minds to the truths of revelation and lends intellectual force and missionary vigor to the doctrinal enterprise.

Christian doctrine may be presented as a transcendent and self-consistent system that is arbitrarily determined by the "data" of divine revelation. This is a familiar feature of defensive apologetics, which seeks to prevent doctrine being undermined by secular thought and life. The Neo-Scholastic theology of the earlier decades of de Lubac's theological career was a prominent form of this. However, a method that is primarily concerned with propositional purity and consistency has the effect of isolating doctrine from other theological and intellectual disciplines, thereby marginalizing it within both the academy and the Church.

De Lubac's alternative proposal is that faith and reason together prepare space for doctrine, which complements and completes them. This does not mean that doctrine is nothing more than a function of human intellect or desire. On the contrary, in his doctrinal theology, de Lubac is passionately committed to engaging Scripture, the theological tradition, and Church teaching. He recognizes that doctrine is dramatic. It is impossible to imagine any

---

[30] The contributions of de Lubac, Pierre Chaillet, and other Roman Catholics to their city's spiritual resistance is commemorated in its Centre d'Histoire de la Résistance et de la Déportation (Center for the History of the Resistance and Deportation).

[31] De Lubac, *Theological Fragments*, 91–104.

bolder intellectual enterprise than the human quest to articulate and make public eternal truths that were first communicated in distant history in the spoken word and in written texts. In 1961, de Lubac produced the preface to a compilation of writings by the Roman Catholic convert and dramatist Paul Claudel (1868–1955), in which he quotes the latter's evocation of his response to hearing the chanted words of the Creed:

> When in my village church I hear the *Credo* being said, one article after the other, . . . it seems to me that I am witnessing the creation of the world. I know how much they have cost—each of its expressions, each of those printed statements of eternal truth. I know what convulsions, what wrenchings of heaven and earth, what torrents of blood, what efforts, what parturition of the intelligence and what effusions of grace were required for their emergence. I see those great dogmatic continents, one after the other, rise up and take shape before my eyes, and I see humanity in labor, finally succeeding in tearing from its heart the definitive expression.[32]

In quoting Claudel, de Lubac presents the development of Christian doctrine as painful and costly. He also locates doctrinal proclamation in the context of worship, thereby highlighting doctrine's intrinsically collective locus. This properly contrasts with the interplay of faith and reason, which, being concerned with assent to belief rather than with its content, occurs within the individual believer.

The traditional grammatical form of credal affirmation serves as an important reminder of the epistemological status of doctrine. In the Creed, Christians affirm their belief "in" God, Jesus Christ, and the Holy Spirit.[33] Despite an identical grammatical structure, this belief "in" is different from belief "in" a trusted friend or loved one, such as belief that he will succeed in a task or keep a promise. Each of these amounts to a prediction of the future rather than an

---

[32] Ibid., 428.

[33] Henri de Lubac, *The Splendor of the Church*, trans. Michael Mason (San Francisco: Ignatius Press, 1986), 32–38; de Lubac, *The Christian Faith: An Essay on the Structure of the Apostles' Creed*, trans. Richard Arnandez (San Francisco: Ignatius Press, 1986), 133–43.

affirmation that is true in the present. Belief "in" God is also different from belief "in" extra-terrestrial life, which is solely an existence claim. Although prediction and existence are both aspects of doctrinal affirmation, belief "in" God is predicated on the additional dimension of a relation between the knower and the object of knowledge that itself provides the possibility and content of the belief. For this reason, the Creed has traditionally been affirmed in the grammar of the singular first person. The words "I believe in" are deeply personal, being grounded in the recognition of their object and adherence to it, in which a bond of reciprocity is established.[34] However, doctrine is equally the publicly formulated statement of belief that has been preserved by the Church and handed down through many generations of Christians. This collective aspect is given every time the Creed is repeated by a Christian worshipping alongside others.

Being a theologian in a Church with a formal body of magisterial doctrinal teaching, de Lubac sees no need to undertake the exceedingly long and laborious task of constructing his own systematic theology. Such an enterprise would, for him, be based on a misunderstanding of doctrine as the product of individual human creativity, rather than as a shared possession that is communicated and received as a gift. Rather, de Lubac wishes to understand the implications of doctrine for ecclesiology and exegesis in his intellectual, social, political, and cultural contexts and to reflect on the implications that follow for Christian mission and witness. His doctrinal contributions will therefore be considered under other headings rather than brought together into a systematic whole. Nevertheless, a useful example of de Lubac's methodology is found in his discussion of salvation. This, he recognizes, tends to be viewed individualistically, as a belief in the "survival of the individual soul, its immediate reward, and . . . attaining the vision of the Divine Essence".[35] However, he continues, just as Christians on earth do not live in isolation, neither do the elect. Heaven is no mere aggregation of members admitted gradually, but a true unity that is received as such. Moreover, this unity is personal, rather than a composition of

[34] De Lubac, *Splendor*, 35–36; de Lubac, *Christian Faith*, 147–48.

[35] De Lubac, *Catholicism*, 112–33 (112).

individual persons in extrinsic relationship with each other. Salvation is social, and therefore the "salvation of the community" is the "condition of the salvation of the individual".[36] A powerful image of the general judgment, in which salvation is granted, is presented in Matthew's Gospel following the parable of the talents: just as, on returning from his long journey, the master judges all his servants at the same time, so the Son of Man comes in glory, sits upon his throne, and judges as one all the nations gathered before him.[37] De Lubac also links the doctrine of salvation with that of the resurrection: if blessedness is embodied, then it cannot be enjoyed before the general resurrection, which occurs only at the end of time, as suggested by Ezekiel's vision of the reviving of the dry bones and as graphically portrayed in the Book of Revelation.[38] Hence Bernard of Clairvaux, in a sermon for All Saints' Day, portrays the elect waiting in the antechamber of heaven, unable to gain admittance until the full number of the saved is assembled.[39] Even the saints, he insists, will not enter heaven without the people. In this way, de Lubac expounds the doctrine of salvation by calling into question received understandings, relating salvation to other doctrines, and engaging biblical and theological texts.

De Lubac's theology is profoundly christological. Jesus Christ is the final and complete accomplishment of both human redemption and divine revelation. Just as Christ is the body of the Church, so is Christ the sole and universal key of Scripture. De Lubac attaches great importance to the Trinity as comprising three Persons, emphasizing that it is through this tripersonality that the divine unity must be seen and resisting the replacement by Karl Barth (1886–1968) of the language of personhood with that of modes of being.[40] Nevertheless, he rebuts the notion that the work of Christ is added to by the work of the Spirit. He writes: "The Spirit of Christ enables us to penetrate into the depths of Christ, but he will

[36] Ibid., 120.

[37] Mt 25:14–33.

[38] Ezek 37:1–14; Rev 20:4–15.

[39] Bernard of Clairvaux, *Sermons for the Autumn Season*, trans. Irene M. Edmonds and Mark Scott (Collegeville, Minn.: Liturgical Press, 2016), 154–58 (154–55).

[40] De Lubac, *Christian Faith*, 81–83.

never lead us beyond him."[41] The relation between the Spirit and Christ is comparable to that between Christ and the Father. Just as Christ neither spoke nor acted on his own initiative, but was sent by the Father, so the Spirit does not act or speak of himself, but is sent by Christ to glorify him and to inspire and guide his followers. Rather, the Spirit continues and completes Christ's work by giving believers an understanding of Christ and sanctifying them. It would be entirely wrong, de Lubac contends in multiple places, to suppose that the Spirit reveals new truths to believers with no reference to the work of Christ or the Church. The Spirit was given to believers when Christ was glorified on the Cross, and on the day of Pentecost the Spirit completed the constitution of the Church.[42] There is no need whatsoever to be "set free" by the Spirit from the historic Church, still less from the work of Christ, and the Spirit has no desire to effect such separations. Rather, the Spirit baptizes believers into full ecclesial participation in Christ.

## The Church

In January 1959, the newly elected Pope John XXIII (in office 1958–1963) unexpectedly announced his intention to convene the Second Vatican Council in Rome. This decision had significant implications for de Lubac, who, since the late 1940s, had been out of official favor, for reasons that will be described in the next section. In August 1960, he was rehabilitated and assigned a place at the center of the council's planning, being appointed a consultor to its Preparatory Theological Commission. He subsequently became a theological expert at the council itself, attending the general congregations, which were held in Saint Peter's Basilica in the mornings, and spending the remainder of the day attending business meetings, lecturing, and meeting groups and individuals.[43] As is well known, during the council's first session, the assembled bishops rejected

[41] Ibid., 247–49 (248).

[42] De Lubac, *Splendor*, 206–8. See Mt 27:50; Lk 23:46; Acts 2:1–4.

[43] Jacques Prévotat, "Introduction", in Henri de Lubac, *Vatican Council Notebooks*, ed. Loïc Figoureux, trans. Andrew Stefanelli and Anne Englund Nash (San Francisco: Ignatius Press, 2015), 1:15–43 (30–43); Aaron Riches, "Henri de Lubac and the Second

much of the draft material received from the Preparatory Theological Commission, which was conservative in content and tone, citing, for example, anathemas issued by previous councils and popes. As a mere consultor, de Lubac had had no responsibility for this material. Among the rejected texts was the schema on revelation, which had proposed that Scripture and tradition constitute two distinct sources of divine truth. This suggested that tradition could legitimately develop, and command assent, independently of Scripture. In fact, in the documents that the council actually produced, Scripture and tradition are both extensively cited and frequently interwoven, as is also the case in de Lubac's own oeuvre.

During the council's first intersession, de Lubac was invited to join its Doctrinal Commission and to contribute to two new schemas, which ultimately became *Dei Verbum*, the Dogmatic Constitution on Divine Revelation, and *Lumen gentium*, the Dogmatic Constitution on the Church. De Lubac promoted these documents in conferences and lectures in the years following the council.[44] Moreover, in the summer of 1964, during the council's third intersession, he contributed to the commission's work of revising the hotly debated Schema 13, which would become *Gaudium et spes*, the Pastoral Constitution on the Church in the Modern World. His accomplished critique of atheism prepared him well for this task. The new secular locus for theological reflection and action, which the schema controversially adopted, had its roots in the spiritual resistance of many Church members and clergy to Nazism. Following the courageous examples of de Lubac and his confreres in Lyon, and of many others throughout France, Christians had accepted their new calling to defend the spiritual and political rights of others by means of the laity and the clergy working together.[45] Under Nazi tyranny, the people had truly to be the Church if the Church were to contribute any effective opposition.

Earlier roots for the council's theology may also be found in the social and cultural transformation brought about by the First

---

Vatican Council", in *T&T Clark Companion to Henri de Lubac*, ed. Jordan Hillebert (London: T&T Clark, 2017), 121–56.

[44] Henri De Lubac, *The Church: Paradox and Mystery*, trans. James R. Dunne (New York: Alba, 1969).

[45] De Lubac, *Christian Resistance*.

World War. The upbringing of many clergy and members of religious orders, including the Jesuits, had been pious, rural, and relatively privileged. However, in France as in many other European states, the clergy and members of religious orders were not exempted from military conscription. The war therefore created a social, cultural, and religious melting pot into which de Lubac and countless other young seminarians and novices were plunged. This radically changed their theological concerns and their expectations about how the Church should relate to society.

The opening words of *Gaudium et spes*, which was promulgated by the new Pope Paul VI (in office 1963–1978) at the close of the council, proclaim: "The joys and the hopes, the griefs and the anxieties of the men of this age, especially those who are poor or in any way afflicted, these are the joys and hopes, the griefs and anxieties of the followers of Christ."[46] Themes of de Lubac's that are identifiable in the document include human dignity, creation in God's image, and intellectual sharing in the light of the divine mind.[47] Atheism is also interrogated at length, being understood as a failure of the inward call of conscience as well as a social phenomenon that the Church is called to contest.[48] De Lubac's willingness to engage the secular mind-sets of late modern culture, which was basic to his fundamental theology, became a key component of the council's methodology. The bishops gathered in Rome recognized that it was no longer sufficient to present sacred truths in timeless isolation from their current context. Rather, doctrines needed to be articulated anew and related to modern secular reality through critical engagement with that reality. This missionary agenda was pursued beyond the lifetime of the council by the new Secretariat for Non-Believers, which was founded in 1965 with de Lubac as a member and later became part of the Pontifical Council for Culture.

De Lubac's early works on the Church are *Corpus Mysticum* and *Catholicism*, which were first published in French during the 1940s.

---

[46] Second Vatican Council, Pastoral Constitution on the Church in the Modern World *Gaudium et spes*, December 7, 1965 (hereafter abbreviated as *GS*).

[47] *GS* 12, 15.

[48] *GS* 19–21.

In these, his methodology is largely textual and historical, and although implications for practice follow, they are not the principal object of these studies. Rather, de Lubac wishes to deepen the ecclesiology of his day. In *The Splendor of the Church*, which was first published in 1953 as *Méditation sur l'Eglise* [Meditation on the Church], he engages practical issues somewhat more directly. However, the council, and the events that surrounded and followed it, precipitated ongoing closer reflection, which was sometimes pointed, on concrete issues of Church polity. These works include *The Motherhood of the Church*, *Particular Churches in the Universal Church*, and *A Brief Catechesis on Nature and Grace*.

The council's heritage has been passionately debated by both defenders and detractors. For his part, de Lubac was concerned that, even while the council was still in session, what he termed a "para-council" was in progress around its fringes. The agenda of this second "council" was, he contends, the dismantling of much of historic Roman Catholic doctrine and tradition in favor of a broadly secular humanism. De Lubac's alarm was fueled by the social upheavals that were brewing as the council concluded. During May 1968, he saw Parisian students and striking factory workers occupy buildings and blockade streets, agitating for a new and destructive secular politics. This and the spread of civil unrest to other European countries instilled in him a new caution, and from this point onward he placed greater emphasis on the need to preserve for the future the doctrines and traditions that had been transmitted through previous generations.[49]

De Lubac and the many others who wished to promote the council's true agenda had to tread a difficult path. *Gaudium et spes* had aligned the Church with the aspirations and sufferings of the modern secular world, but its compilers had not expected that, less than three years after its promulgation, many people who embodied that world's joys and hopes would be fighting pitched battles with police and soldiers on the streets of major world capitals. While contesting liberal readings of *Gaudium et spes*, de Lubac remained assured of the truth of the basic intuition that, because there could be no

[49] Henri de Lubac, *More Paradoxes*, trans. Anne Englund Nash (San Francisco: Ignatius Press, 2002), 97–98.

autonomous secular sphere, the Church needed to engage vigorously with the modern world and speak directly to it.

Nevertheless, misunderstandings about de Lubac's intention may arise among interpreters of the council when the sacred is over-identified with the Church and the secular is over-identified with society. Despite his deep concern with ecclesiology, which he delineates in sometimes poetically arresting terms, de Lubac is no proponent of an ecclesiastical triumphalism. On the contrary, he discusses at length how this was the error of the so-called "political Augustinianism" of medieval theologians like Giles of Rome (ca. 1243–1316): to equate the Church exclusively with a heavenly city of God and society exclusively with an earthly city of political power, which, being such, needs to be subjected to the spiritual power of the Church. Opposing this distorted reading of Augustine, de Lubac pictures the heavenly and the earthly cities, not as discrete institutions, but as distinct principles. Both, he avers, are "*mystical* societies, as secretly intermixed in history as they are adverse in principle".[50] The state does not need the Church to grant it legitimacy. Rather, the state possesses its own secular legitimacy, just as the Church has her proper spiritual legitimacy. Neither requires endorsement by the other. Rather, each is part of God's plan for ordering the world.

Indeed, in a broad historical perspective, the origins of secularization may be traced to occasions when the Church assumes too much earthly authority, rather than to instances when the state, on its own initiative, seeks to disempower the Church. De Lubac regarded the work of Marsilius of Padua (ca. 1275–ca. 1342), the apologist for the Holy Roman Empire who argued that secular political power was founded independently of, and in competition with, the Church and in competition with her, as a mirror image of the "political Augustinianism" just referred to, which viewed papal approval of political authorities as essential for their legitimacy.[51] The birth of the modern state, this suggested, was provoked by misguided attempts by the Church to assert direct political power. When appropriating the legitimate temporal authority that the civil

[50] De Lubac, *Theological Fragments*, 251–52.

[51] Ibid., 281–83.

power exercises under God, the Church sows the seeds of secularization.

Nevertheless, de Lubac recognizes that if secularization is to be combatted, it is essential that the Christian faith continue to be manifested in outward, visible, and institutional forms. He endorses the dialectical and dogmatic theology reestablished within Reformed Protestantism by Karl Barth (1886–1968) and inflected by Dietrich Bonhoeffer (1906–1945) as a response to Nazi tyranny and the complicity of many Christians.[52] Yet de Lubac sees a new context as requiring new methods, above all a reappraisal of the anti-religious and anti-institutional message that many readers of Barth and Bonhoeffer have reasonably taken from some of their key writings. De Lubac suggests that this was partly rhetorical. In one of the many places in which he quotes *Mystici corporis*, the 1943 encyclical of Pope Pius XII (in office 1939–1958) on the Church as the Mystical Body of Christ, de Lubac asserts that the sacraments, faith, laws, counsels, traditions, and ministry that the Church sustains are essential for preserving the objectivity of faith—a point that, in broad terms, Barth himself came to accept.[53] *Mystici corporis* is certainly the magisterial text that de Lubac most frequently cites, and he regards the doctrine that the Church is Christ's mystical body—as reaffirmed in *Humani generis*, the 1950 encyclical of Pope Pius XII—to be the "key point of theological reflection on the Church of Christ".[54]

What sort of institution should the Church be? De Lubac was wary of the secular bureaucratic models of decision that the panoply of secretariats, commissions, and conferences spawned by the Second Vatican Council had unwittingly promoted, despite serving on some of them himself. In response, he rearticulated specifically theological understandings of institution, decision, and authority, against which the organizational reality could be judged. It was a great mistake, de Lubac believed, to model the Church on secular institutions. These may be defined by purpose and structure, but with the Church, things are different. The Church is produced by

[52] De Lubac, *Christian Faith*, 154–59.

[53] De Lubac, *Splendor*, 289. For Barth, Henri de Lubac, *The Motherhood of the Church and Particular Churches in the Universal Church*, trans. Sister Sergia Englund, O.C.D. (San Francisco: Ignatius Press, 1982), 8, 18, 75–76.

[54] De Lubac, *Splendor*, 99.

prayer and worship, and supremely by the Eucharist, in which the Church's identify as the body of Christ is announced and celebrated. For de Lubac, "the Eucharist makes the Church."[55]

This organic, embodied ecclesiology is far removed from the model of the Church as an administrative bureaucracy. To view the Church as Christ's body is to establish a symbiotic relationship between order and charism. If the Eucharist makes the Church, then new charisms that emerge during eucharistic celebration cannot legitimately be stifled by hierarchical structure and decision. But neither may the current Church order, which de Lubac traces back to the New Testament, be swept aside and replaced by a looser configuration. This is because the Eucharist is a celebration across time and space, instituted by Christ and continued through his apostles and ministers and, especially, his bishops. Uncompromisingly, de Lubac describes the Church as the body that "Jesus Christ instituted on the foundation of the Apostles and which has lasted ever since that time in history".[56] Persisting through the centuries and extending across the globe, the Church reflects this eucharistic universality in concrete form and, possessing an organic universality, the Church is set apart from all secular institutions.

De Lubac recognizes that the Church's most important work is shared by all her members. The greatest and most universal duty of Christians, given at baptism, is to cooperate in God's work in saving the world. This task comprises two dimensions: the collective salvation of the world and the individual salvation of unbelievers, and includes both the "increase of the Church" and the "intensive use of the Church's spiritual treasury".[57] Christian confession cannot be reduced to notional Church membership. On the contrary, the parable of the talents suggests that more is asked of those to whom more has been given.[58]

De Lubac complements this missionary grounding for common Christian life with a theology of priesthood. Continuing his bap-

---

[55] Henri de Lubac, *Corpus Mysticum: The Eucharist and the Church in the Middle Ages*, trans. Gemma Simmonds with Richard Price and Christopher Stephens (London: SCM, 2006), 88. See also similar statements in De Lubac, *Splendor*, 151–53.

[56] De Lubac, *Motherhood of the Church*, 178.

[57] De Lubac, *Catholicism*, 240–45 (241–42).

[58] Mt 25:14–30.

tismal focus, he points out that it is not only clergy who are anointed, at their ordinations, but that at baptism every Christian is anointed and thereby sealed with the Spirit.[59] Similarly, referring to the reclothing of the newly baptized superseding the reservation of vestments to priests, he acknowledges that all Christians have now put on Christ.[60] De Lubac unequivocally affirms that, by virtue of participating in the priesthood of Christ, every Christian is a priest. Drawing on the Exodus imagery of Israel as a kingdom of priests and a holy nation, as well as on the Pauline and Johannine notions of kingly priesthood, he describes a universal priesthood that is a "mystical reality that cannot be surpassed or further deepened".[61]

Notwithstanding his exaltation of universal priesthood, de Lubac clearly distinguishes it from ordained priesthood. Whereas the former is interior and spiritual, the latter is exterior and, it might be added, literal. The exterior priesthood is needed in order that the Eucharist may be consecrated and received by the whole Church. Importantly, de Lubac stresses that, although ordained priesthood exists solely to serve the needs of the Church, it in no way follows that it is a "sort of emanation from the community of the faithful".[62] To interpret it this way would be to devalue the universal priesthood of all believers by suggesting that it is self-grounding. Rather, all priesthood, whether universal or ordained, interior or exterior or spiritual or literal, derives from Jesus Christ.

Already hinted at here is de Lubac's high doctrine of episcopal ministry. In the person of the bishop in his diocese, the Church's universal and particular principles are combined. Committees and regional conferences add nothing fundamental to episcopal collegiality and might even detract from it. For this reason, de Lubac was a strong critic of what he termed the "phantasm of conciliarism", according to which decisions with consequences for the Church's universality should be made by the whole body of bishops meeting together on a regular basis. If such a method of decision were

---

[59] 2 Cor 1:21–22.

[60] Gal 3:27.

[61] Ex 19:6; also Is 61:6; 2 Mac 2:17; 1 Pet 2:9; Rev 1:6; De Lubac, *Splendor*, 133–44 (134).

[62] De Lubac, *Splendor*, 140–41. For an extended late reflection on ordained priesthood, de Lubac, *Motherhood of the Church*, 337–63.

instituted, he feared, the likely effect would be the undermining of bishops' ongoing, locally rooted collegiality. A council such as the Second Vatican Council is, in contrast, an entirely different matter. Although episcopal authority is intrinsically collegial and universal, and bishops do not therefore need to assemble in a single place in order to exercise it, when all the bishops do gather in order to reflect on and articulate Church teaching, they may be said to act "collectively". The purpose of such collective action, however, is to strengthen the normal, geographically dispersed collegial action of bishops. In *The Motherhood of the Church*, de Lubac affirms that it is "more usually through the unanimous teaching of its members, dispersed in space and spread out in time, that the episcopal college watches over and orders the faith and life of the Christian community".[63]

There is, of course, one further instrument by which the Church's universality is preserved: the papacy. The ministry of the church of Rome as the focal point of ecclesial unity is grounded, significantly, in her own identity as a particular church within the whole. In consequence, when exercising her universal ministry, the Roman church is herself bound by the requirements of universality that pertain to any particular church. Avoiding defenses of papal primacy based on the contestable notions of antiquity or unbroken lineage, de Lubac argues for a pragmatic origin. Marshalling evidence as early as Clement, he shows that the church in Rome found herself, by circumstance rather than intent, at the center of a network of churches that was preserved by letter writing and within which her bishop had acquired an arbitrating role.[64] The picture that emerges is of a ministry exercised through encouragement, advice, cajoling, and reprimand, rather than by means of the legal apparatus upon which secular institutions rely. Nevertheless, de Lubac cites three key modern documents that define the doctrines of papal primacy and infallibility. Referring to *Pastor aeternus* (1870), the First Vatican Council's incomplete Dogmatic Constitution on the Church of Christ, he argues that, if the faith of the Church is to maintain its vigor, this needs to be authoritatively defined in for-

[63] De Lubac, *Motherhood of the Church*, 249.

[64] Ibid., 275–335.

mal terms and translated into a language that may be widely understood. However, because of the council's suspension, this constitution was published in a much shorter version than intended, which failed to place papal primacy and infallibility in their wider ecclesial setting. Grounded in Scripture, tradition, and the opinion of the whole Church, de Lubac makes clear, papal infallibility is "in reality that of the Church herself".[65] He also refers to the presentation, in the 1910 anti-Modernist oath of Pope Pius X, of the papacy as the visible foundation of the whole Church, by virtue of being the office of the successor of the apostle Peter. The third document he invokes is Pope Pius XI's 1928 encyclical on religious unity, *Mortalium animos*, in which the magisterial authority exercised by the papacy is presented as a function of that which the bishops collectively exercise on behalf of the whole Church. There can be no doubt that de Lubac regards the preservation of unity through authority as essential in a skeptical age.

## The Supernatural

Joining the Jesuits in 1913, de Lubac suffered firsthand the effects of militant secularism. A decade earlier, the *lois d'exception* had been introduced in France in two stages. In 1901, while Pierre Waldeck-Rousseau (1846–1904) led the government, a measure had been passed requiring state registration by all religious groups. Three years later, under the government of the former seminarian Émile Combes (1835–1921), another legislative measure had banned all teaching by clergy, and religious orders had therefore been obliged to relocate their seminaries abroad. The south coast of England was favored by the Jesuits, and de Lubac went into exile there as a novice.

Although the secular French state did not allow members of religious orders freedom of education within their own country, it required them to return home to fight its wars. His novitiate continued, not in the classroom or in the chapel, but in the mud of the Somme battlefield. The maelstrom of war changed forever the

[65] De Lubac, *Splendor*, 267–73 (271).

outlook of de Lubac and countless other Jesuits from respectable provincial families. Entering fully into the modern secular world, they became truly part of it for the first time. However, this did not diminish the passionate allegiance of many for the Church. Following his demobilization in September 1919, de Lubac returned to his philosophical and theological studies. These included his juniorate in Canterbury (1920), periods at the Maison Saint-Louis, which was the Jesuit philosophate on the island of Jersey (1920–1923), and the theologate at Ore Place, Hastings (1924–1926). The theologate relocated to Fourvière in Lyon in 1926, where de Lubac completed his remaining two years of formation.

In 1920, just a year after leaving the army, de Lubac was therefore in a classroom on a small island being taught Neo-Scholastic theology. He particularly recalls the classes of Father Pedro Descoqs, who followed the methodology of the Spanish Jesuit Francisco Suárez (1548–1617), which established a clear separation between philosophy and theology. "Pure" nature, it was supposed, is the object of philosophy alone, whereas theology is concerned with revelation, which constitutes a different system of truth. Descoqs' "combative teaching" was, de Lubac recollects, a "perpetual invitation to react".[66] On Jersey, de Lubac's desire to contest the Suárezian philosophy of pure nature led his teachers to identify him as a neo-Thomist. Yet, as will be seen, he came to distance himself from the emerging neo-Thomist consensus.

De Lubac's alternative theology of the supernatural began to take shape at the theologate at Hastings, to which he moved in 1924. This was more intellectually open than the philosophate on Jersey. The major new journal *Recherches de science religieuse*, which had been launched in 1910, had in its first two years published twenty contributions by no fewer than seven Hastings scholars. De Lubac was a member of the Sunday discussion group "La Pensée", in which he began to develop his own understanding of the supernatural. The group's convener was Joseph Huby (1878–1948), who, de Lubac states, encouraged him to "verify whether the doctrine of Saint Thomas on this important point was indeed what was claimed by the Thomist school around the sixteenth century, codified in the

---

[66] De Lubac, *At the Service*, 42.

seventeenth and asserted with greater emphasis than ever in the twentieth."[67]

As this background suggests, theological use of the concept of the supernatural was not new. The First Vatican Council's Dogmatic Constitution on the Catholic Faith, *Dei filius* (1870), had defined the Christian religion as a supernatural institution that was, as such, utterly opposed to rationalism and naturalism.[68] It taught that reason may establish the beginning and the end of all created things. However, God has revealed himself and his decrees through the supernatural revelation of his Son. This, *Dei filius* suggested, is because humans have been ordained to the supernatural end of sharing in divine blessings that exceed their power of conception. The supernatural revelation that makes this possible is contained in the Church's scriptural and oral traditions, which were received by the apostles from Christ and by the dictation of the Holy Spirit and have been transmitted through subsequent tradition. In consequence, faith, by which the human intellect and will are fully yielded in obedience to God, is a supernatural virtue inspired and assisted by divine grace.

De Lubac found much to commend in the First Vatican Council's notion of the supernatural, such as its emphasis on divine revelation as occurring through the trinitarian Persons and the handing on of this revelation in Church tradition. However, as has been seen, when engaging his rationalist and naturalist opponents, de Lubac adopted a strategy of undermining them by exposing flaws in their own position rather than by disengaging or condemning. Second, by identifying the source of supernatural revelation as the historical Christ and the Holy Spirit dictating to the apostles, the council appeared to exclude the possibility that elements of this revelation were offered to the Israelites. Third, by associating grace with a supernatural revelation restricted to the Christian era, the possibility that Adam was created in a state of grace appeared to be excluded.

De Lubac saw these points as lending support to the theory of pure nature, according to which the natural and the supernatural constitute two independent orders of existence and understanding.

---

67 Ibid., 35.

68 *Dei filius* 2–3, in *Decrees of the Ecumenical Councils*, ed. Norman P. Tanner, 2 vols. (London: Sheed & Ward, 1990), 2:806–8.

Under the influence of Aristotle, the natural order was viewed as possessing its own self-sufficiency, with humans able to pursue natural ends unaided by grace. The supernatural, in contrast, was oriented to divine revelation, which could be reliably known only through grace. The theory of pure nature was deeply entrenched in this particular conception of the supernatural and was regarded by some as a prudent apologetic stance in a secular era, giving recognition to the autonomy and dignity of human nature, reason, and action. However, de Lubac was deeply concerned that the presumption that natural life could continue without the power of grace had opened the way to a radical modern secularism that sought to refute religious claims entirely.

For de Lubac, the debate about the relation of nature and grace was essentially a debate about the reception of Augustine, especially in the works of Michael Baius (1513–1589) and Cornelius Jansenius (1585–1638).[69] Both these theologians viewed Adam and Eve before the Fall as possessing a good nature and as capable of good moral conduct by their own efforts. For Jansenius, the Fall was catastrophic, because the human depravity that resulted contrasted so starkly with what had preceded. Significantly, for him, grace arose because of sin. These ideas were important because, historically, Jansenism was the French national theology, shaping the minds of many generations of theologians, confessors, and believers. By means of its sharp distinction between nature and grace, it presented a clear opposition between the secular and the sacred, with the secular realm characterized by perversion and wickedness, while the sacred realm provided assured salvation to a few. On this view, the only hope for the world was God's overpowering grace. This was given only to a small minority of people and, once offered, was irresistible. The majority, who did not receive grace, comprised a mass of perdition consigned to hell.

De Lubac identifies the modern grace–nature debate as originating in the Augustinian theologies of Baius and Jansenius. This context is especially prominent in the French theological and national contexts. Nevertheless, he also traces the debate in the work of three

---

[69] David Grumett, "De Lubac, Grace, and the Pure Nature Debate", *Modern Theology* 31 (2015): 123–46.

other theologians. The most proximate of these is Suárez, whose years of work fell between those of de Lubac's principal protagonists and with whom the theory of pure nature is particularly associated. In Suárez' systematic expositions of the theory, *De ultimo fine hominis* (On man's final end) (1592) and the posthumous *De gratia* (On grace) (1619), purely natural ends, appetites, and powers exist in parallel with a supernatural nature, which depends on God and is fully explicable by divine revelation. However, the two systems of nature and grace have no connecting points. This is because Suárez accepts the Scholastic principle drawn from Aristotle that an appetite that is natural, being grounded in a power that is natural, can seek only an end that is natural.[70] There can be no desire for the supernatural that originates in nature but has an object or effects that are disproportionate to it. Suárez also denied that supernatural hope, which has strictly spiritual objects, may satisfy desire. An underlying difficulty with his position, de Lubac argues, is an impoverished conception of finality: "not a destiny inscribed in a man's very nature, directing him from within, and which he could not ontologically escape, but a mere destination given him from outside when he was already in existence".[71] Moreover, Suárez consciously turned the notion of a *state* of pure nature—which had been an hypothesis discussed by theologians that was, as such, potentially valid if certain conditions were met—into an *order* of pure nature that was presumed to be universally valid.[72]

Through his engagement with Thomas Aquinas, de Lubac addresses a major concern about the notion of natural desire for God: that, if such desire is not wholly restricted within the natural realm, then rational creatures attain union with God through their own power. De Lubac distinguishes two uses of the term "natural", indicating either inclination or sufficiency.[73] Because a rational creature may be inclined to an end but nevertheless possess insufficient means to attain it, the natural desire for God is not, in itself, efficacious. In the intellectual nature with which rational creatures

---

[70] De Lubac, *Augustinianism*, 157–59; de Lubac, *Mystery*, 41–42.

[71] De Lubac, *Mystery*, 68–69, also 147–49.

[72] De Lubac, *Augustinianism*, 226–27.

[73] Ibid., 171–75, 219–20.

were created, a superior, spiritual appetite is certainly present: they have an impulse not simply to fulfill their nature but to transcend it. Nevertheless, God, being their supernatural end, must exceed their power of understanding, and in present earthly life they are unable to enjoy perfect beatitude, but are merely capable of a limited participation in beatitude.[74] This participation is due to an obediential power by which the rational creatures are subjected to their Creator, which, because of the incommensurability of Creator and creature, can only ever be partly satisfied. Rational creatures may be granted the means to pursue their end, but not the end itself.

For Aquinas, rational creatures naturally desire not only God but the vision of the divine substance. Judged by the standards of common experience, this proposition may well appear unfeasibly bold. However, desire is determined by end. If rational creatures were assigned an inferior end, such as sentience or mere physical existence, they would be no different from animals or inanimate objects. Moreover, to a single thing only a single end may be assigned. For these reasons, it is necessary both that the end of rational creatures is the vision of God and that rational creatures naturally desire this end.[75] It is also necessary that this end be determinate: no thing is moved to infinity. Rather, as with gravitation, the closer a body approaches its determined end, the more quickly it is moved. Nevertheless, in its attainment, this end is disproportionate to nature, standing in a similar relation to nature as act to potency or cause to effect. The soul is raised up by infused grace, and the intellect is strengthened by the light of glory.[76]

De Lubac endorses much of the theology of Duns Scotus (1266–1308), which he reckons to be much closer to Aquinas than to Suárez.[77] This is perhaps surprising, in view of more recent historiographical critique of Scotus, in which he has been presented as a precursor of modern individualism and secularism. For Scotus, God is the naturally desired end of rational creatures but their supernaturally attained end. Rational creatures are indisposed to their

[74] Ibid., 142, 188–89, 200–201.

[75] De Lubac, *Mystery*, 56, 204–6.

[76] Ibid., 85–88.

[77] De Lubac, *Augustinianism*, 123–25; de Lubac, *Mystery* 85, 116.

true end, which is gradually revealed to them rather than being immediately accessible by means of natural knowledge. However, de Lubac suggests that Scotus viewed this "desire" too naturally, as an innate appetite that amounted to a "weight" of nature like that which, in Aristotelian philosophy, inclines an animal or a stone to its final end. Scotus contrasted this naturalistic desire with an elicited appetite or desire, which could not, as such, be natural.

During the nineteenth century, Jansenist theology had been significantly challenged by neo-Thomism, which had spread into France from Italy. Many fail to realize that, in this period, neo-Thomism exerted a liberalizing influence on doctrinal and moral theology. Neo-Thomists contested the Jansenist notion that the sacred and the secular were fundamentally opposed. Grace was offered, so they suggested, through gifts that were deemed specifically spiritual, such as the sacraments and indulgences. Neo-Thomists argued that human nature included a spiritual dimension that was naturally oriented to spiritual reality, through which grace was received. However, like Suárezians, they were also deeply influenced by the Aristotelian view that a realm of activity exists in which people may pursue the goods that are natural to them by their own efforts unaided by grace.

De Lubac sees as many problems with neo-Thomism as with Suárezianism, arguing for an expanded role for grace but also a continuing place for nature. He develops his own theory of the relation between grace and nature on the theological ground left open by the Council of Trent, which recognized the role in justification of both prevenient grace, by which adults are disposed to God, and of free assent to, and cooperation with, this grace.[78] De Lubac grounds his theory in the doctrine of creation, affirming that creation is the one gift that might not have been given, with all subsequent gifts being an outworking of this original lavish divine act of bringing the world into being, from which everything else has followed. To take the grace of creation seriously, de Lubac argues, means that nature, although fallen, is primordially graced and continues to bear the divine image. The grace of redemption is not, therefore, like the surprise, arbitrary intrusion of a stranger into hostile territory. Rather, the recipient of redemptive grace is already oriented to that

[78] De Lubac, *Mystery*, 169; *De justificatione* 5, in Tanner, *Decrees* 2:672.

grace, being able to recognize it dimly and to accept it. De Lubac wholeheartedly endorses Aquinas' insight that grace does not destroy nature but perfects it.[79] The whole created order is primordially oriented to God and dependent on God, who is its final end.

## The Eucharist and Scripture

For de Lubac, the Eucharist and Scripture are intimately associated in the life of the Church. Together they are the source of the Church and build up her life. In the assembly of believers, Scripture is read and heard, and the Body and Blood of Christ are analogously distributed and received.[80] Moreover, the Last Supper is narrated in the Synoptic Gospels, and its handing on to Christian communities as the Eucharist is justified by Paul.[81] The parallelism of the Eucharist and Scripture is instructive for two further reasons. First, each has a spiritual meaning that, although grounded in literal actions and words, goes beyond them. Rather, through fraction, the spiritual meaning emerges out of the literal meaning. To underline the close relation of eucharistic and scriptural exegesis, de Lubac cites multiple exegetical uses of bread imagery.[82] Jerome (ca. 347–420), who draws on apocalyptic texts, portrays Christ using a winnowing fork to separate the spiritual grain from the literal chaff.[83] With Peter Damian (1007–1072), the kernels of grain are then ground between the millstones of the Law and the Gospel, so that the wheat may be extracted. The loaves broken and distributed to the crowds figure in the books of the Pentateuch (Genesis, Exodus, Leviticus, Numbers, and Deuteronomy), from which spiritual content is extracted, or the seven seals on the scroll of God's mystery in Revelation.[84]

---

[79] Thomas Aquinas, *Summa theologiae* Ia, q. 1, a. 8 ad 2; 61 vols. (London: Blackfriars, 1964–81), 1:30–31.

[80] Henri de Lubac, *History and Spirit: The Understanding of Scripture according to Origen*, trans. Anne Englund Nash with Juvenal Merriel (San Francisco: Ignatius Press, 2007), 406–26.

[81] 1 Cor 11:23–26.

[82] Henri de Lubac, *Medieval Exegesis*, vols. 1 and 3, trans. E. M. Macierowski; vol. 2, trans. Mark Sebanc; 4 vols. (Grand Rapids, Mich.: Eerdmans, 1998–), 2:26–27.

[83] Mt 3:10.

[84] Mk 6:41, 8:6; Rev 5:1–5, 6, 8:1.

The grain, chaff, wheat, and loaves provide apt images for exegesis. Just as these acts constitute and make possible real eucharistic participation in Christ's body, so the fragmentation of Scripture into its different senses by the action of the human intellect allows participation in Christ's word and the understanding of this word.

The second similarity between the Eucharist and Scripture is that each refers to Christ and is fulfilled in Christ. This reference to Christ has multiple senses. In the case of the Eucharist, de Lubac delineates the notion in medieval exegesis of Christ's "threefold body". Traceable to the bishop and liturgist Amalar of Metz (775–850), this developed the New Testament association of the bread of the Eucharist with the body of Christ. In the Roman Rite of the Mass, the bread has traditionally been broken into three parts. One of these has been commingled with the wine in the chalice, one has been consumed by the people, and one has been left on the altar. De Lubac traces the shifting exegesis of how each of these three bread fragments refers to aspects of the Church and of Christ's body.[85] The first fragment, commingled with the wine in the chalice and consumed by the priest, has typically been taken to represent Christ's resurrected body, in which his earthly body and blood are reunited. The second fragment, consumed dry by the people —although, until recent decades, not necessarily during the Mass itself—has frequently been identified with the body of Christ on earth, being received by those living on earth. The third fragment has figured the resurrection, being left on the altar until the end of Mass in the same way as the departed rest in their tombs until the end of the present age. Furthermore, it is this fragment that has been taken to the dying as viaticum. These three fragments may each be identified with a different type of exegesis. The first, representing Christ's resurrected body, is viewed allegorically, with the priest's words and actions signifying doctrinal truths. The second fragment is identified with the body of Christ on earth, by means of a literal exegesis grounded in immediacy and visibility. The third fragment, suggesting the resurrection, points to an eschatological exegesis grounded in Christ's gift of life and its awaited consummation.

---

[85] De Lubac, *Corpus Mysticum*, 268–301.

All this indicates that the Eucharist is, like Scripture, an objective reality that has been transmitted through Christian history and that is generative of belief, devotion, community, and theology. Whereas ordinary food and drink are consumed and destroyed, the recipients of the Eucharist are themselves spiritually transformed and assimilated into Christ's body.[86] The Eucharist is therefore actively celebrated and received by the whole Church. Not only does it refer to past events such as the Last Supper, but it makes present a new reality and nourishes the Church, which is thereby a mystical anticipatory sign of the kingdom of God. Because of this intimate relation of the Eucharist and the Church, each resists interpretation in isolation from the other. This is true even of the understanding of the mode of divine presence in the Eucharist. While accepting the theology of transubstantiation—which posits that, in the Eucharist, the substances of bread and wine are changed into the substances of Christ's Body and Blood—de Lubac prefers the alternative medieval term "confection", which may describe both the change in the bread and wine and the eucharistic transformation of the Church.[87] Although not himself a liturgist, de Lubac advocates the renewal of worship via a deepened understanding of its history. "As we seek to grasp", he writes, "the significance of the rites and formulae by which the treasure of our faith is transmitted to us, the first step necessary is to return to the sources."[88] His proposals include eucharistic presidency by the priest facing the people and the renewal of the evening Easter Vigil liturgy.[89] Both of these are now widespread.

If Christ is the hermeneutical key of the Eucharist, he is also the primary referent of Scripture, through whom diverse texts gain a coherent and convergent meaning. This meaning is unlocked by the Cross, which is Scripture's "sole and universal key" and by which, de Lubac continues, Christ "unites the two Testaments into a single body of doctrine, intermingling the ancient precepts with the

[86] De Lubac, *Theological Fragments*, 71–75 (74).

[87] De Lubac, *Corpus Mysticum*, 83.

[88] Henri de Lubac, "Le sens de la messe", in *Corpus mysticum: l'eucharistie et l'Église au Moyen-Âge: étude historique* (Paris: Cerf, 2010), 399–402.

[89] Henri de Lubac, "Vigile de Pâques 1940", in ibid, 371–77.

grace of the Gospel".[90] Christ's exegesis is active, having been manifested in his life and actions as well as by verbal interpretation. In the present day, it is easy to think of Scripture as deriving its unity from the formal development of a definitive canon of writings. However, de Lubac shows that, even before the process of canonical formation was completed, exegetes regarded Scripture as a coherent whole and often referred to it in the singular. This was possible because Christ was the endpoint and fullness of the scriptural texts.[91] The effort of understanding this fact and its full exegetical ramifications, de Lubac suggests, continues today. Refuting a supersessionist view of the relation of the two Testaments, he states that full account must be taken of the "ever more illuminating light" of the Old Testament in the exegesis of the New Testament. Moreover, whereas exegesis has sometimes been regarded as the study of a historical document, there is now an ever more pressing need to recognize it as the reception of God's Word by the faithful.

The reasons for de Lubac's tremendous interest in the spiritual interpretation of the Eucharist and of Scripture may be understood through his work on Origen. Often dismissed as an obscurantist who enveloped Scripture's literal truth in a fog of allegory, the third-century exegete in fact offers, de Lubac argues, deep wellsprings of doctrinal reflection, following the "long course" that biblical interpretation had run during the nineteenth and earlier twentieth centuries through the "parched lands of rationalism and positivism".[92] Central to de Lubac's case is that Origen's use of allegory is specifically Christian, contesting pagan esotericism and advancing beyond the symbolic representations of the soul and of morals found in Philo (ca. 30 B.C.–ca. 50), the Jewish exegete and earlier Alexandrian. The crucial difference is Origen's rooting of allegory in biblical history, which requires him to attend to Scripture's literal sense. In order to understand how Origen does this, de Lubac contends, it is necessary to examine his biblical commentaries and homilies, rather than relying on the incomplete methodological statements contained in

[90] De Lubac, *Medieval Exegesis*, 1:225–67 (239).

[91] Ibid., 1:247, 265.

[92] De Lubac, *History and Spirit*, 14.

his theoretical texts. De Lubac reminds his readers that, far from promoting rationalism or heresy, Origen played a key role in refuting millenarianism by showing that Christ's reign on earth would be neither literal nor immediate. Moreover, through his spiritual exegesis, Origen showed that, although Christian belief was different from Jewish belief, Christians had no reason to deny Jewish Scripture, because it contained spiritual truths. He thus secured the unity of scriptural revelation, defended threatened faith, and protected ordinary believers.

De Lubac's doctrine of scriptural exegesis will now be described in greater detail. This is important for understanding his whole theology, which is rooted in Scripture both directly, through his own use of scriptural sources, and indirectly, via his engagements with numerous patristic and early medieval theologians. As many exegetical texts show, spiritual exegesis was widespread through much of theological history until it was marginalized by Scholasticism. Moreover, during the nineteenth century, it was advocated by figures including Pope Pius IX (in office 1846–1878).[93] In his four-volume study of medieval exegesis, de Lubac recovers and reframes this exegesis, which is grounded in the recognition of the multiple senses, or meanings, of Scripture. All of these are founded on the *literal* sense, that is, on the narrative of events that precede, encompass, and follow the life of Christ on earth.[94] They include episodes with a factual basis, such as the Babylonian Captivity, the birth of Christ, and the preaching of the apostles, which are literal according to a strict meaning of the term. However, other events, such as those narrated in the opening chapters of Genesis, in the Song of Songs, and in the parables told by Jesus in Luke's Gospel, are read in a *historical* sense rather than in a literal sense, because they have not in reality taken place in the way described. The whole of Scripture is historically true, but not all of it is literally true.

What is the purpose of the many portions of Scripture that are historically true but not literally true, or, to put it another way, that report subjective history rather than objective history? These have a *spiritual* sense, referring to truths beyond the history itself. Exam-

---

[93] De Lubac, *Discovery*, 88.

[94] De Lubac, *Medieval Exegesis*, 2:41–50.

ples include Jacob's vision of the angels ascending and descending upon the heavenly ladder and the chariot imagery of Ezekiel, which may each be taken as referring to different aspects of mental and physical commerce with God.[95] In some instances, however, the spiritual reference is to Christ, such as in Isaiah's suffering servant prophecies and in many of Jesus' own parables.[96] This category of spiritual propositions has, de Lubac argues, a *mystical* sense, being more objective and universal because of a specifically christological meaning. The spiritual and mystical sense may be further distinguished as allegorical, moral, and eschatological.

The *allegorical* sense of Scripture is taught by Scripture itself, preeminently in Paul's letter to the Galatians in his presentation of the birth of the sons of Abraham by Hagar and Sarah. Hagar, who was a slave woman, bore children according to the Old Covenant of the law and the flesh, while Sarah, who was Abraham's wife, bore children of the heavenly Jerusalem, who were set free from the law. Paul writes: "This is an allegory: these women are two covenants. One [woman, in fact] is [Hagar] from Mount Sinai, bearing children for slavery. . . . Now Hagar is Mount Sinai in Arabia; she corresponds to the present Jerusalem, for she is in slavery with her children. But [the other woman corresponds to] the Jerusalem above [she] is free, and she is our mother."[97] This explanation demonstrates the importance of detail in allegorical readings of Scripture, both in the substance of the events recounted and in the different aspects of their interpretation. The specifically Christian form of allegory, which Jewish writers like Philo anticipated, has clear factual reference, supremely to Christ. It contrasts with pagan and Gnostic uses of allegory to communicate hidden meanings or secret knowledge, which were vague and elitist. As Origen recognized, Paul indicates his allegorical method of reading the law in several other places. He favors spiritual circumcision over literal circumcision, regarding the law itself as spiritual.[98] In two places, he employs the Deuteronomic injunction not to muzzle an ox treading out grain in defense

[95] Gen 28:10–17, Ezek 1.

[96] De Lubac, *Medieval Exegesis*, 2:19–20, 93–94; see Is 52:13—53:12.

[97] De Lubac, *Medieval Exegesis*, 2:1–9; Gal 4:24–26.

[98] De Lubac, *History and Spirit*, 77–86; Rom 2:29, 7:14.

of his acceptance of material support from his disciples.[99] Paul also uses marriage, in which the "two become one flesh", as an image for Christ and the Church, while making immediately clear that this mystical reality in no way reduces or replaces the obligations entailed by literal marriage.[100] He states of the events of the Exodus that these happened to the Israelites to serve "as a warning [*týpos*], but they were written down for our instruction".[101] Also noteworthy is the extensive liturgical allegorizing of the letter to the Hebrews, in which the earthly sanctuaries of the tent of meeting and the Temple serve as images for the heavenly sanctuary.

Allegory may usefully be distinguished from *typology*. At its simplest, typology is the use of a person or an action as an example for others to follow. Paul repeatedly stresses the importance of ethical exemplars, or types, in Christian communities.[102] Another kind of typology, also instructional, is the comparison of a historical episode from the New Testament with one from the Old Testament, such as Jesus identifying the cup of wine at the Last Supper with his blood and the turning of the River Nile into blood before the Exodus.[103] However, de Lubac makes clear that allegory, while always dependent on typology, goes beyond it. Building upon historical events and comparisons, Paul had to "divert a word . . . from its ordinary meaning because he was using it to express a new and profoundly original thought", in order to show "how what was written after having taken place *typikos* [as an example] must be understood and lived *pneumatikos* [spiritually]".[104] Allegory thus has a practical aspect that typology by itself lacks, an aspect that closely relates it to the other scriptural senses now to be introduced.

After allegory, de Lubac turns to the *moral* sense. This order of exposition is significant. Scripture's moral meaning is not, for him, to be found in its literal sense, nor is a moral reading or response a prerequisite for the doctrinal understanding brought by allegory. De Lubac is critical of this approach, which was common in patristic ex-

[99] 1 Cor 9:9; 1 Tim 5:18 (cf. Deut 25:4).
[100] Eph 5:31–3.
[101] 1 Cor 10:11.
[102] Phil 3:7; 1 Thess 1:7; 2 Thess 3:9; 1 Tim 4:12; Tit 2:7.
[103] Mk 14:23–25; Lk 22:17–18; Ex 7:19–20.
[104] De Lubac, *Theological Fragments*, 129–64 (131, 133).

egesis, protesting that it has placed Christian morality "ahead of the mystery upon which it in fact depended".[105] Methodologically, this order of exposition has treated Scripture no differently from other possible sources of morals, such as secular literature. In contrast with this naturalistic approach, de Lubac promotes the mystical alternative. This is most properly *tropological* and is, for him, the superior form of the moral sense. Tropology is the turning around of speech, so that it refers to something other than its immediate object within the written text.[106] In this way, tropology is also the turning around of the reader as subject, so that actions and life themselves become an extended, lived exegesis of Scripture, which thereby functions as a mirror, teaching the reader self-knowledge and morals. As Paul states, Scripture was written for human instruction and to encourage steadfastness.[107] Events corporeally performed in distant times and places may now be spiritually performed. As de Lubac put it, this is more than a doctrine of interior illumination of the soul by God. Rather, it is the "doctrine of the interiorization of the biblical datum" in its history and mystery.[108] Biblical accounts of migrations describe the journeying of the soul, while stories of military battles refer to spiritual combat. Just as Christ's Annunciation and Nativity are narrated, so must Christ be conceived and born within every soul. Moreover, as Paul explicitly states, just as Christ was crucified and resurrected, so must his followers die to sin and live for righteousness.[109]

The fourth and final of the senses of Scripture is the *eschatological sense*. De Lubac frequently describes this sense as *anagogical* because it suggests a spiritual ascent. It combines the doctrinal objectivity of allegory with the moral subjectivity of tropology and has two aspects, which are both mystical.[110] The first aspect, which is more obviously designated eschatological and is associated with allegory, concerns the ultimate end of individual people and of the whole universe and the coming and return of Christ. Long ago, God

---

[105] De Lubac, *Medieval Exegesis*, 2:31; also 1:114–15.

[106] Ibid., 2:127–34.

[107] Rom 15:4.

[108] De Lubac, *Medieval Exegesis*, 2:139.

[109] Rom 6:5–14.

[110] De Lubac, *Medieval Exegesis*, 2:179–87.

announced through his prophets a time of universal restoration, until which Christ would remain in heaven.[111] This eschatological meaning is objective, doctrinal, and speculative. The second aspect, which is properly described as anagogical and is closely allied with tropology, is the contemplative drawing of the person of faith into the mystical life and is, unlike the first, realized subjectively. The fact of resurrection with Christ calls the mind to fix upon heavenly things.[112] However, de Lubac believes that the two aspects of anagogy are ultimately inseparable, because the individual believer's spiritual ascent always occurs within the collective eschatological context given by the action of Christ upon and within world history. In the present age, the spiritual transformation of the world is intimated in word and sign, although it is not yet consummated, just as the spiritual transformation of the self is inaugurated but remains incomplete. "The eschatological", de Lubac writes, "is not something simply absent from the present", but is the "foundation of the present and the term of its movement".[113]

Transcending the opposition between the objectivity of allegory and the subjectivity of tropology, anagogy synthesizes and perfects the spiritual senses, revealing their "dynamic unity" and "reciprocal interiority". Its greatest symbol is Jerusalem, which "condenses . . . the total explication of Scripture and the total exposition of the Christian mystery".[114] It is the angelic heavenly city of Christ. It is the virtuous and faultless soul contemplating and praising God. It is the harmonious Church at peace with herself. In practice, the different senses emerge from each other and return into each other kaleidoscopically. It is not the case, for instance, that Scripture's literal and spiritual senses are in tension or that an anagogical reading justifies the neglect of the moral sense.

Now that the four senses have been enumerated, clearer understanding may be gained of how de Lubac conceives of the relation between the two Testaments. It was earlier stated that he acknowledges Christ to be the primary referent of the whole of Scripture.

---

[111] Acts 3:21.

[112] Col 3:1–2.

[113] De Lubac, *Splendor*, 117.

[114] De Lubac, *Medieval Exegesis*, 2:199–201.

This suggests that the senses may function differently in the New Testament from in the Old Testament and that allegory in particular may be restricted to the Old Testament. Otherwise, it would be possible to view the New Testament as referring to a spiritual truth beyond itself, other than the mystery and fact of Christ. De Lubac is, of course, aware of the extensive allegorizing of some New Testament passages, such as Jesus healing the paralytic at the pool of Bethzatha signifying baptism, or Mary of Bethany pouring perfume over the feet of Jesus figuring the Church's love of him.[115] Indeed, allegory is fundamental to understanding the Gospels because, although they begin with the Incarnation, the events they relate "still belong, to a certain extent, to the era of signs and figures, which is to say to the era of the Old Testament".[116] The New Covenant is not established until the Last Supper, and Christ's true nature is not completely revealed—or, in John's terms, Christ is not glorified—until his death, Resurrection, and Ascension. The writings of the New Testament and the external facts they describe may therefore be allegorized and, indeed, should be allegorized. However, the Testament itself, who is Christ, is definitive and eternal and, therefore, cannot be allegorized. With the New Testament, de Lubac states, "the literal meaning is itself spiritual."[117]

An example of how scriptural exegesis may err is found in the extreme biblical literalism of Joachim of Flora (ca. 1135–1202). Denying the sufficiency of the traditional spiritual exegesis just outlined, the Calabrian abbot complemented this with typic exegesis. Developing a novel doctrine of the "concord of the letter" inspired by the Book of Revelation, he sought to establish the correspondence between a literal reading of the Old Testament and a literal reading of the New Testament. Joachim conceived three ages, or states, of the world, each of which corresponded with the action of a member of the Trinity: the age of science, founded upon the Old Testament

---

[115] Jn 5:19, 12:3.

[116] *Scripture in the Tradition*, trans. Luke O'Neill (New York: Crossroad, 2000), 194–217 (211). This includes excerpts from Henri de Lubac, *L'Exégèse médiévale: les quatre sens de l'Écriture*, vol. 4 (Paris: Aubier-Montaigne, 1964), 106–23, which is otherwise untranslated. A useful compilation of de Lubac's writings on scriptural exegesis, it was first published as *Sources of Revelation* (New York: Herder, 1968).

[117] De Lubac, *Scripture*, 204.

and the work of the Father; the age of the Church, associated with the New Testament and the work of the Son; and the age of spiritual understanding, identified with the Book of Revelation and the Holy Spirit. He supported this scheme with detailed tabulations, calculations, and chronologies, in such a way that the "idea of discovering a secret or deciphering a riddle" replaced the notion of "going deeper into a mystery".[118] With the capture of Jerusalem from its Crusader defenders by Muslim forces in 1187 in view, Joachim believed that history had reached a critical point of transition into the third age. This would bring the victorious resurgence of a regenerated Christianity, with a quasi-monastic contemplative order supplanting the existing institutional Church. De Lubac regards this as utopian hubris, charging Joachim with insufficient respect for tradition and untamed curiosity. Moreover, it was Joachim's refusal of the unifying power of true mysticism, which is centered on Christ, that made possible his subordination of the allegorical, moral, and eschatological senses to a doubled literal sense. Rather than effecting the usual transition from the literal to the spiritual, he exchanged one literalism for another. In every age, de Lubac suggests, superstition, anthropomorphism, and mythography provide tempting substitutes for responsible and accountable exegesis.

The transformative aspect of reception that de Lubac recognizes in the Eucharist also applies to Scripture. The end of scriptural assimilation is the conversion of both the reader and the world, so that Scripture's meaning is to be found, not ultimately in written words upon a page, but in the world, where the true mystery resides. The principal divine authorship is thereby not of words but of the world, of which Scripture is a reading. Christ provides the key to this primary text, exegeting it in his birth, life, death, Resurrection, and Ascension.

## Buddhism

During the 1930s, de Lubac had taught a course on the history of religions at the Catholic Theological Faculty in Lyon. In the 1950s,

---

[118] De Lubac, *Medieval Exegesis*, 3:327–419 (343).

when he was constrained from publishing theology, he rekindled his interests in religion with a detailed study of Buddhism.[119] The authorities in Rome did not regard his interests in Buddhism as theological and so permitted him to pursue them and to give private talks. Impressed by the Asian artefacts at the Musée Guimet in Paris, de Lubac became absorbed by the Pure Land Buddhism that had taken root in Japan. Relatively unknown in the West, this is nevertheless the variety of Buddhism that, he rightly perceived, bears the greatest similarity to Roman Catholicism.

The standard Roman Catholic response to Buddhism in the 1950s, and much later, has been to dismiss it as at best exotic superstition and, at worst, as an "Eastern" form of atheism. In his study of de Lubac, the Swiss theologian and former Jesuit Hans Urs von Balthasar (1905–1988) suggests that this was his subject's own view.[120] In fact, de Lubac saw well beyond these stereotypes. Following intellectually the missionary path trod by Jesuits as far back as Saint Francis Xavier (1506–1552), he refused to concede that a religious movement as ancient and noble as Buddhism was purely secular and made no reference to the sacred. On the contrary, several features of Buddhism in its True Pure Land (Shin) form fascinated him. Shin's spatialized conception of spiritual birth includes the imagery of a Pure Land, which has similarities with the Christian idea of heaven. Its devotion to the person and name of Amida Buddha mirrors Christian devotion to Jesus Christ. The repetition of the name of Amida, known as *nembutsu*, may be viewed as a corollary of Christian prayer and, most obviously, of the ancient Jesus Prayer, "Lord Jesus Christ, Son of God, have mercy on me, a sinner."

Moreover, de Lubac sees several controversies within the Roman Catholic theology of his day paralleled in Shin debates. What are the respective roles in salvation of self-power (*jiriki*) and other-power (*tariki*)? How close does prayer bring the believer to God, or are good deeds more important? Is human life entirely corrupt, or does

[119] David Grumett and Thomas Plant, "De Lubac, Pure Land Buddhism, and Roman Catholicism", *The Journal of Religion* 92 (2012): 58–83.

[120] Hans Urs von Balthasar, *The Theology of Henri de Lubac: An Overview* (San Francisco: Ignatius Press, 1991), 54–59.

it contain seeds of hope? Through his study of Shin Buddhism, de Lubac was able to pursue indirectly many of the questions that his superiors had prohibited him from exploring in an explicitly Roman Catholic context. He never regards Buddhism as a path to salvation in the same way as Christianity is and is, indeed, highly critical of Western forms of Buddhism adopted in conscious rejection of Christianity. However, he argues that, in places where the Gospel has not been heard, Buddhism may rightly be viewed as containing elements of sacred truth.

De Lubac's first volumes on Buddhism, which were published between 1951 and 1955, were ground-breaking and helped to set the tone for a more open attitude to Buddhism within the Magisterium.[121] This is reflected in successive drafts of *Nostra aetate*, the Second Vatican Council's Declaration on Non-Christian Religions. The document had begun life focused on the single issue of the Church's relations to Jews, with its first version articulating a theology of election that sought, in the shadow of the Holocaust, to overcome anti-Semitism. However, in the summer of 1964, during the council's second intersession, de Lubac was appointed a founding member of the Secretariat for Non-Christians, which, in 1988, became the Pontifical Council for Interreligious Dialogue.[122] At this point, the first reference to Buddhism was introduced into the schema that would become *Nostra aetate*, in its third draft. The reference was strengthened in the text's fourth and final version, which alludes to Amida Buddha in its reference to a "higher source" of illumination beyond the self, distinguishing this from self-centered paths of enlightenment. Buddhism, "in its various forms", the final declaration affirms, realizes "the radical insufficiency of this changeable world; it teaches a way by which men, in a devout and confident spirit, may be able either to acquire the state of perfect libera-

[121] Henri de Lubac, *Aspects du bouddhisme* (Paris: Cerf, 2012). The first volume was translated by George Lamb as *Aspects of Buddhism* (London: Sheed & Ward, 1953), and its opening chapter is reprinted in *Communio* 15 (1988): 497–510. The second volume was translated by Amita Bhaka in the *Buddha Dhyana Dana Review* 12, nos. 5–6 (2002), and 13, no. 1 (2003), at www.bdcu.org.au/bddronline. *La Rencontre du bouddhisme et de l'Occident* (Paris: Aubier, 1952; Cerf, 2000) is untranslated.

[122] De Lubac, *Vatican Council Notebooks*, 1:36–38.

tion, or attain, by their own efforts or through higher help [*superiore auxilio*], supreme illumination."[123]

## De Lubac and His Circle

The Society of Jesus, which de Lubac joined at age seventeen, is a worldwide religious order founded in 1540 by Saint Ignatius Loyola (1491–1556). From their inception, Jesuits have devoted themselves to educational, intellectual, scientific, and pastoral work. Although like monks and friars in professing vows, Jesuits are highly mobile, which sets them apart from many other orders. They travel widely to undertake missionary and other work in a wide range of secular contexts. For de Lubac, as for other Jesuits, the order was an extremely close community whose members, even when geographically separated, offered one another intense support.

De Lubac edited the works of many other theologians and philosophers, many of them fellow Jesuits. However, his engagement with Pierre Teilhard de Chardin is notable because it includes four authored books. Moreover, in his memoirs, de Lubac refers to Teilhard more times than to any other thinker.[124] Teilhard had produced a considerable body of work combining theology, philosophy, and evolutionary science, much of it in essay form, but had published very little owing to official censure. Following his death, Teilhard's oeuvre was published in France by an editorial committee, with volumes rapidly translated into other languages including English. Essentially an interwar thinker, Teilhard had sought to interpret classic theological topics, such as matter and spirit, action and passion, causation, Christology, mysticism, and the Eucharist, for a globalized and evolutionary world and, for this purpose, took Scripture's

---

[123] Pope Paul VI, Declaration on the Relation of the Church to Non-Christian Religions *Nostra aetate* (October 28, 1965), 2. See Mikka Ruokanen, *The Catholic Doctrine of Non-Christian Religions according to the Second Vatican Council* (Leiden: Brill, 1992), 124–28.

[124] Henri de Lubac, *Mémoire sur l'occasion de mes écrits* (Paris: Cerf, 2006), 504. Teilhard is mentioned 64 times and Aquinas is referred to 63 times.

moral and eschatological senses especially seriously.[125] He wished to address both Christians and a wider public.

By the time Teilhard's works were being published, however, they were read and interpreted far more liberally than would earlier have been likely. During the 1960s, Teilhard became synonymous for many with a New Age spirituality that existed independently of the institutional Church and that appraised all religions as equivalent manifestations of a single truth. However, de Lubac was at pains to show that this was a serious misreading of Teilhard, even suggesting that Teilhard was among the inspirers of his own doctrine of the supernatural. As early as 1918, Teilhard identified faith in Christ with the "integration of the natural in the supernatural" and, in correspondence exchanged while de Lubac was developing his own theory, sharply critiqued the notion that the supernatural is in competition with a nature presumed to be static.[126] Moreover, Teilhard confidently believed the Roman Catholic Church to be the essential center of the progressive spiritualization and conversion of the world.[127] De Lubac was justly concerned that Teilhard tended too far toward a naturalistic exposition of Christian truth, focusing on its outworking in material, spiritual, historical, and evolutionary processes, rather than on objective biblical and doctrinal teaching. He also thought that Teilhard was too concerned to speak to an age that he regarded as technical and scientific and, in so doing, went too far in adapting classic theological language. However, de Lubac also recognized the value of such an effort of speech and translation and, in his own later work, acknowledged the importance of mysticism, which was basic to Teilhard's vision. In any case, de Lubac's approach to his confrère was, as with far older theological sources, one of careful reading and fair assessment.

De Lubac produced studies of the works of other French clergy. Among them was the Jesuit theologian and chaplain Yves de Montcheuil (1900–1944), who was martyred by the Gestapo after being

---

[125] David John Ayotte, *Globalization and Multicultural Ministry: A Teilhardian Vision* (Mahwah, N.J.: Paulist Press, 2012), 33–59.

[126] Henri de Lubac, *The Religion of Teilhard de Chardin* (London: Collins, 1970), 127.

[127] Henri de Lubac, *The Faith of Teilhard de Chardin and Note on the Apologetics of Teilhard de Chardin* (London: Burns & Oates, 1965), 186–96.

arrested during a pastoral visit to members of the Resistance. De Montcheuil had articulated an active conception of Christian faith, finding its expression in a reinvigorated Church life and a passion for social justice.[128] Located in Paris, he played a key role during the war years in writing for and distributing the *Cahiers* and *Courriers du Témoignage chrétien* in the occupied northern zone. De Lubac also published writings and reflections on Paul Claudel.[129] A poet and a Roman Catholic, Claudel was able, de Lubac suggested, to deploy allusion and analogy to capture some aspects of the Christian tradition better than most theologians, communicating the grandeur of the faith in its outward manifestations as well as in its interior inspiration in the hearts of believers.

De Lubac was also an indefatigable editor of the correspondence that so often sustained the Jesuit community of his era. Three volumes of Teilhard's letters to his parents during his years of formation, although theologically insignificant, illuminate the life and concerns of a Jesuit student of the early twentieth century.[130] Although Maurice Blondel was not himself a Jesuit, his philosophy and friendship sustained many, and de Lubac collated the letters that he and Teilhard had exchanged in 1919, adding extensive annotations. The exchange covered topics such as action, the supernatural, and mysticism and is important in showing Blondel's influence on Teilhard as well as de Lubac's affinity with both figures.[131] De Lubac published a series of letters from Étienne Gilson (1884–1978), the prolific historian of medieval philosophy, covering the related topics of metaphysics, epistemology, the supernatural, Thomism, the vision of God, and

---

[128] Henri de Lubac, *Three Jesuits Speak: Yves de Montcheuil, 1899–1944; Charles Nicolet, 1897–1961; Jean Zupan, 1899–1968*, trans. K. D. Whitehead (San Francisco: Ignatius Press, 1987), 13–60.

[129] De Lubac, *Theological Fragments*, 423–41.

[130] Pierre Teilhard de Chardin, *Letters from Egypt, 1905–1908*, trans. Mary Ilford (New York: Herder, 1965); Chardin, *Letters from Hastings, 1908–1912*, trans. Judith de Stefano (New York: Herder, 1968); Chardin, *Letters from Paris, 1912–1914*, trans. Michael Mazzarese (New York: Herder, 1967).

[131] Pierre Teilhard de Chardin, *Pierre Teilhard de Chardin—Maurice Blondel: Correspondence*, trans. William Whitman (New York: Herder, 1976).

Teilhard.[132] His extensive annotations are as informative as the letters themselves. Edited correspondence with other figures remains untranslated. The time and industry that de Lubac devoted to publishing the writings of others is testimony to his deep commitment to theology as a shared, dialogical enterprise.

## Later Years

For much of his adult life, de Lubac did not enjoy good health. On the night of November 1, 1917, while serving in Eastern France, he had been seriously wounded in the head and in his right hand and arm by shrapnel. Two months in hospital and an extended period of recuperation were required, and he did not return to military service until the armistice in November 1918. His tasks then included guarding German prisoners of war, maintaining civil order, and administration. The injury resulted in ongoing bouts of dizziness, earaches, and vulnerability to meningitis, which he did not overcome until 1954, following a full diagnosis and operation.[133] This gave de Lubac almost twenty years of satisfactory health. However, on January 6, 1972, he suffered a serious heart attack, followed by further attacks and health problems that persisted through the remainder of his life.[134]

De Lubac's final two decades were also marked by a growing frustration with the leadership of the Roman Catholic Church in France and with the Jesuit Order in France. He thought that Roman Catholics in France had been failed by their bishops, who, in the wake of the Second Vatican Council, had wrongly associated collegiality with a doctrinal and administrative distancing from the Holy See, a large and bureaucratic national organization that stifled the charisms of individual bishops, and a preference for national activities over diocesan roles. De Lubac perceived these failings to be

---

[132] Étienne Gilson, *Letters of Étienne Gilson to Henri de Lubac*, trans. Mary Emily Hamilton (San Francisco: Ignatius Press, 1988).

[133] Georges Chantraine and Marie-Gabrielle Lemaire, *Henri de Lubac*, vol. 4 (Paris: Cerf, 2007–), 1:547; De Lubac, *At the Service*, 19.

[134] Chantraine and Lemaire, *Henri de Lubac*, 4:508.

responsible for the rise of the conservative movement around the French missionary archbishop Marcel Lefebvre (1905–1991), who founded his own seminary in Switzerland and, from 1976, ordained his own seminarians without diocesan approval.[135]

During the same decade, de Lubac developed similar disquiet with the Jesuit Order in France. In 1974, the issues reached a head with three separate events. First, de Lubac's longstanding friend and collaborator Jean Cardinal Daniélou died of a heart attack during a pastoral visit to Mimì Santoni, a woman who was said to be a prostitute. Speculation about the circumstances abounded within the order, which, in de Lubac's assessment, amounted to a "slanderous campaign" fueled by the media and motivated by "fratricidal hate" for the legacy of Daniélou and of others of his generation, including himself.[136] Secondly, France's four separate Jesuit provinces were merged into a single province centered in Paris. The Jesuit house at Fourvière in Lyon—the country's ancient Christian heart—was closed, and de Lubac was required to move to Paris. Thirdly, the Jesuit order's thirty-second General Congregation began in Rome and committed the Jesuit order to promoting social justice. This gathering had the effect, de Lubac averred, of stoking the campaign of agitation, subversion, and even abuse against Pope Paul VI to which French Jesuits, he contended, made their full contribution.[137] Previously, in 1968, de Lubac had rebuffed an invitation from Yves Congar to sign the "Declaration for the freedom of theology", which was promoted by the editors of the journal *Concilium*. His fellow Jesuit Karl Rahner and the Dominican Edward Schillebeeckx had, along with Congar and Hans Küng, drafted the declaration, but de Lubac thought that it imperiled Church unity, which was at that point, he argued, threatened more by the undermining of the Magisterium than by restrictions on free theological speech.[138]

---

[135] Ibid., 4:490–92, 591–97.

[136] Ibid., 4:518–25; De Lubac, *At the Service*, 160.

[137] De Lubac, *At the Service*, 158–59.

[138] Chantraine and Lemaire, *Henri de Lubac*, 4:440–44; De Lubac, *At the Service*, 366–67. For the text, Hans Küng, *Reforming the Church Today: Keeping Hope Alive* (Edinburgh: T&T Clark, 1990), 177–80.

De Lubac also had concerns about the direction in which mainstream Roman Catholic theology was moving, offering an extended critique of Schillebeeckx' exposition of the Church as the sacrament of the world. He objects that the Belgian Dominican, in his theological exposition of the key conciliar texts *Lumen gentium* and *Gaudium et spes*, advocates implicit Christianity. Rather than presenting the Church as the unambiguous source of the sacralization of the world, Schillebeeckx sees the Church as manifesting, through a process of *de*sacralization, the sanctification of the world, supposing the world to possess sanctity independently of the Church or of revelation.[139] De Lubac is at pains to stress that he is not claiming that the Church should not repent of her errors or that she should not closely attend to the realities of secular life. Nevertheless, in order to transform the world, the Church needs to recover her identity, not as the sacrament of that same world, but as the sacrament of Christ, who confronts the world.[140] For this reason, de Lubac robustly contests Schillebeeckx' 1967 commendation of Christian involvement in Marxist-inspired political revolutions to overthrow established political orders and install alternative regimes. To advocate such enterprises is, he protests, to conflate world history with salvation history.

By the late 1970s, de Lubac's capacity to participate in theological debate was limited by steeply declining health. However, two events brought him new hope for the future of the Church: the 1978 election of the archbishop of Kraków, Karol Wojtyła (1920–2005), as Pope John Paul II and the 1981 appointment of Aron Jean-Marie Lustiger (1926–2007) as archbishop of Paris.[141] At the Second Vatican Council, Wojtyła and de Lubac had worked together on the draft of what became the pastoral constitution *Gaudium et spes*, and de Lubac had provided the preface for the French translation of his book *Love and Responsibility*.[142] The two had exchanged letters several times a year, and the Polish cardinal's spiritual resistance

---

[139] De Lubac, *A Brief Catechesis on Nature and Grace*, trans. Brother Richard Arnandez, F.S.C. (San Francisco: Ignatius Press, 1984), 191–235.

[140] De Lubac, *Splendor*, 202–35.

[141] Chantraine and Lemaire, *Henri de Lubac*, 4:567–68, 578–79.

[142] Karol Wojtyła, *Amour et responsabilité* (Paris: Dialogue/Stock, 1965), 7–9; de Lubac, *At the Service*, 171–73.

to Communism from behind the Iron Curtain was grounded in a conviction of its evil similar to de Lubac's. Lustiger also had Polish ancestry, but with the important difference that he was a teenage convert. In the words of his epitaph in the crypt of Notre-Dame Cathedral, he was born Jewish, became Christian by faith and baptism, and, like the apostles, remained Jewish. Lustiger's mother had perished in the Auschwitz concentration camp, and he represented the continuity of the Jewish and Christian faiths that de Lubac had expounded since the Second World War. De Lubac praised Lustiger's spiritual leadership of the Church in Paris, and, following de Lubac's death, Lustiger lauded de Lubac's spiritual witness against Nazism and was as well a key advocate for the publication of de Lubac's collected works in French.[143]

Pope Paul VI had considered making de Lubac a cardinal in 1969, but it was Pope John Paul II who finally did so, in 1983.[144] Being almost ninety, de Lubac was exempted from episcopal consecration. It is appropriate that the pope who had personally aided Jews in occupied Poland and had helped to speed Communism's fall chose to honor an old friend who had himself done much to counter persecution and secularist political ideology, also at personal risk, over the course of a long life. At his death in 1991, de Lubac was the oldest cardinal. Following his funeral Mass at the Cathedral of Notre-Dame in Paris, at which Lustiger presided, his ashes were interred in the simple Jesuit plot in the Vaugirard cemetery, which is overlooked on all sides by apartment blocks, alongside those of his confreres, including Daniélou. In order to reach the site, the visitor passes by the far larger plot reserved for army and navy veterans who died at the nearby Hôtel des Invalides. This juxtaposition might seem incongruous, but it reminds visitors of de Lubac's own belief that, in human life, there is a proper secularity through which sacred purposes are worked out.

[143] "Hommage au cardinal Lustiger", in de Lubac, *Mémoire*, 313–27; Jean-Marie Lustiger, "Souvenirs et presence du cardinal Henri de Lubac", in *Henri de Lubac et le mystère de l'Église*, Études lubaciennes 1 (Paris: Cerf, 1999), 219–24.

[144] De Lubac, *Vatican Council Notebooks*, 1:39.

## Conclusion: Reading de Lubac

As a theologian in a Church with a Magisterium, de Lubac had neither the need nor the desire to refound Christian doctrine on first principles. De Lubac, instead, wished to rearticulate doctrine and its implications for a new age, speaking both to theologians and to a wider public.[145] Some of his works, such as those on the supernatural and on scriptural exegesis, are of a scale and complexity that indicate their intended audience to be professional theologians. However, de Lubac produced his works on the Church for a wider audience. The best known of these is *Catholicism*, which has been through multiple printings and offers a powerful synopsis of the essence of Christian belief.

Different agendas and audiences required different styles. De Lubac's studies directed primarily to professional theologians frequently overflow with a tremendous volume of source material, to the extent that his authorial voice is sometimes obscured. However, such works successfully build cumulative cases, and de Lubac clearly believed that sources may speak for themselves. Only in the appendix to *Catholicism* does he offer a series of extracts with no commentary or analysis whatsoever. In other works, such as *The Discovery of God* and *A Brief Catechesis on Nature and Grace*, exposition and argument are in balance. A different genre is on display in *Paradoxes of Faith* and *More Paradoxes*, which are volumes of aphorisms, grouped by theme, that de Lubac compiled over the course of his life.

For the systematic theologian, some classic topics are easier to identify and appraise in de Lubac's corpus than others. Constructive engagement is not helped by the fact that many of the English translations of his works lack an index. Nonetheless, scriptural exegesis, anthropology, sin, salvation, and ecclesiology are the most prominent topics. It is initially less clear where to look for a coherent doctrine of God, Christology, or pneumatology. However, de Lubac regards these major doctrinal topics as approachable only via the revelation contained in Scripture, as this has been received and articulated by the Church, and by means of interior reflection.

---

[145] De Lubac, *Splendor*, 236–67.

His work on these subjects is therefore dispersed, and, if a coherent view is to be developed, a synthetic effort is therefore required of the reader. The precise nature of de Lubac's profound and provocative theological legacy is a matter of ongoing debate and will be evaluated in the concluding interpretive postscript.

## Note on Sources

De Lubac's referencing is copious. Footnotes are retained in whole or in part if they refer to material quoted in the main text or to significant primary or secondary sources that contribute to an understanding of de Lubac's methodology or form part of his argument. For detailed study, de Lubac's original texts should be used, and their pagination is given within square brackets.

Quotations, titles, phrases, and words that appear in languages other than English are given in English translation. Some translations follow published versions as indicated. If a work is available in a modern translation with a title that is not a literal translation of the original or has been significantly discussed using such a title, it is this new title that is generally given.

Following the sources are biographical and bibliographical details of the theologians whom de Lubac cites. English translations of relevant works are given if available.

I am extremely grateful to Ryan Tafilowski for editorial assistance, Philip Marsden for digitization, and to Anne Englund Nash for her work on the manuscript.

I

# The Discovery of God

*On Easter Monday, 1915, de Lubac left Saint Stanislas College, the Jesuit novitiate in Hastings on the south coast of England, to answer a summons to military service. He was nineteen years old. In the army, his new companions included many who were skeptical about Christianity. One was a trainee teacher who was neither an atheist nor a believer, and de Lubac talked with him and with others about his faith. He dates his earliest reflections on the nature of faith to these conversations with unbelieving friends. Much later, he compiled his reflections in a slim volume, with the intention of offering it to a "few friends who had little faith".*[1]

*When compiling this volume, de Lubac also made use of material on the origin of religion, which he had taught at the Catholic Theological Faculty in Lyon from 1929. He argued not only that human belief in God is innate, but that belief in a single God is fundamental to human culture. This "primitive monotheism" thesis conflicts with understandings of monotheism as a historical development of earlier polytheistic belief. Of the book, de Lubac wrote: "The numerous testimonies about the graces of light occasioned by these pages have brought me a superabundant consolation for the trouble they caused."*[2] *He had not intended the book to be read as a theological treatise. It nevertheless received considerable criticism from conservative theologians, who accused de Lubac of fideism. This is the view that belief may be founded on faith alone, with reason playing no part. De Lubac was also charged with ontologism, which is the theory that the first object of intellectual knowledge is*

[1] Henri de Lubac, *De la connaissance de Dieu* (1945; Paris: Témoignage chrétien, 1948). See de Lubac, *At the Service of the Church: Henri de Lubac Reflects on the Circumstances that Occasioned His Writings*, trans. Anne Elizabeth Englund (San Francisco: Ignatius Press, 1993), 41–42.

[2] De Lubac, *At the Service*, 42.

*the immediate intuition of God and of the divine ideas, with human concepts being merely derivative of this prior intuition.*[3]

*To rebut both charges, de Lubac produced a much enlarged version of his earlier work, which was translated as* The Discovery of God. *He here shows how his ideas about the origin of faith are fully consistent with those of the Christian theological tradition. Notably, although the book's topic is the relation of faith and reason, de Lubac does not, in his own words, "insist inordinately on the exposition of proofs for the existence of God".*[4] *Rather, he wishes to understand the intellectual impulse that impels the quest for such proofs. Another of the book's achievements is its reappraisal of negative theology. It is easy to associate the notion that man lacks knowledge of God with agnosticism or even with atheism. However, de Lubac views the negative moment of unknowing as allowing access to a "more fundamental positive exigency, there at the beginning and constantly recurring", which defines the "human spirit in its relation to God". He presents this dependence of positivity on negativity as "diametrically opposed to the extrinsic and restrictive rationalism" of neo-Thomism, which knows only positive knowledge. De Lubac also wishes, however, to counter the "undue inflation" of negative theology that he sees occurring in response to extreme rationalism, which, in the aftermath of the Second World War, was leading toward atheist existentialism. Moving, in de Lubac's terms, in an atmosphere of natural theology, this book draws on historic Christian sources in order to transcend the opposition of positivity and negativity, examining both the "ways by which we go to God" and those "by which God draws us to him".*[5]

---

[3] Ibid., 310–11.

[4] Henri de Lubac, *Sur les chemins de Dieu* (Paris: Aubier, 1956); De Lubac, *At the Service*, 80–81 (80).

[5] Postscript to Henri de Lubac, *The Discovery of God*, trans. Alexander Dru with Marc Sebanc and Cassian Fulsom (Edinburgh: T&T Clark, 1996), 205–20 (220).

## *The Origin of the Idea of God*

[p. 20] All attempts to find a "genesis" for the idea of God—like the attempts to "reduce" it to something else by explaining its genesis—err in some respect or other. The idea of God is a unique idea, distinct from all others, and it cannot be fitted into any system. It strikes down like a flash of lightning, and can be seen cutting through the history of humanity; it plays havoc with the laborious syntheses of ethnologists and historians, and upsets the evolutionary schemes and the erudite "physiologies of religion." Once the intelligence reaches maturity, the idea of God germinates spontaneously.

But however indestructible it may be from then on, it does not immediately shine forth in all its brilliance. And equally it is very far from being so fully and peacefully established in the mind that it holds undisturbed sway. On the contrary, one is tempted to think that, like the seed sown in the Gospel, it fell among thorns and thistles and was quickly stifled by the incredible proliferation of myths.[6] Or else, if it bears fruit, it seems as though the fruit were so closely intertwined with the luxuriant vegetation of the wild seed that there was no longer any way in practice of removing the latter without uprooting the former. Insofar as religion co-exists in this way with a myth, it lends the latter a power of seduction which is, in the end, turned against religion itself. The gods thus secretly nourished by the idea of God are parasites and prevent the true God from emerging. . . . Hence the "deluge of idolatry"[7] that covers the face [p. 21] of the earth. So that in order to attain to religion pure and undefiled, it seems as though we had to sacrifice all these gods, instead of purifying them or testing their worth, and retaining those whose claims prove authentic. Man frees himself from superstition through atheism[8] . . . only to fall once again into

---

Excerpted from Henri de Lubac, *The Discovery of God*, trans. Alexander Dru with Marc Sebanc and Cassian Fulsom (Edinburgh: T&T Clark, 1996), 20–33, 59–65, 145–54.

[6] [Mt 13:1–23; Mk 4:1–20; Lk 8:1–15.—Ed.]

[7] Bossuet, *Elévations sur les mystères* [Uplifting of the soul on the divine mysteries], 7e semaine [7th week] (*Oeuvres*, ed. F. Lachat [1862], ch. 7, p. 135).

[8] Is this not the case, in practice, with Buddhism? Its founder, no doubt, does not

superstition. Or else . . . or else. . . . There seems no limit to the hypotheses man can construct. How, then, can he break out of the circle? Whichever way he takes, his reason is faced with difficulties and with a thousand illusions to overcome before he can emerge triumphant! And in most cases how great is the uncertainty and how many are the errors! And even in the cry of monotheism itself—so rationally well-founded after all—one can often detect a certain lack of assurance:

"O stay of the earth, and you who are enthroned above it, whoever you are, thought can approach you only with difficulty. Whether you are Zeus, or the Supreme Necessity, or the human spirit. . . ."[9]

. . . Unless, that is, God himself intervenes to break the fatal circle and elects a trusted servant who is charged with the task of announcing him to his brethren.[10] Which, as the author of the Epistle to the Hebrews tells us, may happen "at sundry times and in diverse manners."[11]

It is only natural that the idea of God should be, at one and the same time, ready to emerge and yet menaced with suffocation; for mankind—made in the image of God, though sinful—while destined to grope its way slowly up, is nevertheless obsessed from the first moment of its awakening by a call from above. From the very beginning two tendencies have been at work to retard and deflect man's natural impulse towards [p. 22] his creator. One of these tendencies results from the very conditions in which the intelligence

---

deny the gods, but declares them all incapable of assuring the salvation of men; they themselves need to be saved, and the Buddhas are above even the greatest of the gods.

[9] Euripides, *The Trojan Women*, ll. 884–886. [Euripides (ca. 480–ca. 406 B.C.) was a Greek tragic poet who was controversial for his sensitivity to women and other less-privileged members of society. His play is set in the aftermath of the sack of Troy, while its women are being taken away into slavery and are mourning the loss of their homeland.—ED.]

[10] Cf. Vatican I, the Constitution *Dei filius* ch. 2, *De revelatione*: "It is indeed thanks to this divine revelation that those matters concerning God which are not of themselves beyond the scope of human reason can, even in the present state of the human race, be known by everyone without difficulty, with firm certitude and with no intermingling of error" (Acta Concilii Vaticani, ch. 250). (Eng. trans.: Norman P. Tanner, ed., *Decrees of the Ecumenical Councils*, vol. 2: Trent to Vatican II [Washington, D.C., 1990], p. 806.)

[11] Hebrews 1:1. . . .

is obliged to work in order to triumph, little by little, over the darkness; the other, according to the teaching of the Catholic faith, is the immediate fruit of an original moral deviation. Both tendencies, the natural and the perverse, supplement and reinforce one another in obstructing the royal road of the mind, and tempt it aside among the myriad labyrinthine paths of magic and myth. There is the tendency to confuse the Author of Nature with the Nature through which he reveals himself obscurely, whose characteristics we cannot help employing in order to think of him; and there is the tendency to forsake an exacting and all too incorruptible God in favor of something inferior or fictitious. When these tendencies work together, the categories become lifeless and rigid. The world itself becomes more dense. And what should have been a sign becomes a screen. The initial vision is dissipated almost before it is perceived . . . and the divine star disappears behind its "gross shadow":

> [p. 23] Le feu, le vent, l'air subtil,
> La voute étoilée, l'onde impétueuse ou les flambeaux du ciel
> Sont regardés comme les maîtres du monde.

> (Fire, wind and the subtle air,
> The starry vault, the impetuous swell or the torches in the sky
> Are regarded as the masters of the world.)

In the furthest recesses of our consciousness, "the glory of the incorruptible God," before it has had time to shine with all its brilliance, is exchanged for the gods of nothingness or untruth. . . .[12] Or at least the God who is really close to us has been put at a distance—to remain for a long while the unknown God. Even to those who still preserve a memory of him, he becomes a forsaken God. And so it becomes necessary to rediscover him by stages, groping and fumbling and sometimes thinking that we have lost him. Even at times

[12] Wisdom 13:2; Romans 1:23 (with allusion to the story of the golden calf; cf. Psalm 105:19–20); Jeremiah 2:11: "And my people have exchanged their glory for that which does not exist!" Cf. Racine, *Hymnes traduits du bréviaire romain* [Hymns translated from the Roman Breviary], Monday at Lauds:

> Star of which the sun is merely a crude shadow,
> Sacred day, from which the day borrows its brightness.

when the knowledge of God seems to have made decisive progress, he is still easily conceived of as an individual with human passions, or, on the other hand, as a vague and diffused Force. When we think we have exhausted the idea of God, it is no more than a sort of *materia prima* [prime matter], a being as indeterminate and as close to nothingness as empty space; or else it becomes a principle wholly lacking in inwardness, an abstraction with no power of irradiation. Each new formula seems more discouraging than the last and, by reaction, provokes its contrary. The spiritual gain is never definitive, though this alone could stabilize and nourish the intellectual gain. The better is transformed into the worse, and the great force for good in human affairs is enslaved to profane ends: once again man deifies his needs, his interests, his passions, his ignorance and his follies. . . . And then what should have been [p. 24] progress takes the form of negation. More often than not, the gods of fable are supplanted by the Divine instead of by the Living God. Religions and morals close in mortal combat. For man's inwardness is the fruit of his victory over the gods. . . . But from time to time, nevertheless, a ray of pure light filters through. The pagans themselves have their "hidden saints," and the true God chooses his prophets where he will.[13]

There are many facts which make the Marxist theory, and theories like it, plausible.[14] The whole religious system varies and presents different characteristics according to whether man is a hunter, a shepherd, or cultivates the soil. And among unbelievers Marxists

---

[13] Clement of Alexandria, *Stromata* [Miscellany] 5, ch. 6, 35, n. 2: the candelabra of the temple, symbol of Christ, "illuminating in various ways and by multiple fires" the men who believe and hope in him. See also Jean Daniélou, *Les saints "païens" de l'Ancien Testament* [Holy pagans of the Old Testament] (1956). . . .

[14] [The political theorist Karl Marx (1818–1883), who was born in Prussia but spent the second half of his life in London, developed a materialist understanding of history. According to this, social change is the product of economic relationships, and religion, by presenting future life as heavenly rather than earthly, is a mere panacea for social ills. However, the relationship between Marx' own theories and Marxist analysis is disputed. Marxists sought to apply his theories in societies where industrial development was at an early stage (e.g., Russia) rather than completed (e.g., Britain). Moreover, his materialism suggests that theory has no constructive function in society.—ED.]

are not alone in emphasizing this sort of law. Research as a whole confirms it, and the historical-cultural school has made it the principle of religious evolution and has applied it rigorously to all forms of religion, apart from supernatural revelation. They have classified the religion of "pastoral" peoples, of those who "gather fruits", of the "hunters" and of the "planters". . . . Similarly, it has been observed that in a civilization where the horse dominates the economy, the gods adored are chivalric, etc. It is also a fact that the gods of small states, bounded by narrow frontiers and centered upon themselves, are unlike the gods of the great cosmopolitan cities. As the social group expands from tribe to city and then from nation to empire, the cosmic consciousness is ordered and organized accordingly, and involves a series of parallel transformations in rite and myth. It is perfectly true, therefore, that myths and [p. 25] rites reveal and mirror social conditions—which in their turn are closely dependent upon economic conditions—and in consequence these religions tend to lend their constraints to reinforce economic conditions. Yet, to be perfectly just, it should be noted that, for all its social abuses, religion thus envisaged consecrates the very principle of society; thanks to the social and mental coherence which it ensures, it contributes more than any other element to enabling man to live, which is the prime condition of progress.

There is, however, something else to be taken into account: the essential point. One might perhaps say that Marxism, like rationalism, is quantitatively right—somewhat in the same way that determinism is true in respect of the greater part of human action, at least as far as appearance is concerned. Historical materialism is one of those basic truths which cannot fail to convince at first sight, but which is of no help to those who desire to penetrate to the heart of the real. Where experience is concerned, do not the false and the insignificant attract infinitely more attention than the substantial and authentic? The fakes and illusions of the mind, its habitually lazy or bastard forms, its repeated failures, its standardized products, like its sudden unforeseen errors, are all plainly visible, and the observer cannot fail to see them. The area they cover is vast; they encumber the scene. Whereas the thing that counts most, the first sign of change, and the seed of things to come, is almost always rare and hidden, though its action may be widely diffused and may permeate everything. But even if it happens to be noticed, it still needs to be envisaged from within if it is to be appreciated at its proper value; by a method, that is, which has nothing to do with statistical methods and is beyond the scope of empirical observation. There is every reason to think, for example, that the Marxist analysis, applied conscientiously and as intelligently as possible twenty centuries ago, in Palestine, would have overlooked the humble fact summed up in a name: Jesus of Nazareth—as in fact the Jewish and Roman historians overlooked it. That almost imperceptible fact slipped through their nets, and if it happens to be caught in the mesh of learned explanations, it is emptied of its explosive force.

Nevertheless, there are certain broad lines which are too prominent to remain entirely concealed from any who will simply open their eyes. We are told, for example, that the cult of a God without form mirrors an age of trade with distant parts, and a banking system. Is monotheism the result, then, of the slow unification of the powers of the earth?—How are we, then, to explain the history of India, where profound systems of religious philosophy and exalted forms of adoration blossomed in a primitive [p. 26] economy and a politically amorphous society? And, above all, have people read the precepts of the Jewish Decalogue? (Their precise date is not, in this context, of great importance.) "Hear, O Israel! . . . I am the Lord thy God. . . . Thou shalt have no other gods before me. Thou shalt not make thee any graven image. . . . For I, the Lord thy God, am a jealous God."[15]

It does not require any special powers of observation to distinguish two kinds of "monotheistic" religion in our Western world, in spite of their multiple implications and their diverse origins. The first is, at least partly, the fruit of social and political development as well as of reflection. Little by little the pantheons are formed in the image of what happens on earth. The gods are organized, a hierarchy is formed, and their very number and variety begin to suggest the unity of the divine.[16] In the end the head of the divine society grows

[15] Deuteronomy 5:1–8.

[16] Cf. Maximus of Tyre: "Now there is found throughout the whole world a teaching

into the supreme god, while the remaining gods are no more than his manifestations or his serfs.[17] As a nation comes to know the gods of subject nations, it amalgamates them with its own by understanding them as equivalent in a way that is at once enriching and unifying. If, perchance, there is competition, the gods of the vanquished, themselves defeated, are eliminated, unless, indeed, they are adopted by the conquerors or become demons. . . . Such, with a hundred variations, is the case in Babylon and in Egypt, among the ancient Indo-Europeans, and in the Achaemenid Empire,[18] as in the Hellenistic world and in Rome under the Empire. . . . Can the result be said to have been all gain, politically, culturally, and for thought? For the most part, yes, and sometimes the profit was very considerable. But can it be said to mark religious progress, properly [p. 27] speaking? Not always, and sometimes not at all. Even in cases where anthropomorphism was transcended, the goal reached was hardly more than an abstract Divine or divinized Nature: *Aequum est quidquid omnes colunt, unum putari: eadem spectamus astra, commune coelum est, idem nos mundus involvit. . . .*[19] (It is right that whatever everybody worships should be considered one thing: we behold the same stars, the heavens are common to us all, the same world embraces us.) The concentration of gods has not given birth to God!

In the second type of monotheism, on the contrary, the one God affirms his uniqueness with a fierce, exclusive jealousy. "There is no God but God." He is the result neither of concentration nor of syncretism, whether political or intellectual. He imposes and sanctions a new order of values. He is the God who cannot be reached by way of the gods; the path to him leads through conversion and

according to which there is one God who is king and father of all things, and many gods who are sons of this god, co-regents with him. Thus say the Greeks and the Barbarians."

[17] Cf. Dio Chrysostom: "Some people assert that Apollos, Helios and Dionysius are identical to one another, and simply gather together all the gods into a single force of power."

[18] [The First Persian Empire (ca. 550–330 B.C.) established by Cyrus the Great. It extended westward from Persia as far as Palestine, Egypt, Asia Minor, and the Black Sea coast.—ED.]

[19] Symmachus, *Relatio*, n. 10. . . .

the breaking of idols—those made with hands and those fashioned in the heart. He is the God who throws down his gauntlet to the gods of Nature—just as the unknown young David threw down his challenge to the celebrated giant Goliath.[20] A God who must be followed, though it involves leaving the country of one's fathers behind one. . . . A God who leads into the unknown. A God who scandalizes those he does not attract. And before his face "the gods of the nations" are nought but "wood and stone": vanity, nothingness, "the abomination," "sin," "filthy" and "impure," "corpses." They are the "non-gods." "Do not forsake the Lord and adore the gods of nothingness."[21] "Behold, the Lord will come on a white cloud and all the works of the Egyptians will be swept away before his face."[22] "A jealous and exclusive God, who divides everything and leaves nothing standing before him." Just now we were dealing with an easygoing Principle which justified the practices of polytheism and consolidated the dominions of the flesh, while remaining in itself the possession of a small [p. 28] élite of the wise. Now we find a Being in no sense abstract, though purely spiritual; a living Being who, although invisible, acts; an intransigent Being who demands that all worship should be addressed to him, and who wishes to be recognized by all men; a transcendent Being, though nonetheless powerfully personal, who overflows the boundaries of all the cities of the earth; not a cosmopolitan God, but a God who is to be, if he is not already, the universal God.

The second form of monotheism alone is charged with power. It alone is pregnant with religious progress, for it is the source of a radical metamorphosis in the theory and practice of religion. It alone can promote moral and social progress, even where it does not actually initiate it. The God of this monotheism is the only God who can be the object of faith in the full sense of the word.[23] In its encounter with the first form of monotheism, the second form

---

[20] [1 Sam 17.—Ed.]

[21] *Secrets of Enoch*, ch. 2.

[22] Isaiah 19:1. . . .

[23] Cf. the analyses of St. Augustine, of Faustus of Riez, of St. Anselm (*Monologion*, ch. 76–78); . . . of St. Albert the Great and of St. Thomas on the formula "credere in Deum" [believing in God]. . . .

makes no attempt to compromise or to compose the differences between them; it must, in the first place, be victorious over it. *Hebraeorum Deus a Romanis non receptus, quia se solum coli voluerit.* (The God of the Hebrews was not accepted by the Romans, because he wished that only he should be worshipped.)

Then, perhaps, it may utilize the first form of monotheism to express and complete itself or in order to spread abroad, in that way leading the first form to its goal. Now we do not find the second form of monotheism [p. 29] appearing in the great unified states at the conclusion of periods of expansion and conquest, any more than at the end of periods of profound speculation, or in the wake of economic changes. As far as can be seen from the hopeless state of the sources, the religion of Zoroaster,[24] "the least pagan of pagan religions," a religion whose divine forces are not gods so much as the "attributes of the unique divinity",[25] arose in one of the most remote provinces of Iran, far from the focus of culture which existed at that time in Babylon, and before the era of syncretism[26] was opened by the conquests of Cyrus. The history of Judaism and of Islam, too, belies all the theories of the development of religion, which only invoke factors which are foreign to it. Israel was a small nation with a rudimentary economy, a crude philosophy, and a civilization far less developed than that of its great neighbors, who each in turn crushed it. If Israel was quick to profit from their wider conceptions, especially during the exile, it did so for its own ends, and in order to clothe the God which it alone affirmed in more magnificent array. Moreover, it was during the Captivity, in a period of ruin and defeat, that the Israelites celebrated the triumph

[24] [Known also as Zarathustra, a semi-mythical Iranian prophet whose teaching inspired the later religion of Zoroastrianism (Mazdaism). The seventeen poems attributed to him are known as Gathas. De Lubac saw their teaching as anticipating aspects of Christian belief, including creation, a savior, eschatology, and a future divine judgment (Henri de Lubac, *Catholicism: Christ and the Common Destiny of Man*, trans. Lancelot C. Sheppard and Sister Elizabeth Englund, O.C.D. [San Francisco: Ignatius Press, 1988], 158–63). —Ed.]

[25] Jean-Pierre de Menasce, O.P., "Le monde moral iranien [The Iranian Moral World]," *Les morales non-chrétiennes* [Non-Christian moral systems] (Journées "Ethnologie et Chrétienté" [Paris, 1954]), p. 42.

[26] [The mixing of different religions in such a way that the boundaries separating them become unclear.—Ed.]

of their God.[27] As for the Arabs before the Hegira,[28] they can hardly be said to have been united. The idea of God in its highest manifestations and in its humblest forms always bursts and overflows social as well as mental categories. One may indeed say "the Spirit [blows] where it [wills]."[29]

A lasting religion must have roots, and its birth depends upon a series of conditions which are not all of them of a religious order. No Christian need be astonished at the fact, for he knows the place occupied in religion, even in its revealed form, by the idea of "the fullness of time." Supernatural is not equivalent to superficial. The divine does not exclude the human. Nor is it arbitrarily superimposed upon it. But in this sphere, once again let us be on our guard against mistaking conditions for causes.

[p. 30] In paganism, the progress of reflection tended towards the elimination of the gods. Through Christianity, faith in God has promoted the development of consciousness. Man, called by God, has come to know himself by learning to know his vocation. He has become a person forever, to himself.

If *God* is given the same name as the *gods*, it is not because of some parentage, however remote: as though, for example, the one were the perfection, the sublimation, or the unification of the many. It is in order to mark the fact that the others never had but a borrowed, or rather a stolen, existence. God comes into his own, into the rights which, ever since the day when man turned away from him, have been usurped by idle phantoms or by the forces of evil.

There are some who think that the one God is the product of a religious *evolution*. Scattered at first in a dust-cloud of sacred beings, the divine slowly takes form; a hierarchy is organized, and by a

---

[27] [The Babylonian Captivity is dated from the fall of Jerusalem (597 B.C.) to the permission granted to the Israelites by the Persian King Cyrus the Great to return to their country (539 B.C.). The capture of Jerusalem, the subsequent exile, and its ending are recounted in 2 Kings 24–25; 2 Chron 36:17–23; Ezra; Jer 39–43; and Daniel.—ED.]

[28] [The migration of Muhammad and his followers from Mecca to Medina (622), to which the birth of Islam is dated.—ED.]

[29] [Jn 3:8.—ED.]

gradual process of concentration is ultimately raised into a supreme divinity, while all the other powers created by the mythical imagination become from thenceforward its servants. Then, at leisure, it is purified, spiritualized, and refined—perhaps to a vanishing point.

There are others, on the contrary, who hold that the one God is posited at a single stroke by a religious *revolution*. He affirms his position instantaneously in opposition to all else. An individual God who rejects the other gods. A certain conception of the divine which springs up in all its exclusiveness, in opposition to the conceptions entertained up to that time, when man has tired of them either because he no longer perceives their value or because he recognizes their emptiness.

Both theses are based upon careful observation, and each of them deserves to be given full weight, though if one considers the living God of religion rather than the supreme principle of philosophy, there is more historical truth [p. 31] in the second theory than in the first. The God of the Bible is named: he is Yahweh, and affirms his uniqueness by raising up and forming his own people, distinct from all others, by imposing a particular legislation upon them, and through his Prophets he makes a mockery of the gods made with hands. The God of the Gospels is no less personal: he is the heavenly Father, and Christians can only look upon the gods of paganism, if they treat them as having any real existence whatsoever, as demons. Nevertheless, it is true that the formative, intransigent phase, during which monotheism or monolatry is established, is closely followed by an enveloping movement, a phase during which, without allowing himself to be in any way contaminated, the victorious God takes over and uses to his advantage all that is true in the thought and worship that had gone astray. The phase of opposition is succeeded by a phase of absorption, so that the two theses would appear to be complementary rather than contradictory.

Yet neither theory goes to the root of the matter. Neither goes back to the source. In reality, the idea of the one and transcendent God does not [p. 32] arise historically as the result of criticism or in the wake of disillusionment. It is not the fruit of an immanent dialectic whether revolutionary or evolutionary. Nor is it obtained as the result of a synthesis, as though in answer to the need and impulse to unify the fragmentary expressions of the divine; nor is it an antithesis, as though man had become conscious at last of the vanity of his age-old gods.[30] Neither integration nor contrast can explain it. What we take to be cause is in truth effect. The idea of the one God springs up spontaneously at the heart of consciousness, whether as a result of the exigencies of reason or of some supernatural illumination, and imposes itself upon the mind of itself, of its own necessity. In fact, the clearest instance shows God revealing himself, and in doing so dissipating the idols or compelling the man to whom he reveals himself to tear them from his heart: *Reverberasti infirmitatem aspectus mei, radians in me vehementer et contremui amore et horrore*[31] [You have beaten upon the weakness of my sight, shining upon me with power, and I shook with love and dread]. First comes the "radiation," while the light and the attraction, interwoven with fear, emanate from it. The phenomenon of "reverberation" exposes the infirmity of human conceptions, and sets them in the full light of day, and the man whom God has touched is filled with horror at the thought of the phantoms which he had engendered. The faith which is born in him liberates him from superstition.

At the very beginning, then, there is an encounter, a contact, a certain apperception, or whatever term may, according to the case, be applied to it—an illumination of the intellect, vision, hearing, faith. The antithesis comes second, and the synthesis, insofar as one may use the expression, comes last.

The first moment alone, in fact, counts. There is Abraham, hearing the call which tears him from his country and his ancestral cult; and Moses, receiving the Law on Sinai; Isaiah, contemplating the

[30] [De Lubac here alludes to influential skeptical movements against religion. In the 1890s and 1900s, Modernists such as Alfred Loisy (1857–1940) had called into question the biblical grounding and institutional Church setting of Christianity, supposing that a purer form of theism might arise without them. For Ludwig Feuerbach (1804–1872), the idea of God compensated for the failure of human consciousness to realize itself in the world. G.W. F. Hegel (1770–1831) viewed Christianity as the consummate religion produced by the concrete resolution, by means of synthesis, of the conceptual contradictions inherent within earlier religious forms. However, some of his followers proposed that his evolutionary dialectics in fact entailed the wholesale rejection of institutional and doctrinal Christianity. In his dialectical theology, Karl Barth (1886–1968) emphasized the antithesis between the revelation of Christ and the sinful lives of people. —Ed.]

[31] St. Augustine, *Confessions*, bk. 8, ch. 10, n. 16.

majesty of Yahweh in the Temple. . . . Jesus, moved by the Spirit and conversing with the Father.[32] In none of these cases is there any suggestion of a "dialectic", of the swing of the pendulum, the alternation of "for" and "against"—no trace of relativity. All forms of dialectic, whether historical or not, and whatever their mode, imply contrariety and negation. Whatever the spring of the dialectic, one term is always called forth by another. The swing of the pendulum does not imply the introduction of a new principle. Dialectic is a powerful weapon because it corresponds to one of the essential processes of the mind. But when it tries to engender thought, instead of organizing [p. 33] it, its soul is a blind necessity. It throws no light on the inwardness of the beings which at each step, and turn by turn, it posits; or rather those beings have no inwardness; they are terms which are wholly relative to those with which they form a series. Once the idea of the living God has fallen like a seed into consciousness—whether by the light of reason or as the result of a supernatural revelation—it certainly is subjected, like all other ideas, to dialectic. In a sense more than any other idea, since it becomes the principle of perpetual "ferment" which works unceasingly in it. Nonetheless, it remains substantial and positive, and that is what ensures its victory. Far from corresponding to a phase in human dialectic, it is, on the contrary, dialectic which plays the intermediary role, linking in its process a reality already perceived and a mystery surmised, without ceasing to be sustained in its movement by a presence. . . .

Observe, again, how much more striking it appears in the concrete dialectic of history. Religious monotheism, even as we owe it to Israel and Christ—and this is true in some small measure in certain analogous cases—is illuminated by the divine source. Before being a belief, and, *a fortiori*, before becoming a tradition or an idea, it was a vocation, and remains one as long as it preserves its authentic vitality. Its formation bears no trace of the dialectical movement of *ressentiment* [hostility] in the Nietzschean sense.[33] Abraham did not find the true God by turning against the gods of his ancestors; he had to struggle in his heart to abandon them: his faith had to

---

[32] [Gen 12; Ex 19–31; Is 6.—ED.]

[33] [See Friedrich Nietzsche, *On the Genealogy of Morals* 1:10–12.—ED.]

be a victory. Jesus did not preach the vanity of this world like the Buddha,[34] or the vanity of the gods who canonize it, because they are the mythical form of its very substance: he proclaimed the Kingdom of Heaven in which his soul already breathes, and he reveals the Heavenly Father's love in and through his own person. In that sense, too, the Apostle's words are verified: There is only Yes in him.[35]

## *The Proof of God*

[p. 59] Where the proof of the existence of God is concerned, the simplest classic form is, in itself, always the best. It provides the permanent scheme, which survives all the superficial technical adjustments which each thinker, each age and every school find it necessary to introduce. It continues feeding the thought of those who think they can do without it—for "the proof which every man needs in order to attain full certainty is so easy and so clear that one hardly notices the logical process which it implies."[36] That is what Fénelon[37] calls "a sensible, popular philosophy open to any man free from passions and prejudices."[38] In principle, as well as for the straightforward, honest mind, "the merest glance reveals the hand that has made [p. 60] everything."[39] Movement, contingence, exemplarity, causality, finality, moral obligation: the eternal categories[40] are the starting-points open to man; they are always

[34] [An Indian ascetic who lived and taught several centuries before the birth of Christ. —Ed.]

[35] 2 Corinthians 1:19. Cf. Karl Barth, *Dogmatik im Grundriß* [Dogmatics in outline] (1948), p. 42: "Where the true God is recognized, the idols crumble into dust and He alone remains." . . .

[36] Scheeben, *Handbuch der katholischen Dogmatik* [Handbook of Catholic dogma], vol. 2: *Gotteslehre* [The doctrine of God] (Freiburg, 1948), p. 15.

[37] [François Fénelon (1651–1715) was a tutor in the court of King Louis XIV and archbishop of Cambrai (1696). However, he was viewed as supporting quietism, which privileged wordless contemplative prayer above formally structured meditation, and the king later confined him to his archdiocese.—Ed.]

[38] Fénelon, *Traité de l'existence de Dieu* [The existence of God], pt. 1, ch. 1, n. 2.

[39] Ibid., n. 1.

[40] [These are the Five Ways of proving God's existence plus the moral proof associated with Kant and Blondel.—Ed.]

to hand and always resist his critique; they are as contemporary as man and his thought.[41] *Ecce coelum et terram: clamant quod facta sint.*[42] (Behold the sky and the earth: they cry out that they are made.) Or quite simply: *Aliquid est, ergo Deus est.* (Something exists, therefore God exists.) "The whole School is agreed that nothing further is necessary."[43]

But if the spontaneous proof[44] which springs up in this way is to impress reflective thought to the fullest possible extent, it will call for unceasing modification, and the resulting commentary will inevitably take the form of a justification, in some respects critical and never quite the same, by the nature of things. This "learned" form of the proof, "designed in the first instance to forestall and answer objections," implies a continual effort, constantly renewed, to adapt it to changing conditions.[45] The need to adapt the proof will seem strange only to a man who has never dreamed of what is implied by the uniqueness of the case. "The sublime and simple operation"[46] which leads to [p. 61] God remains fundamentally the

---

[41] The reader will have noted that I am here opposing the Kantian criticism and all that follows from it.

[42] St. Augustine, *Confessions* bk. 11, ch. 4, n. 6. . . . Cf. Wisdom 13:1, 9.

[43] André Bremond, *Une dialectique thomiste du retour à Dieu* [A Thomist dialectic of return to God], p. 561.

[44] [De Lubac presents the proof of God's existence, not as the conclusion of a chain of deductive reasoning, but as the intuitive apperception of the dependence of the created order on something beyond it.—Ed.]

[45] Régis Jolivet, "A la recherche de Dieu" [In search of God], *Archives de philosophie* 8 (1931), p. 85: ". . . The classic proofs of God are simpler, more obvious, less contentious, and although 'metaphysical,' they assert themselves, in their essential elements, with a sovereign power. Their learned form, designed above all to respond to objections or to forestall them, is not the common form, that which acts immediately on the spirit and brings it to belief. . . . That is why the most 'subtle' and most captious objections . . . usually do not succeed in shaking the belief of the true believer: the simple and clear schema of the demonstration is incorporated into the spirit beyond and in spite of all the aporia of the clever. . . ."

[46] A. Gratry, *De la connaissance de Dieu* [Guide to the knowledge of God], [2 vols., 8th ed. (Paris: Gervais, 1881)] 1:45–46: "If there are true proofs of the existence of God, these proofs should be accessible to all men. For the light of God enlightens and should enlighten every man coming into the world. . . . It is necessary to seek the origin and the reality (of the proofs) in some common and daily operation of the human spirit; then, once this sublime and simple operation has been found, it suffices to describe it and to translate it into philosophical language. Afterwards its scientific value will be

same. The changes in technique, in perspective, and in presentation do not affect the proof itself.[47] God in his eternity dominates the incessant flux of creation, and in the same way the idea of God in us dominates the fluctuations of our intellectual life, imposing itself through those fluctuations with the same unalterable power. The great minds that have spoken about God are all our contemporaries.

Kant tried to prove that the "transcendent" use of causality was illegitimate, but the causality he had in mind was a narrow, scientific category, the specialized category of causation which rules the universe of Newton.[48] Shaped for the ordering of phenomena, it exhausts its virtue in doing so. Kant's causality is, of course, only one example among many. In fact, modern Western philosophies "are singular in one respect: the world they start out from is," as a general rule, "the world constituted and constantly modified by the sciences." There is nothing surprising in the fact that this world is impotent, by itself, to provide a foundation for thought and sustain the movement of thought to the end. For that to be achieved, it would be necessary to dig down beneath the artificial, methodological categories of science to the great natural categories of reason. Then it might be possible to begin discussing the real question: on the one hand the negative critique, the view that the natural categories are illusory; and on the other hand a reflective effort to justify them and purify their spontaneous use.[49]

---

demonstrated." This does not eliminate the importance and the necessity of more technical considerations, in their own place, as we indicate in the text. Cf. Gratry's observation that "there is no reason separate from the higher attraction which seeks to elevate it" (ibid., vol. 2, p. 279). . . .

[47] This is why it was possible to say that the proofs of God "are not so much an invention as an inventory, not so much a revelation as an elucidation, a purification and a justification of the fundamental beliefs of humanity" (Maurice Blondel, *La Pensée* [Thought] [Paris: Alcan, 1934], vol. 1, p. 392).

[48] [See Kant's *Critique of Pure Reason*, pt. II, div. 1, bk. 2, chap. 2, on how "all alterations occur in accordance with the law of the connection of cause and effect" (A189–211/B232–56). Among Kant and other Prussian intellectuals, there was considerable interest in British thought.—Ed.]

[49] In order to free ourselves technically from criticism, the most useful work is certainly that of Joseph Maréchal. Cf. *Le point de départ de la métaphysique* [The starting point of metaphysics], pt. 5 (1926), p. 452: "The transcendent principle of causality expresses

[p. 62] Behind the apparent variations, the skeleton of the proof always remains the same.[50] The proof is solid and eternal: as hard as steel. It is something more than one of reason's inventions: it is reason itself.

All the objections brought against the various proofs of the existence of God are in vain; criticism can never invalidate them, for it can never get its teeth into the principle common to them all. On the contrary, that principle emerges more clearly as the elements with which the proofs are constructed are rearranged. That is because it is not a particular principle which the mind can either isolate and sift so as to determine its limits, or reject out of hand: it forms part of the substance of the mind. It is not a path which the mind can be discouraged from pursuing to the end, or one from which it can turn away, afraid of having taken the wrong road; path and mind are merged together. *The mind itself is a moving path.*

[p. 63] *Causa essendi, ratio intelligendi, ordo vivendi* (the cause of being, the explanation of understanding, the pattern of living). All thought, like every being, and like every act, needs a principle and a term.[51] The mind did not set itself in motion, and its movement presupposes a direction; that is to say, a fixed point. The purely gratuitous is the purely absurd. One cannot do with the economy of God.

If, as many people think, man's adoration of God were his adoration of humanity itself, he would adore it as nature or as an ideal; that is to say, as something realized or realizable. In either case, the object proposed would be no more worthy of adoration than the transcendent God such as he has been imagined to be and, so imagined, subjected to criticism.

---

this complementary and simultaneous revelation of objective contingency and the eminent perfection which measures it." . . .

[50] Many authors have noted this without, however, explaining things in the same way. Cf. Pedro Descoqs, S.J., *Praelectiones theologiae naturalis* [Lectures on natural theology], concerning the five "ways" of the Summa of St. Thomas: "It seems to us that all the arguments can be reduced to one and involve the way of efficient causality as the only proof in the order of scientific discourse" [1:353; 2:15]. . . .

[51] St. Augustine, *De civitate Dei* [The city of God] bk. 8, ch. 4. . . .

If the divinity were conceived as a pure ideal, never capable of realization, always becoming and never necessarily existing, by what right could it still be called "humanity"? And in what sense could so elusive a term be called intelligible—or adorable?

These are three attempts to evade the living God, ways of escape into mystification.

God is not the first link in the chain, the first of a series in the sequence of causes and effects which constitute the world. God is not "a point of [p. 64] origin in the past": he is "a sufficient reason in the present" (in the past and in the future as well, and during the passage of time).[52] How many objections would disappear, how many misunderstandings would vanish, if that simple truth were understood!

God is not merely the principle and the term, at the beginning and at the end: the Good of every good, the Life of all living things, the Being of all beings,[53] he is also at the heart of all things. *In illo vivimus, et movemur, et sumus.*[54] In him we live and move and have our being.[55] But for that [p. 65] presence of the Absolute at the heart

[52] Étienne Gilson, responding to Léon Brunschvicg, in *La quarelle de l'athéisme* [The atheism controversy] (Léon Brunschvicg, *De la vraie et de la fausse conversion* [On true and false conversion], 228). It is enough to recall that St. Thomas admitted the possibility of a world created *ab aeterno*, that is, a world in which innumerable series of causes and effects would succeed each other indefinitely without beginning or end, only to find himself forced to admit that he could not commit the confusion which is the beginning of so many objections to the most classic proof of the existence of God. There must be a prime mover, as Aristotle in effect already said, not because it would be necessary to have the first term in any sort of (temporal) series, but because there must be a first cause in a (hierarchically ordered) series of causes.

[53] St. Augustine, *De Trinitate* [The Trinity] bk. 8, ch. 3, n. 4: "The good of every good." . . . Pseudo-Dionysius, *Of the Divine Names*, 1, 3. . . . St. Bernard, *De consideratione* [On consideration], bk. 5.

[54] . . . Acts 17:28. Cf. John Scotus Erigena, *De divisione naturae* [On the division of nature = *Periphyseon*] bk. 1, n. 2; bk. 3, n. 1. . . . M. Blondel, *L'Action* [Action], p. 346: God "is at the center of what I think and of what I do. . . . To go from myself to myself, I pass through him constantly."

[55] [Acts 17:28 contains Paul's quotation of a pagan poet given during his address before the Areopagus in Athens, after he had walked through the city viewing its idols. He uses the quotation to suggest that, if men may be considered children of God, God cannot be composed of inanimate metal or stone but is the proximate preserver and judge of the world.—Ed.]

of the relative, of the Eternal at the heart of movement, everything would return to dust.

Becoming, by itself, has no meaning. It passes away and vanishes without really becoming at all: it is another word for the absurd. But without Transcendence, that is to say, without a present Absolute installed at the heart of the reality which is in the process of becoming, not depending on it, but working within it, drawing it on, polarizing it, making it really advance, there could only be unending becoming—unless a catastrophe were to come to put a violent end to everything, and the absurd were at last to rediscover its true nature, so to say, by becoming unequivocally nothing. . . .

All becoming is caused by Being. All becoming is turned towards Being. Becoming can only be thought by Being.

The idea of Progress, which magnifies and in some sort hypostatizes Becoming, is one of the emptiest ideas which men have ever forged. Progress deified, it has been truly said,[56] is not only "a race without a rudder," but a race without an end; or rather a race that gets lost without really being run at all. If you do away with the winning post, you do away with the direction. The result is "to create an abstract 'beyond' that shimmers before the eyes of a distraught individual, a will-o'-the-wisp that flies away at his approach."[57] It is tantamount to doing away with progress. "To do away with absolute perfection is to do away with any idea of becoming perfect." There can be no real improvement where there is "neither axis nor goal"; no real progression except by "reaching the limit." If there is becoming, if progress is possible, then one day there must be attainment (or let us say achievement); and if there can be achievement, then there always has been something other than mere becoming.[58]

---

[56] G. Van der Leeuw, "L'homme et la civilization" [Man and civilization], *Eranos-Jahrbuch* 16 (1948), p. 170.

[57] Gaston Fessard, *France, prends garde de perdre ton âme* [France, take care not to lose your soul] (1946), p. 149; see pp. 133–50.

[58] Félix Ravaisson, *La philosophie française au XIXe siècle* [French philosophy in the nineteenth century], 4th ed. (1895), p. 50. Cf. Yves de Montcheuil, S.J., "Une philosophie du devoir" [A philosophy of right], *Mélanges théologiques* (1946), pp. 238–39. Jules Monchanin, *De l'esthétique à la mystique* [From aesthetics to mysticism] (1955), pp. 43–44. . . .

[p. 145] What is the philosopher? And what is the mystic? What is the essential difference between them, if we consider their original "intention" and take them at the root from which they naturally develop?

Should we say that the philosopher makes use of dialectic, where the mystic relies on experience? Does the mystic plumb the depths of Being, while the philosopher tries to discover how thought engenders or expresses it? Could one say that the mystic is concerned with the immediate and the philosopher with mediation?

In fact, dialectic is common to both of them. The only difference is, perhaps, that the one is mainly affective and vital, whereas the other is rational and conceptual. In each case there is experience, though the experience of the philosopher is active and that of the mystic "passive." Certainly there is no more typical dialectic than that which attempts to translate the mystical experience—or at least its tendency—into thought. The alternation of opposites is nowhere seen more clearly, more instantaneously so to speak. . . .[59] It has even been maintained that the most obviously dialectical of Plato's dialogues, the *Parmenides*,[60] is at bottom the most mystical.

[p. 146] Could it be that the mystic tends to see Being as personal, and the philosopher to conceive it as impersonal?

And yet, to judge by many of the facts, the opposite might equally well be maintained. For as philosophy and mysticism reach the summits of their aspirations, they would appear to transcend this opposition in one way or another.

Perhaps it would be possible to indicate the essential difference between them more nearly by saying that philosophy is above all

---

[59] Just as in the case of those cross-hatched designs where empty and full spaces can be seen changing alternately one into the other, there is a continuous alternation of light and shade, of affirmation and negation, identity and otherness. . . . And dialectic does nothing but interpret the experience itself. Cf. William of St.-Thierry, *Letter to the Brethren of Mont-Dieu*, bk. 2, ch. 3, n. 19 . . . : "Exaltation is joined to trembling, when it is understood that God humbled himself even to the point of death on the cross, in order to raise man to a likeness with Divinity."

[60] [This dialogue, about Plato's theory of forms, considers the possible existence of "the one itself" (137b) above the plurality both of forms and of being.—Ed.]

the search for the *unifying One*, whereas mysticism is the search for —or the attraction of—the *one One.*[61]

The philosopher starts from the need to explain, a need which is, at least virtually, a desire for a total explanation. What he desires is to unify diversity, and at the same time to diversify the one; he requires a system of relationships which embraces everything and makes everything intelligible. His ambition is to comprehend the universe. And if in the course of his search he comes upon God—as he cannot fail to do—it will be as an explanatory principle and a support for the world, as a unifying One. *Res divinae non tractantur a philosophis, nisi prout sunt rerum omnium principia.*[62] (The things of God are [p. 147] not treated by philosophers except as the principles of all things.) When the philosopher posits the absolute, it is never the absolute absolutely, but "the absolute in relation to him."[63]

Philosophy is the work of the reason. It is a "science." But God *in himself* is not an object of "science" to natural man.[64] He can neither be comprehended nor even named. And, as St. Thomas

[61] As for ascertaining how this "One" ought to be sought, how can it be found, and whether the very desire which tends towards it should not at the outset be sacrificed, or at least transcended and transfigured—in broaching these questions we find a whole other concatenation of problems into the depths of which we shall not penetrate. At this point we are speaking only of mysticism in general, in its natural roots, not of Christian mysticism. Let us state only that a Christian mysticism cannot be other than a mysticism of love, that love of neighbor in Christian mysticism is the indispensable sign of God's love, that the preferred ecstasy with regard to it is an ecstasy of actions, and that certain forms of high contemplation are utterly incapable of being in conformity with the spirit of Christianity. As Jacques Maritain has written in *Quatre essais sur l'esprit dans sa condition charnelle* [Four essays on the spirit in its carnal condition], p. 144, "the truest theology of supernatural contemplation is to be found less in the theory of an *intuition* of God" than in a doctrine of "divine experience through a union of love," although the genuinely "noetic" range of the impetus towards contemplation should not be denied.

[62] St. Thomas, *In Boethium de Trinitate* [On Boethius' "On the Trinity"], q. 5, a. 4: ". . . And so the things which are common to all things that exist are treated in the context of the principles within which they find themselves placed. . . . There is, moreover, another way of investigating things of this kind, not according as they are made manifest through effects, but according as they themselves manifest themselves. . . . And in this way divine things are treated according as they subsist in themselves. . . . And this is the theology which is spoken of through Sacred Scripture."

[63] Maurice Merleau-Ponty, interpreting Louis Lavelle in *Eloge de la philosophie* [In praise of philosophy] (1953), p. 12.

[64] I am mindful that St. Thomas defined theology as the science of God. . . . But it should also be remembered that theology is not philosophy. Following St. Thomas

says, we do not know "what he is": we only know "the relation of everything else to him."[65] "To deduce God from becoming," or from any other aspect of the world, "does not mean that one rises to a certain direct knowledge of God with the help of becoming; it means penetrating further into the intelligible structure of becoming itself; or, if one prefers, it means knowing God only to the extent to which he is signified by the essential 'transcendental relativity' of metaphysical 'becoming.' "[66] That suffices, in a sense, to define him. In any [p. 148] case, it satisfies the philosopher in the formal sense of that word which we have indicated. As such he does not ask for more:

*Felix qui potuit rerum cognoscere causas!* [Happy the one who was able to know the causes of things.][67]

But that does not satisfy man. It does not satisfy the spirit. The mystical aspiration is greater, more fundamental, and more total than the demands of reason. The mystic reaches out beyond the supreme Cause and the unifying One, which is, so to say, hardly more than a function, and pursues the One itself. He seeks the One in its being and unity. And the least knowledge of that One is worth more in his eyes than the profoundest and most comprehensive knowledge of all else;[68] and for the sake of finding the One, and being united to it, he is prepared to sacrifice the whole universe.

[p. 149] When, as a child, St. Thomas Aquinas exclaimed "I want to understand God," it was not so much the budding philosopher who was speaking as the religious genius, the contemplative, the potential mystic, the saint with an intellectual cast of mind. And

---

himself, whose words are too clear and too often repeated to allow any serious dispute, I maintain that, to the reason of the pure philosopher, "God, in himself, is not an object of science"—a statement which I maintain in the sense in which St. Thomas meant it, and which the context makes perfectly clear, and not in some vague or general sense, since such a statement in isolation would be equivocal.

[65] St. Thomas, *De Potentia* [On power], q. 7, a. 2 ad 11m and ad 1m: "We do not know what God is. . . . The being of God is the same as his substance, and just as his substance is unknown, even so is his being. . . ." "Concerning God, we discover what he is not; what, in truth, he is remains something that is utterly unknown." . . .

[66] Joseph Maréchal.

[67] Virgil, *Georgics*, 2, 490. . . .

[68] St. Thomas, *De Veritate* [On truth], q. 10, a. 7, ad 3m: "The least knowledge which can be had of God surpasses all knowledge that is had of the creature."

insofar as his speculation led him to satisfy that desire, it is not so much the rational science, whose long career in the West he inaugurated, as one of the aspects of the "intelligence of faith" whose ideal and method had been transmitted to him by the Christian tradition.

But when, on the contrary, he insists so emphatically that "we do not know God, but only the relations of all things to him," he is speaking as a pure philosopher. From that point of view, and that point of view only, there is no reason to read regret or nostalgia into the phrase. As one of his surest interpreters writes: "In a natural theodicy it is not God who is in question as the subject of science; it is universal being, the creature. For God is only envisaged and attained as the first cause and not in himself. In other words, there cannot be a natural theology apart from general metaphysics."[69] The God of the philosophers "completes the formula of the world"[70] and fully satisfies their reason.

[p. 150] And yet St. Thomas insists no less that "the intelligence naturally desires to know God in himself."[71] What exactly is that desire? Does it express the rational need to which philosophical activity corresponds, or does it, in its own way, define the mystical impulse in its natural root? Or should one perhaps see in it the fundamental unity of both?

Let us begin by saying—without for the moment trying to decide whether the suggestion reveals a faulty analysis or a deep insight—that, in speaking as he does, St. Thomas merges the two points of

---

[69] Sertillanges, *Les grandes thèses* [Foundations] . . . , p. 75.

[70] St. Thomas, [*Summa theologiae* Ia,] q. 32, a. 1: ". . . The only thing which we can learn about God by means of natural reason is that which of necessity belongs to him, inasmuch as he is the principle of all things. And we have made use of this fundamental principle above in our consideration of God." Q. 12, a. 12: ". . . [Through effects] we can be led to a knowledge of God and whether he exists; and we can also be led to a knowledge of those things about him which of necessity belong to him, inasmuch as he is the first cause of all things and surpasses all things that have been caused by him. Wherefore we know of his relationship towards creatures, that he is, indeed, the cause of all things; and we also know the way in which creatures differ from him, the fact that, in truth, he is not a part of the creatures which were caused by him, and that these creatures are not removed from him on account of a defect on his part, but rather because he surpasses them all. . . ."

[71] [*Summa theologiae* Ia, q. 12, art. 1; *Summa contra gentiles*, bk. 3, chap. 51, 1.—Ed.]

view which we have just distinguished. The "desire to see God," which he regards as natural to us, is certainly, at bottom, mystical in character. It cannot be limited to a desire to comprehend the world. Nevertheless, St. Thomas tries to establish its reality in a purely rational manner, starting from the effects which the intelligence desires to know in their Cause so as to know them fully. With that in view he unfolds a whole argument in the [*Summa*] *Contra Gentiles*, which is inspired by his faith, and which a pure philosopher might no doubt criticize as without apodeictic value—and that is precisely why a certain number of his interpreters consider themselves justified in maintaining that the natural desire in question, being the desire to see God *as cause*, is not the desire to *see God* in the full sense of the word.[72]

In brief, the argument consists in showing that human reason, the reason which is responsible for the work of philosophy, is not satisfied with knowing an effect as long as it does not know the cause. Hence that continuous movement, that permanent disquiet, that unrest which lasts until reason, moving from effect to effect and from cause to cause, at last reaches the supreme cause from which everything derives, and which, by that very fact, explains and so unifies everything.

[p. 151] It is a solid argument. But does it, in fact, prove *all* that it sets out to prove? Is the term of the argument *formally* the term envisaged? In its desire to comprehend the universe, the intelligence cannot abandon its search until it has reached the first cause, and one can therefore say, with every show of right, that there is a congenital desire in the intelligence to know that cause.[73] But between that and saying, as St. Thomas does in effect, that the intelligence desires to know the first cause, not only as the cause of the effects which it aspires to understand—as the universal *propter quid* [on account of which]—but in its essence, in itself and for itself, independently of its effects and of its relations with everything else, there is surely an abyss?

[72] [In the *Summa contra gentiles*, desire is a recurring trope. See especially bk. 2, q. 55, 13; bk. 3, qq. 25–26, 48, 50, 63, 95–96, and 153; bk. 4, q. 95.—Ed.]

[73] Cf. Origen, *In Psalmum* [On the Psalms] 2, v. 8: "But the inheritance of rational nature is the sight of the corporeal and incorporeal things, and of God who is the cause of all these things." . . .

The mystical impulse, no doubt, bridges the abyss at a single leap. The mystic discerns the One in the Unifying cause, and when he meets the Unifying cause he adheres to the One. But can one say that his strength comes to him from the principle which first moved the intelligence to look for the "cause of causes"? Could one even say that the mystical impulse simply continues along the path of reason, that it simply goes further in the same direction? Would it not be better to recognize that the philosopher's reasoning conceals an anagogical [i.e., mystical] dialectic, the inspiration of which is quite different from the general desire to know?

St. Thomas, therefore, seems to have failed in his attempt to establish continuity between philosophy and mysticism, between the dynamism of the intelligence and the desire of the spirit. The doctrine of "the natural desire to see God" is central to his thought, and he has not succeeded in completely unifying it.

No one will succeed where he has failed. The attempt, strictly speaking, [p. 152] is no doubt impossible. The mystical impulse does not exactly prolong metaphysical inquiry; it does not repeat or extend the work, though it can animate it and, in return, be stimulated by it. The root, in each case, is different, the end is different, and the basic procedure no less so. Philosophical inquiry rises analytically from effect to cause, in virtue of a rational necessity. The mystical impulse rises from effect, perceived as a sign, to that same cause, by a movement which cannot be wholly justified by pure reason—for if it were an argument, there would be more in the "conclusion" than in the "premises"—but which springs from a need of the spirit no less imperious in its demands than the demands of reason, or more precisely, from the magnetic attraction of Being through its signs. The philosopher may rest from his inquiries in contemplation, once the effect is fully understood; the mystic, in the end, will reject all signs—though he will never quite finish doing so—in order to rest in the contemplation of God alone.

[p. 153] There is, however, something artificial about the distinction originally established. However well-founded it may be, it posits the "philosopher" and the "mystic" as abstract beings. It distinguishes two functions of the mind. But while it is true that the functions of the mind are diverse, we must not forget that the spirit is one. The intelligence is steeped in it, and no philosopher worthy of the name would be content to remain for good and all imprisoned in his specialty, even if it were the knowledge and explanation of the whole. Philosophy is always pushing back the frontiers of thought. The philosopher is more than a philosopher, and cannot be reduced to a precise definition. His knowledge of the world is equivalently, or at least becomes inevitably, the perception of his own inadequacy. And the labor of elaborating an intelligible world does not save him from "the nostalgia [*nostalgie*] of Being."[74] The greatness of St. Thomas is to have recognized this.[75] By a process which pure reason alone does not suffice to justify, but which the spirit satisfies, or rather insists upon, he was able to penetrate and explore the ways by which the intelligence moves to the point at which he discovered the spiritual appetite within it. In his very philosophy, the philosophical endeavor develops into a mystical flight. The human spirit becomes conscious of its total nature and of its high vocation. He explores all its dimensions and, going beyond the techniques and specializations which obliged him, as it were, to divide himself in two, he seeks to rediscover the simplicity of the mind's essential act. The formal distinctions [p. 154] and oppositions tend to be reabsorbed into unity, although without ever quite reaching it.

---

[74] This is true even of Descartes, so often accused since the time of Pascal of only being interested in God for the sake of possessing the world. See in particular the well-known *Letter to Chanut*.

[75] [This is typically associated with twentieth-century existentialism, and especially with Heidegger's notion of *das Heimweh* (homesickness). However, by tracing nostalgia much farther back to Aquinas, de Lubac suggests that it has unacknowledged theological origins.—Ed.]

2

# The Christian Faith

*Around 1960, de Lubac began a series of discussions with a group of youth chaplains. He had become concerned that, following the Second World War, a crisis of faith had developed that was characterized less by the clash of ideas than by a repulsion from any notion of supernatural reality.*[1] *In* The Christian Faith, *which was prompted by these encounters, de Lubac seeks to counter this secularism by rearticulating basic Christian doctrine. He structures his exposition around the Apostles' Creed. This Creed has traditionally been attributed to the twelve apostles assembled on the day of Pentecost under the direct inspiration of the Holy Spirit, with each apostle contributing an article. This suggested setting for its production vividly presents both its divine source and its unavoidably human origin. Nevertheless, de Lubac describes how this tradition of a twelvefold confession has tended to obscure the Creed's trinitarian character, with its fundamental structure being given by the statements of belief in God the Father, in his Son Jesus Christ, and in the Holy Spirit.*

*De Lubac had long recognized the apologetic value of trinitarian doctrine. In the opening lecture for his course in fundamental theology, delivered at the Catholic Theology Faculty in Lyon in 1929, he subjects the perennial standard assessment of the Trinity offered by theologically weak preachers—that it is incomprehensible, but not irrational—to searing critique. "Many apologists have ignored", he protests, "the wonderful light that an acquaintance with the Trinity brings to reason and the remarkable power of reason to enter into the conception of the Trinity."*[2] *Notwithstanding the dogma's "sublime difficulty", revelation and reason should not disengage each other in its exposition. Rather, because mankind was created in the image of the Trinity*

---

[1] Henri de Lubac, *At the Service of the Church: Henri de Lubac Reflects on the Circumstances that Occasioned His Writings*, trans. Anne Elizabeth Englund (San Francisco: Ignatius Press, 1993), 131–32.

[2] Henri de Lubac, *Theological Fragments*, trans. Rebecca Howell Balinski (San Francisco: Ignatius Press, 1989), 91–104 (99–100).

*and is destined to share its likeness, the depth of human nature will "never be understood if it is not illuminated by a ray coming from the unfathomable brightness of trinitarian life". Indeed, de Lubac argues that Christian theological anthropology is fundamentally, not dualistic, but tripartite. For Paul, flesh and spirit are not two distinct parts of human nature, but contrasting orientations of the whole person, either to sin or to freedom. Paul articulates his true anthropology in his concluding greeting to the Thessalonians, that their spirit, soul, and body may be kept complete and blameless at Christ's coming.*[3] *It is by perceiving these traces of the Trinity in the world that de Lubac is drawn into trinitarian doctrine.*

[3] Henri de Lubac, *Theology in History*, trans. Anne Englund Nash (San Francisco: Ignatius Press, 1996), 117–200 (117–29); 1 Thess 5:23.

[p. 85] *The Economic Trinity*

There has always been an awareness in the Church that the creed, however brief and in whatever state it might be, contains the totality of the faith. This was so even at the time of the christological formulas. As for the earliest trinitarian formulas, they grew, not by the addition of new articles placed at the end of the first three, but by the explanation or development of each of these. This was the case for the *forma antiquissima* [most ancient form], the ancestor of the Roman Creed, which, as we mentioned, goes back to the middle of the second century. We can ascertain this from the fact that, having been transmitted from Rome to Egypt very early on, it was maintained there without any change for a long time. Each of the three articles is itself composed of three parts, which gives us, if you wish, a total of nine articles. There may have been a symbolic intention behind this arrangement, or perhaps there was a desire, after the event, to justify it by appealing to the mystical significance of the numbers. This detail is of little importance to us. But the text is significant. "I believe in God, the Father almighty—and in Jesus Christ, his only Son our Lord—and in the Holy Spirit, the holy Church, the resurrection of the flesh."[4]

[p. 86] This God in whom the Christian thus declares that he believes, this God who is all his faith and in whose name he has come to ask the Church for baptism, is not merely some remote, inaccessible divinity whose reality compels the recognition of man's intellect; he is not merely that divinity that man glimpses as best he can through the created universe—and often mistakes, just as much in the loftiest flights of his thinking as in his grossest mythologies, for the universe itself—and about whom he attempts to say something in his halting language; that mute divinity of whom, at best, we must say that man conceives of him only from the outside and without finding any way of communicating with him. God has so

Excerpted from Henri de Lubac, *The Christian Faith: An Essay on the Structure of the Apostles' Creed*, trans. Brother Richard Arnandez, F.S.C. (San Francisco: Ignatius Press, 1986), 85–115. Some translations from Latin have been made with reference to *La Foi chrétienne: essai sur la structure du symbole des apôtres*, ed. Peter Bexell (Paris: Cerf, 2008), 543–44.

[4] H. Lietzmann, *Histoire de l'Église ancienne* [History of the ancient Church] 2 (. . . Paris: Payot, 1937): 109. . . .

to speak laid bare his own inner life by unveiling his designs to us. "Having spoken in times past through the prophets, in these last days he has spoken to us through his Son."[5] He himself has spoken about himself. He has revealed himself to men, Father, Son and Spirit; the one God, the living God. Men, if they do not refuse to believe him, and if they consent to allow themselves to be penetrated by it, will never cease to be filled with wonder before this partially revealed mystery.

> A divinity without a superior degree that elevates or an inferior degree that lowers; equal in all respects, the same in every way. . . . This is the infinite connaturality of three infinitudes.[6] Each one is wholly God, considered in himself, the Son as well as the Father, the Spirit as well as the Son, each preserving his own personal character: God, the Three considered together. Each one is God because of their consubstantiality; the Three are God by reason of their monarchy. . . . No sooner have I begun to think of their Unity than their Trinity bathes me in its [p. 87] splendor. No sooner have I begun to think of their Trinity than their Unity again takes hold of me. When one of the Three presents himself to me I think that this is all, so filled is my eye, so completely does the rest escape me; for in my mind, too limited to understand even a single one of the Three, there remains no place to give to the other Two. And when I join all Three in a single concept I see a single flame without being able to divide or to analyze the unified light.[7]

Obviously, it is not under this form that the revelation of God in Jesus Christ took place. When God told man about himself, he did not leave man to his own devices. The mystery of the Trinity was not made known to us as a sublime theory, a celestial theorem, with no connection with what we are and what we must become. God, the Creator of our world, has chosen to intervene in our history. It is by acting in our favor, by calling us to himself, by bringing about our salvation, that he has made himself known to us. Our faith in

---

[5] Heb 1:1–2.

[6] [In Classical Greek philosophy, infinity is associated with matter, quantity, and imperfection. However, in Christian theology, God may be regarded as infinite on the grounds of being the source of the forming principle of matter that does not itself require any such principle. This is a relational understanding of infinity.—Ed.]

[7] St. Gregory Nazianzen, *Discours* 40, chap. 41. . . .

him, which is a response to his call, cannot be separated from the knowledge that he has given us of his activity in our midst.[8] "As the snow and the rain come down from heaven and do not return there until they have watered the land and made it fertile and fruitful, so too the Word which issues from my mouth will not return to me without having fulfilled its mission."[9] The structure of [p. 88] the Creed reflects the Word of God at work in the world, transforming the history of mankind into salvation history; it tells us of that all-powerful Word accomplishing the work for which it was sent.[10]

Even for Israel, the inconceivable marvel did not consist in some internal characteristic of the divinity which Israel alone would have knowledge of. It consisted in the fact that the absolutely free and sovereign Being had decided to communicate with men, to give them access to the realm of his holiness. This grace was at the same time an unheard-of exigency, "delivering the creature from his proper place in the land of slavery and bringing him into a 'land' which is God's."[11] Such is the revelation that finds its accomplishment and apogee in Christ: "God", says St. Peter in the home of the centurion Cornelius, "has sent his Word to the children of Israel. . . . You know what has taken place in all of Judea."[12] Jesus himself, in reply to the messengers sent by John the Baptist, tells them to relate to their master "what you have heard and seen".[13] If every act of revelation is in the last analysis a revelation of the Trinity, the entire revelation of the Trinity is a revelation through action, and all this action is directly concerned with man.

This can be expressed by using the word with which the Fathers of the Church commonly summed up this revealing act: "economy" (οἰκονομια) We need not go into detail here concerning the meanings that this word can have. "Economy" (*dispensatio*) means administration; [p. 89] and from this meaning there flows first of

---

[8] Vatican II, dogmatic constitution *Dei verbum*, chap. 1. . . . Not to widen the topic unduly, we leave aside here what refers to the revelation which, in revealing himself to us, God makes of us to ourselves.

[9] Is 55:10–11.

[10] Msgr. Cahal Daly, *We Believe* (Ardagh, 1969), 8.

[11] Hans Urs von Balthasar, *Herrlichkeit* [The Glory of the Lord], vol. 3, 2: 164.

[12] Acts 10:36–43. . . .

[13] Mt 11:4.

all that of design, then that of disposition. In the language of the Fathers—if we leave aside Tatian and Tertullian, who use it to designate the inner organization of the divinity[14]—it refers to all of God's work, in all its phases and under all its aspects: creation, providence, history, the works of nature and those of grace.[15] It is the accomplishment of God's design on earth; it is the mystery of man's salvation[16] taking place within creation and unfolding through time; *dispensatio temporalis* [temporal dispensation],[17] which is condensed entirely in the *dispensatio carnis* [fleshly dispensation],[18] i.e., in the [p. 90] redemptive and divinizing Incarnation,[19] or, as Gregory of Nyssa says, in "the divine mystery of the 'economy' according to man", so as to expand to "the 'economy' of the Church". "The entire mystery", says St. Cyril of Alexandria,[20] "is the kenosis [of the Lord] and his abasement in the carnal economy. . . . He took on the form of a slave, οἰκονομικῶς because of us."[21] St. Paul had said the same thing previously when he spoke of the "economy of the fullness of time", which was to bring about God's "beneficent design" in the world.[22]

---

[14] Tertullian, *Adversus Praxean* [Treatise against Praxeas], chap. 2. He distinguishes in God the *substantiae unitas* [unity of substance] and the *oeconomiae sacramentum quae unitatem in trinitatem disponit* [sacrament of the economy that disposes to unity in Trinity] (. . . see chapters 3, 9, 13, 23, 30 . . .). We are simplifying here a bit what he says. . . .

[15] In its biblical and patristic sense, the word goes beyond the meaning of "salvation history". . . . André Feuillet, *Le Prologue du quatrième Évangile* [The Prologue of the Fourth Gospel] (Paris: Desclée de Brouwer, 1968), 43, where the author distinguishes, following St. Paul, a double mediation by Christ: "cosmic" and "soteriological". This overemphasis on history is, in Protestantism, a characteristic of the Calvinistic tendency.

[16] "Sacramentum salutis humanae" [Sacrament of human salvation]: St. Hilary, *De Trinitate* [On the Trinity], bk. 2, no. 1.

[17] Augustine, *De vera religione* [Of true religion], 7:13; 55:110. . . . Basil, *On the Holy Spirit*, chap. 15, no. 34: "The Economy of God our Savior regarding man." . . .

[18] Origen, *In Jesu Nave* [On Joshua, son of Nun], hom. 3, no. 2. . . . Eusebius, *Démonstration évangélique* [Proof of the Gospel], bk. 3, preface. . . . Cf. Eph 1:9.

[19] Irenaeus, *Adversus haereses* [Against the heresies], bk. 4, chap. 33, no. 7. . . . Severus of Antioch, *hom.* 90: "In addition to theology, there is also the Economy, a marvel beyond our comprehension . . . ; for Isaiah adds, 'See, this live coal has touched your lips; it will take away your iniquities and wipe out your sins' (6:7). It is clear that this live coal symbolizes the Emmanuel." . . .

[20] *Vie de Moïse* [Life of Moses] [ed. Daniélou, *Sources chrétiennes* 207–8].

[21] [*Glaphyrorum in Exodum* (Elegant comments on Exodus)] PG 69:396B, 301D. . . .

[22] Eph 1:9–10.

From the fourth century onward, the Fathers habitually distinguished the two parts that make up all sacred science (what we today call "theology") by using the two contrasting words: "economy" and "theology".[23] Like them we shall maintain that it is through the [p. 91] "economy", and only through it, that we have access to "theology". Even more, all of "theology" remains marked for us with the seal of the "economy". "We believe in one God . . . who sent his Son, . . . who sent the Holy Spirit."[24] It is in this sense that we can agree with the formula used by a contemporary theologian, Gerhard Ebeling, who writes: "The doctrine about God and the doctrine about salvation are identical."[25] This too was what the language of Scholasticism wished to express by saying that the (internal) "processions" of the Persons of the Trinity are known to us exclusively through their (external) "missions"; or again, in the words of St. Thomas Aquinas, that we glimpse the "*occultum divinitatis*" [hiddenness of divinity] only through the "*mysterium humanitatis Christi*" [mystery of the humanity of Christ], in whom the entire "economy" resides—and is transcended.[26]

For this distinction does not create a separation—quite the contrary. In no way does it mean that nothing concerning the internal "processions", nothing concerning "theology", properly speaking, is accessible to us. In no way does it mean that the doctrine about God must be reduced to the doctrine about salvation, for in that case the latter would risk being purely illusory doctrine. "If the Incarnation", says Cyril of Jerusalem, "were pure imagination, then salvation too would be pure imagination."[27] [p. 92] St. Athanasius described the being of the Trinity solely in terms of its external activity, but this was the structure of God's immanent life which the great defender of the "consubstantial" thereby wished to reach,

---

[23] There are innumerable examples. Clement of Alexandria used a synonym, distinguishing between "theology" and "prophecy" (4th *stromata* [miscellany, i.e., *Stromata* 4], chap. 1). . . .

[24] Tertullian, *De praescriptione* [The prescriptions], chap. 13 . . . ; *Adv. Praxean* [Treatise against Praxeas], chap. 2. . . .

[25] *Wort und Glaube* [Word and faith], 490. . . .

[26] Cf. Yves Congar, *Situation et tâches présentes de la théologie* [The situation and present tasks of theology] (Éd. du Cerf, 1967), 10: "God reveals the 'in-himself' side of his mystery in the 'for-us' aspect of the union of grace and the Incarnation."

[27] *Quatrième Catéchèse* [Fourth catechetical lecture], chap. 9. . . .

although always in a human manner. St. Ambrose explained that the Word of God, whose profound majesty is secret, incomprehensible, and unspeakable, became recognizable for us through his humanity —but he certainly thought that in this abasement *pro captu nostro* [according to our capacities] we do indeed recognize him. In other words, neither the Fathers of the Church nor any other authorized witness of our Christian faith have ever thought that our knowledge of the Trinity was condemned to remain purely "functional". For it is indeed true, and it is essential to say, that "God, in his supernatural revelation, teaches us nothing that does not concern our salvation",[28] that the whole gospel is *evangelium salutis* [the gospel of salvation],[29] that the proclamation of the gospel is *salutis praeconium* [the proclamation of salvation]; but precisely, the salvation of man is God himself.

"The expression of the faith", we are told, "must respect the mystery of the faith and avoid making any [p. 93] ontological affirmations."[30] There, at least if one wishes to interpret it strictly, we have a statement which in its second part depends more on the anti-intellectual and anti-objectivistic currents in contemporary thought[31] than on a reflection upon the Christian faith as made known to us by the primitive writings.[32] This thesis has found

---

[28] Pierre Grelot, *Sens chrétien de l'Ancien Testament* [The Christian sense of the Old Testament] (Tournai: Desclée, 1962), 425. Cf. the *Benedictus:* "*ad dandam scientiam salutis plebi ejus, in remissionem peccatorum eorum*" [to give knowledge of salvation to his people by the forgiveness of their sins] (Lk 1:77).

[29] Acts 13:26. Eph 1:13.

[30] *Le Christianisme au XX siècle* [Christianity in the twentieth century], June 16, 1966.

[31] According to R. Bultmann, the formula "Christ is God" is false whenever one understands by the word "God" a greatness that can be objectified, whether it be in the Arian or the Nicean sense, in the orthodox or liberal one; the expression is correct if by "God" one understands the events of God's action. *Glauben und Verstehen* [Faith and understanding] 2:246–61. . . . But how can one speak of "God's action" without objectifying to some degree the word "God"? And if one does not admit that our intelligence includes a power of self-criticism, one will perpetually waver between an untenable objectifying thought and an equally untenable agnosticism.

[32] For instance, as Thomas F. Torrance observes, the presence of the Spirit who had come upon the Apostles was already for them "an ontological reality", in *L'Esprit Saint et l'Église* [The Holy Spirit and the Church, ed. S. Dockx] (Paris: Fayard, 1969), 40.

support in Bultmann's philosophy, which proposes an "existential" interpretation of the biblical texts.[33] Bultmann seems to begin by setting up a kind of radical (and entirely fictitious) opposition between the idea of a revelation accomplished "outside of ourselves" and which would not affect us at all and that of a revelation which, in order to affect us, would tell us nothing and could tell us nothing beyond the actuality of our existence. Revelation, he declares, "brings us absolutely nothing if we expect it to make known to us some teaching which man cannot attain to by himself, [p. 94] mysteries which must remain sacrosanct once they are communicated to us; but it brings us everything if we expect it to enlighten man about himself and to help him understand himself."[34] Given that sort of dichotomy (at least if one seeks to adhere to it systematically), it seems to us that, while trying to avoid an imaginary Charybdis (or one imagined by some "extrinsicists" who do not know what they are talking about), one would inevitably fall into a Scylla in which all the reality of revelation would be engulfed. Indeed, one would reduce Christianity "to a transcendental condition of man's understanding of himself, whether it be a question of thought, life, understanding or action". But to reduce it to this would be "to annihilate it".[35]

Bultmann's undertaking, wrote Karl Barth[36] in his famous address *The Humanity of God*, simply brings us back to

---

[33] [Rudolf Bultmann (1884–1976) was a Lutheran New Testament scholar at the University of Marburg.—Ed.]

[34] *La Notion de révélation dans le Nouveau Testament* [The concept of revelation in the New Testament]. . . .

[35] Hans Urs von Balthasar, *L'Amour seul est digne de foi* [*Love Alone Is Credible*], trans. R. Givord (Paris: Aubier, 1966), 61.

[36] [Karl Barth (1886–1968) was a Swiss Reformed pastor and theologian. While serving the community of Safenwil (1911–1921), he was opposed to the First World War launched by Germany on France and to the support of his former teachers for it and began to reject liberal theology. From 1921, he taught at the universities of Göttingen, Münster, Bonn, and Basel. De Lubac admired many aspects of his theology and his opposition to Nazism. The two met in Paris in June 1956 for Henri Bouillard's high-profile defense of his massive thesis on Barth. After this, they enjoyed shark-fin soup in a Chinese restaurant, where their discussion of justification disturbed other diners (De Lubac, *At the Service*, 70).—Ed.]

> the anthropocentric myth. . . . It is certain that existentialism demonstrates once again the particular truth taught by the ancient theological schools when it repeats that we cannot in any way speak of God without speaking of man. Provided that it does not at the same time bring us back to the old error according to which one could speak of man without first, and very concretely, making reference to the living God![37]

[p. 95] Without wishing to subscribe in any way to this "old error", but in a concern for exegetical reserve, Mr. Oscar Cullmann nevertheless usually adopts a rather restrictive position.[38] "The New Testament", he has written, "cannot and does not propose to give us information about the being of God considered apart from the act by which he reveals himself; all research into 'being' in the philosophical sense is totally foreign to it." Thus formulated, the remark is acceptable; but it could also be turned around; one could say with just as much reason that the New Testament does not claim to speak to us of an act considered without any relationship with the one who performs it, since by that act the latter "reveals himself". It is also true that

> the early Christian writings speak only of the God who reveals himself, of God as turned toward the world, in other words, of the history which unfolds from the "beginning" of John 1:1, up to the "all in all" of 1 Corinthians 15:28, i.e., from the instant at which the Word began to issue forth from God as his creative Word, to the moment when the Son to whom the Father has subjected all things will submit himself to the Father after everything else has been subjected to him.[39]

But this assertion bears within itself at least a part of its own corrective, since none of this "history" would be what it is if it did not unfold between the two extremes which encompass and explain it.

---

[37] [Karl Barth,] *L'Humanité de Dieu* [The humanity of God] (Geneva: Labor et Fides, 1956), 40; cf. 37.

[38] [Oscar Cullmann (1902–1999) was a Lutheran New Testament scholar and church historian at the universities of Strasbourg, Basel, and Paris. He played a significant role in developing Lutheran–Roman Catholic ecumenical links.—Ed.]

[39] Oscar Cullmann, *Christologie du Nouveau Testament* [The Christology of the New Testament] (Paris: Delachaux et Niestlé, 1958), 286.

Indeed, Mr. Oscar Cullmann himself states this very well in a more recent book: "If the Bible, from beginning to end, speaks of the action rather than of the being of God, Father, Son and Holy Spirit, it is still God's being which is manifested in [p. 96] that action, and insofar as it is action." When the author adds that this being of God "can and must be the object of dogmatic reflection, but not of exegetical analysis",[40] this is merely a question of semantics or of determining the limits between two disciplines; the word *exegesis* being taken here in a narrow sense, in conformity with modern usage, to designate only the first phase of textual analysis.

The history of Christian thought shows us, at all events, that the second phase, that of dogmatic reflection, has followed hard upon the first. This had to be, not only as a pragmatic necessity but as a logical one as well. The ontological theandric character of the Incarnation had to be explained and defended so that the paschal soteriology might be understood and preserved. The Fathers of the Church in fact had a clear perception that "the mystery of the death and Resurrection of the Savior is unintelligible without the mystery of his personality."[41] An analogous process followed with regard to the "Spirit of adoption", the one in whom alone we can say that "Jesus is the Lord."[42] One can, no doubt, consider that the later developments of the doctrine sometimes lacked due sobriety; one can expose in these developments an intellectualism as shallow as it was unrestrained; one can likewise discern the influence of certain systems of thought which were not essential to the expression of the faith and which sometimes were even harmful not only to its simplicity but to its very purity. Still, this does not prevent the transition from the first phase to the second from constituting in itself a legitimate procedure, [p. 97] indeed, an indispensable one. "Theology" already exists potentially in the "economy"; it is in a way required by it.[43]

---

[40] Id., *Le Salut dans l'histoire* [Salvation in history] (ibid., 1966), 11.

[41] J. P. Joussa, *Le Salut, incarnation ou mystère pascal* [Salvation: Incarnation or Paschal Mystery?] (Paris: Éd. du Cerf, 1968), 8–9 and 386.

[42] Rom 8:15; 1 Cor 12:3.

[43] Cf. Yves Congar, in *Mélanges M. D. Chenu* (1967), 156–57. . . . Cf. Paul Tillich, *Systematic Theology*, 1:157: "The doctrine of revelation is based on a trinitarian interpretation of the divine life and of its manifestation to itself.". . . On the oneness of the

So there is an essential difference, nay, an unbridgeable gap, between the idea of an "economic" revelation and the idea of a purely functional one. Those who wish to reduce the former to the latter sometimes appeal to a passage from Luther where they say they can hear an authentic echo of the New Testament affirmations:

> Christ has two natures: what does that have to do with me? If he bears this name of Christ, magnificent and consoling as it is, it is because of the ministry and the task he took upon himself; that is what gives him that name. That he is by nature both man and God, this is something for himself. But that he consecrated his ministry and poured out his love to become my Savior and my Redeemer, that is where I find my consolation and my good. . . . To believe in Christ does not mean that Christ is a person who is both God and man, for that is of no help to anybody. It means that this person is Christ; that for our sake he came forth from the Father and descended into the world. . . . It is from this office that he derives his name.[44]

Without taking into account the paradoxical character [p. 98] of so many of Luther's statements, and without trying, either, to understand the polemical edge of this eloquent passage, Ritschl[45] and Harnack[46] in the last century quoted it in an attempt to justify their Christianity without dogmas.[47] Others have imitated them since. Before their time, Ludwig Feuerbach had also drawn his inspiration from it in a wrong sense; carrying to the extreme "the anthropocentric virtualities of Luther's *pro me, pro nobis* [for me, for

---

"economic" Trinity and the "immanent" Trinity (i.e., the Trinity in itself), see further Karl Rahner, *Écrits théologiques* [Theological investigations] 8:129–36 and 98–103, and also chap. 5 of *Mysterium salutis* [Kerygma and dogma] 2 (1967).

[44] *Erlanger Ausgabe* 35:207–8. [From an untranslated weekday sermon on Exodus 12 in which Luther explores the chapter's spiritual sense.]

[45] *Die christliche Lehre von der Rechtsfertigung und Versöhnung* [The Christian doctrine of justification and reconciliation] 3 (3rd ed.): 374, note.

[46] *Dogmengeschichte* [History of dogma] 3 (3rd ed.): 564, in the epigraph of the last book. . . .

[47] [Albrecht Ritschl (1822–1889) and Adolf von Harnack (1851–1930) were both Lutheran church historians and theologians. Ritschl taught at the universities of Bonn and Göttingen, and Harnack, who was born in Estonia, held positions at the universities of Giessen, Marburg, and Berlin.—Ed.]

us]",[48] he had concluded that Luther's Christology, freed from all theology, was no more than a "religious anthropology", and he had sought to find in this the path that leads to an absolute anthropocentricity, denying any other divinity but that of man.[49] Still, on this point as on many others, Luther also offers us the opposite point of view. Take, for instance, his sermon for Christmas in 1521:

> We must learn to know Christ well and the relationship that exists between his two natures, the divine nature and the human nature, for on this point many people are in error. . . . As regards Christ's words, the capital question is to discern which of them belong to his divine nature and which to his human nature.[50]

[p. 99] He also says in his *Great Catechism*: "I believe that Jesus Christ, the true Son of God, has become my Lord", etc.[51] On the other hand, it is certain that he never gave up his faith in the fundamental Christian dogmas.

Dietrich Bonhoeffer[52] was, therefore, not entirely wrong when he stated that "for Luther it is the person who gives meaning to the work", and that "there is no access to the work except through the person."[53] For Bonhoeffer, it was Melanchthon, not Luther, who reduced the person of Jesus Christ to his work, i.e., dogmatic Christology to soteriology, according to his famous formula: "To know Christ is to know his benefits, not to consider his natures and the modalities of his Incarnation." In fact, however, it seems very difficult to oppose Luther on this point to his disciple, Melanchthon. The formula given by the disciple is a faithful echo of the first passage we quoted from the master, and neither of them necessarily

---

[48] Henri Arvon, *Feuerbach, sa vie, son oeuvre* [Feuerbach: his life, his work] (Paris: P.U.F., 1964), 39–40. Karl Barth took up again the *pro me* of Luther but with a totally different stress: *Dogmatics* . . . (Geneva: Labor et Fides), vol. 4, 1 (1967), 135–36.

[49] *Principes de la philosophie de l'avenir* [Principles of the philosophy of the future]: "Protestantism no longer concerns itself. . . with what God is in himself but only with what he is with regard to man . . . ; it is not longer theology—essentially, it is only Christology, i.e., religious anthropology." (Trans. Louis Althusser, 1960, 128.)

[50] *Oeuvres* [Works], French trans., 10 (Geneva: Labor et Fides, 1967), 303.

[51] Second part, art. 2, no. 27.

[52] [Bonhoeffer (1906–1945) was a German Lutheran theologian who taught at the University of Berlin but took an uncompromising stand against Nazism, for which he ultimately paid with his life. He ministered in London and northern Germany.—ED.]

[53] *Wer ist und wer war Jesus Christus?* [*Christ the Center*] (Hamburg, 1962), 25 and 39. . . .

requires an exclusive meaning. While attributing the entire Creed to trust in the forgiveness of sins, which sums up all of Christ's benefits, Melanchthon, like Luther, professed his belief in each of the other articles of traditional dogma. On occasion both of them freely express themselves in a paradoxical, antithetical way which one should not always take literally. Still, their language does indicate a tendency. Neither Luther nor Melanchthon—nor Calvin either, for that matter—"pauses to analyze [p. 100] the *being* of the eternal Son of God made man, i.e., to describe the hypostatic union; rather, they proceed directly to the explanation of his redemptive work"; their entire perspective remains soteriological.[54] With Luther most particularly, his customary language manifests a thought which is "less concerned about knowing Christ's inner mystery than about hearing his promises and the sovereign call of his voice"[55]—and even, we must admit, "a certain scorn for all intellectual dogmatic statements, which he considers as only a side issue in true religious life".[56] There was present in this, at the very least, a certain tendency which history has revealed to be dangerous.

Luther was, no doubt, imbued even to the marrow of his bones with his Catholic atavism, with the doctrines concerning Christ and the Trinity; his imagination and his sensibility naturally played within this framework; his religious experience, it seemed to him, found in these doctrines its normal intellectual, spontaneous and solely legitimate expression.[57] For him, the words *pro me* thus referred, as has been said, "to God's objective intervention in Christ, that saving act, independent of man, by which man is delivered from himself"; while among some of his successors, "concentration on the meaning which the gospel assumes for me, here and now, independently [p. 101] of past historical events, leads to an egocentricity

[54] Alexandre Ganoczy, *Le Jeune Calvin, genèse et évolution de sa vocation réformatrice* [The young Calvin: Genesis and evolution of his reforming vocation] (Wiesbaden, 1966), 141–42, speaking of Luther's *Little Catechism* and the first edition of Calvin's *Institutes*.

[55] René Marlé, *Bultmann et la foi chrétienne* [Bultmann and the Christian faith] (. . . Paris: Aubier, 1967), 134.

[56] Yves de Montcheuil, *Leçons sur le Christ* [Lessons on Christ] (Paris: Éd. de l'Épi, 1949), 53. . . .

[57] [Martin Luther (1483–1546) was an Augustinian friar who, through his preaching and writing, was an early Reformer. De Lubac accurately identifies his Catholic theological sensibility.—Ed.]

in which the meaning of *pro me* is entirely drawn away from its objective pole to its subjective pole." It follows that then "the gospel disappears in favor of man's existentialized self-understanding; the very reality of God is reduced to what he signifies for me, in the needs and contingencies of my own life"—and no divine action comes to deliver me from this prison. Obviously, there are many sorts of influences under which, here or there, such a reversal takes place. We may, however, observe that this consequence is logical enough: if one begins with an experience in which the person of Christ tends to disappear behind his gifts, if the Incarnation is looked upon as a simple prelude to the redemption, it is quite natural to find oneself being carried away to a more and more subjective theology.[58]

How then can we fail to recognize, despite the misuse, a certain legitimacy in the assertions of Ritschl and Harnack, of Bultmann today, and, before their time, of Hegel, when they cite Luther as their reference? For the great Reformer, Hegel tells us, what is required of man is his feelings, his faith, to such an extent that the principle of subjectivity, of reference to the self, is not only recognized but is declared to be the only important thing. One can in fact find in Luther two more or less [p. 102] reconcilable concepts of faith; but the emphasis in the first text we quoted from his writings does not deceive us about what is most personal, most deeply rooted in his thinking: "That lively sentiment which he called faith breaks out in it with such strong naiveté that it immediately transcends all the logical consequences he draws, and which his successors had to spend three centuries to develop slowly."[59]

Who could fail to see at the same time, when this aspect of Luther's thinking comes to a point of exclusive domination, what a contrast exists between it and the Catholic concept by which Luther lived and which has left so many traces in his works? For Catholicism, the dogmatic affirmation, without constituting by itself alone the act of faith, is essential in order to nourish and orient the latter. It always

---

[58] Here we summarize T. F. Torrance, "Cheap and Costly Grace", *The Baptist Quarterly* 22 (1968): 291–96.

[59] Pierre Rousselot, *Études sur la foi et le dogmatisme* [Studies on faith and dogmatism] (unpublished course of lectures in Latin; Paris Theological Faculty, 1909–1910).

maintains the primacy of objective being over personal meanings and appropriations. Such an attitude is not aimed at satisfying intellectual curiosity, which would transform the Christian into a detached spectator of the object of his faith: in religious matters such curiosity "is always out of place and sometimes dangerous" because it is contrary to the submissive disposition which must be that of the believer, and it destroys or at least weakens the spontaneous movement of his faith. But maintaining this primacy of being is something "necessary for religious living itself. One must know who Christ is in himself if one wishes to understand his function."[60] The doctrinal character of faith is not opposed to its existential character: the latter [p. 103] always presupposes the former to avoid becoming an illusory dream or an anthropocentric withdrawal. Thus, today we see Christians belonging to certain sects that have issued from the Reformation, who are disturbed by the destructive subjectivism they can see at work and who, aware of the source from which this springs, deplore what they think was an overreaction against the "Roman error" and call for a "turning backward" on this very important point.[61] "Everything depends on what Jesus Christ, the Son of God, was. The significance of his acts, in his life and in his death, depends on the nature of his personal being. It was *he* who died for us; *he* who redeemed us by *his own* offering in life and in death."[62] The Christians who speak in this fashion have thus come back precisely to what Fr. Pierre Rousselot[63] wrote sixty years ago:

> *Christ has two natures; what is that to me?*—But the substantial reparation of humanity lies in that very fact. But this joining of the divine and the human touches and heals what is most profound and most

[60] Yves de Montcheuil, loc. cit.

[61] [The situation described sharply contrasts with the objective, state-based early Reformation.—Ed.]

[62] T. F. Torrance, art. cit., 297.

[63] [Pierre Rousselot (1878–1915) was a French Jesuit theologian. Conscripted early in the First World War, he became an army officer and was killed in battle at Éparges. His key works were *The Eyes of Faith*, trans. Joseph Donceel (New York: Fordham University Press, 1990); *Intelligence: Sense of Being, Faculty of God*, trans. Andrew Tallon (Milwaukee, Wis.: Marquette University Press, 1999); and *The Problem of Love in the Middle Ages: A Historical Contribution*, trans. Alan Vincelette with Paul Vandevelde (Milwaukee, Wis.: Marquette University Press, 2001). In the quotation, he obviously echoes Luther.—Ed.]

inalienable in me, my very nature. *Christ has two natures; what is that to me?* But every living intelligence is directly, personally, profoundly involved in this central fact of the history of being, which brings divinization to creatures. *At the moment that affects the depths of being itself, it affects the depths of my own being.*[64]

Now, through the dogma concerning Christ we are [p. 104] immediately led to the dogma of the Trinity; "Trinitarian doctrine in itself can be justified in biblical terms only as the background for the doctrine of the Incarnation"—but that background is "indispensable".[65] This is, precisely, let us repeat, what revelation teaches us, as we find it recorded in the pages of Scripture and faithfully summed up in our Creed. True, "the New Testament, while presupposing the pre-existing divine being and the divine person of Christ, does not consider them in terms of their origin and nature but in terms of the reparation they accomplish in salvation history."[66] It is no less true that through this manifestation we distinctly perceive the unique relationship between Jesus and God, the relationship between his person, the Father and the Spirit. So then, if one admits the distinction between the disciplines, as Mr. Cullmann proposes we should, one should specify, in the very spirit of the latter, that exegesis or, if one prefers, biblical theology, "cannot be self-sufficient but needs to be completed by dogmatic [p. 105] reflection which must clarify the implications of the biblical data. This has been the object of the great councils",[67] which have themselves been prepared from the earliest times.

Even though it be a light inaccessible to reason, the divine Trinity is the unique hypothesis which permits us to throw light in a phenomenologically correct manner, and without doing violence to the data given us, on the phenomenon of Christ as he makes himself constantly present in the Bible, in the Church and in history. Everywhere in Scripture . . . the absolute image of God is necessarily cosignified in the image of the economy of salvation which emerges. To suppose

[64] Rousselot, [*Études sur le foi*].

[65] Hans Urs von Balthasar, *La Gloire et la croix* [The Glory of the Lord] I (1965): 368. . . .

[66] O. Cullmann, in *Choisir* (Geneva, August 1960) 21; and, speaking of Melanchthon, *Christologie du Nouveau Testament* [Christology of the New Testament], 285. . . .

[67] Jean Daniélou, *Recherches de science religieuse* 55 (1967): 124–26.

> that Paul, for instance, had in view *only* a Trinity dependent upon the economy shows no less theological poverty than would dogmatics that offhandedly enter into the categories of the inner life of the Trinity without keeping in touch, as regards form and content, with the event of the Trinity manifested by the economy of salvation.[68]

In the Epistle to the Ephesians, St. Paul speaks of the "mystery of the benevolent will" of God toward men, and of the "economy of this mystery",[69] i.e., of the design hidden in God from all eternity, and of its fulfillment in the course of time, which is now revealed in Jesus Christ. When the Fathers of the Church in their turn speak of "the mystery of the economy" or, as [p. 106] Clement of Alexandria calls it, "the economy of God", the "salvific economy",[70] they join into a single expression the two successive parts that made up Paul's idea. Whereas, in this expression, "mystery" means more especially the totality of the divine plan and its ultimate end, "economy", according to the profane meaning of the word (i.e., organization, inner arrangement, or administration), rather designates the totality of the means chosen by God for the execution of his plan, namely, the series of *magnalia Dei*, of [great] deeds accomplished in view of man's salvation. For the Fathers, as for St. Paul, these deeds culminate in the "economy" par excellence, in the unique fact of the Incarnation which Paul himself calls "the mystery of Christ".[71] For him as well as for the Fathers, this mystery of the economy introduces us into the mystery of theology.[72] The [p. 107] "economic" aspect of this "*theologia*" naturally leads them to inquire into the "theological" depths of the "oikonomia". Knowledge of God's works cannot fail to throw some indirect light on God himself, a

---

[68] Hans Urs von Balthasar, *L'Amour seul est digne de foi* (Paris: Aubier, 1966), 111–12. Cf. *La Foi du Christ* [The faith of Christ]: Total faith "goes beyond the Lutheran viewpoint of pure confidence and obviously goes much farther than 'holding as true' the dogmatic truths, a simple caricature of the Catholic concept." (Ibid., 1968, 14 ss.)

[69] Eph 1:9–10 and 3:8–11.

[70] *Stromata* [Miscellany], bk. 2, chap. 2, 4; chap. 6, 29; bk. 3, chap. 5, 20. *Paedag.* [Christ the educator] 8, 1, chap. 6, 25, 3, etc.

[71] Eph 3:2–5. . . .

[72] Cf. Thomas F. Torrance, "The Implications of Oikonomia for Knowledge and Speech of God in Early Christian Theology", in *Oikonomia, Heilsgeschichte als Thema der Theologie* (Hamburg, 1967), 223–38. . . .

light which eliminates many unworthy or insufficient ideas rather than providing us with positive enlightenment.

> The mystery of the Trinity is the expression at one and the same time of the proximity and of the remoteness of God with regard to his creatures. For the Trinity is revealed to us only to the extent in which it makes possible our elevation and our redemption through the work of salvation. This Trinity of salvation presupposes a Trinity in and of itself, dwelling in light inaccessible, whose names, derived from this work of salvation, tell us nothing about the Trinity itself. So, it is in the mystery where God draws closest to us that we best perceive how infinitely far above us he is.[73]

When Christian reflection has succeeded in drawing from the "mystery of the economy" the implications concerning "theology", we can begin to study to a slight extent the Trinity "in itself"; and, proceeding according to a logical plan, we can do this even before coming to consider the work of human salvation. This process was begun, as we mentioned above, in the celebrated *Theological Discourses* of St. Gregory Nazianzen and in the other Cappadocian Fathers.[74] We also find it to some extent in the work of St. Augustine. In 390, in [p. 108] his *De moribus Ecclesiae* [*Of the Morals of the Catholic Church*], Augustine still adhered entirely to the primacy of the "economic" point of view: he showed, in the Church, the Spirit leading to the Son, by whom the Father himself is known.[75] But in 393, in the *De fide et symbolo* [*Faith and the Creed*], we find the order reversed: "To faith in the eternal realities we also add the temporal mission of our Lord, which he deigned to take upon himself for our sake and to fulfill for our salvation."[76] Again, in 396, in the *De agone christiano* [*The Christian Combat*]:

> Faith . . . includes eternal realities which carnal man cannot understand and also temporal realities, past and future, which eternal Providence has accomplished and will accomplish for man's salvation. . . .

---

[73] Erik Przywara, *Philosophie de la religion catholique* [Philosophy of the Catholic religion], 2nd part, *in fine* [conclusion] (in German, Munich-Berlin, 1927, 65–66).

[74] It was given added impetus at this time by the struggle against Arianism.

[75] Bk. 1, chap. 17, no. 31: "This is the work of God's simple, pure charity. . . . Inspired by the Holy Spirit, she brings men to the Son, i.e., to the Wisdom of God by whom the Father himself is known." . . .

[76] Chap. 4, no. 6. . . .

> Thus, believing in the immutable Trinity, let us also believe in its temporal action for the salvation of the human race.[77]

However, even though we adopt this logical and descending order, contrary to the ascending order of discovery, it should never make us forget that our knowledge of the Trinity always remains tied to our knowledge of its action, and that, from this action itself, the total and [p. 109] final form will never be defined. The revelation of the economy of the mystery always leaves unsolved "the mystery of the economy". *O altitudo!*[78]

This is something which even the most intrepid theologians, those at least whom Catholic tradition recognizes as fully its own, have never forgotten. Continually, "the Greek Fathers connect the relationships between the Divine Persons with their relationships with creatures."[79] Their language is extremely cautious; one can say the same of Tertullian and even of Justin. "The Creator of the universe", says the latter, "has no name because he was not engendered. . . . Father, God, Creator, Lord and Master are not names but titles suggested by his benefactions and his deeds."[80] The school to which St. Gregory Nazianzen belonged is also the one which did battle to defend the unfathomable mystery of the divinity against the satisfied rationalism of the Anomeans, those men, says Theodoret, who made "a technology out of theology".[81] Gregory Nazianzen himself declares that "no prophet ever penetrated the Divine Substance, as Scripture testifies; none of them either beheld or explained God's nature."[82] And his friend, Gregory [p. 110] of Nyssa, commenting on the Apostle's words about "the name which is above every name",[83] says: "The only thing appropriate to him is to believe that he is above every name, for the fact that he transcends

[77] Chap. 13, no. 15, and chap. 17, no. 19. . . .

[78] [These are the opening words of the Vulgate translation of Rom 11:33a: "O the depths of the riches and wisdom and knowledge of God!"—Ed.]

[79] Théodore de Régnon, *Études sur le dogme de la Trinité* [Studies on the dogma of the Trinity] 3 (Paris, 1898): 70.

[80] *Seconde Apologie* [Second apology], chap. 6, nos. 1–2. . . .

[81] Theodoret of Cyr, *Résumé des fables hérétiques* [Compendium of heresiology], bk. 4, chap. 3. . . .

[82] *Discours* 28, chap. 19. . . .

[83] Phil 2:8.

every flight of thought and that he is beyond being comprehended under any name constitutes the proof of his greatness, a greatness that man cannot express."[84] Drawing the conclusion implied in this, John Chrysostom prescribes for every Christian the only conceivable attitude, which is one of submissive adoration. "Would you, a man, take part in scrutinizing God? You would outrage him if you curiously sought to grasp his essence. . . . The indiscretion which scrutinizes him draws down his indignation."[85] St. Hilary shows an equal reserve.[86] As for St. Augustine, in many passages he criticizes those who imagine that they can understand God.

> Better to recognize your ignorance than to presume to know. . . . To attain God through one's mind, in some slight degree, is a great blessing; but to comprehend him is impossible.[87] If you have understood, then it is not God![88] It is good for you to falter in praising God, for when you praise him without being able to explain what you would wish, your thought expands within you, and [p. 111] this enlargement makes you more capable of receiving the one you praise. . . .[89] God is ineffable; if, not being able to express what he is, you are still bound not to be silent, what remains for you to do except to rejoice in your heart that you can find no words?[90]

Nor should we accord too much importance to the reversal of procedure which we noticed in Augustine's works; this merely affects a certain order of catechetical exposition, not Augustine's fundamental attitude or the movement of his faith; and his great treatise *De Trinitate* [*The Trinity*] itself explores the inner relationships of the divine Trinity only after an exploration of the human soul, as revelation alone allowed him to undertake. If we now question St. Bernard, we shall find him as severe as the Cappadocians[91] or

---

[84] *Contra Eunomium* [Against Eunomius], bk. 12 . . . ; bk. 1 . . . ; many other passages. . . .

[85] *Sur l'incompréhensibilité de Dieu* [On the incomprehensible nature of God] . . . ; especially hom. 2: 124, 126, 140.

[86] *De Trinitate* [The Trinity], bk. 11, chap. 47. . . .

[87] *Sermo* 117, no. 5. . . .

[88] *Sermons* 52 and 53. . . .

[89] *In ps.* [Expositions on the Psalms] 145, no. 4. . . .

[90] *In ps.* 32, 2; *Sermo* 1, no. 8. . . .

[91] [Basil of Caesarea, his brother Gregory of Nyssa, and Gregory Nazianzen, who lived during the fourth century in Cappadocia in central Anatolia.—Ed.]

St. John Chrysostom in condemning the audacity shown by man when he assumes the role of a "scrutator" [examiner], of an *effractor Majestatis* [burglar of the throne]; with the Book of Proverbs he predicts that such a man will be "crushed by glory".[92] No doubt, he explains, it is possible for man to approach the Divinity, but he must do it *quasi admirans, non quasi scrutans* [marveling, not examining], and this presupposes that the initiative comes from God; the only thing proper for man, at any time, is to examine diligently the mystery of the divine will so as to obey it in all things.[93] Finally, we know that [p. 112] St. Thomas Aquinas shows the link which unites the "processions" and the "missions",[94] and we are also aware of the index of rigidly restrictive analogy to which he assigns all his investigations, apparently so sure of themselves, concerning the being of God.[95] In short, if the "economy" really opens to us the way leading to "theology", the latter always maintains in the last analysis —it should have maintained in all cases—the finest of the meanings it has in the Christian language: praise and silent adoration in the recognition of the unfathomable mystery.

On the other hand, the very terms in which revelation is given to us, and the faith of the first generation of Christians which these terms express, suggest a certain "homogeneity" in the supraconceptual order "between God's being and his manifestations", or, as the Greek Fathers also put it, between the θεὸς πρός ἑαυτόν and the θεὸς πρός ἡμας, the "God for himself" and the "God for us":

---

[92] [This refers to the Vulgate translation of Prov 25:27: "He that is a searcher of majesty shall be overwhelmed by glory" (Douay-Rheims). A *scrutator* was a legal official. The passage in Bernard of Clairvaux, *On the Song of Songs* 62, 3 (4), refers to Paul's diffident description of his own heavenly rapture (2 Cor 12:2–4) and is rendered by Kilian Walsh: "What other mortal then would presume to involve himself by his own attempts at an awesome scrutiny of the divine majesty, what insolent contemplative would force his way into those dread secrets? The scrutinizers of majesty described as invaders are not, I think then, those who are rapt into it, but those who force their way in" (*On the Song of Songs*, 4 vols. [Kalamazoo, Mich: Cistercian, 1971–1980], 3:155).—ED.]

[93] *De consideratione* [Five books on consideration], bk. 5, no. 6. . . .

[94] [*Summa theologiae* Ia, qq. 27–43, which deals with the Trinity, opens with the procession of the Divine Persons and culminates with their mission. The following six questions concern creation.—ED.]

[95] Cf. Prima, 9 [*Summa theologiae* Ia], [q.] 13, a. 10, ad 5: "*Ipsam naturam Dei, prout in se est, neque Catholicus neque paganus cognoscit*" [neither a Catholic nor a pagan knows the nature of God in itself].

> No doubt . . . God remains a mystery; and the Apostle Paul speaks of the "profound depths of God".[96] . . . But God reveals himself as a hidden God. He makes himself known in his mystery. . . . This permanent dialectic between the revealed God and the hidden God comes out [p. 113] strongly in the Incarnation. . . . God is himself totally present in his Word. In his Word, God makes himself known as the holy and merciful God. He makes himself known as what he really is.[97]

This is precisely what Newman,[98] following the whole of Catholic tradition, said in 1841: "Christianity is a supernatural history, almost a pageant; it tells us what its Author is by telling us what he has done."[99] Hans Urs von Balthasar[100] repeats the same thing to us today:

> Beyond existence and essence the constitution of being becomes clearer; it appears to us only in "not holding onto itself", in going out of itself to take flesh in concrete finiteness. This permits finite creatures to receive and to understand him as he is in himself, as the one who does not seek to preserve himself. Thus are they initiated by him into the love that gives without ceasing. . . . Thanks to the sign of God who abases himself in becoming incarnate and empties himself in death and the absence of God, one can throw some light on why God, as the Creator of the world, has already gone out of himself and has descended below himself; it is because it corresponded to his own being, to his absolute essence, to reveal himself, in his

---

[96] [Rom 11:33.—ED.]

[97] Roger Mehl, *La Théologie protestante* [Protestant theology] (Paris: P.U.F., 1966), 10–11 and 62. For Mr. Mehl, this "homogeneity" is a postulate which is "undoubtedly much more stressed in Protestant than in Catholic theology".

[98] [St. John Henry Newman (1801–1890) was a prominent Anglican priest and theologian who converted to Roman Catholicism and, like de Lubac, became a cardinal late in his life. In 1841, he was still an Anglican.—ED.]

[99] "The Tamworth Reading Room" (1841), in *Discussions and Arguments on Various Subjects*, 296. . . .

[100] [Hans Urs von Balthasar (1905–1988) was born in Switzerland and joined the Jesuits in Germany. He studied theology in Lyon (1933–1937), where de Lubac mentored him, but left the order in 1950 to establish his own secular religious institute and continue his theological work. For his time in Lyon, Paul Silas Peterson, *The Early Hans Urs von Balthasar: Historical Contexts and Intellectual Formation* (Berlin: de Gruyter, 2015), 293.—ED.]

> sovereign and unfathomable liberty, as the measureless love which is . . . the height and depth, the length and breadth of Being itself.[101]

[p. 114] So, without ceasing to cry out in adoration with St. Paul, "*O altitudo*" [O depth], the Christian's faith dwells in St. John's affirmation: "*Deus caritas est*" [God is love].[102]

The "economy", the unfolding of divine action in favor of man, comes about, one might say, in three phases. Hence three successive series of operations which are different in nature, and each of which is attributed by our Creed to one of the three Persons—even though it has always been understood that never does any one of them act separately from the other two. So, the works of creation belong to the Father, the works of redemption to the Son, the works of sanctification to the Holy Spirit. This is what Origen explains in the first book of his *Peri archôn* [*On First Principles*].[103] All through tradition we see this same schema used as the framework for elementary catechetical teaching as well as for more extensive works, such as the great treatise of Rupert of Deutz, *De Trinitate et operibus ejus* [*On the Trinity and Its Works*], in the twelfth century. Each of the three series thus distinguished can be more or less fully detailed, but from the beginning they cover together the entire range of history, from creation to the final consummation. From the beginning, the framework is laid down. Before being adopted by the Apostles' Creed, it was used in the primitive preaching, such as we find it in Acts;[104] the entire divine plan of salvation, as explained by the first witnesses of Christ, unfolds in "three historical stages which [p. 115] readily correspond to the three Persons".[105] This is the same framework Luther used, and there is no innovation whatever to be seen in the fact that "the trinitarian division adopted by" the leader of the Reformation in his *Little Catechism* makes the

---

[101] *L'Amour seul est digne de foi* . . . (Paris: Aubier, 1966), 183–86. . . .

[102] [Rom 11:33, 1 Jn 4:8, 16.—Ed.]

[103] *Peri archôn* [On first principles], bk. 1, chap. 3, nos. 5–7. . . . Cf. St. Athanasius, *On the Incarnation and against the Arians*, chap. 8: "The Word became flesh so that we might receive the Spirit." . . .

[104] [Peter in Acts 2:22–36, 3:12–26, 4:8–12, 10:34–43; Peter and the apostles in 5:29–32; Paul in 13:23–39.—Ed.]

[105] Pierre Benoit, *Les origines du symbole des apôtres dans le Nouveau Testament* [The origins of the Apostles' Creed in the New Testament], . . . 45.

Church "only a consequence of the Holy Spirit".[106] For this is, in the Creed, a framework laid down once and for all, which can be neither transformed nor transcended. It measures and encloses the faith. The creed of the Christian faith, which explains the mystery of the "economy", is necessarily and strictly trinitarian.

[106] Cf. Émile G. Léonard, *Histoire générale du protestantisme* [General history of Protestantism] 1 (Paris: P.U.F., 1961): 109.

# 3

# The Church

## Catholicism

*Writing in 1988, Joseph Cardinal Ratzinger described de Lubac's* Catholicism *as an "essential milestone" on his theological journey. He praises de Lubac for "not expressing his own private opinions, which would fade as they had blossomed", but for letting the "Fathers of our Faith speak so that we hear the voice of the origin in all its freshness and astonishing relevance".*[1] *With de Lubac, he writes, "the Fathers become our contemporaries." The later Pope Benedict XVI goes on to describe the fascination that de Lubac's method and sources provoked among theologians in the 1950s, when de Lubac was debarred from publishing any further Christian theology. He also alludes to* Catholicism*'s French subtitle, which refers to the "social dimension of dogma". De Lubac's original intention was to counter excessively individualistic conceptions of the Christian faith by showing how it could only be lived out collectively in the life of the Church. However, Pope Benedict continues, there is now a danger that the Church is viewed in merely sociological terms, whereas de Lubac shows that corporate belonging is, in truth, "rooted in deepest mystery".*

Catholicism *was published in Cerf's "Unam sanctam" series, which was edited by the Dominican Yves Congar. Its first part, which focuses on the Church's social aspect, summarizes some of de Lubac's teaching at the Catholic Theological Faculty in Lyon. The second part, from which this excerpt is taken, collates texts delivered in public lectures that deal with historical dimensions of the Church's identity.*[2]

---

[1] *Catholicism: Christ and the Common Destiny of Man*, trans. Lancelot C. Sheppard and Sister Elizabeth Englund, O.C.D. (San Francisco: Ignatius Press, 1988), 11.

[2] *At the Service of the Church: Henri de Lubac Reflects on the Circumstances that Occasioned His Writings*, trans. Anne Elizabeth Englund (San Francisco: Ignatius Press, 1993), 27.

*Salvation through the Church: The Problem*

[p. 217] Thus we always come back to the Church without ever being able to consider her mystic reality apart from her visible existence in time. She is both at the beginning and at the end, and all that lies between is full of her foreshadowings and her expansion. Seen by the eye of faith the whole religious history of mankind stands out illuminated, its several parts fall naturally into place, and what many were tempted to consider the irremediable conflict between belief in a world-wide call to salvation and belief in the Church as necessary for this same salvation is seen to be resolved.

The problem of the "salvation of unbelievers" has confronted the Christian conscience in tragic guise as a consequence of successive discoveries in geography, history, and pre-history which, while they immeasurably increase the sum of human achievement, seem to diminish in proportion the achievement of Christ. But gradually this problem has been solved by most theologians in the only true Catholic sense. "Not one single drop of grace falls on the pagans", exclaimed Saint-Cyran with a sort of holy enthusiasm.[3] Such a narrow solution has been rejected and condemned, like that of certain Jansenists who, with their idea of a God like to the meanest of men, feared that the "grace of God would be degraded if it were used lavishly". So too has been rejected, as quite [p. 218] inadequate, the solution that has recourse to miracles, for it is of the nature of a miracle that it should be of rare occurrence. How can it be believed that God, contrary to the designs of his Providence, will multiply private revelations? So, lastly, has been rejected the expedient of a natural salvation by which the greater part of humanity, though all

---

Excerpted from *Catholicism: Christ and the Common Destiny of Man*, trans. Lancelot C. Sheppard and Sister Elizabeth Englund, O.C.D. (San Francisco: Ignatius Press, 1988), 217–40. Some translations from Latin have been made with reference to those by Jacques Guillet, Marie-Josèphe Rondeau, and Joseph Paramelle, in *Catholicisme: les aspects sociaux du dogme* (Paris: Cerf, 2003), 495–99.

[3] [Jean du Vergier Hauranne (1581–1643) was a Roman Catholic priest who became the commendatory (honorary) abbot of Saint-Cyran in the Loire, drawing an income from this office to sustain his writing and ministry in Paris. As the patron of Cornelius Jansen (1585–1638), Saint-Cyran was responsible for the introduction of his teaching into France and was opposed to the Jesuits. Jansenism taught that grace is bestowed only on the elect, who are limited in number.—Ed.]

of it is made in the image of God, should be cast into the twilight of Limbo. This thesis, which was taught in the seventeenth century by Trithemius and Archbishop Claude Seyssel,[4] was taken up again by many apologists in the eighteenth and nineteenth centuries to meet the objections of Jean-Jacques Rousseau;[5] but it was too much opposed to the best-established tradition to have any chance of prevailing. Without closing our eyes to the miserable state of many who are "in the shadow of death", we consider, nevertheless, with St. Irenaeus, that the Son, from the very beginning and in every part of the world, gives a more or less obscure revelation of the Father to every creature, and that he can be the "Salvation of those who are born outside the Way".[6] We believe, with St. Cyprian, St. Hilary and St. Ambrose, that the divine Sun of Justice shines on all and for all.[7] We teach, with St. John Chrysostom, that grace is diffused everywhere and that there is no soul that cannot feel its attraction.[8] With Origen, St. Jerome and St. Cyril of Alexandria, we refuse to assert that any man is born without [p. 219] Christ.[9] And, lastly, we willingly allow, with St. Augustine, the strictest of the Fathers, that divine mercy was always at work among all peoples,[10]

---

[4] [De Lubac postdates both figures. Johannes Trithemius (1462–1516), whose surname identifies his Rhineland birth town, became the Benedictine abbot of Sponheim (1483), then of the abbey of Saint James, Würzburg (1506). Seyssel (d. 1520) was the monarchist bishop of Marseille (1515), before becoming archbishop of Turin (1517). —Ed.]

[5] [Rousseau (1712–1778) was a Francophone philosopher and political theorist who rejected the doctrine of original sin, arguing that humans and the created order are inherently good. He promoted religious toleration, but his ideas also contributed to the French Revolution.—Ed.]

[6] *Adv. Haereses* [Against the heresies] 2, 22, 4; 3, 18, 7; 4, 20, 6–7; 4, 22, 2. . . . *Demonstration*, c. 34: "The invisible presence of the Logos has spread everywhere. . . . Through him, everything is under the influence of the redemptive economy, and the Son of God . . . has traced the sign of the cross on everything." . . .

[7] . . . Ambrose, *In Psalm.* [On the Psalms] 118, s. 8, n. 57: "Mysticus autem ille Sol justitiae omnibus ortus est, omnibus venit, omnibus passus est" [But this mystic Sun of justice rose for all, came for all, and suffered for all]. . . .

[8] *In Jo.* [On John], hom. 8, n. 1. . . .

[9] Origen, *In Joannem* [On John], vol. 6, n. 15: "Christ is so powerful that, although invisible because of his divinity, he is present to every person and extends over the whole universe." . . .

[10] . . . *In Psalmum* [Expositions of the Psalms] *88,* s. 1, n. 3: "Non autem clausit Deus

and that even the pagans have had their "hidden saints"[11] and their prophets.[12] In spite of differing explanations of detail and with degrees of optimism or pessimism according to the variations of individual temperament, experience or theological tendencies, it is generally agreed nowadays, following the lead of the Fathers and the principles of St. Thomas, that the grace of Christ is of universal application, and that no soul of good will lacks the concrete means of salvation, in the fullest sense of the word. There [p. 220] is no man, no "unbeliever", whose supernatural conversion to God is not possible from the dawn of reason onward.

But this solution gives rise at once to another problem, and it is important to understand its terms. Christ, in fact, did not confine himself to the accomplishment of the redemptive sacrifice and, in addition, to the proclamation of the good news for the anticipated consolation of a small number. He preached a law, he founded a society. He commanded his Apostles to propagate both. He declared that faith in his person and membership [in] his Church were necessary to salvation. Now if every man can be saved, in principle at least and at whatever hazard, what reason is there for this Church? Is it merely for the purpose of obtaining a better, more certain salvation

---

fontem bonitatis suae etiam alienigenas gentes" [God has not closed off the source of his goodness even to foreign nations]. . . .

[11] . . . *De catechizandis rudibus* [Instructing beginners in faith], c. 22, n. 40 . . . ; etc.

[12] *Contra Faustum* [Answer to Faustus], lib. 19, c. 2. . . . *De Civitate Dei* [The city of God], . . . lib. 18, . . . c. 47 . . . : "Non incongruenter creditur fuisse et in aliis gentibus homines, quibus hoc mysterium [de Christo] revelatum est. . . . Nec ipsos Judaeos existimo audere contendere, neminem pertinuisse ad Deum, praeter Israelitas. . . . Populus enim revera, qui proprie Dei populus diceretur, nullus alius fuit; homines autem quosdam, non terrena, sed caelesti societate ad veros Israelitas supernae cives Patriae pertinentes, etiam in aliis gentibus fuisse, negare non possunt: quia si negant, facile convincuntur de sancto et mirabili viro Job" (609) [It is not unacceptable for us to believe that, in other people as well as the Jews, there were men to whom this mystery was revealed. . . . Nor do I suppose that even the Jews dare to claim that no one has ever belonged to God except the Israelites. . . . To be sure, there was no other people who might truly be called the people of God; but the Jews nonetheless cannot deny that in other nations also there have been some men who belonged, not by earthly but by heavenly fellowship, to the true Israelites, the citizens of the supernal fatherland. And, if they do deny this, they are very easily proved wrong by the example of that holy and wondrous man Job. (Augustine, *The City of God against the Pagans*, trans. R. W. Dyson [Cambridge: Cambridge University Press, 1998], 893).]

for a small number of privileged souls? Or if it be supposed that her presence in the world is necessary in order that grace, which reposes by right in her alone, should be poured out all around her and attain in mysterious fashion the souls even of those who know her not, how can we account for the demand that has been reiterated for the past two thousand years calling for her expansion as the most urgent of all tasks? In any case, how can it still be claimed that the Church is a vital necessity?

On the practical side also the problem is no less acute. Since salvation is made accessible to those who are called (no longer [p. 221] with good reason) "unbelievers", is not the necessity for their belonging to the visible Church diminished to such an extent that it vanishes altogether? By what right henceforward is any obligation of entering the Church imposed upon them? It is not [a] sufficient answer to say: the obligation devolves only on one who encounters the Church. For it might well be asked on what this positive command is founded. And here again it is not enough to reply that between the "unbeliever" and the Catholic the difference as regards the conditions of salvation is considerable. For if this difference, which no one calls in doubt, is only a matter of "more" or "less", how is it to be understood that, though strictly speaking the "less" suffices, yet the "more" should be required? Of course it is always unwise not to choose the most favorable conditions and it is foolish to neglect the means to a fuller life; but it can never be a crime. In a well-known work Fr. Faber[13] remarked (not without some exaggeration) that if we were not blinded by the light all around us the so-called darkness of paganism would seem to us a real light illuminating every man coming into the world.[14] In any case we cannot but admire the attempts of so many missionaries to show us, by dint of human and divine sympathy, the elements of real religion which ennoble the cults even of the most inferior peoples. But if these elements, though mingled with others, are found on all sides, if the darkness, in certain cases at least, is so full of light, where is

[13] [Frederick Faber (1814–1863) was an Anglican convert to Roman Catholicism who founded the London (Brompton) Oratory (1849). At the same time, St. John Henry Newman founded the Birmingham Oratory.—Ed.]

[14] *Le Créateur et le créature* [The Creator and the creature], French trans. (1858), vol. 2, p. 112.

the obligation to seek the additional light that the Church bestows on her children? If an implicit Christianity is sufficient for the salvation of one who knows no other, why should we go in quest of an explicit one? In short, if every man can be saved through a religion that he unwittingly possesses, how can we require him to acknowledge this religion explicitly by professing Christianity and submitting to the Catholic Church?

Of course, the Church militant has no need to be furnished [p. 222] with a systematic answer to all the questions she raises before she can function to capacity. It is enough to know that "she is by divine intention and Christ's institution the only normal way of salvation."[15] And that should be enough for our faith, just as belief in the *Tu es Petrus* [You are Peter] suffices for submission to Christ's vicar [i.e., the Pope] without looking any further. But as Fr. Charles[16] remarks in this connection, "a command, even a divine command, is never the final justification of anything . . . the final justification of the precept is not the precept itself but harmony."[17] And does not the work of theology consist to a great extent in humble search after this harmony? So there is nothing to forbid our trying to explain the assertion of faith on which the missionary activity of the Church is based, and it may be useful at the same time to show how the complementary and the no less certain affirmation of the possibility of salvation for the "pagans" is in agreement with it. Is not this the only way to assure definitive theological recognition for the teaching in their regard, which happily is winning acceptance in our time? For it is certainly important not to leave the smallest opening for that accusation formerly made by the Jansenists against the Jesuits (generally unjustly) of having brought the century to unbelief through their false maxims about the possibility of salvation for men of all religions.

---

[15] *Bulletin des Missions* (Mar.–June 1934), p. 60.

[16] [Pierre Charles (1883–1954) was a Belgian Jesuit, theologian, and missiologist. —Ed.]

[17] "Christi Vicarius" [Vicar of Christ], *Nouvelle Revue théologique* (1929), p. 454.

Surely we can find the required explanation, at least in embryo, in the traditional principles that the preceding chapters have tried to reproduce. The human race is one. By our fundamental nature and still more in virtue of our common destiny we are members of the same body. Now the life of the members comes from the life of the body. How, then, can there be [p. 223] salvation for the members if, *per impossibile* [on the impossible hypothesis], the body itself were not saved? But salvation for this body, for humanity, consists in its receiving the form of Christ, and that is possible only through the Catholic Church. For is she not the only complete, authoritative interpreter of Christian revelation? Is it not through her that the practice of the evangelical virtues is spread throughout the world? And, lastly, is she not responsible for realizing the spiritual unity of men insofar as they will lend themselves to it? Thus this Church, which as the invisible Body of Christ is identified with final salvation, as a visible and historical institution is the providential means of this salvation. "In her alone mankind is refashioned and recreated."[18]

Outside Christianity, humanity can doubtless be raised in an exceptional manner to certain spiritual heights, and it is our duty—one that is perhaps too often neglected—to explore these heights that we may give praise to the God of mercies for them: Christian pity for unbelievers, which is never the fruit of scorn, can sometimes be born of admiration. But the topmost summit is never reached, and there is risk of being the farther off from it by mistaking for it some other outlying peak. This is a fact noticed by many missionaries. It is often more difficult—though in the last resort more worthwhile—[p. 224] to bring to the fullness of truth souls whom a relatively more developed religion has stamped with its mark, though there is no necessity to accuse them on that account of pride and perversion. A critical judgment, not of individual souls—for their

[18] Augustine, *Epist. 118,* n. 33: "Totum culmen auctoritatis lumenque rationis in illo uno salutari nomine atque in una ejus Ecclesia, recreando atque reformando humano generi constitutum est." [All the highest authority and light of reason are in his saving name alone and in his Church alone, to recreate and reform the constitution of mankind]. . . .

precise situation in relation to the Kingdom is never known save to God alone—but of objective systems as found in a society and as offering material for rational examination, shows that there is some essential factor missing from every religious "invention" that is not a following of Christ. There is something lacking, for example, in Buddhist charity: it is not Christian charity. Something is lacking in the spirituality of the great Hindu mystics: it is not the spirituality of St. John of the Cross. And yet those are privileged cases. Outside Christianity all is not necessarily corrupt; far from it, and the facts do not support that supposed law of degeneration in which an explanation was sought for the whole religious development of mankind left, so it was thought, to its own devices. All is not corrupt, but what does not remain puerile is always in peril of going astray, or, however high it climbs, of ultimate collapse. Outside Christianity nothing attains its end, that only end toward which, unknowingly, all human desires, all human endeavors, are in movement: the embrace of God in Christ. The most admirable, the most vigorous of these endeavors needs—absolutely—to be impregnated with Christianity if it is to bear its eternal fruit, and as long as Christianity is lacking, in spite of appearances to the contrary, they only increase that great void in humanity whence arises the cry to the one and only Plenitude, and only make more obvious that slavery from which it stretches out its arms toward its Liberator.

[p. 225] Outside Christianity, again, humanity tries to collect its members together into unity. Throughout the centuries a powerful instinct compels it through an apparent chaos of dispersal and conflict, collisions and strivings, social integration and disintegration, toward a "common life", an outward expression of that unity which is obscurely felt within. But humanity, as we see only too clearly, can never overcome all the opposing forces which are everywhere at work, forces which it contains within itself and is always producing or reawakening. Cities expand yet are always closed societies, they combine together but only to fight more bitterly with one another, and beneath their outward unity there is always the personal enmity of the souls within them. But here is that divine house built upon the rock *in qua* [upon which], according to that marvelous formula of the [First] Vatican

Council,[19] *veluti in domo Dei viventis, fideles omnes unius fidei et caritatis vinculo continerentur* [All the faithful are contained as it were in the house of the living God by the bond of one faith and love]. Here is the marriage house in which heaven is joined to earth. Here is the household in which all are gathered together to eat of the Lamb; here is the place of true sacrifice. Only that Ideal which Christ gave to his Church is pure [p. 226] enough and strong enough—for it did not issue from the brain of man, but is living and is called the Spirit of Christ—to inspire men to work for their own spiritual unity, as only the sacrifice of his Blood can bring their labor to fruition. It is only through the leavening of the Gospel within the Catholic community and by the aid of the Holy Spirit that this "divine Humanity" can be established, *unica dilecta Dei* [the unique beloved of God].

If God had willed to save us without our own cooperation, Christ's sacrifice by itself would have sufficed. But does not the very existence of our Savior presuppose a lengthy period of collaboration on man's part? Moreover, salvation on such terms would not have been worthy of the persons that God willed us to be. God did not desire to save mankind as a wreck is salvaged; he meant to raise up within it a life, his own life. The law of redemption is here a reproduction of the law of creation: man's cooperation was always necessary if his exalted destiny was to be reached, and his cooperation is necessary now for his redemption. Christ did not come to take our place—or rather this aspect of substitution refers only to the first stage of his work—but to enable us to raise ourselves through him to God. He came not to win for us an external pardon—that fundamentally was ours from all eternity and is presupposed by the Incarnation itself; for redemption is a mystery of love and mercy—but to change us inwardly. Thenceforward humanity was to cooperate actively in its own salvation, and that is why to the act of his sacrifice Christ joined the objective revelation of his Person and the foundation of his Church. To sum up, revelation and redemption are bound up together, and the Church is their only Tabernacle.

---

[19] *Constitutio dogmatica de Ecclesia Christi* [Dogmatic Constitution on the Church of Christ], init.

*The Role of the "Unbelievers"*

[p. 227] But if the Church—the historic, visible, hierarchic Church—is thus necessary to transform and complete human endeavor, she herself is by no means complete. She has not even begun her work in some parts of the world. It is a matter of urgency, then, that she should increase, and primarily that her extension should be conterminous with that of the human race. We do not know, of course, what the future has in store for us in this respect, though we may realize fully that our exercise of freedom is continually thwarting God's plans: that ignorance and that knowledge save us from so many illusions. But we cannot doubt that just as of old the mission of Providence in time was to prepare for the first coming of Christ, so now is it to extend the Church everywhere that the Kingdom of God may have more powerful sway in every soul.

As long as the Church has not covered the whole earth and bound all souls together, to increase is a very necessity of her nature. The history of her "missions" is the history of her own growth, is her own history. Her advance is often slow and sometimes it is checked by reverses, such as occurred in the seventh century in face of the overwhelming progress of Islam,[20] or in the eighteenth when Christianity was overthrown in the Far East.[21] The mistaken impression of having already attained to the ends of the inhabited world together with an anticipation of the early approach of the last day combined at times to weaken her effort. Did not St. Gregory the Great himself, the organizer of the English mission, confess that he thought the Church was in her old age and that he had hardly anything left to hope for save the final conversion of Israel? According to him nothing more remained but to retire within [p. 228] oneself and, while rejoicing over victories won, to strengthen one's soul against the attacks of anti-Christ. . . .[22] Yet the Church has ever acknowledged

---

[20] [Through Palestine, Syria, Abyssinia, Egypt, and the Berber coastlands of northern Africa.—Ed.]

[21] [In 1724, Christianity was banned in China by the Yongzheng Emperor, following a dispute between his father and Pope Clement XI about ancestor worship.—Ed.]

[22] *Moralia in Job* [Morals on the book of Job], lib. 19, c. 12, n. 19. . . . Already, for example, Ambrose, *In Luc.* [On Luke], lib. 10, n. 10: "We are nearing the end of time,

her responsibility for all the human race, that human race which the Middle Ages summarized in the threefold posterity of Noah[23] spread out over three continents,[24] but united in their trial and in praise of the Lord like the three children[25] in the fiery furnace;[26] from this humanity they would exclude neither the "Pygmies", the fabulous long-eared Scythians, nor the grotesque "dog-headed ones".[27] From the very first she has always kept her objective before her. A Christian age which deliberately turned away from it would be worse than an age of heresy—is it not, [p. 229] indeed, one of the signs of the true Church of Christ, the indefectible guardian of the faith, that at no time in her history has she ever repudiated this aim?[28] It would amount to a denial of her very being, what

---

and that is why certain maladies of humanity are manifesting themselves, premonitory signs" . . . , etc.

[23] [Noah's three children, Shem, Ham, and Japheth, were traditionally viewed as the progenitors of the Semitic, African, and European peoples respectively (Gen 10).—Ed.]

[24] Paschasius Radbertus, *In Mat.* [On Matthew], lib. 8, c. 17, on the three disciples chosen by Jesus to be present at the Transfiguration: "In his, regni caelestis ordo, et numerus praefiguratur, quod ex origine trium filiorum Noe colligenda est omnis Ecclesia . . . ita ut concussae sint singulae partes terrarum, quae sub tribus describuntur nominibus, ne aut Asia sola credidisse dicatur, verum et Africa simul atque Europa Christi sanguine redempta, de imis ad superna perducitur. . . ." [In these are prefigured the order and number of the heavenly kingdom, because from the three sons of Noah originates the gathering of the whole Church. (Christ's preaching) resounds in the parts of the earth identified by these three names, so that not only Anatolia is said to believe, but also Africa and moreover Europe, redeemed by Christ's blood, are raised from the depths to the heights.] . . .

[25] [Shadrach, Meshach, and Abednego (Dan 3) were young adult Jews working as civil servants in exile in Babylon. They survived being thrown into a furnace after refusing to worship an idol and were promoted.—Ed.]

[26] Honorius of Autun, *Sacramentarium* [Sacramentary], c. 78 (PL 172, 787A).

[27] Portal of Pentecost at Vézelay (Émile Mâle, *L'Art religieux du XIIe siècle* [Religious art of the twelfth century], p. 327). . . . The Eastern records of St. Andrew and St. Bartholomew speak of the conversion of the cynocephalous ("dog-headed"). . . .

[28] It is acknowledged that in their beginnings the Protestant Churches had not this missionary consciousness. On this both Catholic and Protestant historians are agreed. "I cannot forgive the English and the Dutch their neglect," wrote Leibniz, Oct. 1, 1697. Cf. Fénelon, *Sermon for the Epiphany* (1685), first point: "This fruitfulness of our mother in all parts of the world, this apostolic zeal which shines in our pastors alone, which those of the new sects have not even tried to imitate, is an embarrassment to the most famous of the defenders of schism. I have read it in their latest books. They are unable to hide it. I have known the most sensible and upright people in this party confess that

Newman would have called her "Idea". Her Catholicity is both her strength and at the same time a continual demand upon her. She knows "that she was born for nothing else than the propagation everywhere of the Reign of Christ, so as to bring all men to take part in his saving redemption", and that therein lies not the isolated task of some few specialized workers but the "principal office" of her pastors.[29] She cannot forget the prophesies that have [p. 230] always guided her progress and nourished her hope. So long as the Church does not extend and penetrate to the whole of humanity, so as to give to it the form of Christ, she cannot rest.[30]

The Church is a growing body, a building in course of construction. Both metaphors suggest that her completion is not the work of one day. Even supposing in man a complete correspondence with the plans of the divine Architect, the work is long and exacting, and the laying of the foundation stone, that "corner stone" which is no other than Christ, "the first born among many brethren," required, as we know, vast preparations beforehand.

Every created being, in fact, is subject in this world to the law of development. If salvation, which is God himself, is free from it, humanity, in order to receive this salvation, is not so free. Just as for intelligence to dawn in a corporeal organism and shine at last in human eyes it is first necessary that life [p. 231] should arise in the body and that it should discover ever-improving means of communication with the outside world, though its role is solely to prepare itself for receiving this intelligence which is of a high order and which it receives like a grace—the comparison is enlightening, although its details must not be pressed—so did it need thousands of years of preparation for Christ's revelation to be *received* [by] men, and for the divine Likeness in all its splendor to shine in the eyes of his saints; and this is true not only of the Jewish revelation,

---

this radiance, in spite of all the subtleties employed to obscure it, strikes their very heart and attracts them to us." . . .

[29] Pius XI, *Rerum Ecclesiae* [(1926) Encyclical on Catholic Missions]. . . .

[30] Augustine, *In Psalm. 98*, n. 5: "Et si adhuc commoretur particula terrae quae remansit (nondum liberata), non permaneamus in gemitu pro ipsis, ut et illis Deus tribuat intellectum, et nobiscum audiant voces istas, de quibus modo gaudemus" [And if any particular land exists that remains (unliberated), we continue praying for it, that God will grant it understanding and that its voices will pray with ours, as we now rejoice]. . . .

that incomparable stream of light and of enigmas stretching from Abraham to Jesus, but also of all those other, obscurer, more external preparations which went before it or were contemporary with it among the pagans, and of the whole gradual raising up, social, intellectual and material, of fallen man.

[p. 232] Now this wonderful spectacle of divine "economies" cannot be represented as a straightforward development. Spiritual life, like all life, takes shape in a suitable organism only after much hesitation. Outbursts of sudden energy are followed by long barren periods, and not every promise of progress is followed by fulfillment. For every concentration of fruitful effort there is a whole heap of material which seems wasted. One success comes after hundreds of more or less abortive efforts and involves a certain number of miscarriages. And since nature had to produce an unbelievably extravagant profusion of living species so that in the end the human body could appear, we must not be astonished at the strange multiplicity of the forms of religion, before or outside Christianity, shown to us in history.

We must not be astonished, but we must draw the necessary inference and so find the key to our problem. For since a necessary function in the history of our salvation was fulfilled by so great a mass of "unbelievers"—not indeed in that they were in formal error or in a state of degradation, but in that there is to be found in their beliefs and consciences a certain groping after the truth, its painful preparation or its partial anticipation, discoveries of the natural reason and tentative solutions—so these unbelievers have an inevitable place in our humanity, a humanity such as the fall and the promise of a Redeemer have made it.

There is no comparison between their role and that of the scaffolding which, necessary as it is in the construction of a building, is discarded once the building is complete without further thought of what will become of it. For if the heavenly Jerusalem is built of living stones,[31] it is also living beings that go to make its scaffolding. In other words, humanity is made up of persons who have all the same eternal destiny, in whatever category or century their birth has placed them; their relationships cannot be envisaged, then, as just

[31] 1 Pet 2:5. . . .

external [p. 233] ones, as if some existed only to prepare suitable conditions for the development of others, as in Renan's paradox of the coming of a superman.[32] In spite of great differences of understanding and of function, all members of the human race enjoy the same essential equality before God.

As "unbelievers" are, in the design of Providence, indispensable for building the Body of Christ, they must in their own way profit from their vital connection with this same Body. By an extension of the dogma of the communion of saints,[33] it seems right to think that though they themselves are not in the normal way of salvation, they will be able nevertheless to obtain this salvation by virtue of those mysterious bonds which unite them to the faithful. In short, they can be saved because they are an integral part of that humanity which is to be saved.

People speak sometimes of a "supplying"; what we have just described seems in the last analysis the only possible "supplying", one that gives their value to all others for those who have not received the fullness of light. Although in certain cases the "less" seems to suffice—to return to the terms in which our original objection was formulated—the "more" exists and supplies what is lacking that this "less" can suffice, that the "insufficient can be sufficient".[34] More precisely still, there is presupposed not only the restricted precarious presence of this "more" somewhere in the world, but its unrestricted growth and its definitive completion, though in a form that to us remains mysterious. In short there is presupposed both the existence of the Church and the success of her mission. When a missionary proclaims Christ to a people that does not yet know him, it is not only those men or their descendants that hear his preaching, who are concerned with the success [p. 234] of his mission. It is also, it can be said in more than one sense, their ancestors. Indirectly but really it is the whole nameless mass of those who, from the beginning of our race, have done their best in that

[32] [Ernest Renan (1823–1892) was a French philologist whose *Life of Jesus* (1863) presented a heroic Aryan Jesus abolishing a redundant Judaism. Although Nietzsche inveighed against this depiction of Jesus, de Lubac implies that it contributed to Nietzsche's model of the superman.—Ed.]

[33] [The whole assembly of Christ's followers, both on earth and in heaven.—Ed.]

[34] M. Blondel, *Lettre sur les exigences* [Letter on the requirements] (1896), p. 70.

darkness or half light that was their lot. And so it is that God, desiring that all men should be saved, but not allowing in practice that all should be visibly in the Church, wills nevertheless that all those who answer his call should in the last resort be saved through his Church. *Sola Ecclesiae gratia, qua redimimur.*[35]

## *The Obligation to Enter the Church*

We are now in a position to understand the full force of that rigorous and at the same time comforting axiom which, from Origen and Cyprian right down to Pius XI's encyclical *Mortalium animos*, has ever been the expression of orthodox doctrine on the subject we are treating: outside the Church, no salvation.[36] Obviously it cannot mean that no one is ever saved who does not belong exteriorly to the Church, and it is significant that the texts in which it occurs, when they are [p. 235] not addressed simply to schismatics,[37] contain also the immediate qualifying statement which we should expect, excepting the case of invincible[38] ignorance in pagans of good will.[39] But the explanation for which a formula has been found during the last few centuries in the distinction between the body and soul of the Church is neither sufficient nor entirely exact; for the axiom refers, more often than not, not to the soul but to the body of the Church, her social, visible body. Following Innocent III's example, Pius IX is still more explicit: he speaks of the Roman Church.[40]

---

[35] "It is only by the grace of the Church that we are redeemed." Ambrose, *In Psalm.* [On the Psalms] *39*, 1. . . .

[36] Irenaeus, *Adv. Haereses*, 4, 13, 3. . . .

[37] This was most frequently the case in antiquity. Even the symbol of the deluge, which would more naturally apply to the destruction of the infidel, left outside the ark, is applied above all to that of the schismatic. Thus we find in Ruysbroeck, *La loi chrétienne* [The Christian law]: "The unity of the holy Church is like Noah's ark: all those who remain outside the ark must perish. The same holds true for all those who separate themselves from that unity and who set themselves in opposition to holy Church on such and such a point" (*Oeuvres*, French trans., vol. 5 [1930], p. 247). . . .

[38] [Or "unavoidable".—Ed.]

[39] [First] Vatican Council, *Constitutio de fide catholica* [Constitution on the Catholic Faith], c. 3.

[40] Alloc. consist. *Singulari quadam*, Dec. 9, 1854. Profession of faith for the Vaudois, Dec. 18, 1208. . . . Maximus of Turin spoke in the same way of "The Church of Peter", *Sermon 114* (PL 57, 722).

The explanation taken from Suarez also appears to us incomplete: according to this in order to be saved it is necessary to belong, at least in heart and by implicit desire, to the Catholic communion, *voto saltem ac desiderio* [by wish and desire alone]. Whereas these explanations take on again their true force and can be used without danger once it is recognized, by interpreting them collectively, that, for humanity taken as a whole, there can be no salvation outside the Church, that [p. 236] this is an absolute necessity, and a necessary means to which there can be no exception.

In this way the problem of the "salvation of unbelievers" receives a solution on the widest scale, and at the same time no opening is left for compromising laxity. There is no encouragement to indifference. We see now how the Church can, in the words of a theologian,[41] "be merciful to paganism without diminishing her proper character of being the only vehicle of salvation for souls"; and if it is thought that in spite of all these considerations the formula "outside the Church, no salvation" has still an ugly sound, there is no reason why it should not be put in a positive form and read, appealing to all men of good will, not "outside the Church you are damned", but "it is by the Church and by the Church alone that you will be saved." For it is through the Church that salvation will come, that it is already coming to mankind.

Of course the method of this salvation will differ according to whether the unbeliever has or has not encountered the Church. In the second case the only condition on which his salvation is possible is that he should be already a Catholic as it were by anticipation, since the Church is the "natural place" to which a soul amenable to the suggestions of grace spontaneously tends. The "less" is then sufficient—to employ the expression for the last time—not in itself, of its own worth, but insofar as it aspires to the "more", insofar as it is ready to be lost in this "more" directly the exterior obstacles which [p. 237] hide the "more" from it are removed. Far different is the case of the unbeliever who comes in contact with the Church—as long as she is shown to him in her true likeness, he has a strict obligation actually to enter her fold. For if in truth, by the very logic of his correspondence with grace, he already aspires to

[41] Stiefelhagen, quoted in Capéran, *Essai historique*, 2nd ed., p. 475.

her in secret, he would deceive himself if he shirked answering her summons. Those who do not know the Church are saved by her, therefore, in such a way that they incur the obligation of belonging to her even outwardly directly they come to know her.

Since the solution that has just been sketched is founded on principles laid down by the Fathers, it also allows us to harmonize their testimony to the Church as the sole means of salvation with their testimony quoted at the beginning of this chapter to the universal action of our Savior. Indeed it is very noticeable that when the Fathers allow the pagan world something of the light of Christ they generally set this light in a prophetic relationship with the full light of the Gospel, and that they see the Church that is to come in the lives both of the holy people of the Gentile world as well as of the righteous under the Old Law. So, for St. Irenaeus, it must be said without exception of all the saints who lived before the time of the Gospel that, in a sense, "they heralded Christ's coming and obeyed his Law."[42] According to Clement of Alexandria: "Just as God sent prophets to the Jews, so did he raise up in the midst of Greece the most virtuous of her sons and set them as prophets amidst their nation."[43] When St. Augustine, in connection with Job the Idumean [Edomite],[44] speaks of a vast "spiritual Jerusalem",[45] he does not use this term in any sort of opposition to the visible Church, as the soul of the Church might [p. 238] be opposed to its body, but only to the material city of which it was a figure. And when St. Leo lays down that from "most ancient times the mystery of man's salvation has known no interruption", he thereby emphasizes very strongly that unity which binds together the innumerable means of salvation and wonders at their providential variety.[46] The visible tangible link between the Old and New Testaments admits of no doubt, historical continuity being presupposed by the very transformation: so that of all the Gentiles that are saved it will be said, as of the Jews themselves, that they were "in the Old

---

[42] *Adv. Haer.*, 4, 27, 2. . . .

[43] *Stromates* [Miscellanies], lib. 6, c. 5. . . .

[44] [That is, neither an Israelite nor a convert to the Israelite religion.—ED.]

[45] *De Civitate Dei*, lib. 18, c. 47. . . .

[46] *In Nativ. Domini* [On the Nativity of the Lord], s. 3, c. 4–5. . . .

Testament",[47] that they were "saints of the Old Testament".[48] It matters little whether Scripture mentions them or not: we know that many are not mentioned there. Moreover, certain pages are eloquent for those who can read them aright: for example, does not Scripture give a part to Gentile[49] as to Jew [p. 239] in the genealogy of Christ?[50] The emphasis laid on this detail shows that the Fathers saw in it the sign of a more fundamental collaboration between the two peoples. Indeed, did not Jews and Gentiles down through the six ages of the world replenish with the same water, that water one day to be changed by Christ into wine, the water-pots of humanity? Jews and Gentiles were all related to the same Christ, waited for him and—especially in their sufferings, those sufferings which never spare the righteous—prefigured him.[51] Thus all prepared for the universal Church; and she does not hesitate now to recognize them as her members.[52]

---

[47] Agobard, *Adv. Fredegisum* [Against Fredegis], c. 20: "In Veteri Testamento, non solum omnes Patriarchas, sed multos etiam in gentilitate positos credimus invisibili chrismate unctos; per quam unctionem membra Christi, et unum corpus cum omnibus ad aeternam vitam praedestinatis fierent" [In the Old Testament, we believe that not only all the patriarchs, but many of those living in paganism, received an invisible chrism, by which they became members of Christ and a single body of all predestined to eternal life]. . . .

[48] Paschasius Radbertus, *In Mat.* [On Matthew], lib. 10, c. 22. . . .

[49] [Mt 1:1–16 includes Tamar, Rahab, Ruth, and Bathsheba (the wife of Uriah). Lk 3:23–38 achieves a comparable inclusivity by tracing Christ's genealogy back earlier than Abraham, to God and Adam.—Ed.]

[50] Augustine, *Sermo 51*, [nos.] 14–15. . . .

[51] Rupert, *De divinis officiis* [The worship of the Church], lib. 4, c. 4: "Omnium quippe sanctorum a mundi constitutione una fuit salus et exspectatio, Passio Redemptoris, et concordibus eorum dictis praenuntiata, gestisque praefigurata est, ac velut uni subjecta soli, diversis licet ex locis eamdem imaginem multa reddunt specularia: sic plures sancti diversis temporibus ac meritis venientes, praecurrentes Salvatorem, unam eamdemque variis figuris ejus praefiguraverunt passionem" [Indeed, from the foundation of the world all the saints had only one salvation and expectation. The Passion of the Redeemer was foretold by the agreement of their testimonies and prefigured by their actions. Like when, exposed to a single sun, many mirrors in different places reflect the same image, so a company of saints of diverse times and distinctions preceding the Savior prefigured under various figures the same Passion]. . . .

[52] Paschasius Radbertus, *In Mat.* [On Matthew], lib. 9, c. 20: "Salvator noster . . . quasi Dominus ac paterfamilias habet vineam, universam scilicet Ecclesiam, quae ab Abel justo usque ad ilium ultimum electum qui in fine mundi venturus est colligitur. . . . Ac per hoc quicumque ab initio mundi salvati sunt, in hac vere quasi palmites in vite manserunt. . . .

[p. 240] We can therefore conclude: as Jews or Gentiles, although they lived before the visible coming of Christ, must be described as saved by Christ and not merely by the Word, so, though they lived before the appearance of the visible Church among them, they are saved not by belonging in a purely spiritual, intemporal manner to the soul of the Church, but by means of a very real though indirect and more often hidden bond with her body.

---

Omnes una Ecclesia sunt, unaque vinea de vite, quae Christus est, propaginata" [Our Savior . . . as Lord and household head has a vine, namely, the universal Church, that gathers in the just from Abel to the final electee added at the end of the world. . . . From the creation of the world, whoever has been saved truly remains in this as branches on a stem. . . . All are a single Church, a vine grown from a stem, which is Christ]. . . .

## The Theological Foundation of the Missions

*De Lubac's ecclesiology developed in the shadow of the Nazi persecution of the Jews, first in Germany and then, by 1941, within France itself. For de Lubac, it was theologically significant that Nazi persecution had been first against the Jews. As Israel, the people first chosen by God, the Jews had modelled God's relationship of covenant and trust with the world to all people. In them was therefore rooted the mystery of Christ's election of his Church.*

*This text originates in a lecture given in January 1941 at the Catholic Theological Faculty in Lyon and was published soon after in the journal of the* Union missionnaire du clergé. *In it, de Lubac situates his developing spiritual resistance to Nazism in the context of the Church's mission to the world. Strikingly, this is unfolded out of the mission of Israel to the world.*

*De Lubac was convinced that the evil of Nazism would not be successfully resisted by armed force alone. Rather, because the evil was of spiritual proportions, the resistance required was also spiritual. In his memoirs, he writes of the government: "Pétain and his ministers, like most of the men of the Third Republic, seem to have been completely unaware of the formidable spiritual drama that was relentlessly pursuing its course and of the diabolical hurricane with whose violence any attempt to compromise could only intensify."*[53] *Accommodation, appeasement, and turning a blind eye might sometimes be appropriate to the normal run of political life but were entirely inadequate as responses to an encroaching secularist dictatorship that had as its object nothing less than the annihilation of God's chosen people.*

*It is important to grasp not only what de Lubac was opposing, but also the positive ends for which he was working. On several occasions, people within the checkered underground world of opposition to Nazism sought to draw him into their campaigns. These included representatives of the French Resistance, whose methods of operation de Lubac regarded as just as questionable as those of the Gestapo; a brother of General de Gaulle, the leader of the Free French, who wished to unify all opposition under his command; and a British agent parachuted in for a secret meeting. De Lubac rebutted all these advances.*[54] *The mission to which he was committed was wholly peaceful: to expose and contest the erosion of the sacred, to subject the secularist Vichy regime to*

[53] *Christian Resistance to Anti-Semitism: Memories from 1940–1944*, trans. Sister Elizabeth Englund, O.C.D. (San Francisco: Ignatius Press, 1990), 21.

[54] Ibid., 144.

*vigorous theological critique, and to show how Christian identity was a function of Jewish identity.*

[p. 369] The Church's missions fulfill one of Christ's orders.

After his Resurrection, Jesus, Saint Matthew tells us, [met] his disciples on a mountain in Galilee. Approaching them, he spoke to them thus: "All authority has been given me in heaven and on earth. Go, therefore, teaching all nations, baptizing them in the name of the Father and of the Son and of the Holy Spirit, teaching them to observe all that I have commanded you."[55] Nearly the same scene occurs at the end of Saint Mark, where the words of Jesus immediately precede the Ascension: "Go through all the world and preach the gospel to every creature."[56] Saint John gives the cenacle [upper room] as the framework for the same conversation, on the evening of the first Sunday: having wished peace to his disciples who had gathered together, behind closed doors, for fear of the Jews, Jesus adds these solemn words: "As my Father has sent me, so I send you"; then, breathing over them, he says to them: "Receive the Holy Spirit; those whose sins you forgive, they will be forgiven of them. . . ."[57]

These texts, let us note, are the foundation charter of the Church. Previously, there had been distant preparations; there had been the day-to-day education of the chosen apostles; there had been the proclamation and the promise: "I say to you that you are Peter, and on this rock I will build my Church, and the powers of hell will not prevail against her";[58] there had been the mystical birth on Calvary, when, from the pierced side of Jesus, water and blood flowed out, symbols of the sacraments and of vivifying grace. . . .[59] Now, it is the express foundation. Now these same texts are also the foundation charter of the missions. It is by sending them to

---

Excerpted from "The Theological Foundation of the Missions", in *Theology in History*, trans. Anne Englund Nash (San Francisco: Ignatius Press, 1996), 367–427.

[55] Mt 28:16–20.

[56] Mk 16:15. Cf. Acts 1:7 and Lk 24:27.

[57] Jn 20:19–23; cf. 17:18: "As you have sent me into the world, I also send them into the world."

[58] [Mt 16:18.—Ed.]

[59] [Jn 19:34.—Ed.]

preach the gospel to every creature that Jesus hands over to his apostles his divine powers. Missionary work will therefore not be a supererogatory work, it will not be as if on the periphery of the Church's activity: it is her primary work, it constitutes a part of her essential activity. Without a play on words, it is *her mission*: "Ecce, ego mitto vos."[60] In the person of the Twelve, the Church is *sent*. This is what an Instruction addressed on December 8, 1929, for [p. 370] the Congregation of the Propaganda to all mission Superiors recalled: "The Church, which has received the mandate of her divine Founder, . . . continues the mission of Christ on earth—*ipsius in terris consequitur missionem*—not seeking anything but to lead the whole human race to the knowledge of Christ and to lead it, through the observation of the evangelical law, to heavenly glory."

Now this goal has not yet been attained. How far we are from it, even today! Insofar as it has not been fully accomplished, Christ's order thus still resounds with as pressing an urgency as ever in the consciousness of the Church. It merges, for her, with her *raison d'être* [reason for being]. The Church is essentially missionary because what we call her *missions* are nothing but the primary means by which she accomplishes her *mission*. She is therefore not only missionary in some of her members, charged with a specialized function. She is so in all her members, jointly responsible for a common growth. She is so especially in her entire hierarchy, in her bishops and in her supreme pastor. It was to all his reunited apostles that the Savior delegated the mission that he had received from his Father: it is the whole episcopal body, successor of the apostolic college, that is jointly responsible for it today. Pius XI stressed this recently in his encyclical *Rerum Ecclesiae* [On Promoting Catholic Missions], addressing all his brothers in the episcopate: each of them not only has charge of the diocese that is particularly confided to him, but, called into union with all the other bishops to govern the Church of God, participating with them in solicitude for all the churches, he must never cease to hear the call that goes up from pagan lands and souls and contribute, for his part, to responding to it.

[60] [Mt 10:16: "Behold, I send you forth."—Ed.]

"Go, teach all nations":[61] these words have launched the Church, for twenty centuries, onto all the routes across the vast world. Without more reflection than Peter dashing over the water before his master,[62] she goes. She claims neither reasons nor guarantees. How would she contest an order from which she draws her very existence? Besides, whether these words were pronounced under the circumstances related by Saint Matthew or whether they must rather be understood as a stylized [p. 371] memorial of the highest instructions left by the resurrected Lord; whether they are simply the direct echo of his teaching or whether the experience of the first years in Palestine and Syria were necessary so that this teaching, clearly understood at last, could thus be gathered into a formula, as some historians say and as the very account of the Acts seems to suggest: in any case, the essential fact is incontestable. The Church became aware of herself only by waking to the missionary duty that her Founder had traced for her,[63] and it was at first by this duty that she explained herself in her own eyes.

She was prepared for it by the prophets and by the whole history of Israel such as the Holy Books, read and commented on in its assemblies, unfolded it to her. The extraordinary understanding that she possessed from the beginning of this extraordinary history is one of the greatest spectacles offered to the historian; and despite all that is arbitrary, strange or antiquated in the exegetical methods that we see used by the Christians of that era, from Saint Paul or Saint Matthew up to Saint Justin or Origen, in the course of their controversies with the Judaism of their time, we must recognize that they have seen correctly. They are only capitalizing, with varying degrees of success, on an extraordinary intuition, the very one of the Church. The latter, with an infallible gaze, is penetrating to the heart of a reality whose meaning henceforth escapes the blindfolded eyes of the Synagogue. Succeeding the patriarchs and the prophets, she knows herself to be the heir of the Chosen People and of its hopes. She knows herself, as Saint Paul says, to be the true Israel,

---

[61] [Mt 28:19.—Ed.]

[62] [Mt 14:28–30.—Ed.]

[63] [Léonce] de Grandmaison, "L'Expansion du christianisme d'après M. Harnack" [The spread of Christianity according to Prof. Harnack], *Études*, 96:470–71.

Israel according to the spirit,[64] because she alone, thanks to the spiritual revolution of the gospel, can bring to a conclusion the work for which Yahweh had raised up Israel. So that, supposing that Jesus had not formally given the watchword that we have seen, she would have known just as well that this was her task, the magnificent and necessary task for which she alone in the world was suited.

The missionary idea in Israel did not arise in a single stroke. It had first been necessary for the God of the patriarchs and of Moses to be universally recognized for centuries as unique, and for the exclusive cult of which it was always jealous to become, in its adorers, strictly monotheistic. "You will adore only me alone. Listen, Israel, your God [p. 372] is one!"[65] If the monotheistic principle is already contained in the monolatric[66] order, it did not appear there immediately. And, once formulated,[67] it did not produce all its consequences immediately. The conviction that the God of Israel was the one true God of all the earth did not lead right away to the conclusion that this God had to be known and adored by all peoples. A day came, however, when the Jews found themselves faced with this problem, with apparently contradictory givens: Yahweh, the one God, is the God of all; he is, however, nonetheless the particular God of Israel; his worship remains linked to the observation of the Torah and to the service of the Temple in Jerusalem, where he has established his dwelling.

Two types of solutions were then adopted, of which the Bible has preserved many a trace for us.

Some cherished a hope that was as simplistic as radical. Since the divinities of the nations were only vain idols or evil powers, they would vanish, it was thought, before Yahweh, and those who served them would one day be exterminated.[68] Then Yahweh would reign alone, and his people would possess the earth. That would be Israel's

---

[64] [Rom 9:3–8.—ED.]

[65] [Deut 6:4–5.—ED.]

[66] [Monolatry is the belief in multiple gods but the worship of only one god.—ED.]

[67] For example, Isaiah, chapters 44 and 45, etc.

[68] Is 30:27–33. The Rabbot Midrash, on Song of Songs 7:4, will say: "Often it is said that the pagan nations would be entirely destroyed once the Messianic Kingdom opened. The world was created for Israel, in such a way that, at the end, the other people will be burned and annihilated."

great revenge. Others, animated by a less fierce sentiment, reconciled their national particularism more successfully with the awe-inspiring perspective that their faith opened to them; they hoped that a day would come when the pagans, conquered, would be converted to Yahweh, less by an attraction of the heart than by being forced to admit his power:

> And the glory of Yahweh will be revealed
> and all flesh without exception will see it.[69]

Then all will go up to Jerusalem to pay tribute, humanity being organized around Israel as if around a caste of priests for the praise [p. 373] of Yahweh and the service of his people. Such is, for example, the vision by which one prophet from the time of the Exile strengthens his oppressed brothers:

> Barbarians will appear and pasture your flocks,
> foreigners will be your laborers, your vinedressers;
>
> And you, you will be called priests of Yahweh,
> men will name you ministers of our God.
>
> You will eat the substance of the nations,
> you will be glorious with their magnificence.[70]

The extermination or subjection of the pagans:[71] this first type of solution was nevertheless not the only one. Some Israelites did

---

[69] Is 40:5. Cf. Ps 46:11:

> Be still, and know that I am God:
> I rule over the nations, I rule over the earth.

Cf. Sir 36:1–5.

[70] Is 61:6. Likewise, 60:1ff., verses 10–11:

> The sons of the foreigner will build up your walls,
> their kings will be your servants. . . .
> And your gates will always be open,
> they will be closed neither day nor night,
> To lead to you the wealth of the nations,
> and their kings at the end of the caravans.

[71] See also, for example, Ezekiel 28:21–22; Micah 7:15–17; or Zechariah 14:12–19, where the universalist perspective appears as much like a punishment for the Gentiles as like a blessing; for them, it is a question of servitude rather than liberation. And Psalm 47:4:

> Yahweh subjugates peoples to us,
> he places the nations under our feet. . . .

not place boundaries on the generosity of their God or restrictions on their hope. These were undoubtedly a very small number, but through them the Spirit passed. They were par excellence those men whom Saint Augustine was to call: men living under the Old Testament but not of the Old Testament; proclaimers of the New Testament in the midst of the Old: "homines in Vetere Testamento, non autem de Vetere Testamento. . . ."[72] This summit of prophecy appears to us particularly in the second part of the book of Isaiah, which has been called the Book of the Consolation of Israel. Its author does not promise to the exiled and battered people a brutal revenge; rather he shows Yahweh's solicitude extending to the sons of the foreigner:

> [p. 374] I will bring them to my holy mountain,
> I will make them joyful in my house of prayer;
> Their holocausts will be acceptable on my altar,
> for my house will be called:
> The house of prayer for all peoples.[73]

Yet, in this same second part, among all the poems relating to the Servant of Yahweh, arise poems in which Jewish universalism becomes missionary. In the person of this mysterious Servant, Israel no longer waits in inactivity for the day when the entire earth will know its God, but it becomes aware of the mission dispensed to it to work toward the coming of that day:

> Listen to me, O coastlands,
> and hearken you distant peoples!
> Yahweh has called me from my birth,
> from my mother's womb he has named my name.

> He has said to me:

> It is too little that you should be my Servant
> to reestablish the tribes of Jacob
> and restore the preserved of Israel;

[72] *Sur l'épître aux galates* [On the letter to the Galatians], no. 43.
[73] Is 56:6–7, 54:2: "The tents of Israel will expand. . . ." . . .

I will make you a Light of the nations,
  to carry my salvation
  to the ends of the world![74]

The Servant of Yahweh is therefore not only the suffering Just One, Redeemer of his people: he is at the same time the one who proclaims everywhere the Law of Yahweh; he is the one sent, the missionary:

[p. 375] Be attentive, people, to my voice;
  nations, lend me your ear!
For from me will come doctrine,
  my Law will be the light of the peoples.

My justice approaches, my salvation comes,
  my arm will be justice for the peoples,
It is I whom the Isles await,
  it is in my arm that they hope.[75]

What is this Servant? Is he a particular man? Is he the personification of Israel? We know the discussions of the exegetes, the multiplicity of solutions proposed. At one time it seems clear that it refers to an individual, and at others it is the people itself that seems definitely designated. Perhaps it is good that a certain ambiguity remains, perhaps this very ambiguity has a profound significance: How could the prophetic Spirit have separated Christ from his Church?

The same universalism whose inspiration stirs the book of Isaiah appears in more than one psalm:

---

[74] Is 49:1 and 6. And 42:1–4:

Here is my Servant whom I uphold,
my chosen one in whom my soul is pleased.
I have put my spirit into him,
he will show the Law to the nations. . . .

He will faithfully show the Law,
he will not tire or grow weary,
until he has established it on the earth,
and the Isles wait for his doctrine.

[75] Is 51:4–5.

> I will sing praises to you among the peoples, O Adonai,
> I will sing praises to you among the nations!
>
> I will recall your name in all the ages,
> and the peoples will praise you forever![76]

And during the time that followed the Exile, the great fact of the Dispersion of Israel in the midst of the nations is interpreted by some as a providential fact, permitting the Chosen People to accomplish its missionary vocation. It is understood in this way by the author of the Book of Tobit, who sums up his teaching in the song that he places on the lips of the old Tobit after the disappearance of the angel Raphael:

> You are great, Lord, in eternity,
> and your reign extends to all the centuries. . . .
> [p. 376] Celebrate the Lord, children of Israel,
> and praise him before the nations,
> For he has scattered you among the nations that do not know him
> so that you might recount his marvels and so that you might make known to them
> that there is no other all-powerful God but him alone.[77]

Yet, on the other hand, the Sinai covenant remained, inviolable, along with the Law and its thousand observances, and the more time that advanced, the more rigorous became the measures of protection and isolation of the holy people. "I have separated you from the peoples so that you might be mine!": this order from Leviticus (20:26) is reinforced, from the time of the Exile, by the group of Ezekiel and his disciples. It was reinforced again, upon return to the holy land, by Nehemiah and by Esdras. Thanks to the persevering work of the scribes, the holy people was not only separated; it was, so to speak, sequestered, like the Holy of Holies of the reconstructed Temple. It was just as true in the Dispersion as on the soil of the homeland: "The Jews", says Haman to his sovereign Ahasuerus in the little book of Esther, "are a nation living apart among others,

---

[76] 57:10; 45:18. Cf. 47:2.

> All you peoples, clap your hands,
> celebrate Yahweh with shouts of joy! . . .

[77] Tob 13:1–4.

and their laws differ from the laws of all other nations."[78] The attempt at the Hellenization of Palestine, under Antiochus Epiphanius,[79] provoked an even stronger reaction: it was from this time that, along with the revolt of the Maccabees, the constitution of the Hasidic faction dates,[80] a faction which would become famous under the name of Pharisees, which is to say, the "separated".

Thus the Jewish people, with its twofold treasure: its worship, always more national, and its God, always more universal, became a living contradiction. It was not simply a question of two currents confronting each other, between which it would be permissible to choose. The conflict was more internal. This whole religion was summed up in two demands that seemed incompatible. How could it renounce its universal mission, which was its whole reason for being and which alone explained it to itself? But how could it devote itself to it without [p. 377] denying itself, since its structure was so rigorously and narrowly determined? No child of Israel could forget the words of Deuteronomy: "Yahweh has chosen you for himself to be a particular people among all the nations that are on the surface of the earth."[81]

Hence an inextricable situation. To get out of it, some sought refuge in a solution of despair: without abandoning in principle the great views of the future bequeathed by the prophets, they left it to God alone to take care of achieving them; the conversion of the Gentiles and the Messianic peace by which it would be followed would be the work of a miracle by Yahweh, in the day of his power: this is the solution that can be called eschatological.[82] Others, animated by

[78] Est 3:8. And the letter of Pseudo-Aristaeus (second century B.C.): "Our law-giver, instructed in all things by God, has enclosed us within inviolable barriers and within walls of iron, so that in nothing we mix with other nations, we keep body and soul pure."

[79] [Antiochus IV Epiphanes was king (175–164 B.C.) of the Greek Seleucid empire (312–63 B.C.), which had been founded following the death of Alexander the Great. His persecution of the Jews precipitated the Maccabean revolt, after which they secured political independence (143). In combination with Parthian and Roman pressure, this led to the collapse of the empire.—ED.]

[80] [1 Mac 2:42, 7:13–14; 2 Mac 14:6.—ED.]

[81] Dt 14:2.

[82] For example, in Psalm 86:9–10:

> All the nations that you have made will come
> to lie prostrate before you, Lord,

true zeal but hindered by the rigors of the Law, could only meagerly open the door of the Kingdom halfway to those they converted—the "proselytes", those who "feared God": a bastard compromise that, despite what they said, constituted a regression. Others, finally, transforming their theocracy into an arrogant "nomocracy",[83] no longer thought of anything but making the Law a definitive "fence" that would no longer merely protect Israel but also reject forever the scorned Gentiles. Such was the celebrated Akiba, commenting on the verse from the Song of Songs "My beloved is white and red":[84]

> When they hear these praises, the peoples of the world say to the Israelites: We want to go with you, we want to seek him with you. But the Israelites reply to them: You have no part with him; my beloved belongs to me, and I to him.[85]

By this third solution, which prevailed increasingly with a number of its representatives, Israel renounced its mission, it closed its ear to the call from above. It was definitively twisted, it seems, by this aggravated, defensive reflex.

[p. 378] Its whole history ends therefore in an impasse. If we forget for a moment that Christianity is going to come out of it, Judaism of the first century appears to us, according to an expression of Alfred Loisy, like "a singular religion that can no longer be that of one nation and that cannot be that of the world".[86] No means for Israel to be faithful both to its vocation and to its being, no means of surviving without losing its reason for living—unless through a transformation of its whole self, through an extraordinary and unforeseeable change, through a death according to the letter for a rebirth according to the spirit. Now, that very thing had

---

and give glory to your name.
For you are great and you work wonders:
You alone are God!

[83] Joseph Bonsirven, *Sur les ruines du Temple* [On the ruins of the Temple], 142.

[84] [De Lubac refers to the Vulgate version of the Song of Songs 5:10. A clearer meaning is given by: "My beloved is radiant and ruddy."—ED.]

[85] [Mekhilta d'Rabbi Yishmael 15:2, i.e., exegesis of Ex 15:2 in the Jewish rule of scriptural exegesis attributed to the early-second-century Rabbi Ishmael ben Elisha. Akiba was notable among the Jewish rabbis in promoting an allegorical interpretation of the Song of Songs and thereby defending its canonicity.—ED.]

[86] See also J. Bonsirven, *Le Judaïsme palestinien au temps de Jésus-Christ* [Palestinian Judaism at the time of Jesus Christ], 1:71–72.

been proclaimed. The message of it has been confided to the most interior and tender of the prophets, Jeremiah:

> See, the days are coming, declares Yahweh,
> when I will make with the House of Israel and
> the House of Judah a new covenant;
> Not like the covenant I made with their fathers
> on the day when I took them by the hand
> to lead them out of the land of Egypt. . . .
>
> But here is what the covenant will be
> that I will make with the House of Israel
> when those days have come, declares Yahweh:
> I will place my Law within them,
> and in their hearts will I write it,
> And I will be their God,
> and they will be my people! . . .[87]

It is from this passage, quoted at length by the Letter to the Hebrews,[88] that the term "New Testament" originates. A wonderful anticipation! Such was in fact to be the work of the Messiah. So it was not without a profound feeling of its vital need and of the meaning of its history that, as the "fullness of time"[89] approached, Palestinian Judaism was centered in the expectation of the promised Messiah. The voice of the prophets had long since ceased to resound, and yet never [p. 379] more than at the beginning of the Christian era had the liberator of Israel been anticipated.

This anticipation itself was full of new contradictions, and one can say that it, even much more than our present faith, took place, according to the words of the Apostle, "per speculum et in aenigmate".[90] So it is not surprising that, when the Messiah finally appeared, many of his own did not recognize him: having themselves become that "nation without understanding" of which Deuteronomy spoke.[91] But, for the little flock, docile to the illuminations

---

[87] Jer 31:31–33.

[88] Heb 8:8–12.

[89] [Gal 4:4.—Ed.]

[90] [1 Cor 13:12. The Vulgate "per speculum in enigmate" translates the Greek literally: "in an enigma by means of a mirror".—Ed.]

[91] Dt 32:21; cf. Rom 10:19.

of the Spirit, the horizon that had seemed closed was torn open: Jesus does not come to destroy but to complete; he comes to fulfill all hopes, to remove all contradictions. Beyond Moses, he accomplishes the promise once made to Abraham: "All the families of the earth will be blessed in you."[92] The old Simeon can sing in his joy: "Lumen ad revelationem gentium, et gloriam plebis tuae Israël [A light for the revelation of the Gentiles and the glory of your people Israel]." For, heir of Israel, Jesus transforms it into the Church.

When, having returned to his Father, the resurrected Christ sends his apostles, as we saw at the beginning, to preach the gospel to every creature, he is thus only clarifying the meaning of his whole work, expressing a conclusion that is self-evident. When he speaks as the Son of God, he speaks at the same time as the son of Israel. He confides to his disciples the mission he received from his Father and that which he inherited from his people. Since he is son of missionary Israel, the Church that he founds to continue Israel can only be missionary.

Missionary Church, Catholic Church, this is in fact all one thing. One characteristic of the true Church, catholicity is not properly speaking a thing, an objective given, a reality that is in some way material and tangible. At least it was not so at first. It is still only very slightly so today, and it will perhaps never be so fully, if it is true, as a number of theologians have thought, that the "torch of the gospel, which [p. 380] must go around the universe", illumines new regions only by letting those that it had first visited fall back into shadow.[93] But whatever might perhaps be too confident in this hypothesis, it is certain that catholicity is not only an empirical fact. It is an essential attribute and not a superadded accident. It is above all a fact of consciousness. It is an idea and it is a force. It is an ambition and it is a necessity. The Church is catholic because, knowing herself to be universal by right, she wants to become so in fact. Her catholicity is her vocation, which is mingled with her being. She

[92] Gen 12:3.

[93] Fénelon uses the idea in his famous Sermon for the feast of Epiphany: "The river of grace, it is true, is not dried up; but often, in order to water new lands, it diverts its course and leaves only dry sand in the old canal. Faith has not died out, I admit; but it is not bound to any of the places it illumines; it leaves behind it a frightful night for those who have scorned the day, and it carries rays of light to purer eyes." Cf. Amos 9:7.

has been aware of this vocation from the first day; she will remain faithful to this vocation until the last day. The rest, the alternatives of success and failures, advance and retreat, do not always depend on her, and her nature could not be affected by them. But insofar as she has not attained the dimension of the world, she cries out through the mouth of the Prophet: "Angustus est mihi locus, fac mihi locum ut inhabitem [This place is too narrow for me; make room for me to dwell in]" (Is 49:20).

It is Saint Gregory of Nyssa who assures us of it,[94] and all the Fathers say it to us with him. For them, the Church can only be coextensive with the *oikoumenè* [economy]. Now, this is not simply because the *oikoumenè* was then a synonym for the Roman Empire. Despite the illusions that several of them entertained on the subject of the actual extension of Christian preaching, and despite the rhetoric which they too often devote to celebrate its triumphs, they cannot ignore the fact that paganism remains intact in certain regions. In expressions such as "per orbem terrae Ecclesiae latitudo diffusae" [the breadth of the Church is spread throughout the whole world], Origen is proclaiming a necessity, proceeding from the idea that he forms of the Church, rather than pronouncing a judgment of fact.[95] Saint Augustine himself knows that the Ethiopians, for example, have not yet received the gospel, and the same is true, in Africa, for innumerable barbaric nations, "barbarae innumerabiles gentes".[96] So, when he argues against the Donatists that [p. 381] their church is not catholic, what he reproaches them for is not at all so much the small extent of their territory as their claim to be satisfied with it, to have confined the church to it without concern for other peoples, and to settle all problems among themselves, *inter Afros* [among Africans]. What, on the other hand, he admires and loves in the *Catholica* is the fact that, without ever agreeing to restrict herself to any one place, she goes "from East to West", "from sea to sea", to sing over the entire universe the ever-new song of universal charity.[97] She perceives the call of those "isles"

---

[94] Discourse on the baptism of Christ (PG 46, 577). Cf. Is 49:20.

[95] Second homily on Genesis, [no.] 5. . . .

[96] *In Psalmum* [Expositions of the Psalms] 71, [nos.] 11–12; *Epistula* 197, [no.] 4; 199, [no.] 46.

[97] *In Psalmum* 149, [no.] 7. . . .

that the Prophet once evoked, and she knows that it is she who has the mission to respond to it. For she applies to herself what the prophets proclaimed. Everywhere she reads herself in their oracles. It often requires an effort to find Christ there, so wrapped in mystery is his divine Person, but as for her, she recognizes herself there clearly, and to the degree that her mission is accomplished, she is aware that the prophecy is also accomplished.

Dynamic catholicity and missionary impulse: there is no difference between the two. Or, if one insists on finding one, let us say that this catholicity implies that impulse, that this catholicity is its authentic and sincere self only if it is extended in that impulse, in order to take form, insofar as God makes it effective, in a realized catholicity.

## The Sacrament of Jesus Christ

*During the five years following the end of the Second World War, de Lubac regularly led retreats, study days, and seminary conferences for his fellow priests. These included presentations and many opportunities for conversation, of which* The Splendor of the Church *is a product. In the book's introduction, de Lubac states, in his usual modest fashion, that it is not a systematic treatise, still less a work of original research. Rather, in the book, he undertakes to "meditate, in the light of faith, on certain aspects of the mystery of the Church", drawing, as in* Catholicism, *on some of the key texts of the Christian tradition.*[98] *De Lubac regarded this task as especially urgent in the aftermath of the war, in order to rekindle an authentic sense of the Church in the minds of young clergy. Hence the book was originally titled* Méditation sur l'Église (*Meditation on the Church*). *De Lubac was dissatisfied with what he considered to be the triumphalism of its English title, which was by no means a literal translation of the original.*[99] *The book was also translated into Italian, catching the notice of Giovanni Battista Montini, who in 1954 had been consecrated Archbishop of Milan and would in 1963 become Pope Paul VI.*

*De Lubac makes clear that the book was completed before the promulgation, in August 1950, of Pope Pius XII's encyclical* Humani generis, *which charged unnamed Roman Catholic theologians and philosophers with diluting traditional doctrine and failing to respect magisterial teaching authority. Its publication in 1953 was not, therefore, an act of submission to a conservative ecclesiology. Rather, the study indicates de Lubac's unwavering passion for, and obedience to, the Church.*

---

[98] Henri de Lubac, *The Splendor of the Church*, trans. Michael Mason (1986; San Francisco: Ignatius Press, 1999), 9; also De Lubac, *At the Service*, 305.

[99] De Lubac, *At the Service*, 77.

[p. 202] The Church is a mystery; that is to say that she is also a sacrament. She is "the total *locus* of the Christian sacraments", and she is herself the great sacrament that contains and vitalizes all the others.[100] In this world she is the sacrament of [Jesus] Christ, as [Jesus] Christ himself, in his humanity, is for us the sacrament of God.[101]

That which is sacramental—"the sensible bond between two worlds"[102]—has a twofold characteristic. Since, on the one hand, it is the sign of something else, it must be passed through, and this not in part but wholly. Signs are not things to be stopped at, for they are, in themselves, valueless; by definition a sign is something translucent, which dissolves from before the face of what it manifests—like words, which would be nothing if they did not lead straight on to ideas. Under this aspect it is not something intermediate but something mediatory; it does not isolate, one from another, the two terms it is meant to link. It does not put a distance between them; on the contrary, it unites them by making present that which it evokes.

[p. 203] On the other hand, sacramental reality is not just any sign, which is provisional and can be changed at will. It is essentially related to our present condition, which is not one embodied in the epoch of figures pure and simple, nor yet one that includes the full possession of the "truth". The second aspect of its twofold

---

Excerpted from *The Splendor of the Church*, trans. Michael Mason (1986; San Francisco: Ignatius Press, 1999), 202–21. This volume is a reissue of *The Splendour of the Church* (London: Sheed & Ward, 1956). The translation has been checked against the original and corrections have been made. Some translations from Latin are made with reference to those by Nicole Duval and Isabelle Isebaert-Cauuet in *Méditation sur l'Église* (Paris: Cerf, 2003), 432–35.

[100] Council of Florence, *Decretum pro Jacobitis* [Decree on the Jacobites, i.e., the Syrian Orthodox Church], 1441–42: "Tantumque valere ecclesiastici corporis unitatem, ut solum in ea manentibus ad salutem ecclesiastica sacramenta proficient" [The value of the unity of the body of the Church is so great that the sacraments of the Church bring salvation only to those who remain in it]. . . .

[101] See the Ambrosian missal, Preface for the first Sunday of Advent: "manifestans plebi tuae Unigeniti tui sacramentum" [manifesting to your people the sacrament of your first-born Son]; St. Augustine, *Epist.* 187, no. 34: "Non est enim aliud Dei mysterium, nisi Christus" [There is no other mystery of God than Christ]. . . .

[102] Joseph de Maistre, "Lettre à une dame russe" [Letter to a Russian woman], in *Oeuvres*, 8:74.

characteristic, which is not to be dissociated from the first, thus consists in this: that it can never be discarded as something that has outlived its usefulness. We never come to the end of passing through this translucent medium, which we must, nevertheless, always pass through and that completely. It is always through it that we reach what it signifies; it can never be superseded, and its bounds cannot be broken.

In Christ also we find this twofold characteristic. "If you had known me, you would without doubt have known my Father also. . . . Philip, he that seeth me seeth the Father also."[103] Nobody, even at the highest peak of the spiritual life, will attain a knowledge of the Father that will dispense him, from that point onward, from going through him who will, always and for all, be "the Way" and "the Image of the invisible God".[104] And the same holds good for the Church. Her whole end is to show us Christ, lead us to him, and communicate his grace to us; to put it in a nutshell, she exists solely to put us into relation with him. She alone can do that, and it is a task she never completes; there will never come a moment, either in the life of the individual or in the life of the race, in which her role ought to come to an end or even could come to an end. If the world lost the Church, it would lose the Redemption too.

The New Testament, which founded the Church by giving her the inheritance of Israel, is also the "last Testament". The Church is not like the Law—a "pedagogue" [teacher], necessary to the growing young but rightly dispensed with by maturity. "The divine education" entrusted to her with reference to us [has] [p. 204] the [same] duration [as] time itself, and in it we already have, not a heralding or a preparation more or less remote, but "the whole coming of the Son of Man".[105] And she is constantly present in the dialogue of the soul with its Lord. She intervenes actively at every phase of it, but without any inhibiting effect on its intimacy, which, on the contrary, she guarantees. A man who believes himself to be a prophet or rich in spiritual gifts must remind himself that before all else he is bound to submit to the commandments of his Lord as

---

[103] Jn 14:7–9.

[104] Col 1:15; Jn 14:6.

[105] Origen, *In Matt. Series* [Commentary on Matthew series], 47.

they are declared to him by that Lord's Church—otherwise he will prophesy in vain and all his gifts will merely lead him to his own destruction.[106] One who gives way to the temptations of a false spiritualization and wants to shake off the Church as a burdensome yoke or set her aside as a cumbersome intermediary will soon find himself embracing the void or end up by worshipping false gods. If a man begins by using her as his support and then comes to believe that he can go beyond her, he will be nothing more than a mystic run off the rails. Those who anticipate a future "setting-up of the Heavenly Jerusalem", which will inaugurate "a new period of history" on earth and finally assure "the complete triumph of the spiritual", may imagine that they are prophesying a return of the human race into paradise lost;[107] but in reality, the thing is no more than a diseased and pride-ridden dream. It was thus that the heretical Tertullian said: "Hardness of heart reigned until Christ, and the weakness of the flesh endures till the Paraclete",[108] or again: "The Law and the Prophets taught the world's childhood; its youth was brought to flower by the Gospel; now, through the Paraclete, it reaches maturity."[109] The proclamations of a Third [p. 205] Age, an age of "contemplatives" succeeding the age of "Doctors", or a Church of John to follow that of Peter,[110] or a future Kingdom of the Spirit following the actual Kingdom of Christ and the discipline of his Church—these have all generated disastrous schisms. They may, certainly, give, from time to time, a new attractiveness to the original Montanism,[111] which they transform into a sort of

---

[106] 1 Cor 14:37–38: "If any seems to be a prophet or spiritual, let him know the things that I write to you, that they are the commandments of the Lord. But if any man know not, he shall not be known."

[107] René Guénon, *Autorité spirituelle et pouvoir temporel* [Spiritual authority and temporal power] (1930), pp. 151–52.

[108] *De monogamia* [On monogamy], chap. 14.

[109] *De velandis virginibus* [On the veiling of virgins], chap. 1.

[110] See Joachim of Flora, *The Ten-Stringed Psaltery* (p. 156 in [Emmanuel Aegerter trans.]), and again: "Just as the veil of Moses was drawn aside by Christ, so that of Paul will be drawn aside by the Holy Spirit" (p. 157)—to all of which St. Bonaventure replied in his *In Hexaemeron* [On the six days of creation], collatio 16: "Post novum Testamentum non erit aliud" [After the New Testament there will be no other]. . . .

[111] [A Christian movement originating in the mid-second century that claimed to have received new revelation from the Holy Spirit. Tertullian was among its adherents.—Ed.]

philosophy of history, according to the tastes of the age; they may well sometimes make their appearance entangled with thinking of a high order; but they are nonetheless for all that mere Utopias, and of a dangerous variety too.[112] . . .

[p. 206] From the moment when [Jesus] was glorified, the Spirit was given to us, and it was this gift of the Spirit on the day of Pentecost that completed the constituting of the Church.[113] [p. 207] Thus the age of the Spirit is in no sense something still to come; it coincides exactly with the age of Christ:[114] "The communicating of Christ—that is, the Holy Spirit."[115] The Spirit teaches us "all truth" but neither speaks of himself nor seeks his own glory, any more than [Jesus], the Father's Envoy, sought his own glory.[116] Faithful to the mission he received from him in whose name he was sent to us, he makes us understand his message—"brings it to mind"—but adds nothing to it. He comes, as it were, to put the seal on his teaching; he opens our awareness to his Gospel but does not transform it. He spoke often before the coming of [Jesus], but that was solely to proclaim [Jesus'] coming—"who spake by the Prophets".[117] And he has continued to speak since [Jesus] returned to the Father, but only to bear him witness, as [Jesus] bore witness

[112] It was perhaps a certain tendency to justify the Church too much on natural grounds and to forget the role the Holy Spirit normally plays in her that made Joseph de Maistre somewhat indulgent to the *illuminati* by way of compensation. See the eleventh conversation of the *Soirées de Saint-Pétersbourg* [Saint Petersburg dialogues].

[113] 1 Th 4:8; 1 Cor 2:12; Jn 7:39: "Now this he said of the Spirit which they should receive who believed in him; for as yet the Spirit was not given, because Jesus was not glorified." . . .

[114] Rom 8:9–10: "if the Spirit of God dwells in you. Now if any man have not the Spirit of Christ, he is none of his. And if Christ is in you. . . ." See also Gal 4:6. . . .

[115] St. Irenaeus, *Adversus haereses*, bk. 3, chap. 24, no. 1.

[116] Jn 12:49–50; see also Saint-Jure, *L'Homme spirituel*, pt. 1, chap. 1; Jules Monchanin, "Théologie et mystique du Saint-Esprit", [*Dei verbum*], no. 23, p. 76: "A mystique of the Holy Spirit is not a mystique of the Holy Spirit alone, but the mystique of Christ par excellence and the mystique of the Father too; it is a perpetual invitation to pass through appearances, to pass through the Scriptures and dogma and the liturgy—which it maintains and perfects by interiorizing them—to contemplate without end the *prosodos* and *exodos* of a deified creation, and—with an even greater love—the going-out and returning-again of the Trinity."

[117] [The Nicene Creed, echoing Heb 1:1.—Ed.]

to the Father;[118] it is all for proclaiming [his] unique lordship and never in order to substitute himself for [him]. In a word, the Spirit is "the Spirit of Jesus".[119]

[p. 208] There is no other Spirit than this Spirit of Jesus, and the Spirit of Jesus is the Soul that animates his body, the Church.[120] Just as the letter of the Law drew together the first People of God, so the Spirit forms the new People of God.[121] Today we are "in the Spirit" as we are "in Christ", and we may say, with St. Paul, that we have been baptized in one single Spirit to form one single body, or, as St. Basil comments, in one single body to form one single Spirit.[122] The Church is "the society of the Spirit".[123] And it is in the Church that the Spirit glorifies Jesus, just as it is in her, the "House of Christ", that he is given to us[124] in a "final and eternal alliance".[125] It is a bad business when an attempt is made to separate the Church from the Gospel; a bad business when people want to get rid of the spiritual leaven that she mixes into the meal of humanity,[126] and when anyone tries to "extinguish the Spirit"[127] in the Church. But it is an equally bad business when anyone claims to set the Spirit's flame free by rejecting the Church.[128]

---

[118] Jn 14:26, 15:26, 16:13–14; see also 7:39, 20:22. . . .

[119] 1 Cor 12:3; and see St. Basil, *Treatise on the Holy Spirit*, chap. 18; Acts 16:7.

[120] St. Augustine, *Sermo* 268, no. 2: "Quod est spiritus noster, id est anima nostra, ad membra nostra, hoc est Spiritus sanctus ad membra Christi, ad corpus Christi, quod est Ecclesia" [What our spirit, that is our soul, is for our members, the Holy Spirit is for the members of Christ, for the body of Christ, which is the Church] . . . ; also Rom 8:9; 2 Cor 3:17; Gal 4:6. . . .

[121] 2 Cor 3:6–11; Phil 3:3; and also 1 Cor 12:13; Eph 4:4, etc.

[122] St. Basil, *On the Holy Spirit*, chap. 26, no. 61, commenting on 1 Cor 12:18. . . .

[123] "Societas Spiritus"—St. Augustine, *Sermo* 71, chap. 19, no. 32. . . .

[124] Pseudo-Bede, *In Joannem* [On John] (PL 92, 862a–b); St. Augustine, *De Trinitate* [On the Trinity], bk. 15, chap. 19, no. 34.

[125] St. Justin, *Dialogue*, chap. 11, no. 2.

[126] See Origen, *Scholia in Lucam* [Explanations of Luke], 13, 21: "Accipi potest mulier pro Ecclesia, fermentum pro Spiritu sancto." [The word "woman" may be taken for the Church, fermented by the Holy Spirit.]

[127] 1 Th 5:19. Or to prevent the perpetual rejuvenation of the deposit entrusted to the Church and the actual vessel that contains it (see St. Irenaeus, *Adv. haeres.* 3, 24, 1).

[128] Or to prophesy another Gospel beyond that of Christ, which is preached by the Church; see Joachim of Flora's *Liber introductorius in expositionem in Apocalypsin* [*Introduction to the Exposition of the Book of Revelation*], chap. 5: "The first of the three ages of the world unrolled under the reign of the Law; the second was initiated by the Gospel and

[p. 209] The Church is the sacrament of [Jesus] Christ. This means, to put it another way, that there is between her and him a certain relation of mystical identity. Here again we encounter the Pauline metaphors and the rest of the biblical images, which the Christian tradition has continually explored. One and the same intuition of faith is expressed throughout. Head and members make one single body, one single Christ;[129] the Bridegroom and the Bride are one flesh. Although he is the Head of his Church, Christ does not rule her from without; there is, certainly, subjection and dependence between her and him, but at the same time she is his fulfillment and "fullness".[130] She is the tabernacle of his presence,[131] the building of which he is both Architect and Cornerstone. She is the temple in which he teaches and into which he draws with him the whole Divinity.[132] She is the ship and he the pilot,[133] she the deep ark and he the central mast, assuring the communication of all those on board with the heavens above them.[134] She is paradise and he its tree and well of [p. 210] life;[135] she is the star and he the

lasts up till the present; the third will begin toward the end of this century; indeed, we can already see it opening, in a complete spiritual liberation. . . . This age of spiritual understanding, which is about to open continuously before us, will be under the reign of the Holy Spirit. . . . The angel held an eternal Gospel; and what do we find in this Gospel? Everything that goes beyond the Gospel of Christ" (trans. Aegerter, 2:90–118).

[129] St. Augustine, *In Psalm.* 54, no. 3. . . .

[130] Eph 1:23; also Joseph Huby, *St. Paul: Épîtres de la captivité*, pp. 167–71.

[131] Berengard, *In Apocalypsin* [On the Book of Revelation] (PL 17, 884b–c, 937b); see also Ex 25:8.

[132] Origen, *In Lucam* [On Luke], hom. 18 and 20 (pp. 123–24 and 132 in Rauer's edition); St. Augustine, *Enchiridion* [Handbook], chap. 56. . . .

[133] St. Hippolytus, *De antichristo* [On the Antichrist], chap. 59.

[134] Hugh of Saint-Victor, *De arca Noe moralia* [Noah's moral ark], bk. 2, chap. 7: "Columna in medio arcae erecta . . . ipsa est lignum vitae quod plantatum est in medio paradisi id est Dominus Jesus Christus in medio Ecclesiae suae, quasi praemium laboris" [The mast erected in the midst of the ark . . . is the tree of life planted in the midst of paradise, that is the Lord Jesus Christ in the midst of his Church, as a reward for labor]. . . .

[135] St. Irenaeus, *Adversus haereses*, bk. 5, chap. 20, no. 2 . . . ; Hugh of Saint-Victor, *De arca Noë morali*, bk. 2, chap. 9: "Dominus Jesus Christus in medio Ecclesiae suae quasi lignum vitae in medio paradisi plantatus est, de cujus fructu quisque digne manducate meruerit, vivet in aeternum" [The Lord Jesus Christ is planted in the midst of his Church as the tree of life planted in the midst of paradise. Whoever is found worthy of eating its fruit will live eternally] . . . ; Richard of Saint-Victor, *Allegoriae*, bk. 1, chap. 6: "Fons qui est in paradiso, Christum significat. Quatuor flumina fontis, quatuor sunt Evangelia

light that illuminates our night.[136] He who is not, in one way or another, a member of the body does not receive the influx from the Head; he who does not cling to the one Bride is not loved by the Bridegroom. If we profane the tabernacle, we are deprived of the sacred presence, and if we leave the temple, we can no longer hear the Word. If we refuse to enter the holy house or take refuge in the ark, we cannot find him who is center and crown of both. If we are contemptuous of paradise, we are neither fed nor given drink. And if we persuade ourselves that we can do without this received light, we remain perpetually plunged in the night of ignorance. . . .

Practically speaking, for each one of us [Jesus] Christ is thus his Church. We may think of her particularly under the aspect of the hierarchy, remembering [Jesus'] words: "He that heareth you heareth me: and he that despiseth you despiseth me";[137] or again, we may think of the Church as the whole body, the whole assembly at the heart of which he is and manifests himself, and in the heart of which the praise of God rises continuously in his name.[138] But in either case the same thing holds good. Joan of Arc's words to her judges[139] convey at one and the same time the depths of the *mystique* of belief and the practical good sense of the believer: "It seems to me that it is all one, [p. 211] [Jesus] Christ and the Church, and that we ought not to make any difficulty of it." These words of a simple believer are also a summing-up of the faith of the Church's Doctors.[140]

---

Christi" [The source in paradise signifies Christ. The four rivers flowing from there are the four Gospels of Christ] . . . ; etc. See also 4 Esdras 103, 52, on Jerusalem: "Vobis apertus est paradisus, plantata est arbor vitae . . . , aedificata est civitas" [Paradise is open to you, the tree of life is planted . . . the city is built].

136 Origen, *First Homily on Genesis*, no. 5, etc.

137 Lk 10:16; Mt 10:40.

138 Ps 34:18, 25:12, 67:27.

139 [Joan of Arc (ca. 1412–1431) was a young warrior who helped to relieve Orleans but was captured by the city's Burgundian and English besiegers. She was put on trial, found guilty, and executed, technically on a heresy charge based on her wearing men's clothing (Deut 22:5).—Ed.]

140 St. Augustine, *De doctrina christiana* [On Christian doctrine], bk. 3, chap. 31, no. 44: "Christi et Ecclesiae, unam personam nobis intimari" [It is announced to us that Christ and the Church are a single person] . . . ; St. Gregory the Great, *Moralia in Job* . . . bk. 35, chap. 14, no. 24: "Christus et Ecclesia, id est caput et corpus, una persona est" [Christ and the Church, that is the head and the body, are a single person] . . .

Whatever the difficulties we encounter and the disturbances that threaten to throw us off our balance, we should always keep a firm hold on that equivalence. Like Ulysses bound to the mast in self-defense—in spite of himself—against the voices of the Sirens,[141] we should, if need be, hold on, without eyes or ears for anything else, to the saving truth formulated for us by St. Irenaeus: "Where the Church is, there is the Spirit of God, and where the Spirit of God is, there is the Church and all grace, and the Spirit is Truth; to sever ourselves from the Church is to reject the Spirit"—and in virtue of that "to shut ourselves out of life."[142] We should always share the belief of St. John that it is impossible to understand the Spirit without listening to what he says to the Church.[143] We should remember that there is no substantial hope of unity outside that institution which received the promises of unity. We should hold as an absolute principle that there can never be a valid reason for separating ourselves from her. We [p. 212] should try to understand the traditional axiom formulated by Origen—"No one is saved outside the Church"[144]—both in its magnificent breadth and in all its exacting rigorousness, as far as we are concerned. We must grasp the breadth because, as St. Augustine explained, "in the ineffable prescience of God, many who appear to be outside are within"; they are of the Church at least "by wish or desire", while "many who seem to be within are without", and "the Lord knows his own" everywhere.[145] But we must also grasp the rigorousness, for he who "cuts himself off from the [c]atholic communion" and "goes out of the House" of salvation "makes himself responsible for his own death".[146] So that we must never give any place to the disastrous idea of "breaking the bond of peace by a sacrilegious

[141] [In Homer, *Odyssey* 12, this is the only way that the mythical Greek king was able to satisfy his curiosity by hearing the singing of the Sirens, who were female sea demons, without being killed by them.—Ed.]

[142] *Adversus haereses*, bk. 3, chap. 24, no. 1. That is why the Church is "arrha incorruptelae, et confirmatio fidei nostrae, et scala ascensionis ad Deum" [the pledge of incorruption, the confirmation of our faith and the stairway ascending to God].

[143] See Rev 2:7, etc. . . .

[144] *In Jesu nave* [On Joshua], hom. 3, no. 5. . . .

[145] *De baptismo* [On baptism], bk. 5, chap. 27, no. 38. . . .

[146] [Ibid.], chap. 19, no. 25, and chap. 4. . . .

usurpation".[147] And it is no use flattering ourselves that we can still remain "in the society of Christ" although we have put ourselves outside the Church. As St. Augustine puts it, "to live by the Spirit of Christ, one must remain in his body";[148] [p. 213] and again: "[It is] in proportion as one loves the Church of Christ that one has within the Holy Spirit."[149]

It is possible that there may be many things in the human context of the Church that deceive us. And it is also possible that we may be profoundly misunderstood within her, without the things being our fault; we may even have to undergo persecution within the very heart of the Church—that has happened—though we should be wary of presumption in interpreting our own case thus. In such a situation patience and loving silence will be of more value than all else; there is nothing to be feared in the judgment of those who do not see the heart,[150] and we can comfort ourselves with the thought that the Church never gives Christ to us better than on these occasions when she offers us the chance of sharing in the likeness of his Passion. We shall continue to serve by our witness the faith she will continue to preach. The trial may be all the heavier if it comes not from personal ill-will but from a situation that may appear to be impossible of solution; for in such a case wholehearted forgiveness and forgetfulness of self are not enough to carry one through. However, we should be glad before "the Father who seeth in secret" for participating thus in that *veritatis unitas* [unity of truth] which we ask for all on Good Friday. And we ought certainly to be glad if we are, in this way, able to buy at the cost of spiritual suffering that very personal experience which will lend power to our words when it becomes our responsibility to help steady some fellow Catholic whose faith has been shaken—as did St. John Chrysostom when he said: "Do not separate yourself from the Church! No power is as powerful as she. The Church is your hope; the Church is your

[147] [Ibid.], bk. 2, chap. 6, no. 7. . . .

[148] Quoted by Cardinal Feltin in his pastoral letter for Lent in 1951, *Le Sens de l'Église*. . . .

[149] St. Augustine, *In Joannem* [On John], tract. 32, no. 8. . . .

[150] St. Robert Bellarmine, *De romano Pontifice* [On the Roman Pontiff], bk. 1, 4, chap. 20.

salvation; the Church is your refuge.[151] She is higher than [p. 214] heaven and bigger than earth. She never ages, and her vitality is eternal."[152]

The Church—the whole Church, the only Church, the Church of today and yesterday and tomorrow—is the sacrament of Christ; strictly speaking, she is nothing other than that, or at any rate the rest is a superabundance. Yet there are many, who do not by any means wish to be her adversaries, who misconceive her nature, seeing only her human greatness. Without considering themselves obliged to modify their opinions according to her teaching or to enter into her spirit, they show her "every variety of respect" and sometimes even go so far as to feel for her a sort of "filial affection".[153] Some of them are particularly struck by the power of order and conservation she stands for; they admire her long enduring, her wonderful stability amid the storms of the age, the prudence of her government, the principle of authority that she maintains, the social cohesion that she guarantees, and the reconstruction she gives us hope of. For them she is, even more than the announcer and guardian of the Gospel, the awe-inspiring inheritor of the Greek and Roman worlds. For some, she is simply anti-this or anti-that; others see in her a great force of dynamism and progress, which jolts the nations out of their inertia, fills the hearts of a chosen few with the passion for justice, and imparts to the whole of history an impulse that cannot be checked. The humanists may praise her for having, during the Dark Ages, preserved ancient culture in her monasteries and perpetuated in our midst the miracle of Mediterranean civilization; they are grateful to her for her encouragement of the arts and have a connoisseur's appreciation of the beauties of her liturgy, although as a rule they know only of its Latin form, or at

[151] [In the context of the homily, literally. The Byzantine consul Eutropius (d. 399) had sought refuge in the Church of the Holy Wisdom in Constantinople. As patriarch, John protected him, justifying his actions to his congregation in at least two sermons, even though Eutropius had not previously respected the right of others to sanctuary. After leaving the church, Eutropius was arrested and later executed.—Ed.]

[152] Homily [2], *De capto Eutropio* [On the capture of Eutropius], chap. 6 . . . ; quoted in the encyclical *Satis cognitum*.

[153] See Alexis de Tocqueville, letter to Arthur de Gobineau, January 14, 1857, in *Correspondance*, 2d ed. (1909), p. 306.

[p. 215] any rate restrict their serious attention to that form alone. There are very intelligent men, much aware of the problems of their day, who feel confidence in her as the only spiritual force capable of mastering those problems and, in the long run, resolving them. Praise is freely given in many quarters to her civilizing influence, her moral discipline, the magnificent panorama of her educational and charitable work, and the care she bestows on each of the phases of human life.

[We] are by no means unmoved by all this admiration, praise, and hope. Despite the limitations of them, the view they give is nearly always accurate and penetrating in some respect at least. There can never be enough said about the profound humanity of the Church, particularly in our own day, when the noble word "humanism" has been more and more monopolized by the enemies of God, and that with the consent of Christians themselves.[154] But as soon as essentials are misconceived, the wrong turning is not very distant. We no longer understand the Church at all if we see in her only her human merits, or if we see her as merely a means—however noble —to a temporal end; or if, while remaining believers in some vague sense, we do not primarily find in her a mystery of faith. Under such circumstances the very things admired in her are denatured, and her praises are mere vanity—if indeed they do not become blasphemies.

[p. 216] Often, for example, she is seen as a sort of museum piece slowly emptying of life, so that all admiration for her is directed to her past. Or again, she sometimes becomes the battlefield of opposing forces, fought for by this party against that; each wants to

[154] Among many other similar statements on the part of the hierarchy, see Leo XIII, encyclical *Militantis Ecclesiae* (August 1, 1897), à propos the tercentenary of St. Peter Canisius: "Re ipsa ostendere, fidem divinam non modo a cultu humanitatis nullatenus abhorrere, sed ejus esse veluti culmen atque fastigium . . . naturam non hostem, sed comitem esse atque administram religionis" [in reality to show that the divine faith, far from being abhorrent to human culture, constitutes in fact its apex and summit . . . that nature is not the enemy but the companion and helper of religion]. Msgr. Charles Moeller has justly observed: "Far from seeing in the humanistic approach of the Jesuits a concession to sick modern minds, and viewing Jansenism as the abiding Christian attitude, we should, on the contrary, maintain that the former is one of the most fertile adaptations the Church has ever made in the whole course of her history" (*Humanisme et sainteté* [Humanism and sanctity], [1946], p. 217). . . .

claim as its own the right to deploy her moral forces against the other. Each party calls on her to declare herself a supporter of the cause for which it has proclaimed a crusade—this group enlists her in the service of "reaction", that in the service of "revolution". As soon as one party seems to have succeeded in gaining control, the opposition turns from her, and the former's reasons for prizing her become so many reasons for the latter's running her down and bringing charges against her. Thus, from time to time, paradoxical situations arise; some people would have us believe that they support the Church although they do not believe in her divine mission, while others start to doubt her because she does not follow them in the path of their dreams. On occasion she may seem to have let herself be compromised, for the Spirit who presides over her does not give infallible clearsightedness or energy to all those who are her representatives or claim her support, and he does not guarantee them against *faux pas* [false paths]. There may be not only politicians but churchmen too who try to make the Bride of Christ the instrument of maneuverings at the purely human level.[155] But the Church is aware of what she is and faithful to what she believes, and it is [p. 217] not long before she asserts her independence—upon which, resentment wells up on every side. Some reproach her bitterly with leaving her traditional defenders in the lurch in order to fall in with the fashions of the time, and the more full of praise they were before, the more bitter and violent they are then. They get to the pitch when they are ready to view her as a power "foreign to the West and outside our classical civilization";[156] while at the same time others—equally wide of the mark—write her off as obviously spent, stupid, and ineffective and consign her to the past for good.

[155] His Holiness Pope Pius XII, Christmas message, 1951: "The divine Redeemer founded the Church with a view to passing on through her to humanity his truth and grace until the end of time. The Church is his mystical body. She is wholly of Christ, and Christ is wholly of God. Politicians (and sometimes even churchmen) who want to make the Bride of Christ their ally or the tool of their national or international political groupings, strike at the very essence of the Church and damage her own life; in a word, they degrade her to that very level on which the struggles of temporal interests are fought out. That remains true, even where ends and interests are involved which are legitimate in themselves."

[156] See Pierre Lafue, "L'Église et la civilization", *Mercure de France* (December 15, 1927), p. 525.

Thus initial misunderstandings bear their fruit. Even among so-called staunch Catholics and even when it is the faith itself that is in question, there are, unfortunately, few who really take their decisions with reference to their faith—that is, for reasons that are of the faith; in view of which it is scarcely surprising that "men of the world"—particularly, perhaps, the best among them—are always, sooner or later, scandalized by the Church—that is, if they *are* just "men of the world" and no more. It does not matter whether they want to change her or to keep her as she is; they will always be impatient at what they consider her timidity and her lukewarmness, though beneath the surface she is, of course, much more "involved" and far more ardent than they. In fact, the Church does not belong to any party; she is the Church of God. Although she is a witness among men to divine things, she already dwells in eternity.

When the spirit of faith flags within, the contempt of the man outside finds encouragement, and the stratagems and calculations of human wisdom give rise to antagonisms without number. Each man cites one of the "outside" doctrines or parties in order to secure a triumph for his own ideas over those of another—who is, in fact, his brother. When this happens, the quarrels of the Church's own children do not merely weaken the Church; they disfigure her in the eyes of the [p. 218] world: "The sensual person perceiveth not these things that are of the spirit of God."[157] For my own part I will go so far as to say that if the Church were not what she claims to be—if she did not, essentially, live by faith in Jesus Christ, the faith proclaimed by Peter on the road to Caesarea,[158] I should not wait for her to deceive me at the human level before I separated from her. For in that case not all her benefits on the human level, nor all her splendor, nor all the riches of her history, nor all her promise for the future would be able to make up for the dreadful void at the heart of her. The hypothesis is of course not merely false but impossible; yet were things so, all those good things would be the garish trappings of an imposture, and the hope planted by her in our hearts would be a deception, and we should be "of all

[157] 1 Cor 2:14.

[158] [Mt 16:13–20; Mk 8:27–30.—Ed.]

men most miserable".[159] If [Jesus] Christ is not her wealth, the Church is certainly destitute;[160] if the Spirit of [Jesus] Christ does not flourish in her, she is certainly sterile. If [Jesus] Christ is not her Architect, and his Spirit is not the mortar that binds together the living stones of which she is built, then her building is indeed fallen into ruin.[161] If she does not reflect the unique beauty of the face of [Jesus] Christ,[162] the [p. 219] Church is without beauty, as she is if she is not the tree whose root is the Passion of [Jesus] Christ.[163] The knowledge on which she prides herself is false, and the wisdom that is her ornament is false, if both are not summed up in [Jesus] Christ;[164] if her light is not "light illuminated", coming wholly from [Jesus] Christ,[165] she certainly has us captive in the shadow of death. All her teaching is a lie if she does not announce the Truth which is [Jesus] Christ; all her glory is vanity if she does not find it in the humility of [Jesus] Christ. Her very name is something foreign to us if it does not at once call to mind the one Name

---

[159] See 1 Cor 15:14–19. Newman said in 1831, with that somber pungency that sometimes marked the first part of his career: "Much more unworthy has been the practice of boasting of the admission of infidels concerning the beauty or utility of the Christian system, as if it were a great thing for a divine gift to obtain praise for human excellence from proud or immoral men" (*Fifteen Sermons Preached before the University of Oxford between A.D. 1826 and 1834* [London, 1900], p. 71).

[160] *Epistle to Diognetus*, chap. 6, no. 2.

[161] Origen, *In Gen.* [On Genesis], hom. 2, no. 4: *In Lev.* [On Leviticus], hom. 7, no. 2. . . .

[162] St. Ambrose, *In Psalm.* 48, no. 11. . . .

[163] St. Augustine, *Sermo* 44, no. 2: "Unde haec tanta pulchritudo [Ecclesiae]? De nescio qua radice surrexit, et ista pulchritudo in magna gloria est. Quaeramus radicem. Consputus est, humiliatus est, flagellatus est, crucifixus est, vulneratus est, contemptus est; ecce hic species est; sed in Ecclesia gloria radicis pollet. Ergo ipsum describit sponsum illum contemptum, inhonoratum, abjectum: sed modo videre habetis arborem, quae surrexit de ista radice et implevit orbem terrarum. *Radix in terra sitienti*" [From where does this great beauty (of the Church) come? From whichever root it grows, its beauty is in great glory. Let us search for the root. It was reviled, humiliated, flagellated, crucified, injured, scorned: this was its appearance, but in the Church the glory of the root prevails. It thus shows the Spouse scorned, dishonored, rejected, but you can now see the tree that has grown from this root and fills the whole earth. It is a root in the earth for the thirsty]. . . .

[164] See St. Augustine, *De Trinitate* [On the Trinity], bk. 13, chap. 19, no. 24, . . . , etc.

[165] Origen, *In Gen.* [On Genesis], hom. 1, nos. 5–7.

given to men for their salvation.[166] If she is not the sacrament, the effective sign, of [Jesus] Christ, then she is nothing.

The Church's unique mission is that of making [Jesus] Christ present to men. She is to announce him, show him, and give him, to all; the rest, I repeat, is a superabundance. We know that she cannot fail in this mission; she is, and always will be truly, the Church of Christ—"I am with you all days, even unto the consummation of the world."[167] But she should also be in her members what she is in herself; she should be *through* us what she is *for* us. [Jesus] Christ [p. 220] should continue to be proclaimed through us and to appear through us. That is something more than an obligation; we may go so far as to say that it is an organic necessity. The question is, do the facts always answer to it? Does the Church truly announce [Jesus] Christ through our ministry?

The question is certainly one that should be asked. The problem it raises is more than one of the moral order or one of individual conduct. It is a cue not so much for exhortation as for reflection. The problem is not one of stirring up or redirecting a zeal that is always flagging but of protecting that zeal against perpetually recurrent dangers; and if this is to be done we must periodically fix our eyes on the essential in its divine simplicity, without getting any false ideas about the inevitable complexities of action.

The Acts of the Apostles, which tell us the story of the first period of the Church, also show us, from start to finish, this proclaiming of [Jesus] Christ. They open with the words of the risen [Lord] to his disciples—"But you shall receive the power of the Holy Spirit coming upon you, and you shall be witnesses unto me in Jerusalem, and in all Judea and Samaria, and even to the uttermost part of the earth."[168] And they close with the description of Paul "preaching the kingdom of God and teaching the things which concern the Lord Jesus Christ".[169] Every day, in Jerusalem, the Twelve went to the Temple or to some particular house, "teaching and preaching

[166] Acts 4:12.

[167] Mt 28:20.

[168] Acts 1:8.

[169] Acts 28:31; see also Rom 1:1, etc.

Christ [Jesus] without ceasing."[170] When they were hunted out of the holy city, the first Christians [p. 221] at once, in their dispersal, spread abroad "the word";[171] when the deacon Philip, going down from Jerusalem to Gaza, meets on his way a man of good will who is reading the Prophet Isaiah without being able to understand what he reads, he sets to work to explain matters by proclaiming [Jesus].[172] Again, the men of Cyprus and Cyrene who come to Antioch have no business more urgent than proclaiming the Lord Jesus;[173] at Thessalonica, Paul and Silas act in exactly the same way, as soon as they have entered the Synagogue.[174] Paul writes to the Corinthians: "For we preach . . . Jesus Christ our Lord: and ourselves your servant[s] through [him]."[175] The whole of the newborn Church acted and spoke "in the name of Jesus Christ";[176] she is always doing what the angels did by night over Bethlehem —bringing "to all the people" tidings of great joy; for, she says, a Savior is born to you, and he is [Jesus] the Lord.[177]

---

[170] Acts 5:42.

[171] Acts 8:4: "They therefore that were dispersed went about preaching the word of God."

[172] Acts 8:35.

[173] Acts 11:20.

[174] Acts 17:1–3.

[175] 2 Cor 4:5; see also Col 1:25: Paul became "a minister" to "fulfill the word of God"; Eph 6:18–20: "[Pray] for me that I may open my mouth with confidence, to make known the mystery of the Gospel, for which I am an ambassador in chains: so that therein I may be bold to speak according as I ought."

[176] Acts, *passim*. . . .

[177] Luke 2:10.

## Childbirth and Education

*For much of de Lubac's life, secularism was a feature of French national politics, whether of the Third Republic, which prohibited Christian schooling, or the Vichy Regime, which collaborated with the Nazis. However, following the Second Vatican Council, de Lubac believed the Church to be threatened by a secular mind-set from within. This was a departure from the council's true teaching in* Lumen gentium, *its dogmatic constitution on the Church. De Lubac's detailed concerns will be described in the text following this one, which forms a small part of his response to this ecclesial secularism.*

The Motherhood of the Church, *which was first published in 1971, began as a lecture for the Cini Foundation on San Giorgio Island, Venice.*[178] *The council had given rise to new centralized bureaucratic structures within the Church as well as to regional bishops' conferences, which were, in some cases, beginning to develop their own permanent bureaucratic apparatus. In contrast, the Church growth that de Lubac wished to promote was spiritual. The role of the bishop as the personal local embodiment of ecclesial universality was, for him, vital to such real growth and to promoting the particularity of local churches within an overarching universality. In* Particular Churches in the Universal Church, *which was published together with this text, de Lubac explores this matter from an ecclesiological perspective, focusing on institutions. In this excerpt, however, his viewpoint is theological. Of considerable interest is his selection and deployment of female gender images. Within Roman Catholic theology, the female has traditionally been equated with the feminine and, thereby, with the passive reception of divine revelation, whether directly, from a male deity, or indirectly, through a male Church hierarchy. Such an approach is evident in parts of de Lubac's own work, such as his 1968 study of Pierre Teilhard de Chardin's "The Eternal Feminine".*[179] *In this later (1971) study, however, de Lubac uses images including childbirth, motherhood, and education to portray active and relational living and growing in the Church.*

[178] De Lubac, *At the Service*, 132–33.

[179] Henri de Lubac, *The Eternal Feminine: A Study on the Poem by Teilhard de Chardin*, trans. René Hague (London: Collins, 1971).

[p. 59] The mystery of the Church is not a completely spiritual, celestial, or interior mystery. "It is", writes Father Louis Bouyer, "the mystery of what God has accomplished, and never ceases to accomplish, on earth within a history, within the earthly history in which, by entering into it himself, he has become the principal actor."[180] It is the mystery of a social and visible Church which exists in the midst of the world, which acts through men and whose motherhood is exercised through Word and sacrament indissolubly united.

A few distinct accents are noticeable within the unanimity just observed in ancient tradition with regard to this motherhood, depending on whether [p. 60] the birth of the Christian by the Church is considered in the sacrament (above all of baptism, followed by the Eucharist), or in the proclamation of the Word. But it is not necessary to see any opposition in that, or even a duality, properly speaking. In fact—as anyone with any religious instruction knows—the sacrament is never without the gift of the Word, and the Word itself is sacramental. It is the living Word announced by the Apostles, the Word of God himself, delivered, explained to men. The transmission of this Word by those who are its "servants" is not simple teaching, mere "catechesis". It is, for the one who really wants to open his heart to it, the communication of the life of Jesus Christ, Word of the Father.[181] We have seen that Saint Paul, who did not himself ordinarily baptize, nevertheless considered himself as father and mother of those whom he had raised up to the faith in order to introduce them into the Church. When the *Prima* [p. 61] *Petri* [First Letter of Peter] celebrates the rebirth of those who receive the living Word of God,[182] it is undoubtedly a matter

Excerpted from Henri de Lubac, *The Motherhood of the Church followed by Particular Churches in the Universal Church*, trans. Sr. Sergia Englund, O.C.D. (San Francisco: Ignatius Press, 1982), 59–74.

[180] *L'Église de Dieu* (Cerf, 1970), 196.

[181] [Ibid.], 453: "The Word of God transmitted to the Church by the Apostles is not merely a Word that is entrusted to her, but the Word which gives her being, to the extent of determining forever the essence of her structure and of her mode of life. . . ."

[182] 1 Pet 1:23–25: ". . . renati non ex semine corruptibili, sed incorruptibili per verbum Dei vivi. . . . Hoc est autem verbum, quod evangelizatum est in vos" [. . . born again, not of perishable but imperishable seed, through the living word of God. . . . This word is the good news that was announced to you].

of both the preparatory catechesis and the baptismal formula at the same time. When Saint Irenaeus, in his *Demonstration of the Apostolic Preaching*, writes that the Apostles instituted the Church "by distributing to believers the Holy Spirit whom they had received from the Lord",[183] he is undoubtedly also thinking *per modum unius* [in the manner of one thing] about the concomitant distribution of the Word and the sacrament, considered as a double and unique channel through which the Spirit of the Lord is communicated. And when Paul Claudel exclaims, in the account of his conversion: "Praised be this great, majestic Mother, at whose knees I have learned everything!", it is not a catechism or theology course [p. 62] he has in mind, nor even a sermon; it is above all the liturgy, that sacred act whose unfolding he had followed at *Notre-Dame de Paris* before participating in it.[184]

From another point of view, however, two tendencies in the way of explaining the maternal role of the Church could perhaps be distinguished. This is what Karl Delahaye has attempted, calling them the Greek tendency and the Latin tendency. For this purpose, he compares the language of the Greek Hippolytus and that of the Latin Tertullian:

> For Hippolytus, the Church is a mother through the transmission of baptism. For Tertullian, she is again mother in her care to educate afterwards. The interest of the Greek Hippolytus is directed toward the interior result. For the Latin Tertullian it is more a question of exterior—nearly juridical and disciplinary—concern for the life of believers; those who separate themselves from the Church are "without mother".[185]

[p. 63] Still, antithesis should not be forced by imagining one of those dichotomies which are abused today in so many subjects, particularly this one. The Latins have never neglected the sacrament,

---

[183] *Demonstration*, c. 41. . . . *Adversus Haereses*, l. 3, c. 24, 1: "Those who do not share in the Spirit are not drawing the sustenance of life from the breasts of their Mother." . . . Cf. *Didache*, c. 10, n. 2.

[184] *L'Épée et le miroir* [The sword and the mirror], 198–203. *Contacts et circonstances*, 14: "I spent all my Sundays in Notre Dame, and I went there as often as possible during the week . . ." (*Ma conversion* [My conversion], 1909).

[185] *Ecclesia Mater*, 99. . . .

the baptismal rebirth, the eucharistic mystery; nor have the Greeks, those who have been so interested in the *paideia* [education], underestimated the Church's role as educator. It is precisely Tertullian who says to us in his treatise *De Baptismo* [*On Baptism*]: "You who are going to rise up again from the most holy bath of new rebirth, you who for the first time are going to stretch out your hands towards a mother and, with your brothers, ask the Father for the wealth of his charisms."[186] Like Irenaeus setting forth the vivifying faith which the Church distributes as food to her children,[187] he, too, knows that this faith is much more than a doctrine received by the intelligence thanks to the lessons of a pedagogue. The new Christian receives, he says, "the cutting of faith", borrowed from the tree which has lived and grown each day since the first communities received "the cutting from the apostolic seed".[188] As for Hippolytus, referring to the preaching of [p. 64] the Gospel and to the slow formation of Christians, he declares: "The Church never ceases to give birth to the Word from her heart . . . and because she ceaselessly gives birth to Christ, God and man, she teaches all peoples."[189] Moreover, if Tertullian treats those who separate themselves from the Church as orphans, we have already seen above that this was equally the thought of the Greek Origen. And on the other hand, it is a Latin once again, Optatus of Milevis, who, in the same work in which he discusses schism, exalts the fraternity of Christians born of the same mother by explicitly asserting, not their community of doctrine, but the identity of the sacraments received.[190]

The early Father who best brings together these two aspects of the Church's motherhood is Origen. In uniting them, he adds a variety of harmonics, which will be encountered again, in more or less scattered order, everywhere in subsequent Christian tradition, especially in the West. "With Origen, the image of the *Ecclesia mater* [mother Church] has a profundity never again attained. All the expressions of the [p. 65] life of the Church are summed up in the image of the mother who is ceaselessly giving birth. The preaching

---

[186] *De Baptismo*, c. 20. . . .

[187] *Adversus Haereses*, 1. 3, preface. . . .

[188] *De praescriptione* [On the prescription], c. 20. . . .

[189] *De Antichristo* [On the Antichrist], c. 61. . . .

[190] *De schismate Donatistarum* [On the Donatist schism], 1. 4, c. 5. . . .

of the Word, the administration of baptism, prayers, various works: everything is the activity of the Church giving birth to, developing, and carrying to completion in the heart of believers this gift from God which is eternal life."[191]

Thus the voice of the great Origen is here the voice of all Catholic tradition. It is particularly valuable to listen to it today, at a time when a number of people, giving in to that "bewilderment of dissociation that invades and devastates contemporary thought",[192] tend to loosen the bond between Word and sacrament, or even at times to break it. By minimizing the importance of the second, they believe they are increasing that of the first. In reality, they are misunderstanding the [p. 66] one as well as the other, and all their preaching, or what still goes by that name, is not slow in showing the effects of this. Some very wrongly seek support in this matter from the recent council, under the pretext that the priest (or bishop) is designated there as minister of the Word before his sacramental duty is mentioned. This sequence is perfectly legitimate, and one might even say that it is essential, as obviously corresponding to the reality of things. Jesus did not begin by instituting Christian baptism or the Eucharist. His first apostles announced his death and Resurrection before baptizing those who believed on the weight of their testimony, and the Church, following their example, must always be missionary. But there is nothing in that to authorize the least dissociation of the two tasks, or, *a fortiori*, any contempt whatever for the second task, which has been caricatured as the "sacral and worship function". The gift of the Spirit, which engenders and maintains the life of Christ in us, comes to us through this "great

[191] Delahaye, *Ecclesia Mater* [Mother Church], 120. As much could also be said of Augustine, speaking of the Church as educator of people and nations; thus *De moribus Ecclesiae catholicae* [On the morals of the Catholic Church], l. 1, c. 10, n. 17: "*Illi quos quasi vagientes Ecclesiae catholicae ubera sustentant . . . pro suo quisque captu viribusque nutriuntur, perducuntque alius sic, alius autem sic, primum in virum perfectum; deinde ad maturitatem canitiemque sapientiae perveniunt*" [Those who, like infants, are nursed at the breast of the Catholic Church . . . are nourished according to the strength and capacity of each, so that they come, each in his own way, first, to the fullness of personhood and, then, to the maturity and grey hairs of wisdom].

[192] Étienne Borne, in: *Recherches et débats*, 64 (1969), 35. Cf. Jacques Maritain, *De l'Église du Christ, sa personne et son personnel* (DDB, 1970), 107: "The common intelligence takes pleasure in verbal oppositions."

Mother", who delivers us in an incessant and many-sided activity, both Word and sacrament.[193]

We must understand, moreover, that if the Word [p. 67] is already sacrament, the sacrament itself is Word. If the priest is the "messenger of the Gospel", in the name of the Church, he is still fulfilling that role, in fact eminently fulfilling it, "in the highest way in which the Word is realized, that of the eucharistic celebration, anamnesis of the death and resurrection of Jesus Christ".[194] And it is always through the Word that the priest carries out his pastoral function. He educates and guides the people entrusted to him, not as a mere master of catechetical or theological instruction, but as the father who, not without difficulty, raises his children. Just as missionary preaching was directed toward the eucharistic gathering, so the work effected by the sacramental Word is continued in pastoral preaching.[195] If, therefore, the priestly [p. 68] ministry can be analyzed by distinguishing within it the three functions of Word, worship and government, it must not be forgotten that the reality of this ministry is one; that these three functions cannot be completely dissociated, and that each, considered separately, would inevitably be misunderstood. Finally, of course, the preceding explanations must not be taken in a narrowly sociological sense, which would too often be misleading in every respect, but as the expression of a view of faith that must govern the practice of this ministry through the most diverse situations and forms of action.

If the motherhood of the Church is a reality, its analogy with physical motherhood nevertheless includes, like all true analogy, as much difference as similarity. The Church is not a mother "in the way Eve was"; she does not give birth to a people "whose birth would be a tearing away and the [p. 69] source of innumerable oppositions",[196] as has been witnessed in all of history since the be-

---

[193] Cf. M.-J. Le Guillou, *Le Christ et l'Église, théologie du mystère* (Centurion, 1963), 314. . . .

[194] Karl Rahner, *L'essence du sacerdoce ministériel*, in *Concilium* 43:81. . . .

[195] Concerning the difference between the professor of theology and the preacher of the Word, cf. Georges Chantraine, *Vraie et fausse liberté du théologien* (DDB, 1969), particularly 71–97.

[196] Louis Bouyer, *Le sens de la vie monastique* [The meaning of the monastic life] (Desclée, 1950), 89–90.

ginning. Quite the contrary, through childbirth, her goal is to react tirelessly against this misery that is congenital to our sinful race and to "gather into a single body the dispersed children of God".[197] That is what is expressed in a paradoxical image: whereas, in the physical order, the child leaves the womb of his mother, and, withdrawing from her, becomes increasingly independent of her protective guardianship as he grows, becomes stronger and advances in years, the Church brings us forth to the new life she bears by receiving us into her womb, and the more our divine education progresses, the more we become intimately bound to her. Saint Irenaeus was already saying "one must cling to the Church, be brought up within her womb and feed there on the Lord's Scripture."[198] [p. 70] Saint Cyprian says in his turn: "Anyone who withdraws from the womb of the mother can no longer live and breathe alone: he loses the substance of salvation."[199] In his charity, he also expresses this wish: "If possible, let none of our brothers perish! Let our joyous mother hold enclosed within her womb the unified body of a people in full harmony!"[200]

The same idea is forcefully expressed in the *Banquet* of Methodius of Olympus when he comments upon the twelfth chapter of the Apocalypse [Book of Revelation]: "The Church is with child, and she will remain in the throes of childbirth until Christ is formed and begotten in us." We recognize here the Pauline image. And again, a little farther on: "As long as all the citizens have not returned to their native country, the Church is in the throes of childbirth. She is forming 'psychics' which she brings into the world in order to make 'pneumatics' of them. This is why she is a true mother."[201]

[p. 71] Whether it is a question of the entire history of the human race or of each of our individual lives, it can never be said that Christ is completed in any of us. In consequence, the maternal action of the Church toward us never ceases, and it is always in her womb that this action is accomplished for us. In the past, owing to historical circumstances, particularly the invasions by barbarous

---

[197] Jn 11:53. . . .

[198] *Adversus Haereses*, l. 5, c. 20, n. 2. . . .

[199] *De Ecclesiae catholicae unitate* [On the unity of the Catholic Church], c. 23. . . .

[200] [Ibid.], 230. . . .

[201] *Sermo VIII*, c. 5 and 6. . . .

peoples into Western Europe, she has been able to play in certain human spheres an educative role[202] which was one day to come to an end—but the same cannot be said of her essential role. Her mission of giving birth always remains. We do not cease to draw life from her "as children enclosed in the womb of their mother live from the substance of their mother".[203]

One consequence resulting from this is of great significance. We know Saint Paul teaches that since the fullness of time has come to pass we [p. 72] are no longer children, enslaved by the elements of the world or imprisoned under custody of the Law. For us the time of pedagogues is past. According to the logic of our faith, we must become adults in Christ.[204] On the other hand, Jesus said, "If you do not become like little children, you will not enter the kingdom of heaven."[205] At first glance, these two instructions might appear contradictory. But they are not at all. Nor will we merely say that it is possible to reconcile them, that the Christian can become an adult and still preserve a childlike spirit. Such language would be completely inadequate. In reality, we must speak, not of reconciliation, but of correlation. The more the Christian becomes an adult in Christ, as Saint Paul understands this, the more also does the spirit of childhood blossom within him, as Jesus understands it. Or, if you prefer, it is in deepening this childlike spirit that the Christian advances to adulthood, penetrating ever deeper, if we can put it this way, into the womb of his mother.

"The whole task", says a modern writer, Gilbert Cesbron, "consists of becoming fully adult while [p. 73] remaining fully a child." And he adds: "It is the secret of Christianity."[206] It is in fact a secret, and our human reasoning is powerless to discover it or to reveal it to others. Or better, as Jesus himself says: "Whoever has ears to hear,

---

[202] [During the fifth century and later, in the wake of the disintegration of the Roman Empire, bishops often assumed civil leadership roles.—ED.]

[203] Bérulle, *Discours de l'état et des grandeurs de Jésus* [Discourse on the state and grandeurs of Jesus], 10. Cf. Bossuet, *Sermon sur la Trinité* [Sermon on the Trinity]: "Happy motherhood of the Church! . . . she conceives outside of her womb, she gives birth within her womb . . ." (Lebarcq, 2 [1891], 56). [1 Pet] 2:2.

[204] Gal 3:19–29, 4:1–11.

[205] Mt 18:2–4; 19:14–15.

[206] *Ce que je crois* [What I believe] (Grasset, 1970), 208. . . .

let him hear", or again: "I bless you, Father, for having hidden this from the wise and clever and for having revealed it to little ones."[207] Perhaps, however, we can try to glimpse something of it. In our natural life, in fact, each step toward adulthood is a move away from childhood; it is like a loss of paradise, a step toward old age and decrepitude. But in the spiritual life, on the contrary, all progress is, in the proper sense, a renewal. It is an increase in vitality, it is one more step taken within a substantial newness and consequently always new. He who lives by the movements of the Spirit of Christ goes, as Saint Gregory of Nyssa says, "from beginnings to [p. 74] beginnings" toward a new youth and toward a new spring. It is also what was long ago sung so marvelously by Clement of Alexandria, that heir to an old culture in its decline, who was so keenly aware of Christianity's explosive newness. Many are familiar with the lyrical pages of his *Protrepticus* [Exhortation] on this subject. I would like to quote some similar, lesser-known lines from his *Paedagogus* [Educator]:

> Our title of "children" expresses the springtime of our whole life. The truth that is in us does not grow old. Wisdom is always young. . . . "Like a mother consoles her son", says the Lord (Is 66:13), "I myself will also console you." The mother draws her little children into her arms and we—we seek our mother, the Church.[208]

---

[207] Mt 11:25.

[208] [Bk.] 1, c. 5, 20–21. . . .

## The Council and the Para-Council

*The Roman Catholic Church's International Theological Commission was established in 1969 to provide theological advice to the Magisterium and, particularly, to the Congregation for the Doctrine of the Faith. De Lubac was invited by Monsignor Philippe Delhaye, the Commission's long-serving secretary, to submit a paper to the commission, which was subsequently published in the French edition of* Communio *in 1977. This formed the basis of the* Brief Catechesis on Nature and Grace. *De Lubac's dual aims were to provide a synopsis of the doctrine of the supernatural and to "complete it with an exposition on grace, the liberator from sin".*[209]

*The text here presented is from the book's third appendix. It is instructive in illustrating de Lubac's conception of the achievements of the Second Vatican Council in rearticulating the truths of the historic Christian faith for a new era. De Lubac rightly saw the doctrine of nature and grace as key to this. However, in the liberal postconciliar period, there was a greater need to articulate the awareness of sin as the corollary of grace for personal faith. Some interpreters of the council had seen it giving birth to a "spirit" of change and as endorsing a whole "new theology",*[210] *but de Lubac is highly critical of these notions. His assessment of liberal interpretations of the council is critical and direct and comparable with statements made elsewhere.*[211]

---

[209] De Lubac, *At the Service*, 154; also De Lubac, *A Brief Catechesis on Nature and Grace*, trans. Richard Arnandez (San Francisco: Ignatius Press, 1984), 7.

[210] De Lubac, *A Brief Catechesis*, 251.

[211] De Lubac, *Motherhood of the Church*, 25–27; De Lubac, *More Paradoxes*, trans. Anne Englund Nash (San Francisco: Ignatius Press, 2002), 37–66.

[p. 235] Just as the Second Vatican Council received from a number of theologians instructions about various points of the task it should assume, under pain of "disappointing the world", so too the "postconciliar" Church was immediately and from all sides assailed with summons to get in step, not with what the Council had actually said, but with what it should have said.[212] The matter we discussed in the previous Appendix[213] was only one particular and partial episode, which we need not blow up out of proportion, in a much more general and vast phenomenon which, all polemics aside, deserves to be kept in mind in its various manifestations, examined in its sources and analyzed in its effects [p. 236] by the historians of the contemporary Church. This is the phenomenon which we should like to designate as the "para-Council".[214]

Faithful to the promptings given by John XXIII, the Council wanted to bring about an *aggiornamento* [updating] needed by the Church if she were to renew herself; and it can be said that, despite some tenacious opposition, this purpose was achieved. More truly traditional than some of its opponents, the Council cleared the way which the Church must pursue in order to remain faithful to the mission received from her Lord. What the para-Council and its main activists wanted and demanded was a *mutation*: a difference not of degree but of nature. The question was not whether progress should be slower or quicker, whether some halts were needed between stages, whether the goal envisaged should be nearer at hand or [farther] away, whether, in the same spirit of fidelity, more [p. 237] boldness or more caution would be preferable. The objectives sought by the two sides were not the same.

---

Excerpted from Appendix C of *A Brief Catechesis on Nature and Grace*, trans. Richard Arnandez (San Francisco: Ignatius Press, 1984), 235–60.

[212] The Ultramontanes in 1870 had done the same for Vatican I and continued to do so for a long time; but they too were far from successful in their efforts.

[213] [The idea of the Church as the "sacrament of the world".]

[214] This word has also sometimes been used to designate what went on in Rome itself during the Council. This has been described in the chronicles of René Laurentin, who speaks of "the conciliar and paraconciliar activity" or "the activity at the periphery of the Council": *Bilan du concile* [Assessment of the council] (Paris: Seuil, 1966), 52–53. We do not use the term in this episodic and limited sense but, as the reader will perceive, in a wider and more specifically doctrinal sense.

Which of the two, the Council or the para-Council, has succeeded best? The question is too broad, too ambitious and too premature for us to feel tempted to furnish an answer here. No doubt, faith alone makes us certain that, in the long run, the Council will prevail—and this does not prevent us from perceiving some of its good effects every day. But which of the two received more attention from public opinion? Which has most often inspired those "prophetic" undertakings which led nowhere, those hyperbolic eulogies, those programs that announced Year One of the true Christianity[215] that had been betrayed for the past twenty centuries? Which one, even today, is extolled more highly, is better served by the publicists who are most highly regarded and are in the best positions to make themselves heard and to impose their point of view? Events make it necessary to ask these questions; and perhaps they make the answer no less inevitable. In any case, one thing seems [p. 238] beyond question: among many people, whether partisans or opponents or simply docile followers (all of whom were equally fooled), this para-Council, which often deserved the name of "anti-Council", has been mistaken for the true Council; and whatever in the latter's work did not correspond with the former's program has more than once been neglected or misrepresented.

From among certain intellectuals whose faith was not very enlightened, who lacked real culture and were ignorant of history and who were already more or less led astray by the millenarian delusions of our century, the pseudoconciliar ideology, allied as it was with a considerable portion of the press, recruited many partisans. We shall give only one example of this because it belongs to yesterday and because in a few pages it gathers together, in their most general terms, several characteristic themes of this ideology. We are speaking of a pamphlet, published with praiseworthy intentions; and while its author liked to think of himself as audacious, he did not wish to be considered subversive. Indeed, the publication might even be considered as specially "authorized".

"If the Church herself", we read in this pamphlet, "did not take part in the great mutation of the world, she would no doubt be for-

[215] [De Lubac alludes to the French Revolutionary Calendar, which restarted the numbering of years from 1.—Ed.]

ever disqualified." [p. 239] So what we need is "a Church undergoing rapid mutations", a Church whose "entire content of faith" must be "reinterpreted in terms of the new problems which the world faces", a Church that can no longer be defined "according to a descending schema", but according to "an ascending schema". She will no longer have to transmit a heritage, for henceforth she will "be based less on fidelity to a tradition than on a future that must be invented". She will no longer be "a Church laying down eternal verities" but "a locus for creativity, invention, newness". She will no longer need to "defend the deposit of faith" but must rather adapt herself humbly to "the new art of living" which the world is in the process of beginning. Of course, she will not claim to possess anything "sacred" or to consider herself "the guarantor of the religious". "Urged on by the Spirit", she will have left behind "her old crumbling walls" to build for herself "humble, functional houses, indwelt by love . . . which will be the homes of liberty, where something new and great will take place". In fact, "we do not know what she will be, but we must aid in bringing her to birth. . . ."

"In fact", this idyllic dream, floating about in the ether, if it ever became a reality as it claims it wants to do, might well turn out to be the flowery [p. 240] garden through which we would be led, as so often happens, into an arbitrary "structure", constraining in a different fashion than those structures we knew in the Church of old. The people who produce this kind of prose, made up from end to end of historico-Manichaean slogans,[216] certainly do not see where they are being led and where they risk leading others. One would, of course, be mistaken if one attributed too much importance to many semantic excesses, due either to early enthusiasm for the work of the Council or more simply to the pomposity characteristic of journalism. When we read every day that "a new Church must be planted" or that "today we must start constructing a new Church", and so on, or when on the slightest pretext we hear of the "Copernican revolution" taking place in the Church, we do

---

[216] [Manichaeism was a sect founded in third-century Persia that spread widely. Its creation myths included a cosmological opposition and conflict between good and evil. —Ed.]

not always need to become alarmed. In addition, occasional furtive indications which escape the pens of some of these audacious neophytes are sometimes enough to reassure us as to their profound innocence.[217] Still, is it not usually with the wholesale complicity of the innocents, in troubled periods, that the worst deformations come about?

Without questioning the perfect sincerity of [p. 241] their convictions, it would still be insulting to treat the principal authors or promoters of the para-Council as merely "innocents". The instruments of their thinking are more subtle, more "sophisticated"; and they know the precise purposes for which they are using them. Certainly, some points in their program imposed in the name of "modernity" were softened quickly enough, or were found to be less urgent than they were supposed to be. Thus, the "return of the sacred", however one may understand or evaluate that phenomenon, has inspired some doubts and even caused some changes of opinion in more than one uncompromising protagonist of "profaneness". Thus, again, as a result of causes which are only too well known, "Marxist hope" has undergone a loss of prestige—even though it still wins over a lot of dupes. But all these, as we say today, are only "incidents along the road". On the other hand, it is impossible that in the long run some exacting minds should not perceive the contradiction between what is proposed to them and the actual teaching of Vatican II. But then two or three very simple procedures, taken for methodological principles, make it possible for the apostles of the para-Council to regain their advantage.

The first procedure calls for a certain expertise combined with real attention to the texts. It [p. 242] consists in trying to find in the Council documents, every time that they do not conform with the desired program, traces of internal contradictions, with a view to demolishing their balance in favor of a unilateral thesis. Every effort towards a synthesis—an effort which is necessary everywhere for a correct exposition of Catholic truth, even if it does not always lead to a perfect result—is denounced as a merely political compromise; and the mechanism underlying it must be exposed so as to get

[217] "The introduction of the method of human sciences into biblical study has shown us . . . that the Bible is not a book written at a single sitting." (!)

down to the Council's "true" meaning. A minute (or supposedly such) investigation of the debates, of the amendments proposed and of the successive drafts can be very helpful here, on the condition that one has decided in advance what this "true meaning" should have been. "Today it may be regretted", writes a theologian whose euphemisms deceive nobody, "that the Council did not succeed in proposing a more coherent formulation of the majority consensus which one can read between the lines." He is talking about the second chapter of *Dei Verbum* on "the transmission of divine revelation". A similar remark had been made about the first chapter, on "revelation itself", by the advocates of a so-called existential faith which would not include any determination, any conceptual objectivation.[218] But how does one [p. 243] discern this "majority consensus", supposing that it ever really existed?[219] And if by chance one did discern it, in the name of what principles would one prefer it to the definitive consensus expressed by the morally unanimous vote of the Fathers? Even if one considers these questions from a purely human standpoint, why could not a deeper study have been made to enlighten the Fathers on doubtful points that had passed unnoticed in projects which had not yet been sufficiently thought out? Is this not what happens to all of us? And why could the "majority" never have been enlightened on any point by a "minority" or even by a single member? Finally, why represent [p. 244] everything as a struggle between embattled parties? Anyone who saw at first hand how the Council "operated" and followed step by step the elaboration of the texts themselves can never be taken in by such phantasmagorical notions. We know, of course, that there were discussions, sometimes lively ones, and misunderstandings which needed to be cleared up (for instance, on the meaning of the word

---

[218] . . . On this capital point, in a passage dating back to 1958 which constitutes as it were an anticipated commentary on [chap.] 5 of *Dei Verbum*, Fr. Schillebeeckx had seen things more clearly: "In Holy Scripture, the *fides fiducialis* [trustful faith] is always accompanied by a profession of faith. In other words, the personal, existential act of faith, as a fundamental choice, can never be separated from 'dogmatic faith' in which one's personal option is entirely governed by the salvific reality which is presented. . . ." In *Approches théologiques*, trans. P. Bourgy (Brussels and Paris: Editions of C. E. P., 1965), [1:184]. . . .

[219] Especially in the last case mentioned here, to suppose that some artificial compromise was accepted by the majority is pure imagination. . . .

"college" in the Church's tradition, a meaning that seems entirely forgotten today by most of those who discourse on the subject). But a properly informed person would have a wholly different idea about the Council's work and its results from that of certain commentators who are too prone to "read between the lines". And he would be quite certain that a "majority" favoring a program even very approximately like that of some of the protagonists of the para-Council is a pure myth. This is something that the main players in this game know better than anyone else.

When Vatican II, in *Dei Verbum* (to mention it again), reminds us in complete agreement with Trent[220] that the sole source of Christian revelation is the Gospel and when it specifies, further, that this Gospel "shines forth for us in Christ, who is at once its mediator and its plenitude", several writers pretend to understand that in saying this it had revised Trent by admitting Scripture alone as [p. 245] the sole source and by leaving out Tradition—something which is as contrary as possible to the letter and to the spirit of the Constitution. By the same kind of surgical treatment they drew from *Lumen Gentium*, despite the evidence, a "Church-communion" without any firm structures,[221] a "collegiality" never heard of before,[222] a brand new "people of God", a "non-sacerdotal ministry" with a reduced or confused "specificity", etc. A variant of the same procedure consists in opposing one document to another so as to choose the one that, because of its more particularized point of view or its special terminology, best enables one to sidestep a doctrinal teaching which is more strongly stressed in the other. In short, remarks a theologian quoted above: "in the last ten years Catholic theology" (note this self-definition, this canonization of a group which is expert in public relations) "has been trying to resolve the ambiguities in Vatican II." It has been going at this task with zest, urged on, in addition, by the "spirit of the age" which makes people mistake

[220] [The Council of Trent (1545–1563) met in northern Italy.—Ed.]

[221] As early as 1967 Philips wrote, "The artificial antithesis between a juridical Church and a community of love has caused a great deal of mischief": *L'Église et son mystère au 2^e^ concile du Vatican* [The Church and her mystery at the Second Vatican Council] (Desclée, 1967), [1:274].

[222] See Philips' commentary on the Council's text; ibid., 272–316.

this game of [p. 246] dichotomies, this hunt for antitheses, for the perfection of the critical spirit.[223]

The second procedure, which also includes variations, is even simpler. It does not "fiddle" with the texts. It consists in stating frankly in a given case (and these cases, which may be rather numerous, often concern some of the Council's major texts) the reasons why one should not pay any attention to them.

The Council Fathers, we are told, carried out, and could only carry out, a very imperfect task. Old habits of thought could not be dropped overnight, and these "did not allow the intuitions of Vatican II to produce their effects". So the new doctrine, which was supposedly that which in the depths of their hearts the Fathers really wanted to promote, "did not succeed in finding expression in the official documents". In a word, the Council "was paralyzed by old-fashioned aims". These "aims", consciously entertained, inhibited these [p. 247] "intuitions" (subconscious? unconscious?), and it was the former which were enshrined in the documents themselves. In their turn, alas, the popes, too, remained faithful to these "aims", and by that fact they proved unfaithful to the "intuitions of Vatican II". So it is up to us, the theologians, aware as we are of the needs of the hour and impelled by the winds of history, to discover and to proclaim the doctrine which the Council secretly wished to state without having succeeded in doing so.

There is a slightly different explanation which is less subtle. If the work of the Council is indeed very imperfect, its authors, we are told, were quite aware of it; what paralyzed them was nothing but timidity. They did not dare carry their "intuitions" to their logical conclusions. But after remaining stationary for so long, how could such a prodigious leap be made! The Christian people would not have followed it. No doubt, also, "those of the world's bishops who were not yet capable of following the movement would in practice have paralyzed the Council's decisions." So, one can disregard a certain number of "second-rate documents". Again, the world is

[223] A certain school of exegesis had been practicing this for a long time on certain biblical passages, performing dissections in the name of a logic of thought that considered itself trenchant and was merely narrow. In a single epistle of St. Paul, for instance, or in the entire Pauline *corpus*, it was claimed that the so-called "mystical" passages and the "eschatological" passages could not possibly have been written by the same author.

moving ahead rapidly, so that what was acceptable in the 1960s is no longer so in the 1970s. But, we are further assured, the essential part of the Council's labors remains; [p. 248] it authorized the most startling innovations, for this essential element is not found in the contents of the documents, in the letter, but is entirely contained in its orientation, its spirit. This was basically an "open" Council. "At the time of Vatican II", we are told in one instance, "the Church had a lot of catching up to do, and many things have continued to evolve since then, beginning with the situation of Christianity in our own countries. . . . The Council did not so much lay down a program of reforms that were not to be exceeded as it welcomed a new spirit of renewal with inexhaustible applications."

This last statement would be less open to objection if it were presented under a much less generalized guise. Clearly, in the different decrees of the Council, just as in those of preceding Councils (beginning with the "Council" of Jerusalem),[224] one can find certain purely disciplinary decisions which do not claim to be eternal. There are also judgments and directives applying to certain concrete situations. This is particularly the case as regards *Gaudium et spes*, which is entitled "Pastoral Constitution on the Church in the Modern World", and more especially the case for its second part which deals with "various more urgent problems". It offers several practical considerations which some day will be (and in fact some may already be) [p. 249] out-of-date, at least when taken literally. The Fathers of the Council were not unaware of this inevitable caducity as we can see by this remark at the close of *Gaudium et spes*: "Since we have been dealing here with topics which are in constant evolution, the teaching presented here . . . must be further pursued and amplified" (no. 91, 2).[225] That was why a number of the Fathers would have preferred that several chapters of this second part should be treated in an encyclical, or relegated to an appendix, with annexed documents. After much hesitation,[226] the opposite opinion, which had good arguments in its favor,

[224] [Acts 15.—Ed.]

[225] [For this reason, the document was designated a pastoral constitution rather than a dogmatic constitution.—Ed.]

[226] Cf. the account of some of these incidents in J. Y. Calvez, "La Communauté politique" [The political community], in *L'Eglise dans le monde de ce temps, Gaudium et spes, commentaires du Schéma XIII* (Paris and Tours: Mame, 1967), vol. 2, 289. . . .

prevailed.[227] But the authors who invoke, without real discernment, the "intuitions" of the Council as an excuse for disregarding the letter of the documents themselves seem to forget three things:

1. Not all the work of the Council, far from it, [p. 250] consisted in laying down "a program of reforms" liable to be exceeded or not. The Council reminded us at length, sometimes under a different form, often with additional precise details or by insisting on certain aspects that time had more or less obscured, of many essential points of doctrine and discipline and of the Church's tradition that it consolidated. Even if the remainder of these points should give rise to many reforms, they themselves do not fall under the law of time. It is not legitimate to invoke that law to set aside the teachings of the Church on the eucharistic mystery, for instance, or on the ministerial priesthood. Otherwise, this kind of "progress", without guidelines and consequently without clear directions, would end in dissolution and ruin. This would not be a fruitful, because "homogeneous", evolution, as the great Newman said, but mere change based on the various "models" offered us from day to day by shifting types of political societies, by current ideals of "modernity", by various tendencies to desacralization or secularism. One can judge, therefore, the value one should attach, depending on how it is understood, to the slogan which is so lightly invoked to the effect that the Council "was not a goal but a starting point".

[p. 251] 2. The "renewal" whose "spirit" is invoked is not necessarily what this or that individual, what a particular theologian with his individualistic notions or even that large, powerful group whose work of research was not equal either to its power of affirmation or to the publicity apparatus which it controlled, might consider as such.

3. Finally, openly to contradict on this point or that the doctrinal teaching of the Council is surely not the best way to apply that teaching.[228]

---

[227] Cf. the sensible remarks made by one of the lay observers at the Council, the Anglican John Laurence (ibid., 400): "Many things in the second part of Schema 13 will soon be out-of-date, but that will be a reminder that they must continually be revised and perfected. This does not apply to the first part of the Schema. . . ."

[228] We do not, of course, wish to affirm that the composition of *Gaudium et spes*, or of any other Council document for that matter, is a perfect masterpiece. Such an assertion would be worse than an error, an absurdity.

Still, this famous "spirit of the Council", which those who invoke it most have nourished with their own ideologies, is so seductive and so powerful that it soon obliges its adorers to accept a whole "new theology", the foundation of a "new Church"; and if later on it happens that an unfortunate pope[229] tries to show himself faithful to the truth that the Church has always believed in and that the Council itself once again stated, he finds [p. 252] himself accused by overbearing critics of making himself the "triumphalistic herald" and the "superannuated champion" of "old-time theology". His predecessor[230] had been praised by a certain theologian for having exhorted us to "enter in an enlightened manner into the spirit of the Council", but at the same time he was blamed for having recommended to us in the same sentence "a faithful application of the Council's directions". Indeed, the Council was something wonderful the day it opened, a magnificent inaugural spectacle; but as soon as it began to "make concrete decisions" the charm began to fade, the danger of a "certain rigidity" appeared, and its spirit was no longer free and pure. Under those conditions (so one extremist concludes, logically enough), in order to be truly faithful to the Council one must "begin all over from scratch", without "repeating" anything of what it said. There could be no more complete divorce between the letter and the spirit than this.

Is there anything more opposed to the Spirit of God, as found in the New Testament, any sadder spectacle, than the arrogance of this new breed of spiritualism which many of these manifestoes illustrate so grievously?

We are told by one writer that there is a "logic of conciliar dynamism" which demands that we [p. 253] abandon the "official security", referred to "with a sort of defensive instinct" and in spite of "praiseworthy basic intentions" in the encyclicals of Paul VI; it leads us to oppose this security by facing the "total risk, the risk of not knowing, which is a condition for creative life and continuing interpretations". Another invites us to march ahead fearlessly, allowing ourselves to be carried by "the wind of the Spirit" so as "to invent new ways of believing", etc.

If recourse to the "spirit" of the Council or to "the logic of

---

229 [Pope Paul VI.—Ed.]

230 [Pope John XXIII.—Ed.]

conciliar dynamism" is still frequent, another expression, a vivid metaphor, seems to have become the favorite recently (our time is a great consumer of slogans). Its interpretation, or rather its exploitation, offers infinite resources. Vatican II made a "breakthrough"; or, as others say, it made a "breach" through which we can make a breakthrough. Without being too choosy one may amalgamate the three fatidical [prophetic] phrases, through the breach which the Council opened for us we are making a breakthrough, impelled by the breath of the Spirit. Now we can really feel at ease. We were prisoners; henceforth we are free. The Spirit has delivered us from the Institution.

[p. 254] Each of these three expressions which we hear re-echoing around us has, we admit, a legitimate meaning. It is very true that the letter never suffices without the spirit. It is no less true that the Council did open a breach; and even though such military metaphors are hardly proper here, one can agree that this breach invites a breakthrough. But the spirit does not exist either without the letter; the breach is not opened so that we can throw all the contents into the street; and our breakthrough must not be made in order for us to leave our Mother and go and die of hunger and thirst in the desert.

Words, like things, have their uses; they can also be abused.

The practical consequences of the para-Council, the groundwork for which was laid long before 1960, are in large part responsible for many of the reactions which, mistaking their object, have occurred during the last fifteen years against what many thought came from the Council itself. The [p. 255] evil could only be aggravated thereby. Still, one can hardly expect to find in all the faithful a degree of discernment which would require, in addition to a perspicacious intellect, the means of obtaining objectively valid information, a personal, attentive reading of the genuine texts, sometimes a critical evaluation of certain persons occupying important positions, etc. Confusion was, and in certain places still is, so deliberately fomented that it would be unjust to reproach many Catholics for being victimized by it. These people are not retarded, not instinctively hanging on to defensive positions; they simply want to remain faithful to the beliefs of the Church and have found themselves to a greater or lesser extent involved in inextricable contestations. In the same way, if many were infected by the spirit of agitation and the feverish pursuit of "novelties" during those same years, and did not know how to react, it was because they did not discern (and often enough really could not discern) either the tainted source of this propaganda in favor of "a new Church" or the destination to which it intended to lead them.

However, that the Council was not at the origin of a movement which tends to ruin the faith, and that it did not lend itself to such a result unwittingly by a series of imprecise and equivocal statements or tendentious omissions, is amply demonstrated [p. 256] by the texts themselves, the commentaries by those who were the main authors of the documents and the teachings of the popes who ever since the Council have constantly referred back to the documents. This is no less true for *Gaudium et spes* (the only text that a number of people seem to want to understand—and this is to misunderstand it already[231]) than for all the others. Aware of the upheavals in our society, in which "the best and the worst" are mingled, and ready to hail all forms of progress which in their order can contribute to the rise of a better "humanism", Vatican II still rejected whatever might tend to reduce "man's integral vocation", his "journey to the heavenly [p. 257] city", and to close his mind to "the mystery of faith" (*Gaudium et spes*, nos. 56–57). When it stressed the autonomy of those areas which depend only on man's natural activity, it made clear the distinction between "nature" and the "supernatural", as well as their necessary union. Proposing to apply remedies to the "imbalance" which results from the accelerated "mutations" of our century, it tried to enlighten man regarding the mystery of his own being by presenting to him Jesus Christ, "the same yesterday, today and forever" (*Gaudium et spes*, nos. 5; 9; 10, 2, etc.).

For the para-Council, on the contrary, the Church, which has finally attained adulthood after an infancy that had lasted for twenty centuries, is bringing about "a radical revolution" within herself. She must no longer pretend to interpret the world to us in terms

[231] "If the aftermath of the Council has so often been disappointing, if it gave rise to uncontrolled and sometimes disastrous experiments, one may say that this was due to not having given to *Lumen Gentium* and to the other two constitutions that complete it (on the liturgy and on the word of God) the attention which they deserved": Cardinal Garonne, "*Lumen Gentium*, 15[e] anniversaire", in *L'Osservatore Romano*, French ed. (Nov. 27, 1979), 1–2.

of the Christian faith; she must cease considering herself "as the depositary of the truth"! She must accept generalized "pluralism"; she must proceed to "secularize" herself; she must give herself a "democratic" structure, imitating that of modern states; she must cast aside those old wives tales about "interior life", and so on. Such were some of the fashionable slogans which, openly or in secret, wrapped in nebulous phraseology or not, had been circulating throughout the Western and Christian world ever [p. 258] more and more widely in the years before the Council. The Calvinist Karl Barth was a clear-sighted witness of all this, and the remarks he made about it in his great work, *Church Dogmatics*, transcend, as he himself said more than once, the frontiers of his own confession. The situation within the Catholic Church especially disturbed him.[232] "Inner secularization", he wrote in 1959,[233] "threatens the Church as such: her message, her doctrine, her order and her mission." Some people

> have found fault with what they call the sterile and static differentiation between the *ecclesia docens* [teaching church] and the *ecclesia audiens* [listening church]; but in so doing they have come to question the fruitful, dynamic meaning of this differentiation; by stressing the non-holy priority of some human word they have questioned the holy priority of the Word of God, and they have managed to get rid of it more or less successfully. They talk of a "universal priesthood", understanding by that expression the sovereignty of the individual or of the crowd. They thought they [p. 259] were eliminating priests, theologians and preachers, but in reality they were turning away from the Lord of the whole Church. . . . While they explain and apply (and criticize too!) the Bible and dogma, while they rely on the Holy Spirit (who breathes where he wills) and on conscience to which each man is responsible, they have been able to bring out the notion of brotherhood in Christ, in theory; whereas in practice they have only succeeded in glorifying the ideas, the words and lives

[232] He repeated this to me with deep sorrow a short time before his death; he deplored the fact that certain priests had given up Marian devotion—a devotion which he himself did not practice, but he understood very well that nothing living would replace it in their souls.

[233] Karl Barth, *Dogmatique* [Church dogmatics], trans. Ryser (Geneva, 1972), vol. 4, bk. 3, 35–36. . . .

> . . . of *homunculi*[234] filled with covetous desires; and they sought to make these sovereign in the midst of the Church herself. On the other hand, if "ecclesiastics" and theologians have frequently shown themselves estranged from the "people," they have just as often proved to be entirely too soft and accommodating in their regard, quickly giving in to the latter's "desires", when what was involved would have demanded that they be vigilant, firm and sure guides. . . .
>
> How many Christians with a very limited knowledge of ecclesiastical history give free rein, in dealing with tradition, to their limited common sense and their wandering imaginations; they gaily rush forward and simplify problems in their eagerness to show initiative. . . . [Their introduction into influential positions] opened wide the door to errors and confusions of the most varied sorts that threaten indeed not only an ancient "orthodoxy" or a more recent one but the very understanding of the Gospel itself and its progress. . . .

[p. 260] To these characteristics, noted by a Protestant some fifteen years ago, would we need to add a great many correctives so that the picture might apply to today's situation in a portion of the Catholic Church (the proportions of which should not be exaggerated)? On the other hand, where, without preconceived convictions, would one find in the work of the Council the root of all this, or any sort of justification for it? One must rather admit that, under the influence of the para-Council, it is the capital points very expressly treated by the Council (especially as regards the Church herself) that are most often challenged today. "The evolution of the Church", wrote Réne Rémond, "has taken an entirely different direction from that which the Council expected and which the faithful also hoped for. Yet, for all that, I do not feel that I need to change my evaluation of the Council's work."[235] This, it seems to us, is also the sentiment of John Paul II.

---

[234] [Alchemists were believed to create these very small human creatures.—Ed.]

[235] René Rémond, *Vivre notre histoire* [Living our history] (Paris: Centurion, 1976), 125.

# 4

# Grace and Nature

## Surnaturel

*De Lubac's famous study on the supernatural was twenty years in the making, having been planned while he was studying theology at Hastings and Lyon (1924–1928). Its first three chapters were published in the journal* Recherches de science religieuse *in 1931.*[1] *However, during the 1930s, while he was teaching at the Catholic Theological Faculty in Lyon, he did little further work on the project beyond, in 1939, publishing an outline of its second part in the* Bulletin de literature écclesiastique. *Progress resumed during the Second World War, when he twice fled from Lyon in fear for his life. On the first occasion, in June 1940, German forces were descending on the city as the armistice was being signed and the Vichy regime was established. A group of Jesuits managed to escape to La Louvesc, and de Lubac carried with him a bundle of papers that included his notebook for* Surnaturel. *Three years later, on receiving a warning that the Gestapo were searching for him, de Lubac similarly evaded capture by hiding at the Jesuit house in Vals, again with his notebook and with access to an excellent library.*

Surnaturel *was first published in its entirety in Lyon in 1945, with a shortage of decent printing paper accounting for its poor production quality. It received several favorable reviews in theological journals.*[2] *Nevertheless, in September 1946 a storm of controversy broke, even though, as noted above, portions of the book had been published many years earlier with little critical comment. The twenty-ninth General Congregation of the Jesuit order was being held in Rome to appoint a new Superior General, and in an address written for him by others, Pope Pius XII appeared to censure the theology of*

[1] Henri de Lubac, *At the Service of the Church: Henri de Lubac Reflects on the Circumstances that Occasioned His Writings*, trans. Anne Elizabeth Englund (San Francisco: Ignatius Press, 1993), 35–36.

[2] Ibid., 203–23.

*de Lubac and other French Jesuits. Those with links to the house at Fourvière in Lyon remained under particular suspicion, which peaked in August 1950 with the publication of the papal encyclical* Humani generis, *"concerning some false opinions threatening to undermine the foundations of Catholic doctrine". The text censured those who "destroy the gratuity of the supernatural order, since God, they say, cannot create intellectual beings without ordering and calling them to the beatific vision."*[3] *Some readers understood this to be a reference to de Lubac.*

[3] *Humani generis* 26, in *The Papal Encyclicals*, ed. Claudia Carlen (5 vols.; Ann Arbor, Mich.: Pierian, 1990), 4:179.

## *Divine Exigence and Natural Desire*

[p. 368] Paradox of the human spirit: created, finite, it is not just added on to nature; it itself is nature. Before being a thinking spirit, it is a spiritual nature.[4] Irresolvable duality, as much as indissoluble union. Image of God, but drawn from nothing. Therefore, before loving God, and in order to be able to love him, it desires. Made for God, the spirit is attracted by him. God alone is Love alone without desire, because God possesses nothing of nature that imposes itself on him:[5] pure Being, pure Act, he is also pure Love.

---

Excerpted from *Surnaturel*. This book has not been published in full English translation, although part one is closely followed in *Augustinianism and Modern Theology*, trans. Lancelot Sheppard (New York: Crossroad, 2000). The conclusion, which is reproduced here, is trans. David Coffey in *Philosophy and Theology* 11 (1999): 368–80. Since this was published, a revised version of the remaining parts has appeared as *Esprit et liberté dans la tradition théologique*, trans. Eric Iborra with François van Groenendael and Philippe Vallin, ed. Jean-Pierre Wagner (Paris: Cerf, 2013), 17–196. This latter is a translation from the Italian *Spirito e libertà*, trans. Franco Follo (Milan: Jaca, 1980), because the original French has been lost. The principal difference between the original and revised texts is expanded citation and referencing. In the conclusion, there are several substantive new footnotes that provide expanded definitions of key terms, and these are here excerpted and translated within square brackets.

[4] [This idea of a "spiritual nature", which alone, in a very specific sense, has a direct link with God (cf. Saint Thomas, *Summa theologiae* IIaIIae, q. 2, a. 3, resp. and ad 1), which God has made in his image and which, by the fact of his eminent dignity, depends more than other natures on God. The idea of a nature open in its essence to the completely free and marvelous gift of divine love because it is made with this gift in view, the idea of a being whose end is not, like those of other beings, "proportionate to its nature", of a being who, rather than finding its normal completion in the natural order, finds it only in God, in a transcending [*dépassement*] of the self and of the entire natural order. How has such an idea, which appeared to former theologians [*scholastiques*] so admirable and simple that they would never have thought to question it, become unintelligible and scandalous to some of today's theologians, who have, however, little awareness of the innumerable difficulties presented by contemporary philosophies? It seems to me that one of the reasons is this: they have themselves fabricated an absolute, metaphysical principle, which is the object of immediate evidence, from the highly contestable axiom according to which, as Suarez stated, for example, "the natural appetite is founded only on a natural power" (*On Grace*, prolegomena 4, chap. 1, 8). They take this to be one of the fundamental truths "pertaining to the universal patrimony of the human spirit" (A. d'Alès). They think that, in order not to be heterodox in the manner in which they understand this, any doctrine of the supernatural that is not grounded in their complicated speculations on "pure nature" must be contested.]

[5] Cf. Maurice Blondel, *L'Action* (1936), 1:163–64.

Spirit is thus desire of God.[6] The whole problem of the spiritual life will be to liberate this desire, then to transform it: radical conversion, *metanoia*, without which there is no entry into the Kingdom. . . . But this is not at all our subject. The only thing that we must observe here is that the natural desire is already something totally different from this "biological desire" under whose characteristics it happens to be represented.

---

[6] [Some moral theologians and some spiritual theologians contest this principle, taken in its full force, in the name of the nobility of the moral life, and certainly in the name of the perfect purity that must characterize the adhesion of the spiritual creature to the God of love. Not without reason, they guard against the tendency they perceive to privilege interest and calculation, or to subject ultimate choices to determining factors. . . .

From a historical viewpoint, these judgments are contestable. However, the concern that motivates them deserves consideration. It is important to prioritize the problems and not to confuse their levels. Let us leave simplistic antitheses to Nygren, which are not, like he thought, founded on Scripture. *Éros* and *agapê*, let us briefly say, are not simply opposed, as if mutually exclusive. *Éros* should be understood in two different senses. Considered as expressing a distinction of nature, it should not be assimilated into an egoistic love. "There is a major difference", says Fénelon with good reason, "between what is supposed in an act and the motive or formal reason of that act. When one speaks of the disinterestedness of love for beatitude, one does not at all speak of the necessary and non-deliberative inclination that the theologian designates *appetitus innatus* (innate appetite), but only of intentional acts and their underlying motives" (Letter to M. de Meaux on love; third letter to the archbishop of Paris on his pastoral instruction; *Oeuvres* 3:360 and 2:495; cf. 305 and 411–12). There is a major distinction that neither Bossuet nor the various critics of Fénelon, nor even any recent theologian, has understood. Even if Christian revelation, united to the strength of the Holy Spirit, has come to change radically the spiritual attitude upon which salvation depends, it has not changed human nature and has not exempted it from the ontological laws that govern it. The grace of God always operates in us from the same foundations. In itself, the "desire of nature" is not yet susceptible to any such moral qualification. It is true that Platonic *éros*, like that of Aristotle and Plotinus, is not identical with the "desire of nature" that emerges in the Christian tradition: as it is, it cannot enter into *agapê* without corrupting it. But ideas do not traverse history like blocks. Why not see the profound transformations to which the doctrine of the creation of man and his creation in the image and likeness of God has, among Christian thinkers, subjected this *éros*? . . .

Undoubtedly, anyone is free to describe *éros* as, on the one hand, the egoist desire in which is rooted the being who has not heard the call of the divine *agapê* or who is closed to this call and, on the other hand, as the natural tendency, preliminary to all free activity of being that is performed by God and for God, which is to be completed and surpassed in God. But we do not see how the second of these two realities threatens the purity of *agapê*. It seems to us, on the contrary, that it is this which expresses in man the indefectible condition of the creature, and which constitutes him as the indispensable and permanent foundation (*socle*) out of which *agapê* may grow.—ED.]

The spirit, in effect, does not desire God as an animal desires its prey. It desires him as a gift. It does not at all seek to possess an infinite object: it wills the free and gratuitous communication of a personal Being. If therefore, *per impossibile* [on the impossible hypothesis], it were able on this occasion to capture its supreme good, it would no longer be its [p. 369] good. Does one still wish to speak of exigence? In this case one would have to say that the unique exigence of the spirit here is to demand nothing.[7] It demands that God be free in his offer, as it demands to be free itself (in a completely different sense) in the acceptance of this offer. It no more desires a benefit that it might capture than it desires a benefit it would have to accept.

Thus the absolute gratuity of the divine gift appears as a request of the creature both for itself and for the glory of its God.

A certain truth, but one which often is wrongly interpreted. Is this to say that the desire of God is in us only as a "velleity"?[8] It is concluded in fact that it is necessarily inefficacious and that it is intended to be such. But the expression "inefficacious desire" is equivocal, and the notion of "velleity" is inconsistent. Against a current way of understanding each of them, we maintain that the desire of God is absolute.[9] The most absolute of all desires. To desire the divine communication as a free gift, as a gratuitous initiative, is to desire it with a desire of itself inefficacious, but this is not the same as having, as it is sometimes said, a desire that is platonic, conditional, or conditioned.

Certainly, as we have just seen, it would be contradictory to express such a desire—desire of a gift as a gift—by the term *exigence*. That would be to attribute to its subject the idea of a request, a claim. Now—without even entering here into the question of rights, but simply from the point of view of a phenomenological analysis—to lend it such a character would be to understand it in

---

[7] Cf. Joseph Vialatoux, *Raison naturelle et religion surnaturelle* [Natural reason and supernatural religion], in *Revue Apologétique* 51 (1930), p. 269: "The desire for the supernatural, far from demanding its object, demands on the contrary that its object be not at all able to be demanded."

[8] [A mere wish or inclination.—Ed.]

[9] "The absolute maximum of all rational desire", says Nicholas of Cusa, *La vision de Dieu*, translated by Vansteenberghe, p. 17.

the wrong sense. It is quite the opposite. It is essentially humble —with an ontological humility—placing the spirit in an attitude of waiting. The "I who aspire" is not an "I" who lays claim.— But it would not be less false, in return, to make of it a simple *velleity*. This is not because the object of the desire is too exalted, too difficult, too exquisite, or because it is less absolutely desired. Besides, what would this be other than a velleity in the being itself? Let us understand that we are dealing with a unique case, where paradox is a necessary sign of truth. The spirit desires not only God himself, but God as he cannot fail to be, God giving himself freely, in the initiative of his pure love. Resuming the word *exigence* in a new sense, let us say that, far from being a lesser [exigence], it is a greater exigence.

[p. 370] We must resume again, and thus return to express in all senses, these ideas of desire, exigence, velleity, which we encounter, full of equivocations as they are, in every avenue of our problem.

As soon as one gets into the position of thinking of man, be he of whatever manner and in whatever measure, as a kind of absolute over against God, as soon as one withdraws him to whatever degree (be it only a momentary withdrawal) from God's sovereign domain, one must immediately take care to declare that, this man being obviously unable to demand anything of God, there does not exist in his nature any law so formal, any tendency so essential, that it would *have* to be satisfied in every hypothesis, even if perchance God had not intended it that way at all. To think otherwise would be to oppose the sovereign independence of the Creator.[10]

Now, is not this manner of realizing man, puerile as it may appear

---

[10] [Absolutely ultimate end yet free gift; nature's most profound object of desire yet completely supernatural: thus appears the "vision of God". So have the greatest masters of the Catholic tradition defined it. (In passing, let us note that Saint Thomas speaks not only of a *desiderium naturale* (natural desire), but of a *desiderium naturae* (desire of nature) —a detail that, alone, suffices to exclude some superficial and reductive interpretations of the first expression.) We believe that it is not in suppressing, or in minimizing, one of the two terms of these opposing observations that a satisfactory theory of this will be obtained. That goes for this problem as for all those concerning deep reality. Their solution can be found only in harmonizing an outmoded opposition. This is all the more true when it is a matter not only of human problems but also, as in this case, of the ultimate problem and of supernatural mysteries!]

on reflection, our mind's spontaneous way of operating? Indeed, are we not its slaves? Do we not always have the tendency, despite our affirmations of principle, to conceive of participated being as univocal with Being itself? Forgetting, or at least not "realizing" at depth, our condition of creatures, we reason more or less as if the creation were only a fact, a purely extrinsic condition of our position in being, as if it affected only our origin, and not our very essence. We do not straightway discern the consequences for the very data of the present problem. So we begin by envisaging man in his relationship with God as one might envisage a being of nature in its relationship to an external and finite agent, another being of nature, which by hypothesis must assign him his end. We imagine two beings over against each other, therefore equal in some manner, and we naturally conclude from this that, if the universe has any coherence, all that there will be of essential desire in the first of these two beings will entail in the second an obligation to satisfy it, thus placing the second in a state of dependence on the first. It is only when we remember that the second of these two beings is God himself, and when we perceive that such a state of dependence is incompatible [p. 371] with the divine sovereignty, that we recognize, after the event, the rights of the Creator in placing a restraint on the desire of man. We therefore declare that the desire of God, if it truly is the desire to see him, cannot be an absolute desire, since such a desire would place God in dependence on his creatures. Therefore, if we do not totally deny its existence in man, let us at least weaken it as much as possible. With a force that seems to us necessary we reduce it to the level of a simple "velleity". From the standpoint of our premises, is not this the sole means available to us to avoid sacrilege—or at least to recognize a contradiction in human nature, and insult the wisdom of the Creator for not doing violence to its freedom?

Thus we have exorcised the monster of "exigence". Let us not ask at what cost. Let us not examine too much the value of this inconsistent notion of "velleity", which no reflexive analysis has produced. But was it worthwhile to take the monster so seriously? Was it anything other than a phantom of our imagination? A closer attention to the relations that maintain the creature with its Creator would have allowed us, so it seems, to avoid the steps of which we have been speaking and the unsatisfactory solution to which they lead.

God has not forged for us a nature and one day, so to speak, launched us into existence without foreseeing the significance of his creative action, without surmising the series of "exigences" which he was about to release and which we would not fail to press before him, and especially against him. *Operatur omnia secundum consilium voluntatis suae* [He does all things according to the counsel of his will].[11] Moreover, it would be inexact to say that God is obligated, even against himself; that he is bound, even in knowledge of a cause. If there is in our nature a desire to see God, this can only be because God wills for us this supernatural end which consists in seeing him. It is because, willing it and never ceasing to will it, he therefore sets up and never ceases to set up this desire in our nature. So that this desire is nothing other than his call.

The monster of exigence was therefore only a phantom. We exerted ourselves to resolve a false problem. In reality, the question of exigence *does not arise*. However pressing, in effect, [p. 372] may be the desire of the supernatural, however strict may be in the spirit the need which it expresses, how could one speak in this matter of something human that weighed on God, placing God in dependence on man, since such a desire or such a need, if it is in man, is not of him? It is entirely willed by God. Moreover, whatever were the good reasons for calling it "natural" (since it is essentially in nature and expresses the heart of it), one must add that it is already, in a sense, something divine.

"If, to convey it, these shadows of being are a solid foundation, it is because it itself constitutes their invisible support." Thus speaks Mr. Maurice Blondel of contingent things which prove the necessary unique Being.[12] One can reason similarly on the subject of the desire to see God. If this desire demands, in the sense of which we have spoken, to be fulfilled, it is because God is already at its source, even though "anonymous". The natural desire of the supernatural: it is the permanent action in us of the God who creates our nature,

---

[11] Eph 1:11. Cf. St. Thomas, *Summa theologiae* Ia, qu. 25, a. 5, ad 2: "*Deus non debet aliquid alicui nisi sibi*" [God does not owe anything to anyone except himself].

[12] *L'Action* (1893), p. 344.

as grace is the permanent action in us of the God who creates the moral order. The order of "nature" and the order of "morality", these two orders contain all the conditions—the former essential and necessary, the latter personal and free—required to allow us to attain our supernatural end, and both are contained in the interior of the same world, a unique world that one can call for that very reason, though it may contain some entirely natural elements, the supernatural world.

To suppose a nature that could establish its own exigences would be as absurd as to suppose a freedom that could establish its own merits. God, in crowning our merits, crowns his own gifts. Similarly, in fulfilling our natural desire, he responds to his own call. Like every created being, the human spirit has its limits, naturally insuperable. In no sense and under no title, natural or moral, do we have rights in regard to God. *Deus nulli debitor est quocumque modo* [God is no one's debtor in any way]:[13] this word of [Ockham] is an echo of the whole tradition. It is one of the first axioms of the Christian faith. No confusion of the natural and the supernatural is admissible, no explanation of the latter that harms its perfect transcendence. The gift of God would not be the gift of God if it were not the marvel of marvels and the miracle of miracles. Baianism is just as insane as Pelagianism. [p. 373] Equally irreligious, these two errors are at base identical. Each is explained by the survival of the ancient concept of nature and of man—a survival that is unceasingly favored by our spontaneous ways of thinking—combined with a thesis deriving from the Christian conception. In each case this hybridization produces an equally unfortunate result.

Receiving from Christianity the idea of our last end, let us receive from it at the same time the idea of our beginning. Let us not think of the one without thinking at the same time of the other. Let us remember that our God is he by whom all subsists and that he is the Creator of essences themselves. There exists eternally only a Logos, and this Logos is interior to the divinity: *et Deus erat Verbum* [and the Word was God].[14] If these elementary truths do not leave us, we shall have no need to soften our desire into a velleity. We

---

[13] [William of Ockham, *In I Sent.*, dist. 41, q. 1; dist. 17, q. 1.—Ed.]

[14] [Jn 1:1.—Ed.]

shall understand without difficulty that it contains no threat to the divine freedom, God putting it in us only because he freely wills to give himself to us. We shall understand that the measure of our desire is the very measure of our dependence.

Extremely simple truth, which psychological observation endorses. In effect, since it is expressed in the operations of the conscious life, the desire to see God takes in us the form of a duty before taking that of a need,—of a duty to which our more profound nature consents, but which is not thereby less onerous. This desire is in us, yes, but it is not of us, since it is satisfied only in mortifying us. Or rather, it is so profoundly in us that it is ourselves, but it is ourselves who do not belong to ourselves: *non sumus nostri* [We are not our own].[15] Our proper nature is not our own. And because the truth of our being is to be, in a sense, alienated from ourselves, we waken to ourselves in feeling ourselves *bound*. So well that, completing the formulas at which we have just arrived, we can now say: it is not because man desires him that God is obliged to give himself to him; but on the contrary, it is because God wills to give himself to man that man is obliged to strive to possess him—before understanding that he will only possess him if God gives himself to him.

The saint who examines his conscience finds there nothing on which to pride himself, however great his merits. His humility [p. 374] is no deception, but the expression of truth, more and more deeply plumbed. Likewise the philosopher or the theologian who examines the natural desire by a reflexive analysis:[16] the further he

---

[15] Whence the mixture of attraction and repulsion that the creature feels over against God, its desire to open up and its temptation to close up. Virtual division, congenital to every spirit, but actualized, aggravated, envenomed in us by sin. "*Et inardesco, et inhorresco*" [I both burn and shudder] (St. Augustine [*Confessions* 11, 9]).

[16] We are dealing here, in effect, with a reflexive analysis and not introspection. The desire of the spirit is not an object of empirical psychology. We no longer wish to decide whether this desire can be known by the sole light of reason, or whether the light of revelation must be added. We know that this point is controverted by theologians. Perhaps, moreover, the antithesis has something artificial about it, if it is true that revelation has not been without reverberation on reason itself. Thus, the knowledge of sin, which makes us "stretch out our arms to the Liberator," was historically sharpened by the knowledge of liberation; thus again, more generally, *nusquam se melius deprehendit modus humanae imperfectionis, quam in lumine vultus Dei in speculo visionis* [Nowhere does

pushes his analysis, the less he can recognize an exigence. On the contrary, he will see ever more clearly how it is the expression of the right of God, how it is a divine exigence.[17]

Natural desire, divine exigence: let us try to grasp better the identity of these two terms.

What we will necessarily, with an absolute will, one can say in general, if you like, that we demand it. Let us therefore say this provisionally in regard even to God. But let this be added immediately: we do not demand it because it pleases us to demand it; we demand it because we cannot not will it. It imposes itself on us, it demands that we will it; at the same time as our conscience ignores it, at the same time as our freedom turns away from it. Its exigence is such that we cannot be without it. If therefore we demand it, it is because it first demands this exigence of us. But by the same token it transforms its nature. Necessity of will, rigorous law, received by the spirit and not dictated by it!

That which nature would demand in its own name and by its own act could not transcend nature. It would only be a natural object: which is against the hypothesis, the problem at hand being that of the supernatural. Rather, the predicated exigence would possess nothing of consistency and would only be an impassioned caprice: which again is against the hypothesis, since it has to do with admitting the idea of an essential exigence.

Exigence, therefore; essential exigence, exigence in nature, but which in reality is no more natural in its source than in its object. Exigence which is in command of us. Exigence which consequently can never assume on our side the tone of a claim. Exigence which is exactly the opposite of what we would expect. By it we do not

---

the manner of human imperfection understand itself better than in the face of God in the mirror of vision]: William of St.-Thierry, *Epistola ad fratres de Monte Dei* [Golden epistle], n. 110 (Davy, p. 148).

[17] These explanations suffice, so it seems, to vindicate the word *exigence*, though it may often be better to avoid it because of the abuse that has been made of it. Basically, there would be no more reason to misunderstand it than, for example, the Thomistic expression *capere Deum* [to obtain God] or *capax Dei* [capable of God], about which one should not be scandalized, as if St. Thomas had said "to lay hold of God." Classical expression, which one meets already in the Latin version of the *Peri archôn* [On first principles] and in St. Augustine.

command: we have to obey. Nature obeys its ontological ordination by desire, just as free will must obey the moral law by love.

Exigence placed in man by the Creator, since he made him "in his own image," assigning him "his likeness" as ideal and term.[18] Ever since, this term torments us in our nature, and this ideal torments us in our freedom. "If man," says [John of] Ruusbroec, like a [p. 375] hundred others, "is made in the likeness of God, that is to say, he is made for his grace."[19] Nothing could extinguish "the eternal exigence of the divine unity" which burns in the depths of his being.[20] No more, even if he remain deaf, even if he be no longer sensitive, will he be able to hinder the retention, in the depths of his conscience, of the ideal which must lead him to the term of this unity: "Be perfect, as your heavenly Father is perfect."[21] Term on this side of which the spontaneous drive of our being will never be able to consent to cease; ideal that will never cease to aim at the spiritual drive, conscious or not, which gives rise to our moral life, and which the more humble manifestation of this life supposes in its entirety. Term which can only be attained by the realization of this ideal, and which is confused with it: for if it be true that the law resumes in love, in love also is resumed the eternal law.

Term that we have not chosen, ideal that we have not forged. As the first dominates us, so the second judges us. Both oblige us equally. The first, with a necessitating obligation; the second, with a free obligation. But both, in a manner equally rigorous, absolute, definitive. Such is our vocation as men, as spiritual creatures. Dou-

---

[18] [Echoing Gen 1:26.—Ed.]

[19] *L'ornement des noces spirituelles* [The spiritual espousals], book 2, ch. 58. . . . Cf. St. Bernard, *In Cantic.* [*On the Song of Songs*], Sermo 18, n. 6: *Deus denique est, et nihil est in rebus quod possit replere creaturam factam ad imaginem Dei, nisi caritas Deus, qui solus major est illa* [Finally, God is love, and there is nothing in things which could satisfy a creature made in the image of God except the love that is God, who alone is greater than it]. . . .

[20] [*La pierre brillante*] *The Brilliant Stone*, ch. 3. Ruusbroec adds: "The more the contemplative takes account of this attraction and this exigence, the more he feels them. And the stronger his feelings, the more he burns to be one with God; for he desires greatly *to pay the debt that God demands of him*. The continual exigence of the divine unity ignites in the spirit an eternal fire of love; but from the fact that this spirit pays his debt without respite, there is stirred up in him a perpetual fire." (Vol. 3, pp. 235–36). God, says Ruusbroec again, "is not only liberal and avid, but is liberality and avidity themselves."

[21] [Mt 5:48.]

ble attraction of the living God, without which nothing would be, from which nothing escapes, God who by his eternal permanence will be eternally my misery or my joy, according as I shall have delivered myself to him or attempted to withdraw myself from him.

Finally, from a slightly different angle let us complete our grasp of the same idea, and see how, without the modern hypothesis of "pure nature" and better than with it, the integrity of the supernatural can be saved.

Identically, beatitude is service, vision is adoration, freedom is dependence, possession is ecstasy. When our supernatural end is defined by possession, freedom, vision, beatitude, only one aspect of it is defined. One only envisages it from the *anthropocentric* point of view, which is quite natural, since one is occupied with the end of man. In itself, this point of view is not, [p. 376] however, the principal one, if it be true that God, who created the world out of sheer generosity, nevertheless created it for himself and his glory, *propter semetipsum et ad gloriam suam*.[22] The whole world attains its end thanks to spiritual being, which receives it in him to relate it to its Creator. Spirit gives the world to God in giving itself to him, in an act of total return. Now this act only attains its perfection, that is to say, it is only accomplished in all its purity, in the supernatural order, which is the order of pure charity. Then nothing is lacking to the plenitude of the "sacrifice of praise."[23] Such is the essential aspect, the *theocentric* aspect, under which our destiny is fittingly envisaged from the first, and which must never cease to command the solution of the problem which it raises.

It is impossible, one can object, to admit that man or any creature whatever can demand of God the vision of God, and it is consequently necessary to admit the idea of a natural beatitude. It is impossible, one can reply, to admit that man or any creature whatever can totally escape the sway of the jealous God. St. Augustine said it, in a forceful formula: "*Totum exigit te, qui fecit te* [He who made

[22] Prov 16:4. First Vatican Council, *De fide catholica* [On the Catholic faith], canon 5. Cf. St. Bernard, [Sermon 3 for Pentecost], n. 4: *Omnia propter semetipsum fecit Deus, omnia propter suos* [God made all things for himself, all things for his own]. . . .

[23] [Heb 13:15.—Ed.]

you demands the whole of you]".[24] St. Gregory of Nyssa also said it, resuming the common thought of the Greek Fathers: the spirit must unite itself to God to render him in fullness this external glory, which adds nothing to his Being, but which even the superabundance of his love cannot make him renounce.[25] And to borrow a formula from St. Thomas Aquinas, we shall say that the desire of man cannot be vain, because God cannot be frustrated in his work.[26]

> I shall complain of this advance of the Creator who wants to lose
> nothing of his creation
> and to recover his capital with interest! I accuse the perfidy
> of this interior consent which he has placed in us like igneous seed.[27]

By this reversal of aspects the problem itself is reversed. What is in question now is not any rights we might have over against God, but the rights God has over against us. It has to do with measuring the extent of this.

If, then, one recognizes that the anthropocentric aspect is bound to the theocentric to the point of being objectively [p. 377] inseparable from it, one concludes that there can be for man only one end: the supernatural end, such as the gospel proposes and theology defines as the "beatific vision." But one will no longer risk putting any sort of exigence in human nature. On the contrary, one will have to add that, on the supposition that man does not get from that the least advantage, he would nevertheless owe God much more than that submission, strict and always tinged with self-interest, that

[24] *Sermo* 25. Cf. *In psalmum* [On the Psalms] 103, *sermo* 4, n. 2: *Non exigo participationem sapientiae meae ab eis quae non feci ad imaginem meam; sed, ubi feci, inde exigo, et usum ejus rei postulo, quam donavi* [I do not require a participation in my wisdom of those whom I have not made in my image; but, where I have made, I do demand it, and I expect the use of what I have given.] . . .

[25] *Catechetical Discourse*, ch. 5. . . . Cf. Basil, cited by Gregory Nazianzus, *Oration* 43, ch. 48: *theou te ktisma tugchanon, kai theos einae kekeleusmenos* [I find myself both a creature of God and commanded to be a God].

[26] This is in regard to the redemption: if it had not taken place, says St. Thomas, *cum homo propter beatitudinem factus sit, quia ipsa est ultimus ejus finis, sequeretur quod opus Dei in tam nobili creatura frustraretur* [Since man was made for beatitude—for this was his last end—it would follow that God's work in so noble a creature would be frustrated]. *Compendium theologiae* [Compendium of theology], ch. 199.

[27] Paul Claudel, *La Ville* [2nd ed.]. *Théâtre*, first series, [2:294].

one associates with a purely natural order. He would owe him always service, adoration, love, such as are realized among the blessed. The whole *sacrificium laudis* [sacrifice of praise]. Even if God were constrained to annihilate him at the moment of his corporeal death, he would not be less obliged to strive after him. It matters little, moreover, that this supposition is impossible: without letting us put the infinite Charity in doubt for a single moment, it has no other purpose than better to make appear in its urgency the law of impartiality which commands our relations with God. This remains constant in every hypothesis, because it has its foundation in a radical absence of rights and demands on the part of the creature. This is not because God, being himself charity and impartiality, envisages our service only as a blissful participation in his life, from which results for us some kind of right to the breast that feeds our subjection. Besides, is not the distinguishing mark of the supernatural order the fact that there everything happens outside the categories of right, interest, or commutative justice? These categories, or other analogues, which play such a large role in expositions concerning the state of pure nature, have no application in the creature considered over against its Creator. Here nothing limits the sovereign independence of the God who gives himself. Everything here, in this gift, is explained by Love: *secundum propositum ejus qui operatur omnia secundum consilium voluntatis suae . . . , propter nimiam caritatem suam* [according to his decree which works all things according to the counsel of his will . . . , on account of his exceeding love].[28]

---

[28] Eph 1:11 and 2:4. And again, among a thousand other traditional texts, these beautiful words of St. Bonaventure, *In 2 Sent.* [Commentary on the second book of the Sentences], d. 3, p. 2, a. 3: *Divina lux, propter sui eminentiam, est inaccessibilis viribus omnis naturae creatae; et ideo per quandam benignitatis condescensionem facit se congnosci, ita quod in illa cognitione cognoscens multo plus agatur quam agat . . . Deus refulget in omni creatura tanquam causa in effectu suo, et ex omnibus potest cognosci, et maxime in creatura quae ipsius Dei est insignita imagine. Sed illa refulgentia luminis, per quam videtur Deus facie ad faciem, non est naturae, sed condescensionis et gratiae.* [The divine light, because of its eminence, is inaccessible to the forces of any created nature; and therefore through a certain condescension of kindness it makes itself known, in such a way that in that knowledge the knower is much more acted upon than acting . . . God shines in every creature as the cause in its effect, and can be known from all things, especially in the creature which is in the excellent image of God himself. But that shining of light, by which God is seen face to face, is not of nature but is of condescension and grace.] . . .

## The Mystery of the Supernatural

*Despite the attacks to which de Lubac's* Surnaturel *was subjected, the new Jesuit Superior General, the Belgian Jean-Baptiste Janssens, expressed full confidence in him. Four censors were appointed to review the work objectively. Of these, two raised no serious criticisms, finding the topic to fall wholly within the appropriate limits of free theological debate. Two others, however, expressed concerns. One focused on supernatural gratuity, suggesting that de Lubac held the following three propositions: (i) the call to the supernatural life may be known without the supernatural revelation given in Church teaching; (ii) human nature is itself a supernatural gift of God; and (iii) human nature requires grace in such a way that divine freedom is undermined. The other censor pursued this third point, arguing that de Lubac's notion of human exigency, or need, of the supernatural was in tension with the "essentially* mysterious *character of our elevation to a supernatural destiny".*[29] *This censor also considered that de Lubac's notion implied that "only grace gives access to morally good activity."*

*As a sign of his confidence, the Superior General directed that de Lubac be appointed director of the journal* Recherches de science religieuse. *In 1949, de Lubac published an article in the journal responding to the charges laid against him, in which he stressed the twofold and paradoxical character of the gratuity in question.*[30] *The following year, the Superior General was required by the Church authorities in Rome to remove de Lubac as the journal's director, reserving the role for himself assisted by an editorial committee.*[31] *However, the article provided the basis for* The Mystery of the Supernatural, *which was published in French in 1965, several years after its completion. This was the closing year of the Second Vatican Council, by which time little conservative opposition to de Lubac's work remained. The study appeared alongside its "twin",* Augustinianism and Modern Theology, *which addressed issues in the historical interpretation of grace and nature.*

---

[29] De Lubac, *At the Service*, 259–64 (264).

[30] Henri de Lubac, "The Mystery of the Supernatural", in *Theology in History*, trans. Anne Englund Nash (San Francisco: Ignatius Press, 1996), 281–316; De Lubac, *At the Service*, 61–62.

[31] De Lubac, *At the Service*, 64.

*The Two Tendencies of the Hypothesis*

[p. 37] There can be no doubt that this is the direction in which a large segment of modern theology is tending, for, given its point of departure, it cannot logically do otherwise. It sees nature and supernature as in some sense juxtaposed, and in spite of every intention to the contrary, as contained in the same genus, of which they form, as it were, two species. The two were like two complete organisms; too perfectly separated to be really differentiated, they have unfolded parallel to each other, fatally similar in kind. Under such circumstances, the supernatural is no longer properly speaking another order, something unprecedented, overwhelming and transfiguring: it is no more than a "super-nature," as we have fallen into the habit of calling it, contrary to all theological tradition; a "supernature" which reproduces, to what is called a "superior" degree, all the features which characterize nature itself.

Take, then, the great traditional texts, from Augustine, say, and Thomas, dealing with man's final end and beatitude: they will be systematically brought down to a natural plane and their whole meaning thus perverted. They will no longer be taken to be anything but affirmations of a purely natural philosophy. The "perfection" of human nature spoken of in these texts, a perfection which was recognized as meaning its supernatural consummation, will thus become a completely natural perfection, which can be adequately defined by pure philosophy. "All the doctors of the Church," it will be said, "hold it to be a philosophical truth that man's happiness can be found only in possessing God." But it does not stop here. The theory goes on to describe—against the evidence of the texts upon which it is based—that "possession of God," [p. 38] that supreme good which makes man "perfect" and "wholly satisfies the appetite of the will," as the crowning point of a purely philosophical ethic. It declares this to be the ultimate end of human effort, without any suggestion of help from the supernatural properly so called, without the slightest allusion to any divine initiative, any divine gift. Final end, beatitude, perfection, these three concepts

Excerpted from *The Mystery of the Supernatural*, trans. Rosemary Sheed with John M. Pepino (New York: Crossroad, 1998), 37–52.

taken from St. Thomas are used to designate not merely the same thing, but a thing wholly contained within the limits of the natural order.

To be obliged to misconstrue so profoundly one of the essential elements in the teaching of the great masters is in itself somewhat astonishing. When St. Augustine uttered his famous declaration "You have made us for yourself, O God . . . ,"[32] he never anticipated that one day in the twentieth century this would be taken in a purely natural sense. When St. Thomas Aquinas said "Grace perfects nature,"[33] he did not foresee that what he said about the completion or perfecting of nature would be retained, while the grace which effects that completion would be left aside. When [John] Scotus Erigena gloried in "the pure and direct contemplation of the divine essence" it never occurred to him that people would ever see in it anything other than the happiness "promised to the saints," the happiness spoken of by St. Paul and St. John, the inspired writers of revelation.[34] When Albert the Great explained the contemplation of "the face of God" by describing a "presence of God shown and presented without mediation," he thought thereby to be describing quite clearly and unmistakably the "beatific vision" and nothing else.[35] [p. 39] When St. Thomas further said: "This immediate vision of God is guaranteed to us in Scripture,"[36] he could not have supposed that one day people would attribute to him the idea of another vision of God, equally "direct," which could be obtained without reference to anything promised in scripture. When he spoke of the "contemplation of Heaven, in which supernatural Truth is seen in its essence,"[37] he did not imagine that later "disciples" would come to divide that contemplation into two kinds, of

---

[32] [*Confessions* 1.1 (1).—Ed.]

[33] [*Summa theologiae* Ia, q. 1, art. 8 ad 2.—Ed.]

[34] *De divisione naturae* [On the division of nature = *Periphyseon*], bk. 1, c. 8: "What then shall we say of that future felicity, which is promised to the saints, which we believe to be nothing other than the pure and immediate contemplation of the divine essence itself, as say John and Paul . . . ?" . . .

[35] *Summa theol., Prima*, tract. 3, q. 13, membr. 4, sol.: "It is most fitting that the face of God be called essential, the presence of God shown and revealed immediately, in the way in which it reveals itself to the blessed."

[36] *Summa contra Gentiles*, bk. 3, c. 51.

[37] *Secunda Secundae*, q. 5, a. 1, ad 1um.

which the first while remaining "by essence" [*per essentiam*] would none the less be "purely natural." Nor could he have imagined that those "disciples" would do the same for the "spiritual union [*societas spiritualis*] with God," the "rational union of the mind with God" [*societas rationalis mentis ad Deum*], the "gratuitous love" [*amor gratuitus*], the "love of charity" [*dilectio caritatis*], and so on.

But beyond this, the consequences of making this kind of division and providing this kind of option are quick to follow. Henceforward all the values of the supernatural order, all those which characterize the present relationship between man and God in our economy of grace, will be gradually reabsorbed into that "purely natural" order that has been imagined (and I say "imagined" advisedly). In that order as in the other we will find faith, prayer,[38] the perfect virtues, the remission of sins by infused charity, grace,[39] divine friendship,[40] spiritual union with [p. 40] God, disinterested love,[41] and a docile abandonment to "personal Love."[42] In short, nothing is lacking. Nothing—for there is even a revelation which, while supernatural in origin and mode, has none the less, owing to its object, always been "entitatively natural." One may say, indeed, that the substitution is complete—but I prefer myself to say that the disguise is complete. Everything that now comes to us by the grace of God is thus withdrawn from the "supernatural" properly so called of our present economy, and "naturalized"—at the risk

[38] St. Thomas said (*Secunda Secundae*, q. 83, a. 10, ad 1um): "To pray is proper to the rational creature," and at the same time: "to pray belongs to him that accepts it through grace." . . .

[39] Suarez, *De fine ultimo* [On the final end], Disput. 13, sect. 2, n. 11: "It is probable that God was going to give to man in this state some genus of providence, by which he might turn himself towards God in a natural love beyond all . . ." (vol. 4, p. 149). . . .

[40] Cajetan, *In Primam Secundae* [On the *Summa theologiae* IIaIae], q. 99, a. 9, n. 3: "Man's friendship for God can be understood under two headings: first, simply, through grace and charity; second, relatively [*secundum quid*], that is to say, it can exist between man in pure nature and God to the exclusion of grace"; note that Cajetan still makes it "relatively [*secundum quid*]."

[41] Lessius, *De summo bono* [On the highest good], bk. 2, c. 23, n. 190: "By some excellent natural love" (Hurter ed., p. 375). A. Moraines, *Anti-Jansenius* (1652), p. 201: "I answer, that it is not impossible for there to be any purely natural love of God *propter se* [for its own sake]." . . .

[42] Blaise Romeyer, S.J., "La théorie suarézienne d'un état nature pure" [The Suarézian theory of a state of pure nature], *loc. cit.*, p. 57.

of being attributed afresh to some special intervention by God according to a different "mode." No difficulty is found in speaking of "natural graces", "natural contrition,"[43] of friendship with God "to the exclusion of grace" [*seclusa gratia*] or "purely naturally" [*in puris naturalibus*]; there seems no obstacle in conceiving of a disinterested love of God, a love that is "most excellent" [*excellentissimus*] and "above all things" [*super omnia*], directed towards "the author of nature," and existing as a fruit of "pure nature." Henceforth, everything, from the first beginnings, from the very appetite for happiness, is thus seen in a kind of double way: "The beatitude of man is twofold: one is natural, in whose acquisition the natural appetite rests. . . . The other is supernatural, in whose acquisition the supernatural appetite rests. . . ."[44] This applies to everything, up to the final point, the "perfect beatitude," the "direct vision," and this has recently been said—the "possession" of God.

What remains peculiar to the supernatural order, except the word? Neither Pedro Descoqs, with his "direct natural vision of God,"[45] nor [p. 41] Père Peillaube, nor Charles Boyer with his "natural possession" of God, has stood out from the chorus, so to say, to produce any really personal idea requiring individual consideration. But they have borne a single stream of thought along to its goal; and long ago others had preceded them in this. Ignatius Neubauer, for instance, or Henri Kilber, Sylvester Maurus; or Gotti. The idea of "natural possession" was indeed put forward in the sixteenth century. Suarez, however, felt obliged to refute it[46]—without realizing that he was thereby attacking the logic of his own position. That logic was to triumph among a large proportion of theologians, to such a point that they came in the end to conceive the state of pure nature in all its detail as "a transfer of the concrete, existing

---

[43] F. B. Franzelin, *De Traditione et Scriptura* [On tradition and Scripture] (1870), p. 556.

[44] Medina, *In Primam Secundae* [On the *Summa theologiae* IIaIae], q. 3, a. 8 (Venice, 1590), pp. 45–47.

[45] *Le mystère de notre élévation surnaturelle* [The mystery of our supernatural elevation] chap. 7 (1938). . . .

[46] *De ultimo fine hominis* [On the final human end], Disput. 16, sect. 1, n. 5 (*Opera* [Works], vol. 4, p. 152; cf. p. 145). Cf. St. Augustine, *De Trinitate* [On the Trinity], bk. 15, c. 7, n. 11: "Nothing pertains to the nature of God that does not pertain to the Trinity". . . .

order."[47] In the complete system, the two series—pure nature and supernaturalized nature, or nature called to the supernatural—flowed along parallel channels in complete harmony. But the only intelligible difference, if difference it be, between the two consists in the epithet applied to each respectively. Without anything apparently to distinguish them, one is called "natural," the other "supernatural."[48] In both there is seen a "perfect possession of the highest good," the two being to all appearances identical, though we are told that one is attained "through acts of the natural order" and the other "through most excellent [*praestantissimos*] acts."

Then again, we find on one side the "natural desire" for God which man would have felt in a state of pure nature, and on the other the [p. 42] supernatural hope of the Christian: the object, Suarez tells us, is in both cases "God as the highest good lovable by the love of concupiscence, i.e. to the advantage of the one loving"; only, whereas natural desire envisages God as "natural good of man," supernatural hope sees him as "supernatural good."[49] What illumination do we get from this? The kindred distinction Kilber makes between chaste love and rightful love which presupposes grace when it is supernatural, but does not need it when it is natural, does not really tell us much more.[50] Any means we might have had to apply a different content to each has been taken from us in advance by our being given a concrete definition which applies equally to both. These examples further demonstrate that if, in such a system, the state of pure nature becomes a "transfer of the existing order," it may also happen in reverse that the existing, supernatural order may

[47] Henri Rondet, S.J., "Le problème de la nature pure et le théologie du XVIe siècle" [The problem of pure nature and the theology of the 16th century], *Rech. de sc. religieuse* (1948): 518 (on Suarez).

[48] Thus *Theologia Wiceburgensis, De beatitudine* [The Würzburg theology, on beauty], c. 1, a. 1. The author of this treatise, Ignatius Neubauer, distinguishes natural happiness, "which is the perfect possession of the highest good through acts of the natural order," and supernatural happiness, "which is the perfect possession of the highest good through pre-eminent acts, going beyond what is due, the strengths and exigencies of created nature" (3rd ed., vol. 5, 1880, p. 3). . . .

[49] *De spe* [On hope], disput. 1, sect. 3, n. 4.

[50] H. Kilber, *De gratia* [On grace], c. 1, n. 4: "A pure, right and supernatural love . . . cannot be had without grace properly so-called, I concede; a natural [love], I deny" (vol. 7), p. 160. . . .

become the transfer of a wholly "natural" order: how can one see in this the fulfillment of supernatural hope, or supernatural love? But whichever way we look at it, are we not bound to be forced into a complete nominalism, or even a mere parroting of words? For, having constructed a complete, imaginary "natural" universe, with supernatural treasures which seem no longer to have anything of wonder attached to them, one is then obliged to postulate beyond that universe another, designated as "supernatural" and declared "more excellent," "more perfect," or rather perfect in a different way, but of which there remains nothing else that can be said.

[p. 43] I may add that it seems hardly fitting—to put it mildly—to the reverence which religion, even the "natural" kind, inspires in us for God, for his majesty and his independence, to bestow so readily upon man as something taken for granted and as a "purely natural end," more than many people would once have dared to declare bestowed upon him by the liberality of God himself. In the eyes of those believers of old, the essence of the Godhead was an inviolable mystery, so profoundly hidden that, even in a universe ruled by grace, no creature could ever see it directly. God, they thought, would only be found, even in the light of eternal beatitude, by being forever sought. As we know, several of the Greek fathers tended to this theory; we find it especially in the works of Gregory of Nyssa. Denys, Maximus the Confessor and John of Damascus handed it on to the West. [John] Scotus Erigena was one of those who proclaimed it.[51] Did not scripture tell us that God "dwells in unapproachable light" (1 Tim 6:16)? How, then, can we contemplate him except by means of "theophanies"?[52]

This doctrine of "the impenetrability of the divine secret" seems to have "caused some thirteenth-century theologians to pause for a moment,"[53] as we see from the first proposition condemned in

---

[51] *De divisione naturae* [On the division of nature = *Periphyseon*], bk. 5, c. 23, 27 and 38 . . . ; bk. 1, c. 8 and 10 . . . ; bk. 2, c. 23 . . . ; etc.

[52] Cf. V. Lossky, "Le problème de la 'vision face à face' et la Tradition patristique de Byzance" [The problem of the "face-to-face vision" and the patristic tradition of Byzantium], *Studia Patristica* 2 (1957): 512–37; . . . *The Vision of God* (London, 1963). M. Lot-Borodine, "La Béatitude dans l'Orient chrétien" [Beatitude in the Christian East], *Dieu Vivant* 15 (1950): 85–115. . . .

[53] H. F. Dondaine, O.P., "Hugues de Saint-Cher et la condamnation de 1241" [Hugh

1241 by William of Auvergne, Bishop of Paris, at the instigation of the professors of the university: "Divine essence in itself [*in se*] will be perceived neither by man nor by angel."[54] It did not, then, appear possible to [p. 44] these theologians to admit of more than a certain "unsatisfied longing which for ever binds the blessed spirit to the invisible cause." Hugh of Saint-Cher, in his commentary on St. John's gospel, denied that God could ever be seen "in his essence." Alexander of Hales resisted this line of thought, but Albert the Great remained "very impressed" by it;[55] dealing on several occasions with this "then burning" subject, he allowed that the saints in heaven, like the angels, have a certain though obscure sight of God "as he is" [*ut est*], but no vision of "what he is [*quid est*]."[56] St. Bonaventure still felt obliged to combat the error of those who said that one could not see God "in his essence" but only "in his brightness" (others said "in his glory"). These over-cautious theologians were certainly wrong. Their hesitations and reservations perhaps resulted from an imperfect understanding of the Greek fathers, for they do not seem to have fully grasped the distinction between *phusis* [nature] and *prosōpon* [face or person];[57] and in some of them, their doubts were reinforced by the influence of Avicenna.[58] But the tendency was an old one, though not for that reason running any less counter to the authentic tradition always preserved in the

of Saint Cher and the condemnation of 1241], *Revue des sciences philos. et théol.* (1949): 170–74. . . . Cf. Maximus, [*Explanations of*] *the heavenly hierarchy*, IV.3: "Denys affirms no one has ever seen or will see the inner reality of God, in other words his essence". . . .

[54] *Chartularium Universitatis Parisiensis* 1 (1889): n. 178.

[55] H. F. Dondaine, "Cognoscere de Deo 'quid est' " [Learning what God is], *Recherches de théologie ancienne et médiévale* 22 (1955): 74.

[56] *De resurrection* [On the Resurrection]: "One must distinguish that it is one thing to see God as he is [*ut est*], and another to see who God is [*quis est*]. . . . The most perfect knowledge of God is the vision of his very being with the recognition of the impossibility of attaining his essence [*quid est*]." *In Epist. quintam Dionysii* [*On the Fifth Letter of Dionysius*], dubium 1: "He will be seen of himself neither on earth nor in heaven except 'because' [*quia*] confused, though God himself be seen more clearly or less clearly according to the diverse modes of seeing and of those seeing." *In caelestem Hierarchiam* [The celestial hierarchy], c. 4, n. 5, 8um: "God can be seen essentially [*quid est*] by no one in such a way that the terms of his essence are grasped, neither by man nor by angel." . . .

[57] Cf. Lossky, *loc. cit.* . . .

[58] [Avicenna or Ibn Sīnā (ca. 980–1037) was a Persian philosopher, theologian, physician, and natural scientist.—Ed.]

stream of Augustinianism. Ambrose Autpert[59] [p. 45] and Hugh of St. Victor[60] gave it a battering. Hugh of Rouen did the same.[61] Like Alexander of Hales and St. Bonaventure, St. Thomas had to combat it and justified his position, without sacrifice of God's incomprehensibility, by the distinction he made in imitation of St. Augustine between "seeing what is" [*videre quid est*] or "seeing by essence" [*videre per essentiam*] and "understanding" [*comprehendere*].[62] Finally, the authority of the Church, in an irrevocable decision, removed the last scruples which prevented belief in the ultimate consequence of God's unimaginable love.[63] The fullest meaning could be given to St. Paul's words: "Then I shall understand fully, even as I have been fully understood":[64] thus, in an instant, there were drawn back the "seventy thousand curtains [veils] of light, shadow and fire"[65] which an Islamic tradition sets between the angels and the glory of God. But one must not forget that the same authority was obliged

[59] *In Apoc.* [On the Book of Revelation], bk. 10, commenting on 1 Cor. 13: "What we should know is that there were many to say that, in the region of beatitude, God is in fact seen in his distinctness [*claritas*], but that in his nature he is not seen at all. I certainly marvel that the subtlety of the inquiry deceived them, for the distinctness of his simple and immutable essence is not one thing and his nature another, but his very nature is his distinctness, his very distinctness is his nature" ([*Maxima Bibliotheca Veterum*] *Patrum*, vol. 13, p. 647 F). . . .

[60] *Expositio in cael. Hierarchiam S. Dionysii* [Exposition of the celestial hierarchy of Saint Dionysius], bk. 2, on these "theophanies": "They place them [theophanies] between rational creatures and God, just as intermediary images of the hidden divinity. . . . But in fact these images are their own, the phantoms of vanity. . . . Let them take away their phantasies, by which they strive to overshadow the light of our minds . . . ! I say that, just as a thing cannot satisfy beyond itself, so also can it not stand before itself [*usque ad ipsum*]". . . .

[61] *Contra Haereticos* [Against heretics], bk. 3, c. 9. . . .

[62] *In 4 Sent.* [Commentary on the fourth book of the Sentences], d. 49, q. 2, a. 3: "The saints will see what God is [*quid est*], but will not comprehend him." Cf. a. 1, ad 1um and ad 2um. *De Veritate* [On truth], q. 8, a. 1: "Whoever knows something through its essence [*per essentiam*], knows of it what it is [*quid est*]"; cf. ad 8um.

[63] Cf. 1 John 4:16.

[64] 1 Cor. 13:12. But it must not be forgotten that in the following century, under Clement V, the Church had to make a decision in the opposite direction, with the condemnation of the proposition that "The soul does not lack the light of glory that elevates it to the vision and blessed contemplation [*fruendum*] of God."

[65] [Known as the "Hadith of the Veils", this is prominent in the mystical Sufi tradition of Islam.—Ed.]

in the following century, under Clement V, to take another decision against the opposite excess, and to condemn at the Council of Vienne the proposition that "The soul does not lack the light of glory that elevates it to the vision and blessed contemplation [*fruendum*] of God." And one would like to see, in these theologians who are so sure of themselves and of their natural faculty for seeing the divine essence, something to give even some faint suggestion of the restraint of the Greek fathers, or the scruples of those who took their inspiration from them: one would like to see in these theologians a similar sense of God's transcendence.

[p. 46] There are however some, apparently aware of both the intellectual difficulty and spiritual inadequacy which I have indicated, who seek a way out by means of a distinction that aims to provide a more precise meaning, and therefore a more acceptable doctrine. "Is it absurd," asks Pedro Descoqs, for example, "to conceive of a real vision of God, the author of nature, which would not reveal him according to his inmost perfections which are of the transcendent supernatural order, but, while remaining in some sense proportionate to our nature, would still be intuitive and go beyond the scope of abstract concepts or infused species?"[66] Expressed thus, the hypothesis is very like the opinion put forward by Sylvester of Ferrara in his commentary on the *Summa contra Gentiles*: he considers that there is, in human nature, a genuine desire to see God, but to see him "as cause."[67] But St. Bernard gave the answer to them both long ago, when he said that only someone who does not yet see can think in terms of such distinctions: "many are the words, many the paths, but only One is signified by them, only One is sought."[68] And Vasquez,[69] speaking of Sylvester, made no bones about calling them "frivolous": "For, since the clear vision of God is one, single and indivisible and the blessed cannot by it distinguish in God diverse attributes and predicates, the whole supernatural vision will

[66] *Op. cit.*, 126.

[67] In bk. 3, 51: "We naturally desire the vision of God inasmuch as it is the vision of the first cause, not however inasmuch as it is the highest good. . . ."

[68] *De consideratione* [On consideration], bk. 5, c. 3, n. 27.

[69] [Gabriel Vasquez (ca. 1550–1604) was a Spanish Jesuit theologian and moralist who taught near Madrid and in Rome.—ED.]

consist precisely in its clarity, and from a supernatural principle, without a doubt proceeding from the light of glory."[70]

There has been no lack of theologians to object to these explanations for their vague and extended use of the terms "nature" and even "pure nature," to include supernatural, or at least preternatural, elements. But, though these others are thus aware of the fatal current into which some of the rest are drawn, and themselves resist it, they sometimes only go on to let themselves be drawn along by a contrary logic whose conclusions seem no better. For they are just as ready to give a precise form to their concept of a purely natural "economy"; and while that form is certainly more coherent, "more simple and rational," may it not [p. 47] also be perhaps even more dangerous? In that economy, as they present it, all of man's moral life would depend exclusively on his own innate powers, exercised in full autonomy, "almost as understood by Aristotle."[71] Is not this likely to end in the idea of an order of things whereby man would be cut off from the "superior part of his soul," his "highest faculty," that which makes him *mens*, a mind marked with the image of the Trinity?[72] Does it not lead us to suppose a being similar to that so often presented by rationalist philosophies—both ancient and modern: a being sufficient to himself, and wishing to be so; a being who does not pray, who expects no graces, who relies on no Providence; a being who, depending on one's point of view, either wants only to continue as he is, or seeks to transcend himself, but in either case stands boldly before God—if he does not actually divinize himself—in a proud and jealous determination to be happy in himself and by his own powers? It seems to me that this line of thinking leads

[70] *In Primam Secundae* [On the *Summa Theologiae* IIaIae], disp. 22, c. 2. . . . Cf. *In Primam* [On the *Summa Theologiae* Ia], disp. 118, c. 2 . . . , quoting St. Bernard: "By these words he so intelligently expressed the whole matter, that nothing could be said or desired [to be said] more clearly by anyone who studies Scholastic Theology."

[71] Guy de Broglie, S.J., "De gratuitate ordinis supernaturalis ad quem homo elevatus est" [On the gratuity of the supernatural order to which man is elevated], *Gregorianum* 29 (1948): 463, final note: "Many scholastics understand the economy of 'pure nature' as the order of things in which our moral life is to be conducted only through the innate and properly autonomous power of man (almost as understood in Aristotle). This conception clearly is more simple and rational than any other, it seems."

[72] Cf. St. Thomas, *De veritate* [On truth], q. 10, a. 1 and a. 7, etc. St. Augustine, *De Trinitate* [On the Trinity], bk. 7, ch. 6, n. 12, . . . etc. . . .

to a natural morality pure and simple, which must tend to be a morality without religion—or at least with only a natural religion "which is itself only one natural moral virtue among others."[73]

Such fears are not an invention of my own. A century ago Franzelin[74] demonstrated the dangers in such a conception. The theologians who adopt it, he said, "without a doubt are mistaken."[75] Nor is it any more acceptable with the correction made by Baius. It may indeed happen that this "purely natural" man becomes aware that he cannot completely eliminate God's action if he is to perfect himself; he then denatures [p. 48] it; for he demands of his Creator a happiness "required in justice," and which can only be attained by helps similarly required—whether they be "general" or "special," "permanent" or "transitory." Hence, though not identified with what is "constitutively natural," the supernatural becomes something "natural by requirement."[76] The final result is Pelagianism, or Baianism: in either case we arrive at a hypothetical creature who has no kind of relationship of love with God; at a "beatitude" which the creature requires and which God owes him. In the "purely natural world" where this creature lives, all idea of God's free gift is lost. How can one say that such a picture, in either possible form, is in harmony with any idea we could have (no matter whether from reason or revelation) of the one true God? Is there any justification for formulating as possible a hypothesis by whose terms God must in justice assure man of any beatitude, however "natural"?[77] Is there

---

[73] Etienne Gilson, *The Christian Philosophy of St. Thomas Aquinas* (London, 1957), 338ff.

[74] [Johann Baptist Franzelin (1816–1886) was an Austrian Jesuit theologian who spent much of his life teaching in Rome and was created a cardinal (1876).—ED.]

[75] *De traditione et Scriptura* [On tradition and Scripture], p. 642. Cf. de Broglie, *Conférences sur la vie surnaturelle* [Lectures on the supernatural life], vol. 2, 5th lecture, also stating that "pure nature," if conceived as being without help from God, is an abstraction which can never be realized. Franzelin, *loc. cit.*: "They are without a doubt mistaken who so compare the present order of providence with the state of pure nature that they consider the present state to be void of all supernatural assistance, and with none other to substitute for it than natural aids; then indeed they persuade themselves that such is the state of pure nature."

[76] F. X. Le Bachelet, "Baius" in *Dict. de théol. cath.*, vol. 2, col. 69.

[77] One theologian wrote to me: "If, in the system of pure nature, it must be allowed that man has rights over God and that his end is *owed* to him, that seems to me reason enough to reject the system." . . .

any justification for proposing in this way a possible order in which God would, in the strict and proper sense of the word, owe man something? Is there any real difference between such a hypothesis and the ideal of "rational sufficiency" against which, when it first reared its head clearly in a Christian society, about the beginning of the thirteenth century, "the Christian soul felt an immediate shock of horror, as faced with the concupiscence of the mind, which was the completion of original sin"?[78]

The two kinds of theory we have been looking at in turn do not merely differ in a few details. It is not simply a question of degree. It would be a euphemism to say of those who have followed them that they "are far from having arrived at complete agreement," and it may be asking the impossible of a theologian to tell him, in face of these mutually contradictory explanations, that he "has no right to treat them as illegitimate or illusory."[79] For if he in fact tends towards accepting one, he can hardly help to that extent rejecting the other. They diverge from the start, and seem totally opposed in spirit. These two "purely natural" universes, whose respective protagonists seem, in addition, quite [p. 49] unaware of one another, and which are each presented to us in turn as representing almost the whole of theological thought—for one will be put forward as being the opinion "of most of the scholastics" while the other claims to be the only opinion accepted by "the theologians"—can only be seen as being in almost every way the antithesis of each other. No doubt I shall be accused from both sides of taking an extreme view; and I would certainly agree. I would not claim that any given theologian is so totally committed intellectually to either—although some of the texts I have quoted are in themselves rather disturbing. But my wish here is to draw attention to difficulties which seem to me quite real. As soon as one begins actually to put into words the idea one has been vaguely forming of this "pure nature" with a purely natural destiny, it becomes hard not to fall into one or the other of these two opposing excesses. Otherwise, as I have said, one is left with only a formal hypothesis, quite legitimate, perhaps, but almost empty of meaning, and quite

[78] M. D. Chenu, *op. cit.*, 31.

[79] L. Malevez, *Nouvelle revue théologique* (1953): 689.

incapable of becoming the basis for any kind of system: it presents a human nature of which we can only say, with Père E. Brisbois, that it is "materially" different from the nature known to us,[80] and the absence of any perceptible link between that hypothetical nature and our concrete humanity in regard to the point at issue makes the hypothesis an unusable one.

In these circumstances, it is surely "more simple and reasonable" to return, as I propose, to the earlier position which is hampered by no such hypothesis. Without dogmatically denying that there may be other [p. 50] possibilities, without rejecting any abstract hypothesis which might be a good way of making certain truths more vivid to us, it is surely "more simple and reasonable," when working out a theological doctrine, not to try to get away from reality as we know it. That is, of course, provided that we show—as we must in any case, though without claiming to give a complete elucidation where the mystery is concerned—how one may try to think of the utter gratuitousness of God's gift, that supreme gift which is none other than himself; provided also that we show intelligibly how God can never be under any obligation, any sort of requirement, to give himself to the being he has made, as is clear from the most elementary and basic Christian teaching, recalled in our own day in Pius XII's encyclical *Humani Generis.*[81]

This is what I tried to do first in a quick sketch at the end of my historical study, *Le Surnaturel.* Written in haste at the request of various people, the sketch was in fact too rapid. It was not intended to treat of the whole problem of the supernatural, and indeed only touched on the major lines of it. On the one question it was

[80] Cf. E. Brisbois, S.J., "Le désir de voir Dieu et la métaphysique du vouloir selon saint Thomas" [The desire to see God and the metaphysics of willing in Aquinas], *Nouvelle revue théologique* 63 (1936): 1105: "Prior to any exterior call, the divine call echoes in the depths of human nature and inspires in it a new will which has not been the subject of deliberation. . . . Thus man's call to supernatural perfection materially modifies human nature. . . ." That profound need which characterizes him thenceforth "would never have existed in the will left to its natural conditions." And again, pp. 1109–10: "The psychology of human desire is completely changed."

[81] "Others corrupt the 'gratuity' of the supernatural order, when they assert that God cannot create beings endowed with intellect without ordaining and calling them to the beatific vision." [The reference is pointed because some presumed that this document censured de Lubac's own *Surnaturel.*—Ed.]

concerned with, more than one theologian found it convincing,[82] and a great many declared their positive agreement with me.[83] I received some detailed objections to things I actually said in it, and have taken careful account of these, for which I should like here to thank their authors. The misunderstandings and misconstructions —some of them truly astonishing—which have been put upon it have been sufficiently dealt with by others,[84] and I [p. 51] hope that they will be obvious enough to the attentive reader to make it unnecessary to recall them all. I shall do so only in so far as it is indispensable if further misunderstandings are to be prevented. A few pages of conclusion, however, could not possibly illuminate every aspect of so major and complex a question. They require not merely revision, but completion. That is why, without repeating what had already been said, I presented some further reflections, laying more explicit stress on the "twofold gratuitousness," the "twofold initiative," or the "twofold gift" of God, in an article in *Recherches de science religieuse* published in 1949, following upon the approval and encouragement I received from Rome itself. People whose opinion is worth having have considered the article a useful

---

[82] One may indicate, for instance, the important account by Dom M. Cappuyns, in the *Bulletin de théologie ancienne et médiévale* 924 (Oct. 1947): 251–54; he essentially approves my historical positions, especially the interpretations I put forward of Thomas' teaching. See also G. Philips, in *Erasmus*, I, n. 5 (March 1947), p. 263: "Père de Lubac's demonstration is sound and illuminating. . . . He in no way compromises the gratuitousness of grace . . . , etc." Cf. Antoine Chavasse, *Revue du moyen âge latin* (1946), pp. 352–54; P. Kreling, in *Jaarboek*, 1949; etc.

[83] In a profound study, Anton C. Pegis, President of the Pontifical Institute of Medieval Studies in Toronto, declared his agreement with me, and Gerard Smith, S.J., concluded with only one objection: that I have not affirmed strongly enough the fact that my conclusions are completely based on the premises of St. Thomas (*Proceedings of the American Catholic Philosophical Association* 23 [Boston, 19–20 April, 1949]); *Philosophy and Finality* (Washington, 1949); G. Smith, "The Natural End of Man," pp. 47–61; A. C. Pegis, "Some Reflections on the Problem of the End of Man," pp. 62–79.

[84] See in particular the critical study by Victor White, O.P., "The Supernatural," *Dominican Studies* 2 (Jan. 1949): 62, n. 1: "Quite a number of the more vigorous attacks have been directed against opinions which seem to have been conjured up by the attackers, and will be sought in vain in the book itself"; and again: "It is noteworthy that his thesis seems to have a sympathetic echo particularly among those who approach the subject from his own fields of specialized studies . . ."; and p. 70: "I think his case is far stronger than his critics recognize. He has himself forestalled a number of criticisms in a quite satisfactory manner, and others totally miss the target they are aiming at."

and illuminating one. [p. 52] Others, though equally friendly, have asked for still further elucidation. I therefore decided, in answer to a great many requests, to reformulate and develop the argument in this book. Without the ambition, which I also did not have then, to say the last word on the subject, or even to cover every aspect of it, I will therefore attempt by means of a "calm disputation" [*serena disputatio*],[85] and as the ancients said, *gumnastikōs* [athletically],[86] to take my study somewhat further. I believe that it is possible to do so, as St. Augustine says, "in catholic peace by a peaceful zeal."[87] And it is to this end that I shall start by asking the theologians who base everything on the modern hypothesis of "pure nature," those who, so to say, place their trust in that and that alone, this simple question: Do you think that this hypothesis, as you present it, even were it basically sound, is really useful here? And again: Do you above all think that it is completely adequate, for any even remotely exacting mind, to achieve the end which all of us who profess the same faith agree in proposing to ourselves?

---

[85] St. Augustine, *De duabus animabus* [Concerning two souls], c. 2, n. 2. . . .

[86] Cf. Clement of Alexandria, *Stromata* [Miscellany] 5, c. 1, 11, n. 1 and 4: "Casting aside all party spirit, all jealousy and argumentativeness . . . faith must go forward, not in laziness, but with every effort to discover the truth."

[87] St. Augustine, *De Trinitate* [On the Trinity], bk. 2, c. 9, n. 16. . . .

## A Meditation on the Principle of the Moral Life

*De Lubac is not usually thought of as a moral theologian. In fact, a significant amount of his writing addresses morality. In his scriptural exegesis, one of the four senses of Scripture is the moral, or tropological, sense, by which the reference of the text is turned around so that the text addresses the reader rather than itself. In the text here presented, de Lubac offers a more systematic exposition of moral theology, rooted in his fundamental theology of the supernatural. For him, the personal turning around that constitutes the fact of morality cannot be isolated from the life of faith. Morality is grounded in the supernatural as concretely experienced by human consciousness through reflection. Although this might initially be revealed as a law to which obedience is due under threat of sanction, it is more fundamentally felt and internalized, awakening, purifying, enlarging, and deepening the sense of duty that already exists in humanity, and leading it, through assent, to love.*

*This article, which was among de Lubac's first, appeared in the* Revue apologétique *in 1937. Published before he became well known or controversial, it did not attract much attention. However, it provides a remarkably succinct account of his moral theology, which is indissolubly linked with the act of faith. Especially notable is the debt acknowledged to Maurice Blondel, who had mentored several other Jesuits of de Lubac's generation and earlier. For reasons of prudence, the controversial Roman Catholic lay philosopher is named only once. However, de Lubac's whole understanding of the doctrine of the supernatural developed with reference to Blondel's work and in correspondence with him.*[88] *De Lubac had read Blondel's* Action, *his* Letter on Apologetics, *and other studies, during his time at the Jesuit philosophate on Jersey, as an antidote to the formal curriculum of neo-Thomism. Furthermore, during a trip to Aix-en-Provence, in 1922, he had visited Blondel. In a letter to Blondel, he writes that the latter's "philosophical work had paved the way" for his own theology of the supernatural.*[89] *Moreover, as discussed in the introduction, the very first volume of de Lubac's collected works,* The Discovery of God, *is Blondelian in its orientation.*

---

[88] De Lubac, *At the Service*, 18–19, 183–88.

[89] Letter of April 8, 1932, in ibid., 187.

# I

[p. 418] Doing justice to our divine vocation, in all its grandeur and in all its commanding urgency, is essentially a matter of seeing one thing: Although the resonance and the form of the call differ in each soul, the call itself is not a particular one. In itself, it does not behave as if it were a special obligation added to a whole host of others. It is not a new duty that, at some arbitrary point in our lives, takes its place in the succession of duties that make up our vocation as human beings.

Using today's theological vocabulary, we could say that the obligation to the "supernatural," precisely because of its incommensurability with every other obligation—after all, the supernatural is not only infinitely above man, but also above every nature that could be imagined—is our fundamental obligation. Inscribed in the inmost depths of that real human being who is each one of us, it is the law of our concrete condition. To be sure, [p. 419] it does not furnish us right away with an objective catalog of all of its demands or give a clear-cut view of its end—just as we do not know from the outset everything that nature itself is. In this sense, it leaves room, both in the life of each individual and in the development of humanity, for every sort of progress, "invention," and inspiration, even for revelation itself. We can even say that it always remains anonymous, that it is never the direct focus of attention, even in the lives of authentic Christians. But that is precisely the point: It is already this obligation whose commanding presence we feel in every detail of the moral life, in every duty, even when understood in the rudest or humblest way—just as, according to St. Thomas, it is already the soul that performs the most elementary functions of vegetative life. From the moment consciousness awakens, it is this obligation that tacitly [*secrètement*] guides all the steps by which duty is purified, enlarged, and deepened both in its object and in its form. It is this obligation that guarantees the unity of the moral life under its most diverse guises and throughout its most far-flung stages; that secures spiritual progress against all opposition, sometimes even against

---

Excerpted from "A Meditation on the Principle of the Moral Life", trans. Adrian Walker, *Communio* 26 (1999): 418–28.

resistance in the name of its past achievements; that, lifting humanity above animal life and, from the very beginning, raising it beyond itself, constitutes it in the expectation of divinizing it.[90]

Now, in proportion as this obligation molds man, it tends to reveal its hidden essence. In proportion as it unveils its ideal, it loses the mask it had to wear for the sake of the initial training of the human animal—the mask of a harsh external constraint, of a positive code commanding or forbidding certain particular actions, of a law threatening with arbitrary sanctions. In being [p. 420] interiorized, it becomes all the more demanding. But the obedience that it requires increasingly takes the form of an assent.[91] Thereupon it reveals its true nature as an attraction, the attraction of the Supreme Good. Then, in the final stage, it reveals itself—more intimately, more particularly—as the attraction of Supreme Love: "*Dilexi Te*" [I have loved thee], as a personal vocation within the great vocation in which all share, the creative call of a personal Love. From behind the order imposed by the Law there appears the face of the living God, who searches for his creature and, having made it according to his image, invites it to become his likeness. And the—sometimes terrible—sweetness of this revelation leads to an ever deeper real-

---

[90] Humanity is thus constituted by this thrust [*élan*] that lifts it above nature, like a powerful surge always at high tide. For this reason, we must translate Kant's "love and respect humanity in yourself" into "raise up humanity in yourself," that is to say, imitate God. Indeed, we can add with the boldness that revelation allows us: "Become God by loving him." This is the only commandment. *Prius intenditur deiformis quam homo* [Before treating him as man, you treat him as godlike].

[91] To the same extent it therefore ushers in a higher freedom—and will do so in proportion as the precepts of the positive law increasingly become means. At the extreme, in the state of perfect freedom brought about by perfect obedience, obligation disappears, since it was never anything but a liberating constraint for the sake of this state of freedom. As Augustine puts it: "*Non obligatio, sed delectatio*" [not obligation, but delectation] (*In Joannem tract.* [Lectures on John], 26).

See also the wonderful text from Augustine's *Contra Faustum* [Against Faustus], 1.22, c.27: "*Sancti ad sublimes angeli habent contemplationem et actionem suam: id enim sibi agendum imperant, quod ille contemplandum iubet, cuius aeterno imperio liberaliter quia suaviter serviunt*" [The holy angels on high have a contemplation and action of their own: They command themselves to do what he (God), whose eternal kingdom they serve freely, because with delight, orders them to contemplate]. By contrast, the soul that does not love God, that refuses to obey him, is a slave: "*obligata amore terreno*" [bound by earthly love] (*Enarratio in psalm.* [Expositions of the Psalms], 121, n. 1); "*obligata vitiis*" [bound by vices] (Gregory the Great, *Moral. in Job* [Morals on the Book of Job], 1,1). . . .

ization that obedience has to be more than assent, that this assent has to be a return of love. Such love has to be a gift, the gift of oneself, and the more heartrending this gift is, the more joy springs from it; the more total it is, the higher it raises the personal life of the giver, divinizing and eternalizing him.

Such, then, are the principal stages in which this sacred "*nisus*" [impulsion], which urges all creation to come home to the bosom of the eternal Trinity to find its definitive firmness and stability—"*solidabor in Te, Deus meus*" [I shall be made firm in you, my God][92] —unfolds from the time it begins to awaken consciousness. Everything in the universe proceeds from its impulsion; everything gets its explanation in this divine Will, whose sovereign freedom for us is at first fixed in natures; [p. 421] everything is shaken because of this call and this gift, this pure gratuity, which first present themselves to us in the guise of necessities and demands.

## II

God is love. These three words of the apostle John,[93] upon which the Christian Tradition has never ceased commenting, do not simply account for the whole of reality, as we have just seen that they do. In explaining our destiny, they also put in our hands the key to giving a rational foundation to the moral life, while rescuing us from the clutches both of the *pure obligation* found in Kant's concept of duty and from the *pure factuality* expressed in Pascal's dictum: "*nous sommes embarqués*" [we are (people) already underway].[94]

We must admit, in fact, that the first awakening is a rude one—if not the first awakening of consciousness, which is characterized by a naive spontaneity, at least the first awakening of reflection. All at once we realize that we are out at sea. We are already underway [*embarqués*]—without having wanted or known it—towards a destination that we must execute a thousand troublesome and risky maneuvers to reach. And—I am about to state a paradox, the greatest

[92] [Augustine, *Confessions*, 11, 30 (40).—Ed.]

[93] [1 Jn 4:8, 4:16.—Ed.]

[94] [Blaise Pascal (1623–1662) was a French scholar and theologian with links to Jansenism who died young due to poor health.—Ed.]

of them all, one that raises the most serious problems once we have caught sight of it—this destination is inflexibly demanding. It does not even grant us the right to decide not to reach it, it condemns whatever impotent wish we might have to return to the haven from which we set sail!

To say it without the aid of metaphor: Right from the start we have to confront a fact that we cannot do anything about: We exist, and our existence is already underway. We run up against the obligation to submit to the moral law. There is no option but to accept these things at first as they are. But this acceptance, though still external, can only be temporary and, in a sense, conditional. Indeed, if they were not subsequently justified, understood, and, by the same token, interiorized, this fact [of existence] and this raw obligation would not be just an open [p. 422] wound for us —which is what they are, without hope of cure, as long as Life has not fully triumphed—but a violation, a scandal. Now, the very idea that this could be so is intolerable. True, it would be prideful to balk at this necessary fact, under the sole pretext that we were born without our knowledge or consent, or to rebel against duty because our spontaneous yearnings make us feel out of tune with it. But conscience could never waive its rights, even for the sake (apparently) of submitting more readily. Neither the intelligence nor the will [has] the right, or even the physical ability, to suffer violence. If their need to be able to agree were destined to remain unsatisfied, then we would have the right to rebel. Indeed, let us dare to utter this seeming blasphemy, whose real target is only an idol: We would have to curse God.

In order to claim exemption from obedience, one would, in Saint Thomas's profound phrase, "have to be able to claim exemption from being."[95] This is the strongest imaginable formula for underscoring ontological necessity, the radical dependence which is at the origin of moral obligation in every free creature. Yet this does not resolve the whole problem, for we have not yet explained the specifically *moral* character of obligation. For if I do not consent to being,

[95] *Summa Contra Gentiles*, 1.3, c.1: *"Nec est aliquid quod ab eius regimine excusetur, sicut nec est aliquid quod ab ipso esse non sortiatur"* [There is nothing that can claim exemption from his rule, just as there is also nothing that does not get being from him]. . . .

if being is simply forced on me, why is it not enough for me to force myself to obey? Must, indeed, can my submission be something to which I consent as well? I find myself embarked upon the ocean of life: But I ought to consent to my embarkation. I am rooted in the soil of being, but I have to [p. 423] transform this rootedness by a loving and free assent—a completely interior process, a "*fiat*" that is purely mine, that no necessity preempts. Now, it would be saying too little if I merely admitted that all of this leaves me with a nagging uneasiness, for not only have I failed to satisfy myself, I have not even begun to satisfy God. I have not yet paid him the only homage that is worthy of him—and of myself. I have simply remained bent under the yoke. I can render this homage only if reflection enables me to discover in myself, beneath the appearance of servitude, a natural consent that mediates between pure necessity and freedom in the strict sense, an original assent springing from being itself, which the entire role of my free will is to ratify, whatever the cost—this, I think, is the full meaning locked in Thomas' tightly packed formula. In a word, my entire moral life depends on the fact that the Being that gives me being is not a tyrant, that there is something in me that responds to his call, even more, that this call comes from that deep region which is more mine even than myself. In other words, everything depends on my being able to see, or at least to glimpse obscurely, the pure Love that lies behind the figure of the absolute Master.[96]

[96] Cf. M. Blondel, *L'Action*, 1 (1936), 25: "Pascal observed that we are already underway [*nous sommes embarqués*]. It follows that we must reach land at all costs. Now, in order to present a solution, one that is luminously evident and good, it is not enough to read off a list of compelling demands, which would only provoke a deep-seated protest. Rather, it is necessary to justify this constraint itself, by showing not only that it is just because it is rational, but also that it is intelligible because it is good and because the very ones who suffer it cannot help saying yes as soon as they catch sight of the fullness of meaning and excellence it contains."

See also, L. Lavelle, "Être et Acte" [Being and act], *Revue de Métaphysique et Morale* (1936): 190: "The mystery of Being is not something other than the mystery of our own being; and it is impossible to crack the surface of that mystery until the mind becomes clear-sighted and keen enough to penetrate to the point where we are tied to the Absolute, in other words, to that totally engrossing focal-point wherein we will what we are with an eternal will that bathes each of our particular acts in its light and for which we would joyfully sacrifice everything."

Once I have seen this, I realize that, despite all the protests of my flesh and blood, despite all the soothing reassurances of an illusory experience, rebellion would be rebellion against myself. By rebelling I would be condemning myself to something worse than death: to the deepest, bitterest laceration, to the torments of [p. 424] a never-ending, because impossible, death. How could I say no to God without emptying me, as it were, of myself? "*Deus, interior intimo meo*" [God, more deeply interior to me than I am to myself].[97] An "emancipation" would be the opposite of a liberation, because service is the opposite of slavery. "*Servire Deo, regnare*" [To serve God is to reign].[98]

III

Yet one question remains. By establishing the *general condition* of morality, we have shown that morality is possible in general. But we have not yet shown that it can be realized concretely. In other words, we have yet to identify what might be called the "primitive fact" that will serve reflection as a kind of priming.

To awaken to reflection by an at least provisional ratification of being and of our own life; to set in motion the unfolding of the moral life by an act of humble submission to exigencies whose sacredness inspires in us at first only a constrained respect—all of this is certainly reasonable, and the opposite attitude would be totally unjustifiable. By what right could we dare to assert that, before having made any effort in the realm of thought or of life, we are naturally on an equal footing with Truth, or in a position to judge

[97] [Augustine, *Confessions* 3, 6 (11).—Ed.]

[98] [From Augustine, *Sermons* 64, 3 (PL 39:1867), and a popular medieval motto.—Ed.] Of course, the problem that we are discussing here, while real and fundamental, is nonetheless a bit abstract. Once again, it does not present itself in these terms except to reflex consciousness. Concretely, from the perspective of spontaneous consciousness, there is none of the separation of elements or distinction of phases that were required for the sake of our analysis. *From the very beginning, both of the moral and of the intellectual life, everything is given, even though nothing has yet been "sorted out."* The problem exists, then, but it already contains the solution, at least implicitly, so that, without fully satisfying the intellect's curiosity, it deprives the mind [*esprit*] of any right to avoid dealing with it. There is in our very nature, at the wellspring both of our will and of our intelligence, a "consent to being," which, in a hidden, but real way, works with [*conspire avec*] the moral law and spontaneously justifies obligation.

everything at the bar of our individual tribunal? Is it not actually more natural to assume, if there are some questions that cannot be discussed beforehand, that a question involving our whole being like this must be one of them? Besides, we have every reason to put faith in being. . . . Yet there is something that, more than simply exhorting us to trust humbly from the outset in spite [p. 425] of darkness and constraint, *commands* such humble confidence, which thus loses any resemblance to a favor. This something is, beyond all the reasonable reasons, a sort of interior evidence [*évidence*]. This evidence may not always be easy to perceive clearly, but, once it has been perceived, it can no longer be called into question.

If we can enter into ourselves, we find there a certain disorder of a particular kind: It is as old as our being, runs as deep as its deepest roots, and, as we immediately realize, has no author other than ourselves.[99] We sense that in the inmost core of our will we are not what, at the very same time, we perceive we should be, and we feel that this is true of us personally even before we have performed any particular action. In short, there is an evil in us. It is not identical with us, otherwise we could not judge it to be an evil, but *it is ours*—and it lies at the origin of the humiliation in which we find ourselves. In the depths of our being there is a dis-accord preventing us from being attuned to the demands of what ought to be. There is a secret division within being, and we are its secret accomplices. Let us repudiate this complicity, reject this darkness, and begin to restore harmony within ourselves: Only then will we have the right to demand clarity and to refuse anything that claims our obedience but clashes with our reason or even simply fails to attract us in some way. Of course, we are talking about a life-long project, and the first step will not be completed before our death. But once we have taken the first halting step, perhaps we will already get a glimpse of the dawn and a foretaste of the state of perfect freedom.

---

[99] Not that each individual is, in this sense, the creator of his own disorder. But, while an objective analysis of the individual's awakening to the moral life discerns only the twofold weight of biology and the corrupting influence of society, reflection enables us to reach a deeper level of truth. From this point of view, what is true of humanity can be said of each of its members, and in every spirit, however limited in other respects or imperfectly detached from matter, there is already the whole of spirit—and all spirits.

[p. 426] We lament our wretchedness, but should we not direct our complaint against ourselves? Is not our first duty to acknowledge this? Although this duty is more subtly humiliating than any other, we cannot really look upon it as such. This is one duty at least that we impose upon ourselves in the full light of day.[100] Right from the beginning, the night is pierced by a tiny point of light, which is the initial form of a "*scintilla cordis*" [light in the heart][101] that our darkness can never entirely extinguish. We know that there is an evil in us, an evil that is ours: This is the *light shrouded in mystery*. Nor are we entirely bowed beneath the yoke. Once we have recognized our duty to free ourselves from this evil, it is we who lay it upon ourselves. The rest will follow. Will it follow to our complete satisfaction? It is too soon to tell, but the experience of others lets us anticipate the answer: Is there anyone who has ever regretted putting his faith in being and surrendering to duty? Can anyone name one saint who was sorry for taking [p. 427] the path that he did? But in any case: Although it is both impossible and undesirable to remove this (analogous) risk from the beginning of the moral life, whose full development in fact depends on it, at least we will have avoided any vicious circle.

Since God is charity, that is, pure generosity, we cannot really come to know him as the God of our soul except by taking, or at least trying to take, a generous step ourselves. Laberthonnière[102] used to place a lot of stress, and rightly so, on this essential point, which is also just an application of the old principle that like is known by like. The eye, the ancients would say, would not open

[100] This statement, as well as those that follow, should not be interpreted in any way that might smack of semi-Pelagianism. In saying that we lay this duty upon ourselves, I do not mean to claim that it is not imposed upon us at the same time, indeed, principally by God, or, on the other hand, that we do not also lay upon ourselves all our other duties when the time comes to do so. But that is just the point: This necessary autonomy—which is compatible with the acknowledgment of God's supreme authority—is realized at the beginning of the moral life only in a privileged instance that can therefore serve moral philosophy as a "primitive fact."

[101] [The title of a popular eight-day retreat guide by the German Jesuit Nicolas Elffen (1626–1706), based on Ignatius of Loyola's classic thirty-day *Spiritual Exercises* (Cologne, 1672). Jesuits typically make the eight-day retreat annually.—Ed.]

[102] [Lucien Laberthonnière (1860–1932) was a French priest and theologian with Modernist sympathies, whose work was formally condemned (1913).—Ed.]

to the light if it were not luminous itself. "*In lumine tuo videbimus lumen*" [in your light we shall see light].[103] "But," an exacting critic might ask, "you urge me to take this step, yet how are you going to convince me to do it, assuming that before I take it I still do not know whether this God of generosity exists or whether the Principle of the universe is blind or evil?" The truth of the matter is that this generous step—which has to be the preliminary step only because the darkness within veils God's face from us—is preceded, prepared, and inaugurated by a *step in sincerity*. There is no leap in the dark, no wager. Not even the most exacting reason can object. Whoever does not want to take the path of salvation has only one option: To refuse to enter first of all into himself, to lie to himself because he does not want to humble himself, not before unknown forces that hem him in on every side—strictly speaking, he would be within his rights if that were so—but before himself, in his own eyes, and on his own testimony. His only option, then, is to assert his own righteousness. But such an assertion has nothing to do with logic.

It has been said that conscience [*conscience*] awakens in sin. At the very least one could say with more certainty that, upon reflection, it becomes aware of itself, from the outset, as a consciousness [*conscience*] of sin.[104] A happy knowledge, a happy [p. 428] shame! God, who does not simply bring some good out of some evil, but, in virtue of a power more marvelous than even the power to create, brings *the Good* out of *the Evil*, raises us up by this means. In fact, we have here the most paradoxical instance of the idea that so captivated Pascal: Our misery is always at the origin of our grandeur.

---

[103] [Ps 36:9.—Ed.]

[104] It is well-known that Hegel—whose dialectic translates into abstract language very real human problems—saw *unhappy consciousness* [*conscience malheureuse*] as a kind of starting-point for the whole speculative enterprise. More precisely, it is the *guilty conscience* [*conscience*] where, in my opinion, we have to locate the starting-point of the moral life. It is also well-known that the intellectual matrix of Kant's religious philosophy, which "was decisive for its entire development," was the idea of "radical evil" (cf. V. Delbos, *La philosophie pratique de Kant* [Kant's practical philosophy], 684).

Is not the shock that hits my conscience when it realizes its sinfulness also a sort of reagent that brings out, by contrast, the good that lies more deeply in it and that attunes me to Goodness itself? It is in this way that the intellect, although naturally metaphysical, nonetheless affirms being only because of a first movement of opposition or refusal.

The mysterious first moment of conscience is a fruitful misery indeed! *Felix culpa*! [Happy fault!][105] Does the attraction of God's love no longer fascinate us? Are we in danger—because we ourselves are evil—of seeing in it nothing but a tyrannous command against which we want to rebel? It is at that very moment that we become aware of our sin, which makes us lower our proud heads. And so we have made the first step on the way of acceptance, which will be the way of liberation. "*Iam illuminari coepisti, quia inest confessio*" [You have already begun to be enlightened because there is confession in you].[106]

It is then that the very fact which tempted us to rebellion—"I never asked to be born"—will become a reason for eternal thanksgiving: "We did not seek God, it is he who sought us."[107]

---

[105] [A phrase from the Exsultet, which is sung at the Vigil Mass of Easter Sunday, which refers to the sin of Adam and Eve preceding the redeeming work of Christ and, in this sense, making the latter possible.—Ed.]

[106] Saint Augustine, *In epist. primam Joannis* [On 1 John], tract. 1, n. 6.

We should make it clear that here, too, we are conducting a reflexive, rather than a psychological, analysis. On the psychological level, there would be more grounds for arguing that the consciousness of sin does not become acute until one has first become aware of God's holiness—just as the appeal to revelation becomes evident only on account of revelation itself. "The more you expiate them, the more you will know them. . . ."

[107] Nicholas Cabasilas [The life in Christ] (PG 150, 504).

# 5

# The Eucharist and Scripture

## Corpus Mysticum

*The ninth century saw a major debate about the theological interpretation of the Eucharist. The archdeacon Florus opposed the allegorical liturgical exegesis of the prelate Amalar of Metz with a more literalist interpretation of Christ's real and objective sacrificial presence as directly bringing salvation. An overlapping debate was centered on the abbey of Corbie in northern France, where Paschasius Radbertus, the abbot, was opposed by the younger monk Ratramnus. In this instance, it was the senior party to the dispute who maintained the stronger sense of substantial presence. Whereas Paschasius argued that Christ's body and blood were substantially present in the elements by consecration, Ratramnus understood their presence spiritually.*

*In 1937, while teaching at the Catholic Theological Faculty in Lyon, de Lubac was called upon to examine a thesis written by Father Paul Duc on Florus'* Exposition of the Mass. *In preparation, he reviewed the work of liturgists such as those just referred to and was struck by the shifting interpretations of the body of Christ, under the Latin term* corpus mysticum. *This provided him with the beginnings of his study with the same title. He describes "unravelling the exact sense of the words, tracking down their origin and following their destiny amid dusty texts" as a "painstaking task", which he continued during convalescence from an illness and completed just before the outbreak of the Second World War.*[1] *The fighting delayed the book's appearance until 1944, although it was first published in installments in the journal* Recherches de science religieuse.

---

[1] *Corpus Mysticum: The Eucharist and the Church in the Middle Ages*, trans. Gemma Simmonds with Richard Price and Christopher Stephens (London: SCM, 2006), xxiii; also Henri de Lubac, *At the Service of the Church: Henri de Lubac Reflects on the Circumstances that Occasioned His Writings*, trans. Anne Elizabeth Englund (San Francisco: Ignatius Press, 1993), 28–30.

## *The Eucharist as Mystical Body*

[p. 13] In the thinking of the whole of Christian antiquity, the Eucharist and the Church are linked. In St. Augustine, in the context of the Donatist controversy,[2] this link is given especially particular force, and this can also be said of the Latin writers of the seventh century, eighth century and ninth century. For them, as for Augustine, on whom they are dependent either directly or through other writers, and whose formulations they endlessly reproduce, the Eucharist corresponds to the Church as cause to effect, as means to end, as sign to reality. However, they make the transition from the *sacrament* to the *power of the sacrament* or from *visible form* to the *reality itself* so swiftly, and place the accent so strongly on the Church that if, in an explanation of the mystery of the Eucharist, we encounter the unqualified phrase "the body of Christ", it is often not the Eucharist but the Church which is meant by the term.

Here, for example, is St. Ildephonsus of Toledo (+ 669). In chapter 137 of his *De cognitione baptismi* [*On the Knowledge of Baptism*], he sets out to comment on the affirmation of faith, "*bread is the body of Christ*". Seeking understanding, faith enquires: "*How is bread his body?*" Ildephonsus then replies:

> *What is seen has bodily form; what is perceived mentally has spiritual fruit. Therefore if you want to grasp mentally the body of Christ, listen to the Apostle saying to the faithful, You are the body and members of Christ. . . . Though many, we are one bread, one body.*[3]

[p. 14] Not that Ildephonsus, or the writer from whom he takes his inspiration[4] and who is himself repeating an Augustinian formulation,[5] is thinking of denying the sacramental presence from which this "spiritual fruit" will be the result, any more than by "under-

---

Excerpted from *Corpus Mysticum*, trans. Gemma Simmonds with Richard Price and Christopher Stephens (London: SCM, 2006), 13–19, 248–62.

[2] [This fourth-century dispute in North Africa concerned whether to accept (back into the Church) Christians who had renounced their faith under persecution. The Donatists refused to accept the authority and ministry of clergy who had done so.—Ed.]

[3] PL, 96, 169 D. . . .

[4] It would appear that *De cognitione baptismi* is an adaptation of the *Liber responsionum* (now lost) of Justinian of Valence (c. 640). . . .

[5] Augustine, *Sermo* 272. . . .

standing" he is eliminating the need for faith. As much as Augustine himself, and as much as his nearer master, St. Isidore of Seville,[6] as well as his compatriot Gregory of Elvira,[7] he knows that in order to remain in this body of Christ, which is the holy Church, we must achieve true participation, through the sacrament, in the first body of Christ.[8] But no more than they does Augustine remain so fixated on the Eucharistic presence as to formulate an independent concept of it. "He discovers real union with Christ, not so much through the medium of the real presence, but through the medium of the sign, and this union is not so much individual union as that of individuals among one another in Christ."[9] By a mental process which faithfully reproduces that of the great African doctor, and which finds analogies with more than one of the Greek [p. 15] fathers, Ildephonsus is therefore immediately looking to the "spiritual fruit". It is this alone which he is envisaging and analysing.

His contemporaries and his first successors most often follow him in this. In the following century Florus of Lyon is one example. He was a faithful Augustinian, very much on his guard against anything that could pass for an innovation. In his commentary on the Mass he took up again the formulation already given by Ildephonsus: "*What is seen is one thing, and what is grasped is another; what is seen, etc. . . .*"[10] He repeats it again in one of his tracts against Amalarius, and in order to describe "the saving and heavenly mystery" of the altar, he writes: "*Moreover the bread of the holy offering is the body of Christ not in matter or visible form but in power and spiritual potency.*"[11] Neither for him nor for any of the authors of that time who speak in the same way was the real presence of the Eucharist truly in question. They are certainly neither "dynamists" nor "symbolists" in the explicitly

---

[6] *De ecclesiasticis officiis* [On Church liturgies], Bk. 1, c. 18, no. 8: "He ought not to separate himself from the medicine of the Lord's body, lest . . . he be separated from the body of Christ. . . . For it is manifest that they live who taste his body." . . . These are formulations that derive from St. Cyprian, *De oratione dominica* [On the Lord's Prayer], c. 18. . . .

[7] *Tractatus* [Tractate] 17. . . .

[8] *Op. cit.*, c. 136. . . .

[9] F. van der Meer, *Sacramentum chez Saint Augustin* [Sacramentum in Saint Augustine], in *La Maison-Dieu* 13, p. 61.

[10] *Expositio missae* [Exposition of the Mass], c. 62, n. 5. . . .

[11] *Adversus Amalarium* [Against Amalar] 1. . . .

restrictive sense that is commonly given to those words by historians of dogma. How could they forget the claims made so clearly by their great forebears, claims that they could not avoid quoting in their *florilegia* [anthologies] or making reference to, either in prose or in verse? Above all, how could they contradict this *lex orandi* [rule of prayer], which was finding such powerful expression in that era of the flowering of liturgy in the West?

> *Come, you saints, and receive the body of Christ,*
> *Drinking the sacred blood by which you are redeemed.*[12]

[p. 16] Many of them were taught through a prayer from the Gregorian sacramentary to pray "so that they may be counted members of the one whose body and blood we share."[13] Like Jonas of Orleans, they also knew how to say: "*We are the Temples of Christ, where his flesh and blood are sacrificed*",[14] or even sometimes to repeat after Amalarius: "*Here we believe that the simple nature of bread and mingled wine are changed into a rational nature, namely, of the body and blood of Christ.*"[15] None of them would have been surprised at the verses which St. Remigius, according to his historiographer Hincmar, had had engraved on a chalice:

> *Let the people draw from the sacred blood they receive*
> *The life which the eternal Christ poured from his wound.*[16]

From time to time they also went so far as to distinguish explicitly between two sorts of participation in Christ. The unity of the body that they all received in communion appeared to them as the sign and promise of the unity of the body, which they themselves must form. Nevertheless, this was not yet the era of logic-chopping, of objective curiosity, nor even, at least among the first of them, of the necessary struggles to ensure that the conditions for the efficacy of the sacrament were met. For them, the consecrated bread was certainly the body of Christ—the expressions *sacramentum corporis*

---

[12] Antiphonary of Bangor (seventh century).

[13] Lietzmann, n. 58, 3, p. 36. . . .

[14] *De institutione regia* [On princely rule], c. 13; c. 16. . . .

[15] *Liber officialis* [On the liturgy] 4, c. 24 (PL, 105, 1141 A–B).

[16] Hincmar, *Vita Remigii* [Life of Saint Remigius] (. . . *Scriptorum rerum merovingicarum*, vol. 3, p. 262).

[sacrament of the body] and *corpus* [body] alternated from their pens without any appreciable nuance to their sense—but what they saw from the very beginning in this bread was a figure of the Church:

> *Therefore he took the bread: he wanted this sacrament to involve bread since bread bears a likeness to his Church . . .*[17]

[p. 17] Thus the *bread of the sacrament* led them directly to the *unity of the body*. In their eyes the Eucharist was essentially, as it was already for St. Paul and for the Fathers, the *mystery of unity*, it was the *sacrament of conjunction, alliance, and unification.*[18] It was given to us "*to unite our race*".[19] Was this not the truth inculcated in us by several of its rites and by the terms which described them, such as the word "collect", to which Amalarius alerts us as having been given to the first prayer of the Mass, "*because it begins by binding the people into one?*"[20]

Is this not what is clearly signified by its other name of "communion"? The *synaxis*, that is to say the mystery of communion.[21] So, at least, it is understood by the commentator of Auxerre writing on the First Letter to the Corinthians:

> [p. 18] *Therefore the sacrament of the body of Christ is called supper because of the communion, since it ought to be celebrated in common by all the faithful and righteous. For the one bread signifies the wholeness of the Church.*[22]

I could certainly also cite more than one case, in Christian antiquity, where *communio*—together with the Greek κοινώνια [*koinonia*]—

[17] Candidus of Fulda, *De passione Domini* [On the Passion of our Lord], c. 5. . . .

[18] Etherius and Beatus, *Ad Elipandum* [Against Elipandus] (in 785) (PL, 96, 941 D). . . . Up to and including the thirteenth century, such expressions would be common; it is because it was *the sacrament of unity, the sacrament of fellowship* that, in the eyes of a certain number of theologians, schismatics could not have the Eucharist, since they had placed themselves outside that unity, outside that fellowship. . . .

[19] Paschasius Radbertus, *Liber de corpore et sanguine Domini* [The Lord's Body and Blood], c. 10. . . .

[20] Amalarius, *Eclogae de officio missae* [Selections on the liturgy of the Mass] (PL, 105, 1327 D). . . .

[21] . . . Clement of Alexandria, *Strom.* [Miscellanies], 3, c. 4. . . .

[22] *In I Cor* [On 1 Cor], XI (PL, 117 . . .). . . .

implies no other idea except that of the reception of the sacrament.[23] We can nevertheless be sure that, as Duguet has written,[24] "in the ancient custom of the Church there was no separation between reconciliation and participation in the sacraments, and when penitents were judged to have been made righteous, they were given the Eucharist, in such a way that communion signified both one and the other", that is to say, according to the context, either one or the other, or more often still, both at the same time. From this derives the complex sense encountered in many expressions such as "*to receive communion*", "*to be reconciled by communion*", "*to be separated from communion*", "*to be excluded from communion*", etc.[25] In their turn this is also the origin of discussions by several historians who, in varying degrees of over-enthusiasm, find differences of interpretation where the original documents present them as a unity. In addition, even in the context of the Eucharist, it is not unusual to find *communio* meaning union with the Church, the "*fellowship of Christians*" or the "*catholic communion*"[26] rather [p. 19] than the actual receiving of the sacrament.[27] When there is a desire to distinguish reception from the effect which it is the sacrament's mission to express and bring about, there is often recourse to certain subtle nuances of language. For example, instead of *communio*, we often find instead *communicatio*: thus, in the work of Walafrid Strabo, the first of these two words indicates the bond within the body of the Church, whereas the second is reserved for the act of sacramental communion.[28] Does not the derivation of both these nouns, from the single verb *communicare*, underline in its own way the central truth of this mystery? . . .

---

[23] For example, Jerome, *Ep.* [Letters] 49, n. 15 . . . ; 77, n. 6. . . . Cassian, *Collatio* 23. . . . 1 Cor., 10.16; Acts of the Council in Trullo II. 42. . . .

[24] *Conférences ecclésiastiques* [Ecclesiastical conferences], vol. 1 (Cologne, 1742), p. 287.

[25] The Council of Elvira (v. 300) *passim*. . . . Council of Carthage (348), canon 3, etc. . . .

[26] Possidius, *Vita sancti Augustini* [Life of Saint Augustine], c. 14. . . .

[27] [The Anglican Communion is a modern global example.—Ed.]

[28] *De rebus ecclesiasticis* [On ecclesiastical matters], c. 22.

*Conclusion*

[p. 248] More than anything, this study has shown us why the word *true* supplanted the word *mystical* as a description for the sacramental body. It remains to be seen more precisely why *mystical*, instead of disappearing, took the place of *true* as a description for the ecclesial body.

From the beginning of Christianity, the Eucharist had always been considered in relation to the Church. The "communion of the body of Christ" of which St. Paul spoke to the faithful of Corinth[29] was their mysterious union with the community, by virtue of the sacrament: it was the mystery of one Body formed by all those who shared in the "one Bread". In the same way, from that time on the Church had never ceased to appear linked to the Eucharist. If, for example, we open the *Glossa* [Explanation] on St. Paul, it is not, as might be supposed, with reference to the account of the Last Supper, but with reference to the metaphor of the body, applied by the Apostle to the Christian community, that we read this sentence: "This is the sacrifice of Christians, *so that the many might be one body in Christ.*"[30]

This mutual bond, long perceived as essential, explains the sense of *mystical body* applied to the Church. It is noticeable that it was with reference to the Eucharist that the Church was first given this description; so much so that, in order to study the expression, we have hardly had to leave the Eucharistic context. However, later theologians, who were able to base their teaching on one or two passages from St. Thomas Aquinas, thought that in this case *mystical* was more aptly opposed to *natural*. According to them, it would be more correct to say that "mystical body" was used in contrast to "physical" or natural body. This would appear to be the explanation offered by the Roman Catechism.[31] In itself, this was no mistake; because once the expression was acquired, it is clear that this opposition immediately [p. 249] presented itself, in the way that the *mystical sense* of Scripture is opposed to the *literal sense*. But a temptation developed here, in the case of the Church, precisely as

---

[29] 1 Cor. 10.17–18.

[30] [Walafrid Strabo] *In I Cor.* [On 1 Cor], xii, 3 (PL, 114, 510 D).

[31] P. 1, a. 9, n. 16.

in that of Scripture: the temptation of no longer seeing anything in this metaphor except the metaphor itself, and of considering "mystical" as a watering-down of "real" or of "true". To a greater or lesser extent, many fell victim to it. According to some, "*mystical body*" was merely the same as expressions such as "*the fellowship of Catholics*" or "*the congregation of the faithful*".[32] From that time onwards, there was no group that could not be given this description: that is how Antoine de Rosiers comes to distinguish five principal *mystical bodies*, because, within the assembly of humankind he counts a hierarchy of five societies.[33] Some who remembered that St. Augustine[34] and St. Gregory[35] spoke of a demonic body had no difficulty in speaking in their own turn of a *demonic mystical body*.[36] It is true that other theologians resisted the temptation and protested against such an extensive use of the word, which they considered an abuse. This was the case, in the eighteenth century, with Noel Alexandre;[37] it is the case in our own day with Fr. Prat's interpretation of St. Paul.[38] They do not want the mystical body of Christ to be confused with any sort of "moral entity". There is no doubt that they are right, given that ancient tradition, the faithful interpreter of Scripture, offers us so many ultra-realist statements concerning the ecclesial body. But the temptation itself would have had nowhere to take hold had we been more careful to preserve the original sense of the word that gave rise to this quarrel.

When it was applied to the Eucharist, the *mystical body* meant the *body in mystery*, immediately connected to a *mystery of the body*. [p. 250] From then on it can be understood that during a whole initial period, it seemed natural to distinguish the sacramental body from the historical body, the crucified body: that was to distinguish the sacrament of the Passion from the Passion itself; it did not mean denying the profound identity that it was the sacrament's purpose

---

[32] Philothei Achillini, *Somnium Viridarii* [The dream of the orchard], c. 360. . . .

[33] *Monarchia* [Monarchy], p. 2, c. 6 (Goldast, p. 312).

[34] *De Genesi ad litteram* [The literal interpretation of Genesis], 11, n. 31. . . .

[35] *Moralia in Job* [Morals on the Book of Job], passim. . . .

[36] Thus the author of the titles added to the chapters of *De Genesi ad litteram* [The literal interpretation of Genesis] (PL, 34, 441).

[37] *Theologia dogmatica et moralis* [Dogmatic and moral theology] (1703), vol. 1, p. 50.

[38] *La théologie de saint Paul* [The theology of Saint Paul], vol. 2, 14th ed., p. 344.

to affirm. When the author of the *Opus imperfectum in Matthaeum* [*Incomplete Commentary on Matthew*] wrote, with reference to the vessels on the altar: "*in which not the true body of Christ, but the mystery of his body is contained*",[39] he was not, in his manner of underlining a contrast, giving an exact interpretation of traditional belief. Through the stages that have been described, the expression *mystical body* passed from the Eucharist to the Church: and once again there was, in an analogous sense, a *mystery of the body*. The *mystical body* was the mystery that described this ecclesial body by means of the sacrament, and, in its radical meaning, it could strictly speaking be described as being "contained" in the Eucharist. Then, from the *mystery of the body* it developed into being a *body in [the] mystery*; from the signification itself to the thing signified.

Thus the Church is the mystical body of Christ: that is to say, quite simply, that it is the body of Christ signified by means of the sacrament. *Mystical* is a contraction of *mystically signified, mystically designated*. That is the sense that clearly emerges from the first statement offered to us on the subject in the work of Master Simon: "*In the sacrament of the altar there are two (bodies): that is, the true body of Christ and also* that which it signifies, *his mystical body, which is the Church*."[40]

Is this not a true definition of *mystical*? The generation that preceded Master Simon's had still not reached the definitive version, but there was a definition which heralded it and in some sense called it into being. This is what we find in Gregory of Bergamo. In chapter 18 of his *Treatise*, after quoting St. Paul on the one body formed by all those who share in the one Bread, Gregory writes:

> *That we, though many, are one body, through the life-giving power of the Holy Spirit,* is designated mystically by this sacrament, *and it was clearly expressed in these words by the Apostle.*[41]

[p. 251] Soon it would be altogether natural to call this body mystically signified by means of the Sacrament a "mystical body". Others were to say: *signified body*,[42] and it would mean the same thing.

---

[39] PG, 56, 691. . . .

[40] *Tractatus de sacramentis* [Treatise on the sacraments] (Weisweiler, p. 27). . . .

[41] Hürter, p. 74.

[42] . . . Cf. Nicholas Cabasilas, *Explanation of the Divine Liturgy*, c. 37. . . .

By virtue of the law operating in the transference of idioms, the adjective that described the Eucharist as signifying could pass to the Church as signified—from the *sacred sign* to the *sacred secret.*[43] If we wanted to interpret some intention of restrictive nuance within this new usage, it would only consist in saying that while the particular body of Christ is present "in truth" in the sacrament, the ecclesial body is only present "as a mystery".[44] But we are not dealing here with a restriction relating to the affirming of its reality. Moreover, even when all reference to the Eucharist had disappeared, the expression would continue to be adapted to its object because, as Cardinal du Perron[45] expressed it, "the word mystical is not always used by writers to exclude the reality of the thing, but to exclude imputing to it evidence and comprehensibility."[46] The Church, the body of Christ, is a mystery and, against the flat notion of it conceived in the Enlightenment and repeated by a few followers of liberal Protestantism, it should be maintained that a mystery is what continues to remain obscure, hidden, and "mystical", even once it has been described, signified, and "revealed".

Eucharistic realism and ecclesial realism: these two realisms support one another, each is the guarantee of the other. Ecclesial realism safeguards Eucharistic realism and the latter confirms the former. The same unity of the Word is reflected in both.[47] Today, it is above all our faith in the "real presence", made explicit thanks to centuries of controversy and analysis, that introduces us to faith in the ecclesial body: effectively signified by the mystery of the Altar, the mystery of the Church has to share the same nature and the same depth. Among the ancients, the perspective was often inverted. The accent was habitually [p. 252] placed on the effect rather than on the cause. But the ecclesial realism to which they universally offer us the most explicit testimony is at the same time, and when neces-

---

[43] Odo of Ourscamp, *Quaestiones*, p. 2, q. 266. . . .

[44] Gregory of Bergamo, c. 19. . . .

[45] [Jacques Davy du Perron (1556–1618) was a French theologian, courtier, and diplomat, who became bishop of Évreux (1595) and a cardinal (1604).—Ed.]

[46] *Traité de l'Eucharistie* [Treatise on the Eucharist] (1622), p. 599. Cf. Wycliffe, *De Ecclesia* [On the Church], c. 5; c. 6, c. 18. . . .

[47] Rupert, *De divinis officiis* [*The worship of the Church*], 2, c. 2. . . .

sary, the guarantee of their Eucharistic realism. This is because the cause has to be proportionate to its effect. The authors of *Perpétuité* [*Perpetuity*][48] put it most effectively when they said: one hundred passages from the Fathers

> Only contain the one doctrine, which is that the body of Jesus Christ, being received by the faithful, effects among them a sort of union, which is not only moral, but physical and natural, since it consists in the real union of our body with that of Jesus Christ; by virtue of which it can be said that all these bodies with which Jesus Christ is united by means of the Eucharist form only one body, because they only have one individual body, which is the body of Jesus Christ. Thus these passages are worlds away from contradicting the real presence, on which, on the contrary, they are founded, because the faithful are only united among themselves in one body because the Eucharist, which is the body of Jesus Christ, is united to them.[49]

By virtue of the same internal logic—and this counter-experience has its price—those in modern times who water down the traditional idea of the Church as the Body of Christ find themselves also watering down the reality of the Eucharistic presence. This is how Calvin made efforts to establish the same notion of a "virtual presence" of Christ in his sacrament and among the faithful. The reason behind it is the same in both cases: "because he is in heaven and we are here below on earth".[50] And the pastor Claude, when wanting to set aside the testimony that apologists had extracted from the Fathers in favour of the Catholic doctrine of the Eucharist, found himself obliged to contest the implications of their texts concerning the Church.[51]—How, indeed, could the Church be truly built up, how could its members be gathered together in a truly united body by means of a sacrament that only symbolically contained the One whose body it was meant to become, and who alone could bring

[48] [In 1667, Antoine Arnauld and Pierre Nicole published *La Perpétuité de la foi de l'Église catholique touchant l'eucharistie* (The continuity of the faith of the Catholic Church regarding the Eucharist) to refute Calvinism.—Ed.]

[49] Bk. 5, c. 9. . . .

[50] Sermon 41, commenting on Eph 5:30. . . . [This is a key tenet of Calvin's doctrine of the Lord's Supper.—Ed.]

[51] Cf. *Perpétuité*, 4, c. 9. . . .

about its unity? St. Augustine himself becomes incomprehensible, and his entire mysticism, so full [p. 253] of meaning as it is, evaporates into hollow formulations if, on analysing the implications of his doctrine, we refuse to recognise within it the faith of the common tradition. For him, the Eucharist is far more than a symbol, because it is most truly that sacrament *by which the Church is bound together in this age*,[52] since the water and the wine of the sacrifice, like the water and the blood that flowed down from the cross, are themselves the sacraments *from which the Church is built*.[53] It is a real presence because it makes real.

This link of causality and of reciprocal guarantee between the two mysteries of the Church and the Eucharist cannot therefore be too highly stressed, not only in order to understand the dogma in itself, but also to understand the Christian past. If our theologians sometimes have difficulty—as they loyally admit—in finding the "real presence" in one or other Eucharistic doctrine from antiquity, it is perhaps because they are looking too hard. If they were more simply to ask themselves, without worrying about anything else, what this doctrine was, they would undoubtedly be more successful in seeing that the real presence was implicit in it. But while they are seeking it without finding it, they are failing to pay sufficient attention to certain other essential characteristics, which are precisely those that would reveal that presence to them. They even manage, through an unconscious tactical error, to minimise those characteristics, affecting to see in them only chance considerations, some sort of "morality" without dogmatic significance, whose terms it would be inappropriate to insist on, and which are not even worth keeping. They make great efforts to find excuses for the great Doctors who were implicated in this, and seem not to notice that this flowering [of dogma] that they so disdain has its solid and vigorous roots in Scripture itself.

Negligence of ecclesial symbolism or minimisation of ecclesial realism: these are two faults that often go hand in hand. As has already been established, the general evolution of doctrine tended towards this. The consequences of the controversy with the protestants con-

[52] *Contra Faustum* [Against Faustus], 12, c. 20. . . .
[53] *De Civ. Dei* [The city of God], 22, c. 17. . . .

tributed to making it worse. This is how Bellarmine[54] comes to say nothing about the relationship with the Eucharist. This silence is in such stark contrast with his learning that, in the numerous texts that he quotes, he would seem to be systematically avoiding the repetition of any sentences in which this relationship might be mentioned. At one point, [p. 254] nevertheless forced to allude to it, in connection with several passages of St. Augustine put forward by his adversaries, he is only prepared to examine these passages in order to use them as objections, and he finally concludes that Augustine was only trying to conceal the truth in them: "Let us reply . . . that Augustine with devoted labour disguised the question and proceeded to moral exhortation!"[55] Du Perron argued in the same vein. In his view, the ecclesial doctrine developed by the Fathers in speaking of the Eucharist is only an "oblique, secondary and accessory doctrine", that dwindles into "hyperbolic and allegorical" language. All that they say about it can be compared to a shadow in relation to a body, an echo or "counter-voice" in relation to a voice.[56] Its entire aim is to "recreate the minds of those who read it through the pious cheerfulness and ingenious inventiveness of these allegorical allusions and applications". And if anyone is surprised when the "counter-voice" is sometimes the only one to be heard, or the shadow is so prominent that the body itself does not always appear, du Perron, like Bellarmine, finds an explanation for it in a fact analogous to what would soon come to be called the "arcane discipline". Someone addressing catechumens cannot yet reveal to them the heart of the mystery:

> . . . St. Augustine, out of concern for the Catechumens, interprets the words that our Lord uses in speaking of his body and blood, not as his true and real flesh and his true and real blood, . . . but as the

[54] [Robert Bellarmine (1542–1621) was an Italian Jesuit theologian who taught in Leuven and Rome, becoming a cardinal (1599) and archbishop of Capua (1602). In correspondence, he disputed with the Protestant King James I of England (VI of Scotland). —Ed.]

[55] *De sacramento Eucharistiae* [On the sacrament of the Eucharist].

[56] Comparing (with some accuracy) these two ways of speaking about the Eucharist with the two "understandings" of Scripture that can be found in the Fathers, du Perron does not see that, in his desire to give weight to literal understanding, he misinterprets the traditional terminology.

> moral and political body of Christ, which is understood as the society of his Church . . . This is a moral and secondary understanding, which St. Augustine uses and sustains in order to satisfy the curiosity of the Catechumens, waiting until they are capable of coming definitively to the proper, direct and immediate understanding of these words . . .[57]

Once more, according to du Perron, the same must also be said of works addressed to pagans: within them the Fathers "disguised and masked what they were saying . . . with cloudy ambiguities, in order to keep their profane readers or audience in a state of suspense and [p. 255] incertitude about the true purpose of the Church."[58] However, there exist sermons addressed to the baptized that are not any more explicit. Would true doctrine still remain hidden from those who are already members of the Church? *Perpétuité* does not think so; but, in the sense given there, we are dealing with "moral" discourses, not "dogmatic" discourses. Supposing that his audience "were well-informed about the substance of their faith", the preacher would attempt "only to edify their devotion".[59] Supposedly, therefore, the Fathers were almost always addressing an audience that they still had no right to instruct, or that they presumed were already well instructed! As we have already seen, there were parts of *Perpétuité* that were better inspired than this.

Several more recent historians follow a similar path. They cheerfully divide up the ancient texts relating to the Eucharist into two groups: the first group is made up of "realist" texts, while all the "allegorized" texts are lumped into a second group, which is abandoned. But the so-called "realist" texts are not always as realist as these historians would have us believe, and by abandoning these "allegorized" texts, they sometimes deprive us of the most effective testimony to authentic realism. The fear of "symbolism" proves a

---

[57] *Réplique à la Response du Serenissime Roy de la Grand Bretagne* [Reply to the answer of his majesty the king of Great Britain, i.e., James I] (1620), pp. 879–80; *Traité de l'Eucharistie* [Treatise on the Eucharist] (1622), 55–[5]9.

[58] *Examen du livre du Sieur Du Plessis* [Examination of the book of the seigneur du Plessis] (*Les diverses oeuvres* . . . , 3rd ed, 1633, p. 1100). We know that the protestant Daillé retained this 'discipline of the arcane' (his own phrase) in order to affirm the irremediable obscurity of the Fathers. . . .

[59] Migne, vol. 2, col. 759; cf. 768–78. . . .

poor counsellor here. For example, we find written: "the allegorism of some of the Fathers, whereby the body of Christ is presented as his mystical body or the Church, or again its doctrine, or its teaching, does not permit us to consider those who taught it as partisans of Eucharistic symbolism."[60] How true! In fact it is often quite the contrary. But it is therefore doubly deplorable that, through a desire to escape a negative "symbolist" interpretation, we should deliberately be deprived of an *essential* part of the Eucharistic doctrine of our forebears. It is also deplorable that a theology that sets out to be strictly historical and "positive" [p. 256] should sometimes commit the historical nonsense of lending its own state of mind to an age where a quite opposite state of mind pertains. Ontological symbolism holds in the history of Christian thought —and in Christian thought itself—too important a place to remain unknown or neglected with impunity—particularly in sacramental theology.

It now seems fairly clear how and why *mystical body* passed from Eucharistic usage to ecclesial usage, and what precise significance ought not be attributed to it in one and the other case. Nevertheless, the total significance of the change that ensued can only be fully understood by insisting on the following observations. Of the three terms: historical body, sacramental body and ecclesial body, that were in use, and that it was a case of putting into order amongst each other, that is to say simultaneously to oppose and unite them to one another, the caesura was originally placed between the first and the second, whereas it subsequently came to be placed between the second and the third. Such, in brief, is the fact that dominates the whole evolution of Eucharistic theories.

This evolution should not be imagined as a rupture or a sudden deviation, any more than as a rectilinear development or a simple explanation. It should rather be compared to a circular movement that was no more precipitate or more rigid at any one particular point of its life. Through the effect of this movement, viewpoints were continually but almost imperceptibly changing. Some new aspect would be discovered, which would continue being confused with the one

[60] G. Bareille, *Eucharistie* ([*Dictionnaire de théologie catholique*], vol. 12, col. 1123).

that preceded it, until that one disappeared. New habits of thought came into being, to all extents and purposes without being noticed. The wheel carried on turning, as inexorably, if not as regularly as time itself, and under the influence of whatever mentality was then prevalent, it was the problems, far more than their solutions, that changed. Naturally there resulted a series of interferences, and also a series of misunderstandings between those minds that remained more attached to the past and those that looked more to the future. Discussions arose that were often more lively than was warranted by any real distance that lay between the positions of those who were more attentive to new needs, and therefore eager to detect error in any form of antiquarianism, and those who, on the contrary, had a confused sense that in the abandonment of ancient viewpoints, great riches were in danger of being lost. This is the origin of the double phenomenon of traditional [p. 257] formulations that perpetuated themselves by changing, or mostly that changed gradually in spirit while remaining unchanged in the letter. Furthermore a real doctrinal continuity is maintained here. It is very rare that an innovation, even a slight one, cannot claim authority from some earlier text, and the syntheses elaborated from it all have their roots in the furthest reaches of the past. Between one era and another, as between one Doctor and another, it is often no more than a question of a simple difference of emphasis—admittedly all the more irreducible because they escape the rules of logical discussion. It may be the evolutions, oppositions, and awkwardnesses that I have tried to point out in the course of this study are therefore often rather forced; to those familiar with the entire collection of texts, it may even seem that to comment on them is to be over-scrupulous, perhaps even arbitrary. It was difficult to avoid this trap altogether: but was it not necessary to emphasize somewhat fleeting characteristics in order to grasp them more clearly?

The most serious misunderstanding that arose from such an evolution was certainly, from an historical perspective, the one to which St. Augustine's thinking fell victim. As time went on, it proved fatal that it became more misunderstood, and we see as the centuries go by those who claim to be his partisans dividing into two opposite camps, representing two contradictory interpretations each of which is nearly always equally false. We have encountered various examples of this above. One of the most typical cases is found in Augustine's teaching on reception of communion by the unworthy. These approach the holy table and receive the sacrament. What does the Lord do meanwhile? Not what he did at the Last Supper, where he ate the Passover with his disciples with such delight. He does what he did on the Cross when, having tasted the bitter drink that was offered to him, he refused to drink it. *He does not admit them into his body.*[61] This should be translated as: "he does not incorporate them into himself." This is the habitual perspective of Augustine, who always sees the ecclesial body as an extension of the Eucharist. But once we have, in some sense, divided the ecclesial body from the sacramental body, by a shift in the caesura, the problem of the interpretation of texts of this sort becomes insoluble. The *to be received by Christ* and the *to receive Christ* being from now on separated, it would seem that Augustine, who distinguished them with the most subtle of nuances, by denying the first thus also denied [p. 258] the second. The problem, for Augustine, was that of the fruitfulness of the sacrament, that of its spiritual fruit (*being transformed into the body of Christ*); what happens is that this is made into a problem of validity, a problem of sacramental presence. It was indeed a question of communion; but it would primarily become a question of the effect of the consecration. According to these new perspectives, the reading of Augustinian texts became distorted. They were searched for a response that they could not provide. Do schismatics, heretics and the excommunicated truly receive the sacrament? Do they truly have the Body of our Lord on their altars? This is the question posed from the eleventh century onwards. No, replied a certain number of theologians, such as Gerhoh of Reichersberg: is the Catholic Church not indeed the only place of true sacrifice? "Who could imagine that heretics, especially self-declared heretics and those under a ban of excommunication or interdict, could have Christ present in their liturgies?"[62] Yes, would reply partisans of the doctrine that was to emerge triumphant, while others thought they had found a solution through better distinguishing between the cases that Gerhoh was aiming at and the case of those who were simply

---

[61] *In psalmum* [Expositions of the Psalms] *68*, sermo 2, n. 6. . . .

[62] *In psalmum 23* (PL, 193, 1088 B–C). . . .

unworthy. . . .[63] The two extremist parties could claim Augustine for their own, as well as the third; but if the second is certainly much more justified in doing so, nevertheless it makes equally little sense in each case.[64]

We should not conclude, from all this, that evolution was a negative thing in itself. It was normal and therefore good. Furthermore, it was needed in order to remedy error and to offer a response to the questions inevitably raised by progress in understanding. Preserving the [p. 259] *status quo* in theories and viewpoints has never been and can never be an adequate means of safeguarding the truth. In the present case, many misunderstandings that the ensuing changes brought about were the sorts of inconvenience that all good brings in its wake. But this cannot be said for the mutilations that actually accompanied it in many cases. Could Eucharistic realism not have been safeguarded without the virtually total abandonment of symbolism? What ruination heresy accomplishes here, even when it is vanquished! "Woe to those", we could say, with apologies to Pascal, "who have led the defenders of faith to turn from the foundation of religion", in order to direct speculation about the Eucharist towards external problems of apologetics! These should not have been set aside, but they ended up by absorbing the entire effort of reflection. More scientific than religious, the syntheses that ensued could in no way be definitive. However, rather than in their inevitable fragility, the damage lay in the abandonment that they appeared to sanction. The eighteenth century, as we have seen, had used the stones of our ancient inheritance to build new structures. But evolution was not slow in coming, and if some formulations lasted, they remained all too often nothing but formulations. The Magisterium, from far off, recalled the essence: theology, without contradicting it, did not always listen to it, or merely proved itself its feeble echo.

[63] Honorius of Autun, *Elucidarium* [Elucidation], 1 . . . ; *Eucharistion*, c. 6–10. . . . Cf. Peter Lombard, *Sent.*, 4, d. 9. . . .

[64] One of the last to untangle the ambiguities (before the historical work of the moderns) is Rupert, who still remains close to Augustinianism: *De Spiritu sancto* [On the Holy Spirit], 3, c. 22 . . . ; *De divinis officiis* [The worship of the Church], 2, p. 11, c. 13 . . . and fragment *De sacramento corporis Christi* [The sacrament of the Body of Christ]. . . .

The damage equally affected the domain of the Eucharist and of the Church.

Indeed at one level the constant build-up of Eucharistic piety became more easily oriented towards an overly individualistic devotion,[65] and sometimes proved poorly defended against certain sentimental excesses. This is how one of the most magnificent examples of progress afforded by the history of Christian life was prevented from bearing some of its finest fruit. As for the Church, insofar as, by defending itself against internal and external attack, it managed to give itself or to define for itself the characteristics of its exterior constitution, by that very fact a good many theologians developed an idea of it that was less and less realist, because less and less mystical. The Thomist [p. 260] synthesis, still so nourished on tradition and so highly organised, was too quickly abandoned in favour of theories which were of quite different orientation and too dependent on controversy. Except among a few isolated thinkers, such as Nicholas of Cusa in the fifteenth century,[66] this is how the "mystery" of the Church disappeared from the horizons of thought, as if there necessarily had to be a conflict between the perfection of the "visible society" and the intimate solidity of the "Body of Christ"![67] It seems that it would therefore be of great interest, we might even say of pressing urgency, given the present state of what remains of "Christendom", to return to the sacramental origins of the "mystical body" in order to steep ourselves in it. It would be a return to the mystical sources of the Church. The Church and the Eucharist are formed by one another day by day: the idea of the Church and the idea of the Eucharist must promote one another mutually and each be rendered more profound by the other.[68] *By the food and blood of the Lord's body let all fellowship be bound together!*[69]

I am certainly not so naïve as to think that this living synthesis was never realised in its perfect state in the thinking of the Doctors or

[65] . . . The traditional doctrine was recalled once again by Cardinal Maglione in his letter of 11th July 1939 to Eugène Duthoit (*Semaine sociale de Bordeaux* [Social week of Bordeaux], 1939, pp. 7–8). More recently Pius XII, message of May 1942.

[66] *De concordantia catholica* [The Catholic concordance] 1, c. 6, and 3, c. 1. . . .

[67] Nevertheless, the Roman Catechism (p. 1, a. 9, n. 21).

[68] Scheeben, *Dogmatik* [Dogmatics]. . . .

[69] Oration [on] the Mozarabic liturgy, Julian of Toledo (PL, 96, 759 B).

the practice of the people of any century. The periods from which I have to cull most of the material for my explorations were, as any other, troubled times, eras where disunity and hypocrisy ruled. . . . If the tragic needs of our time plead for us in some sense to reinvent in its first vigour the doctrine whose loss is being the death of us, such an effort at reinvention no more consists in "taking mental refuge in an idealised past" than in "building for ourselves some imaginary refuge" in a future painted according to the whims of our imagination.[70] We must, however, recognise or rediscover the genuine riches bequeathed to us by the Christian past. We need to relearn from our Fathers, those of Christian antiquity and also those of the Middle Ages, to see present in the unique Sacrifice the unity of the "three bodies" of Christ.[71] Such an assessment seems to impose itself all the more because without it [p. 261] the very strength of the corporate aspirations which can currently be felt at the heart of the Church, and which are in particular driving the liturgical movement, cannot be without peril. Here or there, it could degenerate into a naturalist impulse. Indeed there is always a risk of forgetting: it is not the human fact of gathering for the communal celebration of the mysteries, it is not the collective exaltation that an appropriate pedagogy succeeds in extracting from it that will ever in the very least bring about the unity of the members of Christ. This cannot come about without the remission of sins, the first fruit of the blood that was poured out.[72] The memorial of the Passion, the offering to the heavenly Father, the conversion of the heart: these, therefore, are the totally interior realities without which we will never have anything but a caricature of the community that we seek. But the Eucharist does not offer us some human dream: it is a *mystery of faith*. In order to meditate on this mystery of faith, which also encapsulates the whole mystery of salvation, we can finish by borrowing once more one of the voices of antiquity that has spoken to us throughout this book:

> . . . To the one and only Son of God and Son of Man, as to their head, all the members of the body are joined, all those who are re-

---

[70] Cf. Romano Guardini, *Liturgische Bildung* [Liturgical formation], p. 52.

[71] Nicholas Cabasilas, [Commentary on the divine liturgy], c. 38. . . .

[72] Cf. Matthew 26.28.

ceived in the faith of this mystery, in the fullness of this love. Thus it is one single body, it is one single person, one single Christ, the head with its members, who raises himself up to heaven, and in his gratitude cries out, presenting the Church in its glory to God: "Here is bone of my bone and flesh of my flesh!" And, demonstrating that he and the Church are joined in a true unity of persons, he says again: "and they will be two in one flesh".

Yes, this is indeed a great mystery. The flesh of Christ which, before his Passion, was the flesh of the only word of God, has so grown through the Passion, so expanded and so filled the universe, that all the elect who have been since the beginning of the world or who will live, to the very last one among them, through the action of this sacrament which makes a new dough of them, he reunites in one single Church, where God and humankind embrace one another for all eternity.

This flesh was originally nothing but a grain of wheat, a unique grain, before it fell to the earth in order to die there. And now that it has died, here it is, growing on the altar, coming to fruition in our [p. 262] hands and in our bodies, and, as the great and rich master of the harvest is rising up, he raises with him to the very barns of heaven this fertile earth at whose heart he has grown.[73]

---

[73] Rupert, *De divinis officiis* [The worship of the Church], 2, c. 11. . . .

## The Literal Sense of Scripture

*De Lubac's earliest writings on scriptural interpretation date from the 1930s. In* Catholicism, *he devotes a chapter to images from both testaments that have been used to represent Christ, the Church, and Christians.*[74] *For instance, Job seated on his dunghill is both Christ crucified and his persecuted Church.*[75] *In the book that bears her name, the Moabite woman Ruth represents non-Jews being brought into the Church. The Psalms continually refer to Christ. The bride in the Song of Songs is the Church seeking Christ, while Luke's parables make continual reference to both Christ and his Church. In an edited volume, de Lubac outlines the doctrine of the "fourfold sense" of Scripture,*[76] *quoting a common medieval couplet summarizing this: "The letter teaches what took place, the allegory what to believe; the moral what to do, the anagogy what goal to strive for."*[77] *Moreover, much of his book on Origen,* History and Spirit, *deals with the relation between the literal and spiritual senses, especially with regard to allegory and Christology.*

*De Lubac reports that he came to the Greek Fathers late. Like most Roman Catholic theologians, he was less competent with Greek than with Latin, and it was not until 1929, when he assumed his professorship in the Catholic Theological Faculty in Lyon, that he began to study these Fathers seriously. At this time, he began working on* History and Spirit, *gathering material over a period of twenty years. He describes the book as "written with joy."*[78] *Origen (184/85–253/54) had long been viewed as a heretic, being accused of having corrupted Christian theology with the philosophical concepts and methods of paganism. However, de Lubac insisted that he was a man of the Church who was pastorally attuned to the needs of his hearers in the Christian community for spiritual edification from Scripture. In view of the frequent charge against Origen that his use of allegory undermined Scripture's literal*

---

[74] Henri de Lubac, *Catholicism: Christ and the Common Destiny of Man*, trans. Lancelot C. Sheppard and Sister Elizabeth Englund, O.C.D. (San Francisco: Ignatius Press, 1988), 165–216.

[75] Job 2:8–13.

[76] Henri de Lubac, *Theological Fragments*, trans. Rebecca Howell Balinski (San Francisco: Ignatius Press, 1989), 109–27.

[77] Ibid., 109:

> "Littera gesta docet, quid credas allegoria,
> Moralis quid agas, quo tendas anagogia."

[78] De Lubac, *At the Service of the Church: Henri de Lubac Reflects on the Circumstances that Occasioned His Writings*, trans. Anne Elizabeth Englund (San Francisco: Ignatius Press, 1993), 65–66.

*sense, it is striking that de Lubac presents him as an exegete who took Scripture's literal sense very seriously.*

## *Affirmation of History*

[p. 103] Having exorcized the general prejudice that so often makes Origen's allegorism misunderstood and being better informed about his true mind, we can now approach the examination of his doctrine relating to the meaning of Scripture. We will begin at the foundation: the literal sense.

The Bible is full of mysteries. Origen recalls this on nearly every page of his commentaries and homilies. Everything, in the holy history, takes place "in mystery". Everything that was written is mystery.[79] There are so many mysteries that it is impossible to explain them or even to perceive them all. Their grandeur surpasses our strength. Their density is crushing. "See what weight of mysteries overwhelms us!"[80] The more we advance in our reading of the Holy Books, the more these mysteries accumulate. It is like an immense sea, and when we are close to casting ourselves into it, with the little raft constituted by our feeble means, a feeling of fear invades us. . . .[81] Nothing in Scripture is said as if by chance; nothing is related in vain.[82] Secret intentions are hidden everywhere. The least details of vocabulary, the [p. 104] least editorial anomalies are the sign of a new mystery: the Holy Spirit did not will them without profound reasons. The sacred text must therefore be "sounded" everywhere with the greatest care.[83] That is what Origen repeats with respect to everything, and it is what immediately strikes the

Excerpted from *History and Spirit: The Understanding of Scripture according to Origen*, trans. Anne Englund Nash with Juvenal Merriel (San Francisco: Ignatius Press, 2007), 103–18.

[79] HGen [Homilies on Genesis], hom. 4, 2 . . . ; hom. 9, 1 . . . ; hom. 10, 2 . . . ; hom. 15, 5 . . . , and 7 . . . , etc.

[80] HJosh [Homilies on Joshua], hom. 25, 4. . . .

[81] HEx [Homilies on Exodus], hom. 9, 1 . . . ; HGen, hom. 9, 1. . . .

[82] Nothing is said or done "casu, eventu, otiose, fortuiter, inaniter, frustra, communiter" [by chance, by fortune, without purpose, fortuitously, pointlessly, in vain, mundanely]. . . . HNum [Homilies on Numbers], hom. 27, 1: "Non possumus loc dicere de sancti Spiritus litteris ut aliquid in iis otiosum sit aut superfluum" [We cannot say concerning the writings of the Holy Spirit that anything in them is purposeless or superfluous]. . . .

[83] HLev [Homilies on Leviticus], hom. 3, 1. . . .

reader. But this mysterious character of the Bible is not affirmed to the detriment of its historical character. The spirit does not wish to harm the letter. It does not wish to "destroy the text".[84] If the reality of the visible world is a figure for the invisible world,[85] then the reality of biblical history will also be a figure for the things of salvation and will serve as their "foundation".[86] The deeds and gestures of the personages it presents are, in their very reality, full of a mysterious meaning.[87]

Origen fought against Docetism.[88] Now what he did not admit with respect to Christ, he was no more disposed to admit with respect to [p. 105] Christ's preparation in Israel. In his Scripture as in his earthly life, Origen thought, the Logos needs a body; the historical meaning and the spiritual meaning are, between them, like the flesh and the divinity of the Logos.[89] All of Scripture is, so to speak, "incorporated"; like the One whom it proclaims and prepares for, it is "non in phantasia, sed in veritate" (not in fantasy, but in truth).[90] Certainly, just as one must not stop in Christ at the man who is seen but, through the flesh that veils him to carnal eyes, perceive by faith the God who is in him, so one must go through the external history that is offered to us in the Holy Books, particularly in the Old Testament, in order to penetrate to the "spiritual mystery" that is hidden there. But this truth presupposes its opposite. One must believe, first of all, in general, that the things happened as they are recounted. They took place ἐπι τῷ ῥητῷ (in the way stated).[91] The Jews were simply wrong in restricting themselves to it. Against them and those who are like them, "we defend both the letter and the spirit of the Scriptures", not wanting to "curse the letter" any more than to "blaspheme the spirit".[92] [p. 106] All that

---

[84] Cf. MtSer [Commentary on Matthew series] 50. . . .

[85] HGen, hom. 1, 11 . . . and 16 . . . , etc.

[86] HGen, hom. 2, 1. . . .

[87] HJudg [Homilies on Judges], hom. 9, 2 . . . , etc.

[88] [The belief that Jesus Christ's human body, and therefore his suffering, only appear to be real.—Ed.]

[89] HLev, hom. 1, 1. . . .

[90] Cf. MtSer 92. . . .

[91] HJer [Homilies on Jeremiah], hom. 7, 1. . . .

[92] HLev, hom. 14, 1 . . . , and 2: "Nos vero qui ex utroque genere Istrahelitae sumus, et litteram et spiritum in Scripturis sanctis defendimus et litigamus adversum eos, qui ex media parte Istrahelitae videntur, et dicimus quia neque secundum litteram maledici

happened, happened "in mystery":[93] but the mystery presupposes the real event. One must believe "the testimony of the history". "Manente prius historiae veritate" (The reality of the history remains first of all).[94] Thus, when we read that the Assyrians took the children of Israel into captivity,[95] we believe both that the thing once took place and that, for us, it represents the captivity that certain "spiritual Assyrians" make us suffer today.[96] Our theologian is consistent here with himself as were, on their side, the Docetists whom he had to combat. Marcion,[97] rejecting the Jewish Bible, also rejected the humanity of Jesus by denying him any "birth": Origen incorporated in a single defense the reality of his physical body and the reality of his preparation in Israel.

Some might be tempted to reject the literal sense when it seems too improbable. This might be the case for the very act of creation. Why not take it as a sort of Platonic myth, similar to the account of Timaeus?[98] Why not suppose at least a preexisting matter that God would have organized? Origen, however, does not hesitate to accept the account as it is, without concerning himself with the repugnance of Hellenism, and to justify it he argues against the philosophers decisively. He does so, too, in the case of many miracles. As extraordinary as some of them may be, he does not see in that any reason [p. 107] to jump over the "obvious interpretation".

---

oportet neque secundum spiritalem intelligentiam blasphemari" [But we, who are Israelites springing from both races, defend both the letter and the spirit in the Holy Scriptures, and we fight against those who have the appearance of being Israelites. We claim that one should not curse according to the letter nor blaspheme according to the spiritual sense]. . . .

[93] HGen, hom. 9, 1. . . .

[94] CGal [Commentary on Galatians] (1297A). . . .

[95] [2 Kings 17:6.—Ed.]

[96] HEx, hom. 7, 8 . . . ; hom. 1, 3: "When you hear talk about the captivity of the people, believe with certainty that it took place according to the testimony of history but also that it was the sign of something else and that it prefigured the mystery to come". . . .

[97] [Marcion of Sinope (ca. 85–ca. 160) promoted a distinction between a higher, transcendent god, whom he associated with the New Testament, and a creating and preserving god, whom he found in the Old Testament. His Christology was docetic, and he denied the reality of Jesus' human body.—Ed.]

[98] [This dialogue of Plato describes the geometrical ordering of the world by a creator god, or demiurge, according to models known as forms. Unlike most of Plato's other texts, it was widely available to medieval theologians.—Ed.]

The mockery of Celsus[99] does not intimidate him. "God grant", he cries out, "that I be called insane by the infidels, I who have believed such things!"[100] We can see, in the homily that he devotes to Noah's ark, what meticulous care he brings to justify the most precise literal meaning of the most astonishing accounts in opposition to the ironical objections of Apelles[101] and many others.[102] Rather than imitate the incredulous laughter of the heretics and pagan intellectuals, he says again, "must we not admire this construction, which seemed so like a great city?"[103] The story of Abraham, Lot's wife changed into a statue of salt, the ten plagues of Egypt, the passage through the Jordan, the rock struck by Moses, the stories of Balaam, of Gideon, of Deborah,[104] and so on—there is nothing in all of that, either, that he would dream of merely questioning. The miracle of the sun stopped by Joshua[105] does not seem to him to demand long explanations—the facts recounted are so clear; he simply observes in their regard: "These things, which were produced in the reality of history, proclaim to all centuries the wonders of the divine power."[106] Keturah, the spouse whom Abraham received [p. 108] when he was "full of days",[107] can very well be for him dialectics or some other science: that does not prevent him, on the following page, from naming her distant heir the Queen of Cedar [Kedar].[108] It is certainly not the miraculous that embarrasses him!

---

[99] [A Greek philosopher who wrote (ca. 177) the earliest known attack on Christianity, known as *The True Word*.—Ed.]

[100] HLk [Homilies on Luke], hom. 7. . . . What is at issue is the virginal conception of the Savior and the sanctification of John the Baptist. [See Lk 1:41.]

[101] [A follower of Marcion who taught in Rome and Alexandria.—Ed.]

[102] HGen, hom. 2, 1: "Let us see, first of all, what is literally reported about the ark, and, posing the question about it that many customarily bring as objections, let us seek, too, for solutions to them", and so on. . . .

[103] CC [Against Celsus] 4, 41: . . . In his explanations about the ark, Saint Augustine will refer to Origen: *De civitate Dei* [The city of God], bk. 15, chap. 27, no. 3: "Si autem cogitemus quod Origenes non ineleganter astruxit" [If we consider what Origen constructed with no lack of elegance]. . . .

[104] [Gen 11:31—25:11; Gen 19:26; Ex 8:1—12:30; Josh 3; Ex 17:5–6; Num 22–24; Judg 6–8; Judg 4.—Ed.]

[105] [Josh 10:13.—Ed.]

[106] HJosh, hom. 11, 1. . . . The same confidence is found in Hippolytus with respect to Joshua and the sundial turning back under Hezekiah: *Commentary on Daniel*, bk. 1, chaps. 7–8. . . .

[107] [Gen 25:1, 8.—Ed.]

[108] HGen, hom. 11, 2. . . .

Of still many other passages, he could say what he says with respect to the death of Moses,[109] in an expression that sums up in advance the fine Augustinian developments on the miracle: "history at once astonishing in its account and magnificent by its meaning".[110]

Whether it is a matter, moreover, of episodes, as is the case particularly in Genesis and Exodus, as well as in the books of Joshua, Judges, and so on, or of precepts and maxims, as is the case in Leviticus and in the Book of Psalms, his principle is the same: All contain divine depths, but they retain, nonetheless, in the very great majority of instances, their literal significance. The episodes "were accomplished perceptibly"; the precepts had to be or must still be "observed according to the letter".[111] It is always necessary to know this perceptible, literal, historical aspect. It is appropriate to begin by studying it; it normally serves as the basis for spiritual understanding. Sometimes it will be good to pause there awhile. If necessary, [p. 109] a geographical or topographical consideration will come to establish its basis in fact. Thus, for the wells of the patriarchs:[112] "That these holy men had dug out wells in the land of the Philistines, as Genesis assures us, is proved by the marvelous wells that are still evident in the town of Ascalon and that truly deserve to be seen because of the singularity of their structure, different from that of all others."[113] Moreover, certain very simple explanations may "be favored".[114] It happens rather often that the literal meaning of Scripture is useful and edifying by itself, although that is not always the case. This applies to precepts of the law that are confirmed by those of the Gospel. It also applies to the story

---

[109] [Deut 34:1–8.—Ed.]

[110] HNum, hom. 22, 3. . . .

[111] PA [On first principles] 4, 3, 3. . . .

[112] [Gen 26:17–22.—Ed.]

[113] CC 4, 44. . . . What Father Abel says of Cyril of Alexandria could be applied already to Origen: "La Géographie sacrée chez Cyrille d'Alexandrie", *Revue biblique* 31 (1922): 407: "One does not approach an Alexandrian exegete without fearing to see the given facts of history and geography vanish beneath the action of allegorical exegesis. So it is not without a certain surprise that one finds in the commentaries on the prophets coming from the pen of Saint Cyril of Alexandria a true concern for the literal explanation through historical facts and geographical analysis. . . . It is rather intriguing to compare the care that the Alexandrian master brings to treat of geography with the disdain witnessed by one of the masters of the school of Antioch in regard to these questions." . . .

[114] HJer, hom. 18, 4. . . .

of Joseph:[115] "I do not think that Momus[116] himself, so to speak, could find anything to criticize in this event, which furnishes many beautiful lessons, even without going so [p. 110] far as allegory."[117] It also applies to the story of Deborah, of whom the "prima ipsius litterae facies" (the surface of the letter itself) can already bring so much consolation to the weaker sex, even before one examines "quid etiam interioris intelligentiae respiret arcanum" (what secret, inner meaning it might also breathe forth).[118] The very fine homily on the sacrifice of Abraham,[119] all quivering with emotion, which nourished generations of exegetes and spiritual leaders, is content to present the tragic conflict that is played out in the soul of the patriarch between fatherly love and the duty of obedience to God: only one brief paragraph toward the end sketches the significance of Isaac and the ram as figures of the Lamb of God.[120] Thus every time it is possible, "the text of the story edifies us first of all."[121] It is only after having set this forth that we wonder *in addition* what more interior meaning hidden there, what "allegory", might be appropriately drawn from it. We will comment on it "spiritualiter" only after having explained it "simpliciter".[122] In particular, we will beware of the tendency to neglect the literal meaning of certain precepts in order to rise immediately to the "allegory" or to escape through "tropology": such spiritualism is not respectable, and the more refined perfection of which it boasts is in danger of failing in the elementary duties of the Christian.[123]

The immorality of certain acts reported by the sacred writers will no more be a reason to question them than the miraculousness of certain other events. It will merely be one more reason for us to seek the spiritual meaning. For "God, in his wisdom, has disposed [p. 111] all things of this kind so that the goodwill of man will serve him for good ends and his bad will for necessary

---

[115] [Gen 37–50.—Ed.]

[116] [The Greek god of satire.—Ed.]

[117] CC 4, 47. . . .

[118] HJudg, hom. 5, 2. . . .

[119] [Gen 22.—Ed.]

[120] HGen, hom. 8. . . .

[121] HNum, hom. 20, 1. . . .

[122] MtSer 56. . . .

[123] MtVol [Commentary on Matthew] 15, 15–18. . . .

ends",[124] and just as he draws good out of evil, God draws our edification from the least edifying accounts. This is what we should recall, especially when we find in the divine Scriptures "certain faults committed by the holy Fathers": the figurative sense that we draw from it and that serves for our instruction is a kind of redemption of it; "purification and satisfaction are obtained by the Doctors, showing that such acts were images of future things, not so that the faults of the saints be reproached them, but so that we see thereby that sinners themselves contribute to the inheritance and society of the saints."[125] Moreover, let us not cry out too quickly at the scandal! Here we have, for example, the incest of Lot's daughters.[126] It contains a higher teaching, and that is enough to justify the account. But is there not also a way of explaining "what seems to be the most shocking in this story"? We could, therefore, "on the one hand, give it an allegorical meaning and, on the other, even find some defense for it on its own".[127]

It is not that absolutely everything in the Bible must be taken literally. There are, although few in number, certain "purely spiritual" episodes. At times, too, Scripture "intermingles with the history some details that did not take place, others that were impossible, others that might have happened but that did not in fact happen". Thus certain [p. 112] pages or features "do not have a corporal sense".[128] For instance, this assertion from the Book of Joshua: "And Joshua wrote Deuteronomy on stones in the presence of the sons of Israel."[129] That "makes us reflect":

> How can he write so long a book with the sons of Israel remaining there to the end, or even, how could the stones of the altar bear the contents of such a long book? Let them tell me, these Jewish friends

[124] HNum, hom. 14, 2 . . . : "Et propterea puto in divinis voluminibus scripta esse et bonorum gesta et malorum, et ex sinistris dextrisque actibus Scripturas divinas esse contextas, ut intelligamus quia apud Deum otiosa non sunt nec malorum opera nec bonorum" [And therefore I think that in the divine books the deeds of both good men and evil are recorded, and wicked and righteous deeds are woven together to form the divine Scriptures so that we may understand that the works of both good and evil men serve the purposes of God]. . . .

[125] HLev, hom. 15, 3. . . .

[126] [Gen 19:30–38.—Ed.]

[127] CC 4, 45. . . .

[128] PA 4, 2, 5. . . .

[129] [Josh 8:32.—Ed.]

> of the letter, who do not know the spirit of the law. How is one to show here the truth of the story? But, up to this day, when Moses is read to these latter, a veil is set over their heart. For us, on the contrary, who are turned toward the Lord Jesus, the veil is taken away, for wherever the Spirit of the Lord is, there is freedom of understanding. Thus, our Lord Jesus does not need much time to write Deuteronomy, that is, the second law, in the heart and spirit of believers who are worthy of being chosen for the construction of the altar; to inscribe there the law of the spirit.[130]

The spiritual interpretation seems in this case like an expedient intended to find in certain passages a meaning they would otherwise lack—unless it is the overly quick renunciation of finding a meaning in them that serves as an expedient in view of their spiritual interpretation. The latter can also serve to reconcile two apparently contradictory texts.[131] If we are to believe what Origen says, he would resign himself to it only as a last resort; he would abandon the struggle only "reluctantly, conquered by reason".[132] But, be that as it may, he consents to it sometimes a bit quickly, following the example of Clement [p. 113] and Philo. He is not unhappy to embarrass the "friends of the letter" in some subtle exegetical difficulty or to have this additional motive to soar into the sky. "See how he who flees the figurative sense will fall into absurdities on every side!"[133] In particular, he declares the "letter" impossible for having begun with too narrow an intention. How, he says, for example, do we apply the law of Leviticus: "eye for an eye, tooth for a tooth"[134] to the murderer of a newborn who does not yet have teeth? Or again, how can the Jebusites live with the sons of Judah in Jerusalem "to this day", according to what the Book of Joshua says, since the expression "to this day" signifies in the Bible "until the

---

[130] HJosh, hom. 9, 4. . . .

[131] HJosh, hom. 16, 3: "In superioribus dicebatur quia Jesus cepit omnem terram, et hic modo scriptum est quia terra relicta est multa valde. Putasne contraria sibi Scriptura contineat? Sed redeamus ad intelligentiam spiritalem, et in ea nihil invenies, contrarium" [It was said above that Joshua conquered the whole land, and here it is written that a very great part of the land remained unconquered. Do you think Scripture can contain contradictions? But let us return to the spiritual sense, and then you will find nothing contradictory in Scripture]. . . .

[132] HEzek [Homilies on Ezekiel], hom. 3, 2. . . .

[133] MtVol 17, 35. . . .

[134] [Ex 21:24.—Ed.]

end of the ages"? The sons of Judah themselves already no longer live in Jerusalem.[135] This is because, persuaded that everything is given in the Bible "principally in view of the spiritual sense", that "its principal end is spiritual teaching", Origen is always ready to admit, in wonder, that divine providence has scattered accounts and precepts with certain absurd or impossible details, as "stumbling blocks", "in order to urge the most penetrating and attentive minds to search the depths of Scripture and to seek there a meaning truly worthy of God". Whereas, "if the usefulness of the Mosaic law were to appear clearly or if the account were always limpid and consistent, we would not believe there was anything but the natural sense. . . . Following smoothly the easy slope of the discourse, we would abandon in the long run a doctrine that would seem to us to have nothing divine about it, or rather, riveted to the literal sense, we would learn nothing worthy of God."[136] At the same time as he thus admires in these weaknesses of the letter a marvelous pedagogical means employed by the [p. 114] Savior, Origen has a tendency to multiply them in order to make of them an anti-Jewish polemical tool. In his explanation of the law, he is overly concerned to show "quam inconveniens sit Judaica intelligentia" (how unfitting is the Jewish interpretation).[137] "Velim requirere a Judaeis" (I would like to question the Jews);[138] "velim ego in hoc loco percontari a Judaeis" (I would like in this passage to interrogate the Jews);[139] "Patroni litterae Judaei velim videre quomodo asserunt" (I would like to see how the Jews, the patrons of the letter, would answer):[140]

[135] HJosh, hom. 21, 1 . . . ; on Joshua 15:63. . . .

[136] PA 4, 2, 9. . . .

[137] HLev, hom. 3, 3. . . .

[138] HJosh, hom. 7, 5. . . .

[139] HJosh, hom. 5, 5: "Post haec jubetur filius Nave facere cultros ex petra et sedens circumcidere filios Israel secundo. Velim ego in hoc loco percontari a Judaeis, quomodo potest quis secundo circumcidi circumcisione carnali. Semel enim circumcisus quis, ultra non habet quod secundo possit auferri. A nobis vero, quibus dicitur quia lex spiritalis est, vide quam digne et convenienter ista solvantur" [After these events the son of Nun is ordered to make knives of stone and to sit circumcising the sons of Israel a second time. I would like in this text to interrogate the Jews, how anyone could possibly be circumcised a second time with a bodily circumcision. A man circumcised once does not have anything more that could be removed. But see how properly and fittingly we, who have been told that the law is spiritual, can solve these problems]. . . . [Josh 5:2.]

[140] H1Kings [Homilies on 1 Kings], hom. 1, 18. . . .

such are the expressions that generally herald his remarks on some impossibility of the text.

Too convenient a process, based on a singular conception. Here we can speak with some justification of the "escape mechanisms of the allegorical school".[141] Let us recognize at least that they were not perceived to be so. Saint Hilary, for example, would write: "Interpositis enim nonnullis rebus, quae ex natura humani sensus sibi contrariae sunt, rationem quaerere caelestis intelligentiae admonemur" (For when some things that are introduced are contrary to one another according to the natural level of human understanding, we are advised to seek the solution in the heavenly meaning).[142] The [p. 115] same reasoning is found again in Saint Augustine[143] and Saint Jerome.[144] Moreover, we can observe a similar process in Theodore of Mopsuestia himself.[145] We could also say that "this habit of using inconsistencies or oddities in a text as a pretext for finding some new significance in it went back to the beginnings of Christianity. It was one of the preferred arguments of Saint Justin in his polemic against the Jews. It had been the argumentation used by Jesus in confronting his adversaries with the enigma of Psalm 110: The Lord said to my lord" (Mt 22:40). "Such a principle of exegesis", continues Father Guillet, "was based on a justifiable idea, on the conviction that the religious depth of the Bible surpasses human logic. But it requires in its application a familiarity with the

---

[141] Bishop Devreesse, *Essai sur Théodore de Mopsueste* [Essay on Theodore of Mopsuestia] (1948), p. 72. . . .

[142] Hilary, *In Matt.* [On Matthew], chap. 20, no. 2. . . .

[143] Augustine, *In Psalm. 103,* s. 1, no. 18: "Quare quaedam in rebus visibilibus quasi absurda miscet Spiritus sanctus, nisi ut ex eo quod non possumus accipere ad litteram, cogat nos ista spiritualiter quaerere?" [Why does the Holy Spirit mix some apparently absurd matters with the visible facts, unless for the reason that we may be forced to seek the spiritual sense because we cannot accept the literal sense?]. . . .

[144] Jerome, *In Isaiam*, bk. 7 (Is 19:1): "Sed et in hoc et in aliis Scripturarum locis pleraque ponuntur, quae non possent stare juxta historiam: ut rerum necessitate cogamur altiorem intelligentiam quaerere" [But in this and in other passages of Scripture, many things are written that cannot stand as history, so that we might be forced by the necessity of these things to seek for a higher meaning]. . . .

[145] Jacques Guillet, "Les Exégèses d'Alexandrie et d'Antioche, conflit ou malentendu?" [The exegeses of Alexandria and Antioch: conflict or misunderstanding?], [*Recherches de science religieuse*] 34 (1947): 265.

proper style of the Bible that neither Origen nor Theodore could possess."[146] We should not, however, exaggerate the extent of these applications, even in Origen. In fact, the latter rarely abuses the principle he set. When he permits himself to contest the historical literalness of some detail, it is more than once with the [p. 116] well-founded feeling that even those "qui valde amici sunt litterae" (who are great friends of the letter) will be forced to admit to it.[147] At bottom, he denies the literal sense in much fewer cases than he seems to say, and nearly always it is only in minimal points that take away nothing from the substantial historicity of the account. Besides, he himself declares: "In most cases, one can and must save the truth of the story. . . . The really historical episodes are, in Scripture, much more numerous than those that contain a purely spiritual sense."[148]

There is, however, one exception, and a very important one: that of the texts concerning our origins and last ends, those "summa Scripturarum" (high points of Scripture) that are the first and the last pages of it. Origen was clearly aware that they form a category apart in revelation. We saw above how wrong those were who reproached him, through lack of understanding, for having treated the account of our origins as a pagan allegorist treated his myths. The same remark holds true for the declaration on our last ends. Origen reacted against those who, in their interpretation of the eschatological texts, let themselves be deceived by the words and images to the point of concocting "inept fables and empty fiction"; to the point, for example, "of going so far as to believe that after the resurrection one would use bodily food and that one would drink wine, not at all from that true Vine destined for eternal existence, but from a material vine".[149] Led astray by "their carnal taste and their passion", they [p. 117] "go around in an abyss of inane talk

[146] Ibid. Of the two examples he has just analyzed, Father Guillet concludes that "logicians and grammarians of their times, they [Origen and Theodore] did not understand the movement of Hebrew thought, and that the artificial culture of declining Hellenism made them strangers to the lyricism of the Psalms."

[147] HLev, hom. 16, 6. . . .

[148] PA 4, 3, 4. . . .

[149] CSong [Commentary on the Song of Songs], prol. (p. 66).

and nonsense".[150] "They err and are ignorant of Scripture", he said again, those who dream of carnal weddings for the world to come, through an interpretation worthy of the Sadducees.[151] He thereby worked both for orthodoxy and for the strictness of the moral ideal. Without being severe toward the "little children in Christ", who took the foretold return of the Son of Man on the clouds of heaven in the most dull-witted sense,[152] he combated delusive imaginations. He purified the idea of salvation and hope in the kingdom. As we have already seen, he destroyed the millenarian error,[153] which was at that time still powerful and sustained by those *solius litterae discipuli* (disciples of the bare letter) who treated him as suspect himself.[154] At the same stroke, he allowed the Church to accept the Book of Revelation without fear into the canon of Scriptures. For the strongest argument of the millenarists was drawn precisely from that "revelation", which they interpreted literally, so that most of their adversaries saw rejecting it as apocryphal as the only way of combating them. Papias, the Letter of Barnabas, Saint Justin, Saint Irenaeus,[155] Tertullian had let themselves be caught by the symbolic descriptions of the mysterious book. Soon Bishop Nepos[156] would draw his principal argument from it in his *Refutation of the Allegorists*. On the other hand, Caius, at Rome, attributed it to Cerinthus, and still much [p. 118] later certain Eastern Churches would hesitate to receive it.[157] Origen himself, without having to lead any direct com-

---

[150] CPs [Commentary on the Psalms] 1 (533BC).

[151] MtVol. 17, 34. . . . No resurrection at all would be better than the one they imagine. . . .

[152] MtSer 50. . . . Likewise for the trumpet of Judgment of which Saint Paul speaks, etc., 51–52. . . .

[153] [The belief, based on a literal reading of the Book of Revelation, that the world is about to end and Christ will return to reign for a thousand years.—ED.]

[154] PA 2, 11, 2. . . .

[155] Irenaeus rejected in advance any attempt at allegorization: *Adversus Haereses* 5, 35. . . . Chapter 61 of the *Demonstration* does not contradict the doctrine of *Adversus Haereses*, although he emphasizes the spiritual side of the kingdom of Christ. . . .

[156] [An early Egyptian bishop who promoted a literal reading of Scripture, including that of Genesis.—ED.]

[157] Cf. Jerome, *Tract. de ps.* [Tracts on the Psalms] *1* (v. 440): "Legimus in Apocalypsi Joannis (quod in istis provinciis non recipitur liber . . . )" [We read in the Apocalypse of John (which book is not accepted in these provinces . . .)]. . . .

bat in its favor, had the merit of dissipating the millenarian dream while preserving the authenticity of the holy book. He was, in this way, the providential instrument to whom, more than to any other, we owe today the possession of this treasure. Here, too, Newman's observation is proved true: The fate of mystical interpretation and that of orthodoxy are linked together.[158]

[158] [John Henry Newman, *An Essay on the Development of Christian Doctrine* (Cambridge: Cambridge University Press, 2010), 319–27 (324).—Ed.]

## Medieval Exegesis

*While de Lubac worked on* History and Spirit, *he was gathering material for an even larger project: his four-volume study* Medieval Exegesis. *He defines "exegesis" more widely than is usual today. Originally, de Lubac explains, it included "all the successive parts of Christian reflection being exercised on the basis of revelation handed on to us by the Holy Books accepted in the Church: that is, first of all, the 'exegesis' of biblical texts, in the limited sense of our present usage, in its immediacy, as it were; then dogmatics, ecclesiology, moral theology and spirituality".*[159] *In embracing this larger understanding of exegesis, he wishes to bring theology and Scripture into a closer alliance than was typical in his day, contesting the Scholastic tendency to conduct theology with little direct reference to Scripture. However, de Lubac also calls into question approaches to theology that establish particular doctrinal points using supposed proof texts. Rather, Scripture needs to be read as a whole.*

*The fourfold method of scriptural interpretation—distinguishing literal, allegorical, moral, and eschatological senses—marvelously synthesizes, de Lubac states, the whole of Christian faith, thought, and spirituality. "So grossly unappreciated in modern times", he writes, it is "nevertheless still the bearer of promises for renewal".*[160] *These promises were to have been the topic of a fifth volume, which, despite preparatory work, was never written. This volume would have discussed the survival of remnants of spiritual exegesis, its reappearance, misunderstandings of the past, and new perspectives resulting from controversies and the development of critical methods. Readers, therefore, have some liberty to draw their own conclusions about the implications of de Lubac's project for scriptural interpretation today.*

*De Lubac writes that, as his work progressed, he became ever more aware of the extraordinary unity of the two testaments and of the importance of this unity for the whole of the Church's history and doctrine. This theme was prominent in* Dei verbum, *the brief but profound dogmatic constitution of the Second Vatican Council on divine revelation. De Lubac's exegetical method is similar to that in* Corpus Mysticum: *assembling texts in order to identify how key terms have been used and how meanings have shifted over time.*

---

[159] De Lubac, *At the Service*, 86.

[160] Ibid., 83–84.

## *The Unity of the Two Testaments: Evolution and Mutation*

[p. 1:225] Of Origen's two formulas, the one that puts tropology [morality] immediately after history was tripartite right from the beginning, since it was founded on a putative analogy between Scripture and man, insofar as he was made up of three elements. On the other hand, the formula in which allegory precedes tropology would only be quadripartite through some kind of development, or by its being broken up and divided. In its initial simplicity, which contains all that is essential about it, it includes only two members, and these two members are understood and mutually arranged in such a way that nothing analogous can be found, even notionally, outside the Christian faith. What we have here is a theory that, even in its very form, owes everything to this Christian faith, and that, in its content, seeks to give it full expression. It is because he has neglected to make this fundamental declaration that more than one historian has spent vast storehouses of learning in vain, or rather he has ended up falsifying, indeed, conjuring away one of the greatest facts of history.

To summarize the whole thing briefly: the Christian tradition understands that Scripture has two meanings. The most general name for these two meanings is the literal meaning and the spiritual ("pneumatic") meaning, and these two meanings have the same kind of relationship to each other as do the Old and New Testaments to each other. More exactly, and in all strictness, they constitute, they *are* the Old and New Testaments.

In the Book of Revelation, Saint John, like Ezekiel, speaks of a scroll, written within and on the back.[161] "Intus et foris" is how the Vulgate [p. 226] translates it. This is a good translation, since we are dealing with a scroll, the scroll that we see at times in medieval paintings and sculptures. It is held in the talons of an eagle, whereas the three other symbolic animals hold a codex [bound book with pages] that is similar to our present-day books. Most often, as we have seen above, tradition regards it as the book of the Scriptures.

---

Excerpted from Henri de Lubac, *Medieval Exegesis*, trans. E. M. Macierowski, 4 vols. (Grand Rapids, Mich.: Eerdmans; Edinburgh: T&T Clark, 1998–2009), 1:225–41, 261–67; and 3:140–46.

[161] Revelation 5:1; Ezekiel 2:9–10.

Outside it is written in accordance with the letter. On the inside it is written in accordance with the spirit.[162] To understand it, we must pass from one to the other. A spiritual understanding of the Word of God as recorded in the Bible must be acquired. This understanding, which penetrates through the surface of the letter, or which bursts forth from the letter, is commended or distributed in a "spiritual commentary" by all those who have a teaching role in the Church. For those who teach have received "the dispensation of the Spirit" from God, as Saint Paul says.[163] It is "a higher degree of understanding,"[164] a "higher" or "deeper"[165] understanding, "more absolute" than a literal understanding.[166] From it there follows a "more noble,"[167] a "more august"[168] meaning. It is an "interior" understanding, which discerns "internal causes,"[169] whereas the literal sense remains external and superficial. It is a "sublime"[170] and "sacred"[171] understanding, "a more sacred kind of understanding,"[172] which one receives in order to become perfect. This understanding is approached by degrees or stages, by the action of a grace coming from on high. It bequeaths a "sublime" and "divine" meaning to us, lifting us into regions where the mystery of the heavens is opened to us.[173] In it we find the restful state of interior light, in it alone we stand in awe of all beauty, and we taste all the piquant flavor of revelation. It engenders a spiritual joy in each one of us and in the whole Church.

Far from being an invention, the result of a whim or a dream, this understanding has its own structure, which compels us to recognize it. The spirit is not separated from the letter. At first, it is contained and hidden in the letter. The letter is good and necessary,

---

[162] Origen, *In Jo.* [Commentary on the Gospel according to John], Bk. 5, c. 6. . . .
[163] 2 Cor. 3:8.
[164] Origen, *In Gen.* [On Genesis], h. 4, n. 4. . . .
[165] . . . Origen, *In Num.* [On Numbers], h. 22, n. 1. . . .
[166] Hilary, *In ps.* [On the Psalms] *134*, n. 6. . . .
[167] *In Gen.*, h. 17, n. 8. . . .
[168] Jerome, *Adv. Jov.* [Against Jovinian], Bk. 1, c. 22 . . . ; etc.
[169] Origen, *In Jos.* [On Joshua], h. 23, n. 3. . . .
[170] Ambrose, *In Luc.* [On Luke], h. 7, n. 134. . . .
[171] Jerome, *In Is.* [Commentary on Isaiah] . . . (PL 24: 171 A). . . .
[172] Origen, *In Ez.* [On Ezekiel], h. 4, n. 1 . . . ; h. 6, n. 1. . . .
[173] Jerome, *In Gal.* [On Galatians] . . . (PL 26: 390). . . .

because it leads to the spirit. The letter is its instrument and servant. If, in ancient Israel, the chief priest wore two tunics,[174] it was to signal to generations yet unborn this twofold meaning of the Divine Law, consisting of the literal and the spiritual.[175] The spiritual understanding comes to remove the veil that covers the letter or the veil that is the letter, in order to extricate the spirit from it.[176] Or else, in opposite terms, it comes to cover up the poverty of the letter with a royal mantle that transfigures it. Without it, moreover, one sees Scripture without really seeing it. Like the sun breaking through a thick cloud, it lays bare the spirit, like the core beneath the crust, like the grain beneath the straw. It sheds light on all of Scripture, for everything [p. 227] in Scripture should be understood spiritually. Everything in Scripture is "spiritual," everything in it is "intelligible"—but on the condition that one work hard to hear it by an interpretation, a contemplation, and an anagogy that are spiritual. All that Scripture recounts has indeed happened in history, but the account that is given does not contain the whole purpose of Scripture in itself. This purpose still needs to be accomplished and is actually accomplished in us each day, by the mystery of this spiritual understanding. Only then—although it is a direction that is indicated rather than a landmark that is ever attained—will Scripture bear us its fruit in its fullness. Only then will we have the "truth" of it.

If we take all these traditional expressions, but forget the context that determines their importance, we are not, up to that point, really saying anything that cannot more or less be found at the heart of various "religions of the Book," at least as regards what is believed by their followers. In all Scripture that is considered to be revealed, the tradition that refers to Scripture presupposes some hidden meaning, and it is precisely this hidden meaning that is the point of departure for many curious constructs and subtleties of thought. But here we have something that obviates all comparison, imparting a unique

---

[174] [Lev 8:7.—Ed.]

[175] *Decret. Bonizonis* [Bonizo, On the Christian life], Bk. 3, n. 54 . . . ; etc.

[176] Bruno of Segni, *In Gen.* [On Genesis], on Isaac and his blindness: "he did not recognize the spiritual understanding under the veiling cloak of the letter" (PL 164: 205 C); etc.

significance to the "spiritual understanding" of the Christian tradition.

For the Christian there exist two successive "Testaments," which are not primarily or even essentially two books,[177] but two "Economies," two "Dispensations," two "Covenants," which have given birth to two peoples, to two orders, established by God one after the other in order to regulate man's relationship with him. The goal of the one that is prior in time is to prepare the way for the second. But this is not what merits them those respective terms of "old" and "new." The New Testament does not take its name solely from the fact that it comes second in time. It is not merely "modern." It is the last word, in an absolute sense: "the latest thing," "a thing that is new and eternal." It is definitive, eternal: "it is said to be eternal, since it will not be exchanged for another testament in the same way as the old was exchanged for the new";[178] always new, "because it has never grown old,"[179] renewing everything: "it is said to be new, because it speaks of things that are immutable and ever new";[180] "always new, because it is always renewing minds, and never old, because it never withers."[181] It is that "Power of God," "which cannot pass away or grow old."[182] "Whereas the Old Testament never discerns the present except by reference to the future, the New Testament discerns a real present that nothing can call into question. The New Covenant is not repeated. It is completed and fulfilled once and for all."[183] Not only will it not be [p. 228] revoked or perfected, but the way in which it is understood will not change: "the understanding of it never changes."[184]

---

[177] It is in Melito of Sardis (+175) that the first mention of the Old Testament as a collection of books can be found. For the New Testament, we have to wait for the antimontanist author who was writing around 192–[9]3. [See Eusebius, *Church History* 5, chap. 16, 3, where an unnamed writer begins by stating that he has long hesitated to compose his text, in case he appears to be adding to the "New Testament", which may not be increased.] The meaning of the expression is still being debated.

[178] . . . Amalarius, *Ep.* 4 (PL 105: 1334 C). . . .

[179] . . . Augustine, *In ps.* [On the Psalms] *149*, n. 1. . . .

[180] . . . Isidore, *Etym.* [Etymologies], Bk. 6, c. 1. . . .

[181] . . . Bernard, *In vig. nat. Dom.* [On Christmas Eve], *s.* 6, n. 6. . . .

[182] . . . Rupert, *In Ap.* [On the Book of Revelation], Bk. 9, c. 14. . . .

[183] K. Barth, *Dogmatique* [Dogmatics] [French trans., vol. 1, 2, 1 (99)].

[184] . . . Gregory, *In Ez.* [On Ezekiel], Bk. 1, h. 6, n. 17. . . .

Thus there is, in one sense, an opposition between the two Testaments: "one way then . . . another way now."[185] But there is nonetheless a unity. Their relationship is ambiguous. The second arises from the first and does not repudiate it. The second does not destroy the first. In fulfilling it, it gives it new life and renews it. It transfigures it. It subsumes it into itself. In a word, it changes its letter into spirit. To understand the Bible "spiritually" or to understand it "in an evangelical, gospel sense" is all one and same thing.[186] "Now the truth of the Holy Spirit shines without obstruction by any veil of the Old Testament."[187] Correlatively, from the day that this change was made, the first Testament found itself surpassed, obsolete, outdated—"antiquated" in all the parts of its writings that were not in conformity to the new. If, then, one wanted to maintain the literal interpretation as a standard or benchmark, it would become "the letter that kills."[188] Henceforth this Old Testament no longer exists for the believer except in its relationship to the New Testament, which is to say that henceforth it has to be understood in its entirety "according to the spirit." Doubtless this understanding was not meant to negate the interpretation of the Old Testament that was formerly arrived at "according to the letter," but was meant rather to oppose the interpretation of it that would be claimed to be given nowadays "according to the antiquated letter."[189] The ancient Jews, those, at least, who were faithful, understood the writings of Scripture, to the extent that God wanted them to understand it at the time. But those of them who refused to acknowledge the new covenant by refusing to acknowledge Jesus Christ lost their very understanding of these writings.[190] "Henceforth everything that is not understood by way of the Spirit which renews all things is old and antiquated."[191]

Now a transformation like this of the Old Testament in the New is not the consequence of an evolution of minds. Nor is it spread

[185] . . . Rabanus, *In Num.* [On Numbers], Bk. 1, c. 13. . . .

[186] Origen, *In Num.*, h. 11, n. 4. . . .

[187] . . . Isidore [On Exodus] (PL 83: 313 A).

[188] Isidore, *Etym.*, Bk. 6, c. 1, n. 1–2. . . . [2 Cor 3:6.]

[189] . . . Bruno of Segni, *In ps.* [On the Psalms] . . . (PL 164: 696 BC). . . .

[190] Hervaeus, *In Is.* [On Isaiah], Bk. 7. . . .

[191] . . . Gregory, *In 1 Reg.* [On 1 Kings], Bk. 1, n. 9. . . .

out in terms of duration. It comes to pass all at once. It is not a progression by stages. Although it has been prepared for, in the end it is an abrupt transition, it is a wholesale transfer, it is a change of register, by which everything takes on another meaning. Thanks to a new illumination, everything that constituted what today we call the Old Testament—persons, events, institutions, laws, temple, sacrifices, priesthood, etc.—appeared to be changed all of a sudden:

> The inward anxiety of my mind "disturbed me," on account of the sudden introduction of the New Testament for the Old, when, [p. 229] instead of the books of the prophets and the law, which I knew were divine and written by the Holy Spirit, the preaching of the Gospel suddenly filled the whole world.[192]

Properly speaking it is a shift or transformation:[193]

> There is a transformation of the way in which these things are understood, even though the way they are named does not change.

For words denoting transformation and change recur constantly in the texts: "a change of law and of priesthood,"[194] "the transformation of the Old Testament into the New Testament."[195] To use a word that is even more expressive and no less frequent, it is a conversion—a conversion of letter to spirit.

A fact of this kind is not to be confused with the process that can be observed throughout the history not only of Israel, but also—with differences that this is not the place to analyze—in the history of other peoples: a process of spiritualization, of deepening on the basis of initial givens that date back to rougher times. Beryl Smalley wrote that:

> Allegorical interpretation marks a stage in the history of every civilized people whose sacred literature is primitive.

This is the means, in effect, by which is resolved the conflict that has become inevitable between the letter of that which is held to be

---

[192] . . . Bede, *In Cant.* [On the Song of Songs], Bk. 5 (PL 91: 1186 A). . . .

[193] Origen, *In Gen.*, h. 13, n. 3. . . .

[194] . . . Isidore, *L. de variis q.* [Book on Various Questions], c. 12, n. 4. . . .

[195] . . . Peter Lombard, *In ps.* [On the Psalms] *39* (PL 191: 399 A).

normative and the demands of the new intellectual and moral situation.[196] Thus new problems receive an appropriate solution, and progress can be welcomed without the sacred bond being broken and without an alteration of the fervent attachment to venerable teachings or prescriptions. Thus, from a meditation on the ancient Scriptures "there issue forth new Scriptures, a curious mix of fidelity and imagination"; the expressions of a first author are taken up by another and given a new coloration.[197] Furthermore, everything is not always arbitrary in such a process, and the historian often has leave to admire "such a living role that is played by tradition, which ceaselessly makes great works rise again, so that they bear fruit and are extended in time."[198] In the case of Israel, notably, the fact is beyond doubt. It has taken on a great amplitude, and it has borne beautiful fruits. It has, moreover, been pursued, albeit in other conditions, in the bosom of Judaism, after the Christian era. But in this case we are speaking of another fact, one that comes later and is more decisive. [p. 230] Since these facts happen to have been confounded, it is necessary to be somewhat insistent.

The most ancient feast days in Israel were agricultural feast days. They were retained, but transformed into feast days that commemorated the great events reported in the book of Exodus: the flight from Egypt, the gift of the Law, the wanderings in the desert, and the conquest of the Promised Land.[199] But this historic reinterpretation was itself only a first step. At the time of the prophets, the nation's past was idealized, the providential significance became more pronounced and came to be the springboard to higher hopes. Henceforth history served as a key to understanding the present and transformed itself more and more into an allegory of the future. The favors that God visited on his people became the warrants for more precious favors. The old accounts took on a new symbolism. There was, as Jean Daniélou says, "a rooting of the typology in the Old Testament itself." There was, for example, a whole "prehistory of

---

[196] Smalley, 2. . . .

[197] A. Robert, "Le genre littéraire du Cant. des cant." [The literary genre of the Song of Songs], . . . [*Revue biblique* 52] 1945, 201.

[198] J. Steinmann, *Le prophète Isaïe* [The prophet Isaiah], 312.

[199] [Ex 12:33–39, 19–31, 15:22—18:27, Josh 6–12.—Ed.]

patristic interpretation of Exodus": the prophets themselves give notice of "a second Exodus, of which the first was a mere figurative symbol," just as they give notice of "a second cataclysm of which the first Flood was the figurative symbol."[200] For the author of the Book of Daniel, the destruction of the Tower of Babel prefigures the fall of Babylon,[201] and for Ezekiel the description of the first paradise is projected onto his vision of the last Jerusalem.[202] What is more, at the prompting of the Spirit, the sacred authors from generation to generation use the materials brought together by those of previous generations to herald a purer and more interior religion.

> By re-reading and meditating on the ancient texts in the light of recent events or new situations and then re-using them and reworking them, they were led to come to a clearer and deeper understanding of the theological content of these texts and thus to promote the progress of the revealed message.[203]

This is the case, in particular, for Jeremiah, for Deuteronomy, and for the second part of the Book of Isaiah. This "new song" constitutes "a new elaboration and blossoming" of the truths that had already seen the light of day in more ancient times, but had not yet borne their fruit. This is the case with the Song of Songs and Psalm 40, which re-use different themes taken from Hosea, Ezekiel, and second Isaiah to achieve a deeper appreciation of the idea of the union of Yahweh and Israel by making the most of the analogical union of man and woman. This is also the case with Ezekiel, as Renée Bloch has shown in a penetrating study: "Using the [p. 231] materials received from his predecessors, the writer prophet has succeeded in constructing an original work, in order to communicate a new message that answers to the needs of his time." He has rethought "the whole history of Israel and the significance of its great events in relation to the present situation":

---

[200] J. Daniélou, *Sacramentum futuri* [Sign of the future] (1950), 131–[3]2. . . .

[201] [Gen 11:1–9, Dan 2:25–45.—Ed.]

[202] [Gen 2:4–16, Ezek 47:1–12.—Ed.]

[203] Cf. S. W. Baron, *Histoire d'Israël* [The history of Israel], 1 (. . . 1956), 6–8, 133, 182.

> We are in the presence of a reflection which, at a moment of confusion and disorder, anxiously consults with the past in order to find in it the illumination, the answers, the explanations, the assurances, and the hopes that the present, a particularly sombre present, requires. To this end, the prophet harmonizes various texts, especially from Hosea, Jeremiah, and Deuteronomy, in order to clarify them, explain them, and complete them mutually, and to make them react somehow in this mutual interplay . . . to make illumination that is partially new burst forth from them. . . . He takes up oracles of the past, but he inserts them into a whole that gives them a new meaning, a new importance—not *different* from that of the past, but a progressive addition to it—adapted to the needs of the present situation and in conformity with the mission that he has received. . . .[204]

This is precisely the midrashic genre[205] whose importance grew in Israel beginning at the time of the exile and which invaded canonical and noncanonical literature. Knowledge of this genre is indispensable for a sound exegesis of the New Testament.

Let us not suppose that an evolution like this totally escaped the notice of the ancient Christian commentators. They were well aware of one of the essential methods of the prophets: "It is a trademark of prophetic knowledge to recall deeds in order to help in the doing of deeds."[206] They also knew how to recognize the allegorization of previous history, the "mystery" of which was found to have been partially revealed from before the time of Christ. Thus we have Saint Augustine explaining Psalm 113:

> Listen to what is more marvelous: some of the hidden and veiled mysteries of the old books are revealed in part by the old books. For the prophet Micah says this: "As in the days when you came out of the land of Egypt I will show them marvellous things, etc." (Mic. 7:15–19). Certainly you will notice, brothers, that the sacred mysteries are quite manifestly being laid open here. Thus, in this psalm,

---

[204] Renée Bloch, "Ezéchiel XVI, exemple parfait de procédé midrashique dans la Bible" [Ezek 16: A perfect example of midrashic procedure in the Bible], *Cahiers sioniens* 10 (1955): 193–223; 213, 216–[1]7. . . .

[205] [The Jewish rabbinic tradition of commentaries on the written and oral law.—Ed.]

[206] . . . Hilary, *In ps.* [On the Psalms] *62*, 4. . . .

> although the marvellous spirit of prophecy considers the future, it [p. 232] seems, nonetheless, to be recounting things as if they have already happened in the past.[207]

Thus the prophets have already "polished," if we can use such a term, the hearts of the men of their time, to make them catch a glimpse of some of what was foreshadowed by the most ancient history of Israel. According once again to Saint Augustine, this took place:

> so that we might believe that it was not merely apostolic authority that made those figures ours. But this notion was encompassed by the prophets themselves. Their eloquence was of a revelatory kind. Seeing and rejoicing in this revelatory eloquence, we may safely draw out of God's treasury new and old things that are harmoniously related in a mutually coherent arrangement.

It was natural that Deuteronomy drew their attention in this regard. In observing that it enacts "a more evident legislation" than earlier texts, Origen had recognized it as a symbol of "evangelical precepts," that "second law that leads everything to perfection." He had seen it as "that law of the Gospel written in the heart of the believer who hears and retains the words of Christ." Extending his analysis, as was his custom, he had also supposed that it signified the second coming of Christ, which will be "more dazzling and glorious" than his first coming in the humble lineaments of flesh.[208] Others, who drop this latter application, retain the idea that Deuteronomy announced in a more strikingly true and forceful way: the promulgation of the Gospel, a true and definitive "second Law." We find terminology such as: "The Gospel signifies what can be called a second promulgation of the law"[209] and "the Deuteronomy of gospel truth."[210] Had not Saint Paul himself allowed it to be understood, by a subtle exegesis, that a passage from this book of Scripture contained "a prophetic announcement of gospel

[207] . . . *In ps. 113,* n. 4. . . .

[208] *De princ.* [On first principles], Bk. 4, c. 3, n. 13. . . .

[209] . . . Bede, *Q. sup. Deut.* [Questions on Deuteronomy], c. 2 (PL 93: 409 C).

[210] . . . Jerome, *Ep.* [Letters] 78, n. 43. . . .

justice," a kind of "anticipation of the economy proclaimed by Christ"?[211]

Therefore it can be said that "between a biblical theme and its typological patristic exegesis" there are "a certain number of gradual stages that are comprised of the interpretations of this theme to be found in successive biblical authors."[212] Except that it is the author of these last lines who adds that the same theme can therefore be found taken up "by the Prophets, the Psalms, the Jewish Apocalypse, the New Testament, and finally the Fathers of the Church—so many times the theme is taken up by men who are turned towards the future." Now this is what the Fathers and their spiritual [p. 233] heirs would have refused to endorse. In their eyes, the "moment" of the New Testament was not—and it could not be so in the eyes of any Christian—a simple moment in a series, a moment analogous to the "moments" of the Psalms, the Prophets, or the Jewish Apocalypse. In their eyes, this "moment" of the New Testament was—to borrow two words from Karl Barth—the "critical instant," which became the "eternal instant." It was the unique "kairos." The level of Deuteronomy was not fully comparable to it. It was no more true for them than it was for Saint Paul that it constituted a second Testament.[213] They were well aware that, while Saint Paul had been able to "extend" the meaning of the inspired writer without betraying it, this extension of meaning presupposed the unique intervention of the Fact of Christ. Those were writers who, like Origen, in their opposition to the heretic Gnostics, made a greater allowance for the revelations of the Logos before the time of his incarnation. But at the same time, these very writers felt more forcefully the congenital imperfection of our knowledge until the advent of the regime of the New Law, and they were not slow in proclaiming that the coming of the Logos in the flesh, and the Logos alone, constituted "The Coming of

---

[211] St. Lyonnet, "S. Paul et l'exégèse juive de son temps, à propos de Rom 10:6–8" [St. Paul and the Jewish exegesis of his time with regard to Rom 10:6–8], *Mél. Robert* (1957), 498–[9]9.

[212] Daniel Lys, "A la recherche d'une méthode pour l'exégèse de l'A. T." [In search of a method for Old Testament exegesis], *Etudes théol. et rel. 3* (1955), 5, n. 6.

[213] Augustine, *In Hep.* [Writings on the Old Testament], Bk. 5, q. 49. . . .

Truth."[214] With all the more reason, they themselves did not suppose that they were constituting a new "moment" in this coming. A thought of this kind could only have been rejected by them as a blasphemy. They did not take the initiative, in their turn, of interpreting the old texts other than by the past, and neither did they project into the past the new interpretation received from the witnesses to Jesus: they were entirely enthralled by their admiration for the unique, unsurpassable Newness, utterly special and transfiguring everything it touched, that in their eyes constituted the "New Testament." And if they were, in fact, very much oriented toward the future, since every Christian awaits the glorious return of Christ, this was no longer in the manner of the ancient seers of Israel, for they knew that Christ has come, and they were not awaiting another Christ, of whom the Christ of the Gospel would still have been only a kind of prefiguration. Henceforth all their hope could be "none other than the present gift of Jesus Christ."[215] Prepared "from the beginning of the age" by a whole series of stages, salvation had finally come. The transition from shadows to truth had taken place:

> Truth puts the shadows to flight!
> Light gives illumination to the night![216]

Suddenly the Lord had appeared, coming out from the dense forest of allegories, the gloom of which had not been broached up to that [p. 234] point.[217] This is what none of the stages that had marked the progress of Israel's religion had yet accomplished. Without the Lord, who was destined to appear at the end term of all this, all these stages would have been fruitless and ineffectual. "They would be running in vain, if they were not boasting of Christ."[218] And by contrast with this end term, it had to be said indistinctly of all these stages: "all the time before the coming of the Savior remained empty and useless, as it were."[219] This is the

---

[214] Origen, *In Jo.*, Bk. 28, 12. . . .
[215] Cf. K. Barth, *Dogmat.* [Church dogmatics], French translation 1 (1953).
[216] . . . Adam of Saint Victor, *Pâques* [Easter] (Gautier, 26). . . .
[217] Aelred, *De oner.* [On the prophetic burdens of Isaiah] *s.* 28. . . .
[218] . . . Werner, *Defl.* [Compilations], Bk. 1 (PL 157: 821 D).
[219] . . . Helinand, *s.* [Sermons] 7 (PL 212: 535 D).

illumination that had not yet been procured by any of the successive "re-readings" of the Holy Books. None of these "re-readings" was comparable to the "re-reading" made henceforth in the Word and in his Spirit. The "newness of the Gospel" was thus something other than a higher level or rung in an ascent that would need to be continued.[220] Without a doubt, it did not change the conditions imposed on our outlook by our present existence in the flesh. In this sense, it had to be said yet that we were still walking amid "shadows and appearances." At least we were living henceforth "in the shadow of Christ."[221] The Lord Jesus was the unique and incomparable summit: "the mountain of mountains, not one of the mountains."[222] In him, Scripture in its entirety had "once and for all" received its fulfillment. Moses and Aaron had lived. Following the true Joshua, Christians had entered into the promised land of the Gospel.[223] Now they could work hard, in the cheerful boldness of their faith, to relate in detail the great allegory of Scripture. They were well aware that in this endless task they were not in any way extending or completing the total allegorization that had been made once and for all by Christ.

## *The Action of Christ*

It is sometimes said that in order to understand biblical revelation properly it is necessary to have some sense of history, some sense of evolution, that is to say, some notion of the continuity of God's work in time, the uninterrupted continuity of a homogeneous historical development. No assessment could be fairer, so long as one does not ignore, in this very continuity and evolution, "history's character of perpetual creation . . . wherein it is God who acts";[224] so long as one knows how to recognize biblical revelation as "a

[220] Rupert, *In Ez.* [On Ezekiel], Bk. 1, c. 6: "the newness of the Gospel". . . .

[221] Origen, fr. *in Cant.* [On the Song of Songs] (Procope; 181–[8]2). . . .

[222] [Heterius and Beatus], *Ad Elip.* [To Elipandus], Bk. 2, c. 50. . . .

[223] *Libri carolini* [Books of Charlemagne] 1, c. 19. . . .

[224] L. Bouyer, *La Bible et l'Evangile* [The Bible and the Gospel] (1951), 234; cf. 230–[3]1. . . .

series of successive transpositions,"[225] transpositions "that are veritable metamorphoses."[226] But at the same time no assessment could be more incomplete. The history of revelation also offers the spectacle of a discontinuity that has no equal, which makes the traditional [p. 235] idea of allegory, understood in its most profound essence, irreplaceable. This idea was much more than "the expression of a prophetism of progress," as people sometimes say, echoing Edward Caird,[227] and the "theory of evolution," therefore, cannot be sufficient to relay it.[228] In a sense, it is true, the continuity still remains, and one can even say that it is "faultless." Nothing was "improvised." Jesus Christ did not come on the scene "all of a sudden," without preparations, into the middle of an entirely hostile or strange world.[229] The Old Testament was an outline, a rough sketch, a "first draft,"[230] as it were. The New Testament is the fruit of a supernatural tree whose roots and trunk and leaves were the Old Testament, and "it is through the Law that one arrives at the Gospel."[231] The light that bursts forth from the Gospel had begun to gleam in the Law: "Whatever sheds light in the Old Testament flashes forth radiantly in the New Testament."[232] But in another sense, the break is a radical one. The new covenant is not like the old covenant.[233] The people of God would no longer be an ethnic group. The Divine Presence would no longer be localized in one spot, in a material tabernacle. From now on, God would be in Jesus Christ and everywhere. To explain such a contrast, it does

---

[225] C. Charlier, *La lecture chrét. de la Bible* [Christian reading of the Bible], 155.

[226] L. Bouyer, "Liturgie et exégèse sp." [Liturgy and spiritual exegesis], *La Maison Dieu*, 7 (1946). . . .

[227] [Edward Caird (1835–1908) was a Scottish philosopher who became master of Balliol College, Oxford.—ED.]

[228] What moderns seek in the theory of evolution, in order to convey history, is what the ancients would have demanded of the allegorical method. . . .

[229] Maximus of Turin, hom. 55 (PL 57: 355 B). Also Hildegard, *Scivias* [Know the ways], Bk. 3, c. 11 (197, 716 B). . . .

[230] . . . Augustine, *s. Mai.* [Sermons, ed. Mai] 158, n. 1; . . . ; etc.

[231] Isidore, *De ecclesiasticis officiis* [On Church liturgies], Bk. 1, c. 11, n. 1–2. . . .

[232] . . . Aimo, *In Ap.* [On the Book of Revelation], Bk. 2 (PL 117: 1008 D).

[233] Jeremiah 31:31: "Behold, the days are coming, says the Lord, when I will make a new covenant with the house of Israel and the house of Judah, not like the covenant which I made with their fathers. . . ." . . .

not suffice to say that "Israel's soul has matured."[234] The transposition that takes place at this point constitutes "a newness and an overstepping of boundaries as complete as an assumption and fulfillment."[235] Incommensurable with the "perpetual creation" that could be observed up to that point is the "new creation" that consummates it.

Nevertheless, let us recognize that this case is unique, beyond the bounds of all likeness and all analogy. In human history, there are not two "fullnesses of time." In the history of revelation, moreover, there are not a whole series of graduated testaments: after the Old Testament, there are no more testaments except for the New. Even if there were several transitions, there was only one transition, however, the final one, which forever merits the name of "Easter."[236] Only then do we find that "Moses died,"[237] so that another, higher life might take the place of his. Up to that point, it was a time of "shadows." Now "Truth" has come on the scene.[238] Previously it was "the Law and the Prophets." Henceforth it is "the Kingdom of God."[239] Also, whatever may be the astonishing, disconcerting statements which the historian finds himself constrained to make, statements which can put him in the realm of affirmations that are no longer answerable to history alone, a case such as this, more than any other, will, in its singularity, always escape the ken of anyone who does not assume the point of view of faith. The conversion of the Old Testament to the New, or of the letter of Scripture to its spirit, can only be explained and [p. 236] justified, in its radicalness, by the all-powerful and unprecedented intervention of Him who is Himself at once the Alpha and Omega, the First and the Last.[240] It could not have happened other than "through the workings of

---

[234] Although there had indeed been a maturing. Irenaeus, *Adv. Haer.* [Against the heresies] Bk. 4, c. 9, n. 3. . . .

[235] Congar, *Le mystère du Temple* [The mystery of the Temple], 252.

[236] Cf. Augustine, *In Jo.* [On John], tr. 55, n. 1. . . .

[237] Origen, *In Jos.*, h. 1, n. 3. . . .

[238] Jerome, *Ep.* 22, c. 23. . . .

[239] Cf. Luke 16:16; Romans 8:3; Galatians 4:4; Hebrews 1:1–2.

[240] Revelation 1:17. Cf. 1 Cor. 15:45; . . . Hildegard, *Sciv.* [Know the ways], 3, c. 7 . . . ; etc.

Christ."[241] "Ancient Word,"[242] "the one born before the ages," and "the one come at the end of time,"[243] Jesus Christ can say, at the moment of the Incarnation: "It is I who speak; here am I."[244] Furthermore, he can say in truth: "Before Abraham was, before Adam was, I am."[245] "Seed of Abraham, creator of Abraham"; "Lord of the prophets, fulfiller of the prophets";[246] "prototype" of all those who, having appeared before him on the biblical stage, can only be "types" in relation to him, he is at once he "from whom and through whom all prophecy exists."[247] Moreover, he is the Master of the First Testament as he is of the Second. He has made them for each other. He separates them and reunites them in himself. Thus, if such a transition can be made from one to the other, it is because it is a "transition to Christ"[248] and concurrently a "transition that is effected in Christ."[249] If all the "clouds" are dispelled all at once, perhaps this is only by virtue of the unparalleled burst of brightness that is the bright burst of Christ: "On account of his bright glory, the clouds dissipated at the sight of him."[250] If truth takes the place of shadowy darkness by a sudden illumination, it is because that Truth which shines in Christ has come into play: "the Truth of God has appeared in Jesus alone."[251] If there is a "transformation," it is because it happens through Christ.[252] "He did not nullify those ancient signs of things by argument, but he transformed them by fulfilling them."[253] If there is a "change," this change can only be the fact of Christ:

---

241 . . . Pseudo-Augustine, *s.* [*Sermons*] 90, n. 4. . . .

242 Rupert, *In Ap.*, Bk. 2 (PL 169: 865 A).

243 Aimo, *In Ap.*, Bk. 1 (PL 117: 960 C); etc. Mark 1:15.

244 . . . Origen, *Sel. in Thren.* [On Lamentations], 4, 20. . . .

245 John 8:53–58. . . .

246 . . . Augustine, *In Jo.* [On John], tr. 43, n. 16. . . .

247 . . . Hilary, *In ps.* [On Psalm] 54, n. 2. . . .

248 . . . Augustine, *In ps.* 7, n. 1. . . . Cf. 2 Corinthians 3:16.

249 . . . Abelard, *s.* 13 (PL 178: 485 C).

250 . . . Bernard, *In dom. 1 post Epiph.* [On the first Sunday after Epiphany], *s.* 2, n. 1. . . .

251 . . . Jerome, *In Eph.* [On Ephesians] (PL 26: 507 A).

252 "mutatio per Christum," Claudius [of Turin] (PL 50: 1053 C). . . .

253 . . . Florus, *Exp. Missae* [Exposition of the Mass], c. 4, n. 11. . . .

> Coming in the flesh, the Lord changed all the shadowy ceremonies of the Mosaic law by turning them to the light of spiritual life.[254]

If there is a transfer, it is that Jesus Christ, entering into the Holy of Holies,[255] sends us his Spirit. If there is total renewal, it is because the Newness of Christ has intervened. On this subject, the celebrated words of Saint Irenaeus are well known: "by bringing himself he brought all newness."[256] Saint Ambrose says the same thing, in a formula that is no less energetic: "The Lord Jesus came . . . and what was old was made new."[257] If the result of such a "moulting process" is not only total but definitive, if the "Christian meaning of the Bible" is to be found "affirmed henceforth and forever,"[258] it is because, in fact, God has, in successive stages, "led his people in anticipation of Someone."[259] All of biblical history and all of biblical reality had Christ for its unique end.

> [p. 237] The law is a shadow of what is to come,
> Christ is the promised end,
> He is the consummation of all things![260]

> The old law confirms the new and the new law fulfills the old;
> The old things are hopeful, the new are faith-filled;
> But the grace of Christ binds together the old and the new.[261]

In short, the spirit of the letter is Christ. The Gift prophesied by the Law is Christ. "The New Testament is Christ."[262] "The Gospel is Christ."[263] "The breath that comes from our mouth is Christ the Lord."[264]

---

[254] . . . Othloh, *Dial. De trib. quaest.* [Dialogue on three questions], c. 46. . . .

[255] [Echoing Heb 9:11–12.—Ed.]

[256] . . . *Adv. Haer.*, Bk. 4, c. 34, n. 1. . . .

[257] . . . *De int. Job et David* [The prayer of Job and David], Bk. 1, c. 4, n. 12. . . .

[258] G. Auzou, *La Parole de Dieu* [The Word of God] (1956).

[259] [Charles] Hauret, "Comment lire la Bible?" [How should the Bible be read?] *La Table Ronde* (1956), 141.

[260] Adam of Saint Victor, Sequence: "Let the old leaven be purified," [vv.] 19–21 (Gautier, 47).

[261] Paulinus of Nola, *Ep.* 32, *ad Severum* [to Severus], n. 5 (PL 61: 333 A).

[262] . . . Bede, *Q. in Reg.* [On the Book of Kings], Bk. 1, c. 1 (PL 93: 431 A).

[263] . . . Amalarius, *De eccl. off.* [On the liturgy], Bk. 2, c. 20 (PL 105: 1096 B).

[264] Lamentations 4:20. . . .

Therefore, Jesus Christ brings about the unity of Scripture, because he is the endpoint and fullness of Scripture. Everything in it is related to him. In the end he is its sole object. Consequently, he is, so to speak, its whole exegesis. According to Saint Augustine, this is what is meant by mention of the phrase "with a view to the end," which can often be found in the heading of psalms: "When you hear the text of the psalm saying, 'with a view to the end,' let your hearts turn to Christ."[265] Scripture leads us to him, and when we reach this end, we no longer have to look for anything beyond it.[266] Cornerstone that he is, he joins together the two Testaments, just as he joins together the two peoples. He is the Head of the body of the Scriptures, just as he is the Head of the body of His Church. He is the Head of all sacred understanding, just as he is the head of all the elect. He is the whole content of Scripture, just as he contains all of it in him:

> The whole body of Divine Scripture, both the Old and the New Testaments, contain the Son of God. . . . In him is contained all the Law, both old and new.[267]

> All of Divine Scripture is one book, and that one book is Christ, because all of Divine Scripture speaks of Christ, and all of Divine Scripture is fulfilled in Christ.[268]

> The Word of God, the only-begotten Son of God, Our Lord Jesus Christ . . . seems to be a great mainstay of truth, if anyone can interpret Sacred Scripture in such a way that he is mindful of the mystery of it, namely, the Lord himself, who established it.[269]

But this unity in Christ includes yet another aspect, which reveals it even more forcibly. Inasmuch as he is the exegesis of Scripture, Jesus Christ [p. 238] is also the exegete. He is truly Scripture's Logos, in an active as well as a passive sense:[270] "Christ, who alone

265 . . . Augustine, *In ps. 139*, n. 3 . . . ; etc.

266 . . . Cassiodorus, *In psalt., praef.* [On the Psalter, preface], n. 3. . . .

267 . . . Gaudentius, *Tr.* 2, *in Ex.* [On Exodus] (26).

268 . . . Hugh, *De arca Noe mor.* [On Noah's moral ark], Bk. 2, c. 8 (PL 176: 642 C).

269 . . . Godfrey of Admont, *H. dom.* [Sunday homilies] 60 (PL 174: 401 BC).

270 Cf. M. Heidegger, *Essais et conférences* (1958), 251: "logos is at once *legein,* to express, and *legomenon,* that which is expressed."

unlocks an understanding of the Scriptures."[271] It is he alone who explains it to us, and in explaining it to us, he gives an explanation of himself: "The Book opens itself on its own."[272] And who, in fact, other than he himself, could be a better interpreter of himself? It is he and he alone who shows us how, from one end to another, Scripture in its entirety signifies nothing other than the Gospel, that is to say, himself. Even during the time when he lived on earth, he said to the Jews who questioned him: "You search the Scriptures . . . and it is they that bear witness to me."[273] Nevertheless, this could only be by way of anticipation. But one evening, on the road to Emmaus, we see him giving a more explicit teaching to the two men who were traveling with him on the way: "beginning with Moses and all the prophets, he interpreted to them in all the scriptures the things concerning himself."[274] And this second time, unlike the first, presupposes the accomplishment of the mystery. "More and more, the Savior began to reveal the mystery of his Passion, and there is no problem harmonizing this with the Gospel."[275] In this case, he conveys to the understanding an explanation which has been fulfilled in its substance. He invites us to see what has just had light shed on it for all time.

This is because Christ's exegesis, insofar as it is essential and decisive, does not consist of words first and foremost. It is actual. It is Action.

> For every doubt is taken away, and the truth is proclaimed, when the truth is proved not by words, but by actual things.[276]

Before explaining to his disciples on Easter evening how the ancient Scripture bears witness to the New Testament and thus comes to be

---

[271] "Christus, qui solus intelligentiam Scripturarum aperit," Hervaeus, *In Is.* [On Isaiah], Bk. 8 (PL 181: 557 D).

[272] "Liber ipse aperit seipsum." Cf. Bernard, *In die s. Paschae* [Sermon for Easter], . . . on the seven seals, n. 12: "Worthy is the Lamb who was slain, the Lion who rose again, and lastly the Book itself is worthy of opening itself" (PL 183: 280 C).

[273] John 5:39. Godfrey of Admont, *H. dom.* 60 (PL 174: 401 B); etc.

[274] Luke 24:25ff. . . .

[275] . . . Ambrose, *In ps. 40*, v. 15. . . .

[276] . . . Pierre de Corn[ouaille], *Disp. adv. Sim. jud.* [Disputation against Simon the Jew] (ed. R. W. Hunt, . . . 154).

changed into it, Jesus brings about this change. In other words, the prophecies and the figures are made clear by their very fulfillment —and it could not be otherwise. The mysteries of Scripture are "revealed in action."[277] Such, according to Saint Jerome in his translation of Origen, is the double significance of the Greek word used by Saint Luke at the beginning of his Gospel, a word that can only be translated by the conjoined words "fulfilled" and "manifested."[278] "The night will be illumined like day," sings the Psalmist. This is what happens when the Lord comes.[279] At that point "the Gate that faces East opens up, and from it the true Light radiates forth."[280] At that point, "the Old Testament was opened up, and the spiritual understanding that was hidden in it was revealed to believers."[281] "Christ is the illuminator of ancient things."[282]

[p. 239] Jesus is thus a scriptural exegete by virtue of himself, by virtue of all his being, and by virtue of all his mystery. He is an exegete, in principle, from the moment of his Incarnation. This is what Origen explained in the fourth book of his *Peri archôn*, which is too often taken for a treatise on hermeneutics in the narrow sense of the word, as if the only matter discussed in it were the *books* of the Bible and not first and foremost the very *realities* of the twin Testaments:

> The brightness of the coming of Christ illuminated the law of Moses with the shining splendor of truth and lifted the veil that had been placed over the letter. For everyone who believed in him he unlocked all the good things that were enclosed in it.[283]

We can, however, speak in less general terms. Jesus is a scriptural exegete par excellence in the act by which he fulfills his mission, at that solemn hour for which he has come: in his sacrificial action, at the hour of his death on the cross. That is why he says,

---

[277] . . . Autpert, *In. Ap.* [On the Book of Revelation], Bk. 7 (573 C).

[278] *In Luc.* [On Luke], h. 1, Jerome's translation [*plérophoreó*].

[279] Cassiodorus, *In ps. 138,* n. 12. [Ps 139:12 in the modern numbering.]. . . .

[280] Jerome, *Ep.* 121, pref. . . .

[281] Berengaud, *In Ap.* [On the Book of Revelation], v. 4 (PL 17: 874 C). . . .

[282] . . . Tertullian, *Adv. Marc.* [Against Marcion], Bk. 4, c. 40. . . .

[283] . . . *De princ.* [On first principles], Bk. 4, c. 1, n. 7. . . .

in effect: "Behold, I make all things new."[284] That is why he *kills* the shadows and images in terms of their literal meaning and why he makes known the spirit in which the faithful should live. What we have here is a divine alchemy that alone realizes the "virtue of the Lord's passion."[285] "While the Savior hung on the cross, the understanding of Holy Scripture spread throughout the world."[286] In pronouncing the words "it is finished" on that gibbet which is a symbolic representation of the last letter of the Hebrew alphabet,[287] Jesus imparts to all of Scripture its fulfillment.

> In this way, he reveals the whole mystery of man's redemption, which was to be found in hidden form in the twenty-two books of the Old Testament.[288]

His Cross is the sole and universal key.[289] By this sacrament of the Cross, he unites the two Testaments into a single body of doctrine, intermingling the ancient precepts with the grace of the Gospel. By dying, the Lion of Judah obtains the victory that opens the Book with seven seals.[290] He penetrates into the Temple that contains the holy ark.[291] He rends the veil that covered the mysteries of grace.[292] In one stroke, he shows the profound meaning of what was written, and at the same time he opens the eyes of those who place no

---

[284] Revelation 21:5. Cf. 2 Corinthians 5:17; 1 Corinthians 15:47–[4]9; Ephesians 4:28. . . .

[285] . . . Aelred, *S. ined.* [Unedited sermons] (Talbot, 42).

[286] . . . Irimbert, *In Jud.* [On Judges], Bk. 1 (Pez, 4, 196).

[287] [Tav, which in the Sinaitic alphabet is similar to a Latin cross.—Ed.]

[288] Helinand, *s.* [Sermons] 10: "The sign of the cross is correctly represented by the last letter of the Hebrew alphabet, for it brought to an end the figurative expressions of the law and ratified the virtue of charity, which contains the whole law. All the mysteries of human redemption, which lay hidden in the twenty-two books of the Old Testament, were revealed in the cross and were brought to full perfection. For this reason, when the Lord was given vinegar as he hung upon the cross, he said: 'It is finished'" (PL 212: 567 B).

[289] Augustine, *In ps. 45*, n. 1: "Our Lord's cross was a key by which things that were closed were unlocked." . . .

[290] [Rev 5:5.—Ed.]

[291] [Rev 11:19.—Ed.]

[292] [Mt 27:51; Mk 15:38; Lk 23:45.—Ed.]

obstacles in the way, for they need eyes to see this: "through his death he opened the eyes of our mind."[293]

Thus the light of truth bursts forth doubly from the Cross. All of [p. 240] tradition repeats this: "he reveals the spiritual understanding,"[294] "he promotes a spiritual understanding of the eloquence of Sacred Scripture,"[295] "he transforms the shadowy world of figurative expressions into truth,"[296] "he puts an end to the literal and ascribes pre-eminence to a new, spiritual understanding."[297] What the rod of Moses had accomplished figuratively by striking the rock is accomplished in very truth by a thrust of the centurion's lance:

> If Jesus had not been struck, if blood and water had not flowed from his side, all of us would still be suffering from thirst for the Word of God.[298]

Here, then, on Calvary we have the great, open Book of the Divine Plan that is henceforth legible by everyone:

> The divine mind is a great book. . . . The Book of Revelation and Isaiah bear the stamp of that book, and Ezekiel is fed by its open pages. . . . In that book Esdras reads distinctly and openly about the wooden stair of the cross; when the soldier opened Jesus' side with a lance, all the windows of the Christian faith were lit up with blood and water, so that there was nothing covered up that was not revealed. . . .[299]

---

[293] . . . Gregory, *Mor.*, Bk. 29, c. 14, n. 26. . . .

[294] . . . Cf. Gregory, *In Ez.* [On Ezekiel], Bk. 2, h. 9, n. 2. . . .

[295] . . . Autpert, *In Ap.*, Bk. 2: "Thus the key of David opened the door and nobody closes it: because the eloquence of Sacred Scripture, a spiritual understanding of which he promotes among the elect through the grace of his Incarnation, cannot be outlined to any of the Jews because of the veil that covers their hearts" (541 H). Cf. Bk. 3: "Not only could the book not be opened by any of the angels or men, even its seals could not be broken. Which is to say that the sacramental mysteries of Divine Scripture could not be shown as having been fulfilled through them. They had to be shown as being referred to him. You have to understand through all this that how it was fulfilled cannot be understood by the reasoning mind" (477 DE).

[296] . . . Aimon [Haymo of Halberstadt], *In Hebr.* [On Hebrews] (PL 117: 934 A).

[297] . . . Bruno of Segni, *s. in octava Dom.* [Sermon for the eighth Sunday] . . . ([*Maxima Bibliotheca Veterum Patrum*], 6, 700 C).

[298] Origen, *In Ex.*, h. 11, n. 2. . . .

[299] . . . Peter Cellensis, *In annunt.* [On the Annunciation], *s.* 1 (PL 202: 705–6).

Here is "a turning of the page that clarifies everything, like that great illustrated leaf on the missal. Here, painted in red, is the great Page that separates the two Testaments! All the doors open at once, all the conflicts vanish, all the contradictions are resolved":[300]

> That light from on high falls onto earth,
> And drives off the wretched darkness of death;
> Something new is displayed; the old is revealed:
> Now nothing is left closed up and hidden under the letter.[301]

Just as "universal recapitulation" has been accomplished by the sacrifice of Jesus,[302] so, similarly, we find that the ancient Scriptures have been definitively opened and condensed. But also, just as the sacrifice of Jesus is completed by the Resurrection, which is no longer separable from his death, so it is the Resurrection that consummates its double effect. The one who opens the Book is indissolubly "the Lamb who was slain and the Lion who comes back to life."[303] In leaving the tomb, Christ sets aside the [p. 241] stone that covered it, that stone of the letter which, up to that point, was an obstacle in the free flow of the spiritual understanding, that stone which he had already prophetically caused to be removed from the tomb of Lazarus.[304] As the new Jacob, he takes the cover off the well,[305] so that the whole world may henceforth drink deeply from these waters.[306]

---

[300] Paul Claudel, *L'épée et le miroir* [The sword and the mirror], 74.

[301] . . . Walter of Châtillon (end of the twelfth century; Wilmart, [*Revue Bénédictine*] 49, 164).

[302] Ephesians 1:10. . . .

[303] This is why the Book of Revelation makes the lion the first of the four living creatures: Autpert, *In Ap.*, Bk. 3 (466–[6]7).

[304] [Jn 11:4.—ED.]

[305] [Jn 4:6, held by tradition to be the location described in Gen 33:18–20.—ED.]

[306] . . . Remi, *In Gen.* [On Genesis], 29, 2: "The stone placed over the well symbolizes the literal covering with which the spiritual water was covered over. But our Jacob, that is to say, Christ, moved the stone aside, inasmuch as he broke through the surface of the letter and revealed a spiritual understanding of the Scriptures" (131: 106 C); *In Gen.*, 24: "For the person with eyes, the way that leads to the well is the Passion of Christ, which leads us to an understanding of the Scriptures. And we would not be able to understand the things that had been written in the Old Testament, if they had not been clearly fulfilled in the Passion" (99 A). . . .

The Action of Christ in fulfilling the Scriptures and conferring on them, at the same time, the fullness of their meaning, is still compared by Christian tradition to the act of eucharistic consecration. For, in truth, Scripture is bread, but for the Christian this bread does not become the living food that it ought to be until it has been consecrated by Jesus:

> . . . Therefore, it was then that the Lord Jesus took the bread of Scripture in his hands, at the point when, having become incarnate according to the Scriptures, he suffered and rose; at that point, I say, he took the bread and gave thanks, when, to fulfill the Scriptures, he offered himself up to the Father as a sacrifice of grace and truth.[307] . . .

### *The Sense Given by the Spirit*

[p. 261] Such is the deep meaning of the Christian distinction between letter and spirit. It was established right from the beginning with some definite features by the Apostle Paul, who, in this respect, wanted only to be a witness to Christ, the exegete of his Exegesis. What is more, the distinction is unanimous. Regarding it, there is no duality of traditions such as pertains to classifications and explanations that are less fundamental. Without a doubt, the meaning of this distinction is more or less vigorously grasped, more or less clearly analyzed in accordance with the circumstances in question: not all the commentators on Scripture are Origens or Augustines! There is, moreover, no doubt that two family groups of understanding, as it were, can be distinguished. Each of them will prefer to make use of one of the two formulas that divide the triple or fourfold sense between them. We shall return to this subject at a later point. The members of the first of these two family groups are more attentive to the interior principle of the spiritual understanding, which is the Holy Spirit.[308] The members of the second group are especially concerned with its essential Object, which is Christ.[309] More than anything else, the first are spir-

---

[307] . . . Rupert, *In Jo.* [On John], Bk. 6 . . . (PL 169: 443 BD). . . .

[308] Pseudo-Remigius, *In ps.* [On the Psalms]: "the spiritual understanding is not given to just anyone who happens to be doing research. . . . I welcomed the Holy Spirit and he gave me understanding" (PL 131: 757 D). . . .

[309] Jerome, *In Gal.* [On Galatians]: "It is our contention that the person who acknowl-

itual. In Scripture they seek, in a direct way, "an understanding of the spiritual life."[310] The second are above all men of doctrine. In Scripture they seek first and foremost "the spiritual mysteries of Christ."[311] But what is explicit with the one group is found implicitly in the other group, and vice versa. The first have no intention of exhausting the spiritual life by cutting it off from its source any more than the second intend to blaspheme this source by denying or neglecting its spiritual fecundity. They are both well aware that Christ cannot be recognized except through the Spirit, and that this Spirit is always the Spirit of Christ. "The law ought to be understood spiritually in Christ."[312] All of Scripture is evangelical when it is contemplated, as it should be, "in the Spirit of the Lord."[313]

Whether it be to denounce their arbitrariness and archaic character, or, more rarely, to justify them, there is almost always an interest in the methods of ancient exegesis. Its machinery is taken to pieces and its sources are catalogued, but there are no precise questions about the establishment of its methods and what service these methods are meant to [p. 262] perform. Or else we find that the variety of its content is described without any attempt to find the principle which confers true significance on these thousands of details, the principle which establishes and proportions their objectivity, and which assures that they are linked to each other. For the historian, analyses of this kind are not of middling interest. In the end, however, they appear hollow and trifling, or they can even be seriously deceptive, as long as they are not joined to another endeavor. This indispensable endeavor should aim not at explaining the great synthetic idea that is always present as a backdrop to this exegesis by breaking it up into its constituent parts, but rather it

edges all the sacramental mysteries of Scripture and understands them in a lofty way is . . . truly spiritual. The truly spiritual person, moreover, sees Christ in the divine books and does not allow them to be construed in the light of Jewish tradition" (PL 26: 390).

[310] . . . Othloh, *Dial de trib.*, c. 33: "The whole history of the Old Testament concerns these events. All these events, although they have a literal, earthly dimension, are sketched out in such a way as to teach the necessity of seeking an understanding of the spiritual life through them" (PL 146: 102 A).

[311] . . . Autpert, *In Ap.*, Bk. 4 (484 G).

[312] . . . Alcuin, *In ps.* [On the Psalms] (PL 100: 597 A). . . .

[313] Cf. Gilbert Foliot, *Fifth unpublished homily*, . . . cited by Ch. Dumont, [*Collectanea Ordinis Cisterciensium Reformatorum*] [1957], 218.

should aspire to understand this idea in its originality, for it is always being met with in the texts. It is a notion that is asserted on many an occasion, and more than once it is expressed with some magnificence.

Once they are explained, it is possible for these matters to appear quite simple, even too simple. In such a case, one is tempted, after having believed from a distance that the ancient exegesis was composed of whimsical oddities, to see its guiding "principle" as being no more than a banal commonplace. The fact is that we live twenty centuries on from this principle. On the other hand, the opposite situation is possible: it can happen that someone who is glad to take a less inexact view of the principle succeeds in "realizing" its pregnant significance. In that case, instead of participating in the astonishment that has fueled so many speculations on Scripture, a person may be led to pass judgment on their excessive boldness. Perhaps one of the reasons for a judgment like this is that our faith, that faith which these speculations helped to "construct," has subsided somewhat. But let us return to our modest purpose. Let us return to the history that we have undertaken, a simple history of certain words and certain classifications.

"We ought to have a spiritual understanding. After the truth of history, everything should be perceived spiritually."[314] When faced by the unanimity of centuries, a unanimity that abounds with witnesses from the very first generation of Christians right to the time of recent ecclesiastical documents,[315] one has every good reason to be astonished at seeing some contemporary authors not only criticizing certain particular features of a complex theory (certain procedures, applications, and excrescences), but going so far as to reject the naming of a "spiritual sense," to denounce it as equivocal. But then what word in what language cannot lend itself to being equivocal? Furthermore, these same authors speak as if what were at stake here was a matter of mere novelty, a question of terminology arising from a personal choice, indeed, from suspect patterns

[314] . . . Jerome, *In Is. prol.* [Prologue to Isaiah] (PL 24: 20 B).

[315] Including Leo XIII's encyclical *Providentissimus:* "The Church has received this mode of interpretation from the Apostles and has approved it with her example, inasmuch as it stands out in the liturgy." And repeatedly in Pius XII's encyclical, *Divino afflante.*

of thought. [p. 263] Nevertheless, even of late, there has been no shortage of theologians willing to observe that this phrase was of common usage, "shared and often used by nearly everyone." There has been no shortage of them willing to affirm that the reality of the "spiritual sense," denied though it be by certain anti-Catholic writers, was a question of faith.[316]

A healthy scepticism continues to be warranted, too, when it comes to the strong opinion expressed by some exegetes, who have been led to believe that the progress achieved in their discipline these days renders the traditional distinction void in terms of its very basis in principle. This is because they imagine that a distinction of this kind is due entirely to ignorance of scientific method, and they suppose as a result that it can only be justified among the ancient exegetes as a "provisional fill-in." Such an a priori position is not conducive to an understanding of the distinction.

Although the role of scientific method is not to be slighted in any way, the failure nonetheless of the well-intentioned efforts that have been deployed by some in order to absorb the spiritual sense without destroying it could be considered predictable, a foregone conclusion. Thinkers in this school of thought reclaim the spiritual sense in its entirety as a literal sense that is tagged as being "full." They suppose that "if well understood," this "full" literal sense would encompass everything that the ancient tradition asked of the spiritual sense. It would aptly constitute "a scientific demonstration of the ways in which the two Testaments harmonize." This is a noble and generous viewpoint, akin to the viewpoint of certain psychologists—"depth" psychologists—who think that by a method that is still "scientific," but broader, thanks to their "integral psychology," they can rediscover the whole reality of the spirit which the science of classical psychology, operating on the basis of space, has denied or proscribed.[317] Such a point of view captures a measure of reality. The spiritual sense, in its authentic purport, is truly a "full sense." This is the sense that allows us to see how the very prophecies that

[316] . . . [Theodore] de Régnon, [*Études de théologie positive*] *sur la* [*Sainte*] *Trinité* 3, 1 (1898), 146.

[317] . . . Charles Baudouin, *Psychanalyse du symbole religieux* [Psychoanalysis of the religious symbol] (1957), 12–13.

were realized for the first time in the history of Israel "are fulfilled spiritually more truly and more completely in Christ and his Apostles."[318] This is the sense that gives the Christian who reads Scripture "the fullness that can be sensed in it,"[319] that introduces him "to the fullness of the Gospel,"[320] to that "fullness of the Word" which Saint Gregory distinguishes from a simple "fullness of the book." It is the object not of a dead scientific knowledge, but of a living understanding. It is that "full sense" which is recommended by Benedict XV in his encyclical *Spiritus Paraclitus*. One must take care, however, to guard against a possible confusion of schemes and methods. For it is precisely the case that while an examination of the texts puts a person on [p. 264] the track of this "fullness," it is not a fullness that is acquired without the Gospel—and we are not speaking of the Gospels consulted as historical documents, but of the Gospel received in faith. This "full sense" presupposes a transposition that is impossible or unseasonable without "newness of spirit." Thus the only "full" sense whose defining framework is entirely coherent does not seem to be quite the same as what a certain number of recent authors have wished to promote. The genuinely full sense "is situated on the level of faith."[321] It is "an essential requirement of faith."[322] It is the sense that is recognized by the Church and in the Church.[323] Furthermore, the spiritual under-

---

318 . . . Jerome, *In Jer.* [On Jeremiah], Bk. 6, c. 32. . . .

319 . . . Cf. Origen, *In Jer.* [On Jeremiah], h. 21, n. 2. . . .

320 Lanfranc, citing Jerome, *In Col.* [On Colossians], 2, 26. . . .

321 J. Coppens, [*Ephemerides Theologiae Lovanienses*] (1958): 17. . . .

322 P. Grelot, in *Intr. à la Bible* [Introduction to the Bible], 1 (1957), 180. Lagrange, [*Revue biblique*], 9, 141.

323 Let Marian theology stand as an example. Father L. Bouyer says that it is "at once an exigency and a product of the whole Word of God. For the texts where Mary appears by name are a knotted tangle, as it were, of several great biblical themes. These themes, far from appearing in only one or two secondary sections of Revelation, encompass its major ideas. In turn, *once they found the seat of their development in the Virgin of the Gospels,* they underwent an expansion around her. The great Marian tradition is merely this process of expansion. In it we discover how the Church, in reading the Marian texts of the New Testament, recognized what there was in the Old Testament that was oriented to Mary . . ." (*Le trône de la sagesse* [The seat of wisdom], 13–[1]4; the emphasis is mine). And 53: "The Old Testament provides the lines of thought according to which the New Testament itself should be understood. Nevertheless, it provides only a sketch of these lines of thought, which cannot be joined together and fashioned into a complete whole

standing, which is an acknowledgment of it, cannot be a matter of pure technique or pure intellectuality. Whatever supple intellectual factors are brought to bear in determining it, whatever good and reasonable process of change is envisaged in considering the natural approaches that are apt to lead a person to it, the Spirit of Christ cannot be eliminated from it. The spiritual understanding is a gift of this Spirit. "Whoever thinks that he can unlock the mysteries of the Scriptures without the Spirit of God is clearly like someone without light who feels his way in a daze along walls that are strange to him."[324]

This is how the spiritual understanding has always been understood in the Church. This spiritual understanding does not impede the scientific work of the exegete any more than scientific work can replace the spiritual understanding. The "true science" of the Scriptures, in the ancient sense of the word, does not depend entirely on "science," in the precise, modern sense of the word, even though it does benefit from it to a large extent. It is not separable from the "outlook that permits us to recognize Christ."[325] Inasmuch as it has a close connection with faith, it is a connection marked by humility, purity of heart, and perfection of life. What is more, it teaches us about the mystery of the Transfiguration:

> Only those who transcend earthly desires with their understanding perceive the majesty of Holy Scripture, which is fulfilled in the Lord.[326]

In effect, such a knowledge of the Scriptures leads to "eternal life."[327] In its fullness, it becomes identified with the Kingdom of Heaven. It is one of the great models of the science of exegesis, and is not

---

before the coming of Christ. Accordingly Christ does limit himself to a more vigorous clarification of what was given in the Old Covenant. What is produced is a transposition of previous themes that would be impossible without the new fact, the new givens of the Gospel. . . ."

[324] . . . Guibert de Nogent, *Trop. In Os.* [Tropologies on Hosea], 12, 4. . . .

[325] Paschasius, *In Lam.* [On Lamentations], Bk. 2: "and knowledge of the Scriptures is that life by which Christ is recognized and which is prepared as something eternal for believers" (PL 120: 1105 A).

[326] . . . Bede, *In Marc.* [On Mark] 8 (PL 92: 218 B); "many of us read the words of Scripture indiscriminately; but a small number of those who are more perfect understand how its lofty heights shine forth in splendor through the mysteries of Christ."

[327] Aimo, *In 2 Cor.* [On 2 Cor], 3 . . . (PL 117: 618 AB).

under suspicion of scorning or neglecting human labor, which is an aid in disclosing it: "The Kingdom of Heaven, knowledge of the Scriptures."[328]

Between these two kinds of "science," there are, to be sure, many connections—several works of recent vintage have contributed to a better definition of these connections—but this is not to say that they are [p. 265] homogeneous. The gap between the two bears a certain comparison to the one that is observable between the theology of the schools and mystical knowledge within the context of faith. Mysticism can no more turn up its nose at theology than the spiritual understanding can disdain the historical meaning established by exegesis. Nevertheless, mysticism is something other than theology, and cannot be considered a natural extension of it. And like mysticism, the spiritual understanding depends on illumination, which can only be given from on high. It is more apt to be received than to be won or found. Human effort has its part in it, as it does in every salutary work, and every age brings its available resources to bear on it, resources that every individual is invited to incorporate in himself, indeed, to perfect according to his means. But an effort of this nature is never directed merely at arriving at a better historical knowledge. In other words, within the perspective of our problem, the human progress of exegesis consists of our being made to reread the texts of the "New Testament" in the ever more illuminating light of the Old. This is a precious fruit, a very necessary method. It is in this respect, perhaps, that we are most obliged to surpass or set to rights ancient exegesis as studied in this work. But what remains after this, by a converse movement of thought, is "to recover" the Old Testament, to reread it in the light of the New Testament such as it is given to us by faith, and thus to lead it "to the sense that is invested in the Gospel."[329] This is a measure that no longer tends only to a better human knowledge, guaranteeing a greater doctrinal security,[330] but to a better spiritual "edification,"

---

[328] . . . *In Matt.* [Jerome, On Matthew] (PL 26: 90 A). . . .

[329] Rabanus, *In Mach.* [On Maccabees], Bk. 2 . . . (PL 109: 1243 A).

[330] Cf. R. Guardini, *Liberté, grâce et destinée* [Freedom, grace, and destiny]: "As soon as the Old Testament is slighted and devalued, the effect is felt immediately in the New Testament, which assumes by degrees a philosophical and psychological character and loses its significance" (French translation by J. Ancelet-Hustache [1957], 235, n.).

of both the Church as a whole and of each one of us. In this case, it is no longer a historical document that is being studied, but it is the Word of God that is being received, as it is addressed to us "here and now." In any case, this is the twofold movement that characterizes patristic and medieval exegesis. Now it cannot be that we are able, by perfecting or correcting the first, totally to make up the deficiency of the second. "If you want to understand, you can only do so through the Gospel."[331] "Holy Scripture, which speaks of the mysteries of the kingdom of God to spiritual men, is like a parable to men of this world."[332]

This, along with a great many other things, is explained by John of Salisbury when he compares some professors of his time who are overly proud of their scientific knowledge and are rather unspiritual to boot, to the eunuch of the Queen of Ethiopia:

> In the chariot of the eunuch of the Queen of Ethiopia they discuss and read the Scriptures with eyes closed,[333] and they disdain or are [p. 266] unable to see him who "is led like a lamb to the slaughter" (Isaiah 53). . . . In any case, although they are seated on the wheels of Scripture, and are borne by a motion of winged animals, their tongue, when they discuss higher things, licks at the earth, nor do they understand the Scriptures, because the Lord of every kind of knowledge does not open their hearts.[334]

Thus, in the final analysis, it must be said that:

> Scripture does not need human wisdom in order that we might understand what is written, but rather the revelation of the Spirit, so that, discovering the true meaning of the things that are to be found enclosed in it, we may draw abundant profit from it.[335]

Without a doubt, we must do our best, with renewed tools and materials, to imitate the Ancients who studied the Bible "with the

---

331 . . . Origen, *In Ex.* [On Exodus], h. 7, n. 7 (213). . . .

332 . . . [Godfrey] of Admont, *h. dom.* [Sunday homilies] 23 (PL 174: 154 D).

333 [Acts 8:30–34.—Ed.]

334 . . . *Polycr.* [John of Salisbury, *Policraticus*], Bk. 8, c. 17 (PL 199: 784 AB). Cf. [John of Salisbury], *Ep.* [Letters] 284 (in 1168): "What was once said to the Ethiopian eunuch could be said to many professors: 'Do you think you understand what you are reading?'" (319 D).

335 Chrysostom, *In Gen.*, h. 21, n. 1. . . .

sweat of their brow, exercising the subtle genius that is innate in them."[336] It is an illusion "to imagine that it is possible to attain the spiritual meaning of the Old Testament by means of symbolic transpositions, through some sort of puzzle game." But it is no more possible to attain this spiritual sense in its entirety by a scientific knowledge that is purely human, "by definite methods, the methods of religious history," which are suitable "when it is a matter of establishing proofs."[337] Let us not be seduced by scientism, in order to escape illuminism. What is very much needed in the long run is that "the eyes of the interior man"[338] should be opened, for they are susceptible to a light that is different from the light that fills the eyes of the wise and learned. As Richard of Saint Victor says, we must acquire "the eyes of the dove."[339] Saint Jerome observes that: "We cannot arrive at an understanding of Scripture without the assistance of the Holy Spirit, who has inspired it."[340] This is "the spiritual sense, which the Spirit gives to the Church."[341] "When things are revealed by an anointing of the Spirit, the mind undergoes an expansion, which enables it to understand Scripture."[342]

To sum up, science and spirituality are in no wise incompatible. In the normal course of things, they should help and support one another, and it is obviously desirable for them to be joined together in the confines of the same subject area. But it is not divinely decreed that the most learned should necessarily be the most believing or the most spiritual. Nor is it divinely decreed that the century that would see the greatest progress in scientific exegesis would, by virtue of that very fact, be the century that [p. 267] would best understand Holy Scripture. Thus we need both the learned, in order to help us read Scripture historically, and the spiritual men (who ought to be "men of the Church"), in order to help us arrive at a

---

336 . . . Jocelin of Furness, *Vita Walteni* [Life of Waldef], [*Acta Sanctorum*], vol. 1. . . .

337 Cf. J. Guillet, "Deux aspects du sens spirituel de l'Ecriture" [Two aspects of the spiritual sense of Scripture], in [*Analecta Gregoriana*] 68 (1954), 303.

338 Othloh, *L. de cursu sp.* [The spiritual race], c. 3 (PL 146: 146 C). . . .

339 Richard, *In Cant.* [On the Song of Songs], c. 15 . . . (PL 196: 450 B and D).

340 Jerome, *Ep.* [Letters], 120, q. 10. . . .

341 . . . Origen, *In Lev.* [On Leviticus], h. 5, n. 5 (343).

342 . . . H. de Marcy, *De per. civ. Dei* [On the pilgrim city of God], *tr.* 16 (PL 204: 384 D).

deeper spiritual understanding of it. If the former deliver us from our ignorance, the latter alone have the gift of discernment, which preserves us from interpretations that are dangerous to the faith.[343] Saint Augustine compares spiritual men to the hills toward whose summits the Psalmist lifts his eyes:

> "I have lifted up my eyes to the hills."[344] By hills we understand the Church's great and famous spiritual men. . . . Through them, all of Scripture is dispensed to us. There are prophets, there are evangelists, there are good doctors: that is the direction in which I have lifted up my eyes to the hills, from whence my help will come.[345]

Thus the informed theologian knows beforehand that the whole veil is lifted only for the person who queries the sacred text "with zealous piety."[346] Even while he accepts the progress that has been made by scientific knowledge and he takes care not to perpetuate all the forms by which faith in the divinity of Scripture was once freely expressed, he recognizes unequivocally that the existence of a twofold sense, literal and spiritual, is an ineluctable given of the tradition. It is part of the Christian patrimony.[347] But it is so on the condition, of course, that this duality be understood and accepted as tradition imparts it. Thus designating any sense that is judged "edifying, pious, and religious" as "spiritual," in order to contrast it with a sense that is declared to be "banal and vulgar," should be disallowed.[348] This would be to understand the spiritual sense itself in a banal way. Together with the Fathers, let us reiterate that the spiritual sense is the New Testament itself, with all its fecundity, revealing itself to us "as the fulfillment and transfiguration of the Old." The passage from one sense to the other, like the passage from one Testament to the other, thus expresses "the very movement of

---

[343] Cf. Augustine, *In ps. 103*, *s.* 3, n. 5: "Spiritual men who make judgments about everyone and are judged by no one: therefore they are the only ones who have not fallen divisively into heresy and schism." . . .

[344] [Ps 121:1.—Ed.]

[345] . . . *In ps. 39*, n. 6. . . .

[346] . . . Augustine, *De ut. cred.* [On the profit of believing], c. 3, n. 9. . . .

[347] Scheeben, *Dogmatique* [Dogmatics], n. 237 (French trans. by Bélet, 1, 183). . . .

[348] Father Spicq has good reason to protest a practice like this, "inasmuch as hermeneutically the 'spiritual sense' has a very precise meaning that denotes the reality suggested by the literal sense" ([*Revue des sciences philosophiques et théologiques*], 1948, 90–[9]1).

our faith" in some way. If we can now reread all of Scripture "and hear Jesus speak to us in it," this is:

> because Jesus himself has been assimilated to it, after having somehow taken on his body of flesh in it. Jesus revealed the whole mysterious sense of Scripture when he surrendered his body on the cross and poured out his Spirit on the world.[349]

## *Verbum abbreviatum* [The Abbreviated Word]

[p. 3:140] . . . In Jesus Christ, who is its end, the ancient Law found its unity in advance. From age to age, everything in this Law was converging toward him. It is he who, from the "totality of the Scriptures," was already making "the unique Word [Parole] of God."[350] The Word [Verbe] made flesh is the new Esdras who decisively rescues the sacred Books at the dispersion of Babylon,[351] where they ran the risk of being lost, and who renews them while gathering them together.[352] In him, the "many words" of the biblical writers become "one Word" for ever.[353] Without him, on the other hand, the bond is undone: once again the Word [Parole] of God is fragmented into "human words"; words that are multiple, not merely numerous, but essentially multiple, and without any possible unity, for, as Hugh of Saint Victor puts it, "many are the utterances of man, since the heart of man is not one."[354] The incredulous Jew, whose *perfidia* [lack of faith] is a faith turned backwards, consequently has in hand nothing but a Law that breaks apart, a dust composed of memories and superstitious rites. The Christian, by way of contrast, grasps its unity in its principle. The Word made flesh is, for them, the *Verbum abbreviatum*. He comprehends the marvel sung by the Prophet: "God made a shortened Word upon the earth."[355]

---

[349] René Marlé, S.J., "Bultmann et l'A.T." [Bultmann and the Old Testament], [*Nouvelle revue théologique*] 78 (1956), 483.

[350] Rupert, *De S. Spiritu* [On the Holy Spirit], l. 1, c. 6. . . .

[351] [1 Esd. 9:37–48, 2 Esd. 14.—Ed.]

[352] Rupert, *De vict. Verbi* [The victory of the word of God], l. 7, c. 32. . . .

[353] . . . Rupert, *In Jo.* [On John], l. 7. . . .

[354] . . . *In Eccl.* [On Ecclesiastes], h. 13 (PL, CLXXV, 204 D). . . .

[355] [Is 10:23, quoted in Rom 9:28. The Vulgate translates: "For the Lord God shall make a consummation and an abbreviation in the midst of all the land."—Ed.]

In the Bible, under the figures and enigmas that announced it, the Word, which in itself is one, which is none other than the Son of God, still showed itself "diverse and varied." It found itself there once again "dilated" and, as it were, distended.[356] For human beings, "the word of the sacred page" could no longer be anything but a token or down-payment of the divine clemency in regards to them,[357] because it still resounded in [p. 141] a hundred ways, each incomplete, through the heart and mouth of many saints. It was indeed "preached by way of declamation, or signified figuratively, or dreamed through the imagination"; sometimes in word, sometimes in deed, its appearance was always transitory and piecemeal.[358] "Clearly the words disposed by the prophets' pen are many."[359] We ought, while thinking of that ancient epoch, also say: "God has spoken once, and many things are heard."[360] That was the epoch of the Old Testament. But new times have come: "Those words were spoken to a Jew, and a Christian heard" them.[361] The words of the revelation uncover their unity by accepting their final sense in the Spirit. By that very fact, they receive their final permanence. Indeed, just as the eternally uttered Word [Parole] is unique, so now is its human hearing, for time and eternity are joined in the Word [Verbe] made flesh.

Here he is, then, this unique Word. Here he is among us, "coming forth from Zion,"[362] having taken flesh in the Virgin's womb: "God has united all the totality of Scripture, his every word, within the womb of the virgin."[363] "Behold the great Word open before us. Behold the Word unfolded before us, and we can read within it at sight."[364] All the contents of the Law and the Prophets are substantially summarized in this Word, and in him for the first time acquire their whole sense. For this is indeed that self-same Word,

---

[356] Origen, *In Gen.*, h. 14, n. 1. . . .

[357] . . . Peter the Cantor, *Verb. abbr.*, c. 1. . . .

[358] . . . Bernard, *Sup. missus est* [On the Incarnation], h. 4, n. 11. . . .

[359] . . . Rupert, *De S. Sp.* [On the Holy Spirit], l. 1, c. 6. . . .

[360] . . . Ambrose, *In ps.* [On the Psalms] lxi, n. 33–[3]4 [Ps 62:11 in the modern numbering]. . . .

[361] . . . [Ambrose], *In ps.* cxviii, s. 13, n. 6. . . .

[362] Prayer for Advent, *Or. vis.* [Mozarabic Rite], 21. . . .

[363] . . . *Sacramentary of Lyon,* 11th cent., feast of the Annunciation. . . .

[364] . . . P. Claudel, *Un poète regarde la croix* [A poet before the Cross], 61.

born of the Virgin today, that the Prophets had given birth to of old. That was under another form, but it was already under the action of the same Spirit.[365] The Word of God had been truly sent to them, just as it was to be truly sent to Mary, and God has no other word [parole] than his Word [Verbe], his only Son: "God's utterance is the Word of God; the Word of God is his Son."[366] This is so much the same Word [Parole] in the two cases that the exchange between the one and the other even enjoys what theological language calls "communication of idioms".[367] Under the one form as well as under the other, it is in reality entirely one and the same mysterious being, that very divine food which deserved the name "manna," "a name expressing a question or rather wonder," a name which designated its singular efficacy at the same time as its unheard of novelty.[368] Here it is now, total, unique, visible in its unity. The shortened Word, the "concentrated" Word, not only in the first sense that that which in itself is immense and incomprehensible, that which is infinite in the bosom of the Father shuts itself up within the womb of the Virgin, reduces itself to the proportions of a little infant in the stable of Bethlehem—as Saint Bernard and his sons used to retell it, as Mr. Olier retold it in a hymn for the Office of the interior life of Mary, and again just yesterday, Father Teilhard de Chardin[369]—but [p. 142] also, at the same time, in that

---

[365] Rupert, *De S. Sp.*, l. 1, c. 8. . . .

[366] . . . Adam of Perseigne, *Fragmenta mariana* [Marian fragments] (CCXI, 750 D).

[367] [The notion that the properties of Christ's divinity may be predicated of his humanity and that the properties of his humanity may be predicated of his divinity.—Ed.] Helinand, *s.* [Sermon] 4: "For the Jews still find the boy Jesus wrapped in swaddling clothes and lying in a manger, i.e., they read him in the Old Testament wrapped with the simple country words of the prophets and the ragged mysteries of the figures" . . . (CCXII, 513 A); etc. . . .

[368] Helinand, *s.* [Sermon] 3 (CCXII, 502 BC).

[369] *Le Milieu divin* (1957), 168: "Quand le moment fut venu où Dieu avait résolu de réaliser à nos yeux son Incarnation, il lui fallut susciter au préalable, dans le monde, une vertue capable de l'attirer jusqu'à nous. Il avait besoin d'une Mère qui l'engendrât dans les sphères humaines. Que fit-Il alors? Il créa la Vierge Marie, c'est-à-dire Il fit apparaître sur terre une pureté si grande que, dans cette transparence, Il se concentrera jusqu'à apparaître Petit-Enfant." ["When the time had come when God resolved to realise his Incarnation before our eyes, he had first of all to raise up in the world a virtue capable of drawing him as far as ourselves. He needed a mother who would engender him in the human sphere. What did he do? He created the Virgin Mary, that is to say he called forth

sense that the diverse content of the Scriptures disseminated along the ages of Waiting comes entirely together so as to be *accomplished*, i.e., to be unified, to be completed, to be illuminated, and to be transcended in this abbreviated Word. *Semel locutus est Deus*: *God has spoken once*:[370] God pronounces only one word [parole], not only in himself, in his unchanging eternity, in the immovable act by which he engenders his Word [Verbe], as Saint Augustine recalled, but also, just as Saint Ambrose already taught, in time, and among human beings, in the act by which he sent his Word to dwell in our earth. "God has spoken once, when he spoke in the Son": for it is he who gives all the words that he announced their sense, everything is understood in him, and only in him "and even those things that had not been heard before by those to whom he had spoken through the prophets have now been heard."[371]

A twice shortened Word, therefore, since at the moment of his incarnation "He has recapitulated in himself the long unfolding of human history, bringing us salvation condensed in him."[372] A twofold shortening, of a Word which is thus neither mutilated nor diminished. A twofold shortening, that of time and that of eternity, which join together to become just one, as time and eternity join indissolubly together in this shortened Word. A twofold recapitulation, that of the Word [Parole] eternally pronounced in the breast of the Father and that of the Word addressed to men in the sequence of the ages, the first being there to permit the second, and the second also to reveal the first, so that we can and should say, in two crisscrossed senses: "We have heard the shortened Word from the shortened Word."[373] Twofold shortening, twofold recapitulation, but always of one unique Word [Verbe], since God has only one Word in his breast and he proffers only one single Word [Parole], which is never other than this Word [Verbe], this very incarnate Word—so that, again, we can and should say, in two conjoined senses: *God has spoken once, since he has begotten one*

---

on earth a purity so great that, within this transparency, he would concentrate himself to the point of appearing as a child." *Le Milieu divin* (London: Collins, 1960), 125.]

[370] [Ps 62:11.—Ed.]

[371] . . . [Augustine], *In ps*. lxi, n. 18. . . .

[372] Irenaeus, *Adv. Haer.* l. 2, c. 18, n. 1. . . .

[373] . . . Garnier, *s*. 5, *de nat. Dom.* [On the birth of Christ] (PL, CCV, 599 C).

*Word.*[374] A twofold marvel, which for us then is always becoming merely one, made manifest in the mystery of Christmas:

> O brothers, if we piously and diligently attend to this Word which the Lord has made today, he shows us how many things and how easily we can be taught by him! If the Word has indeed been shortened, nevertheless this is so that every word that is unto salvation may be summed up in it, since doubtless it is the Word that sums up and shortens in equity. And this "shortened summary has poured forth justice" (Isaiah 10:23). But what wonder is that, if God's Word has shortened all his words for us, when he willed that he himself be [p. 143] shortened and somehow diminished, so that he might somehow contract himself from his own incomprehensible immensity to the narrowness of a womb, and, containing the world, suffer himself to be contained in a manger?[375]

Yes, a shortened Word, "very much shortened"—"brevissimum"[376] —but, in the highest degree, substantial. A shortened Word, but greater than what it shortens. It is a unity of plenitude. A concentration of light. The incarnation of the Word is the opening of the Book, whose exterior multiplicity henceforward allows one to perceive the unique "marrow," that marrow upon which the faithful have come to nourish themselves.[377] Behold: the Word [Parole] which, by Mary's *Fiat*[378] in reply to the announcement of the angel, till then only "audible to the ears," has become "visible to the eyes, palpable to the hands, able to be carried on the shoulders."[379] Still more: it has become "edible."[380] None of the ancient truths, none of the ancient precepts has perished, but everything has passed into

---

[374] . . . Bernard, *De div.* [Diverse sermons], *s.* 73 (183, 695 B). . . .

[375] . . . Guerric, *In nat. Dom.* [On the birth of Christ], s. 3, n. 3. . . .

[376] Absalon, *s.* [Sermons] 22 . . . (CCXI, 130 C). . . .

[377] Rupert, *In Jo.* [On John], l. 6: "The five untainted loaves of the Mosaic Law, i.e., as many books, and two fish, i.e., the prophets and Psalms, bearing witness at once to the Law and the Gospel. . . . He bears the burden of those loaves and fishes of the Scriptures and does not eat of them; he sweats under the weight of the letter and does not touch with hand or tooth the marrow of the spiritual understanding" . . . (CLXIX, 441 D . . .).

[378] ["Let it be" (Lk 1:38).—Ed.]

[379] Bernard, *Sup. Missus est* [On the Incarnation], h. 4, n. 11 . . .

[380] Helinand, *s.* 3 (CCXII, 503 B).

a better state.[381] All the Scriptures are gathered together in Jesus' hands like the eucharistic bread,[382] and in bearing them it is himself whom he bears in his hands: "so that in substance we may fashion a mere mouthful from the whole Bible."[383] "At many times and under many forms," God had distributed to men, page by page, a written book, in which one unique Word [Parole] was hidden under many words; today He opens up that book for them, so as to show them all those words united in the single Word. "The Incarnate Son," "The Word Incarnate," "The Greatest Book": the parchment of the Book henceforward is his flesh;[384] what has been written down is his divinity.[385] Thus the New Testament succeeds the Old, the Old is rediscovered in the New, the one and the other make just one, and in the same way that in God Unity dilates into Trinity, then Trinity gathers itself in Unity, so the New Testament dilates into the Old and the Old is condensed into the New.[386]

Here then, at last, the highest wish has been realized! Here, at last, unity in all its richness! Behold: the unique Sacrifice, and the unique Priest, and the unique Victim. The great passage has been accomplished, "the crossing over from many sacrifices to the one victim":[387]

> Designated by the Patriarchs in a multitudinous order,
> He is honored in the Law, and sung by the Prophets.[388]

Here then is the perfect holocaust! Behold the holocaust that God will never disdain, the one who remains always before his Face. In

---

[381] Hildegarde, *Scivias* [Know the ways], l. 1, vis. 5. . . .

[382] Rupert, *In Jo.*: "He took the book and opened the book, i.e., the whole of holy Scripture. . . . He received of the divine power to fulfill it in himself, that is, the whole dispensation of which, having been taken up within human nature for our salvation, the opening up of that book is the fulfillment of the holy Scriptures. . . . Hence the Lord took the loaves of the Scriptures in his hands at the moment when, having been incarnated according to the Scriptures, he suffered and rose again" . . . (443 *CD*).

[383] P. Claudel, *Apocalypse,* 50. . . .

[384] [The parchments upon which scriptural texts were written were made from the skins of sheep, calves, and goats.—ED.]

[385] . . . Garnier, *s.* 6 *de nat. Dom.* . . . (PL, CCV 609 D); . . . etc. Cf. Hebr. 1:1.

[386] Jerome, *In Ez.* [On Ezekiel], l. 4, c. 48. . . .

[387] . . . Leo, *s.* 68, c. 3. . . .

[388] . . . John Scotus Eriugena, *De Christi resurrectione* [On the Resurrection of Christ], vv. 23–[2]4. . . .

the [p. 144] eucharistic mystery, it is he whom we hold, completely and entirely. Odo of Cluny explains it in his *Occupatio* [*Occupation*], a poem both grand and poor, which we cite only for the doctrine:

Far off he makes the Word, as he promised, shortened;
Once many various gifts have been cast away,
He offers this one grain and wine to all.
He consecrates this, which undoubtedly becomes short, which was too tall.
Now moderate to eat, and so easy to prepare,
But so sublime, by which it may have the whole godhead.[389]

In this shortened Word, which covers all the earth, behold the remedy for all our wounds, behold the perfect healing:

This alone is enough to purge the world's fault.[390]

Behold the purity of the Gospel! "The evangelical discourse has been shortened and perfected."[391] Moses had spoken well of things, and yet his Law had not at all led to perfection: by just one word of Jesus the ultimate perfection has been taught. "The Word, shortened and shortening, is a healthful summary!"[392] The whole essence of the revelation fits within the precept of love: in this single utterance is contained "the whole Law and the Prophets."[393] But if this Gospel announced by Jesus, this utterance pronounced by him, contains everything, this is because it is no other than Jesus himself. His work, his teaching, his revelation, his word, is himself! The perfection that he teaches is the perfection that he provides. Christ is the fullness of the Law. It is impossible to separate his message from his person, and those who tried to do so had long before been forced to betray the message itself: person and message ultimately constitute just one thing. The shortened Word is the Word all rolled into one: the condensed, unified, perfect Word! The living and life-giving Word. Contrary to the laws of human language, which becomes clear as it unfolds, this Word which was obscure,

[389] . . . l. 6, c. 27–32 (A. Swoboda, 120). . . .
[390] . . . Odo, *ib*., v. 33.
[391] . . . Jerome, *In Is*. [On Isaiah], l. 4, c. 10. . . .
[392] . . . Bernard, *De dilig. Deo* [On loving God], c. 7, n. 21. . . .
[393] Sedulius Scotus, *In Rom*. [On Romans] . . . (CIII, 93 CD). . . .

in appearing under its abridged form now becomes manifest: the Word at first pronounced "in hiddenness" is now "made manifest in the flesh."[394] The abridged Word, the Word always ineffable in itself, and yet explaining everything! The final Word, summarizing everything, finalizing everything, concluding everything, sublimating everything, unifying everything:

> [p. 145] Jesus, shortened yet summarizing Word, bringing the Law and the Prophets to a conclusion with the two-part precept of charity. O summarizing Word, O Word shortening in equity! Word of charity, Word of complete perfection.[395]

This does not involve—as some might have believed or as some have said particularly about Saint Bernard—any "depreciation of the divine Word [Parole] in favor of the divine Word [Verbe]," a depreciation which would happily have remained "completely speculative, and, if one can say so, oratorical."[396] This is a profound teaching, contained in principle in the prologue of the Gospel of Saint John, corroborated by a long series of witnesses and by the liturgy itself. By making visible in the ancient Scripture the manner in which "the unique divine Word [Parole] was already approaching us,"[397] by affirming (in perhaps paradoxical-sounding terms) its ontological bond with that Word in which God reveals himself, this teaching on the contrary magnified it and extended its actuality to the whole duration of Christian time,[398] all the while refusing to canonize the *littera sola* [literal alone] within it. Luther had well understood this, in the best period of his biblical reflections, when, in his first commentary on the Psalms,[399] and then in that on the Epistle to the Romans,[400] he took up that old theme of the "Verbum

---

[394] . . . *Or. vis.*, Oration for Advent (32).

[395] . . . Aelred, *De Jesu duod.* [On Jesus as a boy of twelve], n. 13. . . .

[396] . . . A. Humbert, *Les origines de la th. mod.* [The origins of modern theology], I (1911), 52.

[397] . . . L. Bouyer, *Le sens de la vie monast.* [The meaning of the monastic life] (1950), 260.

[398] H. Urs von Balthasar, *Théol. de l'hist.* [A theology of history] ([French] tr. R. Givord, 1955), 104–5.

[399] *In Ps.* [On the Psalms] ([*Weimarer Ausgabe*] 3, 262).

[400] *In Rom.* [On Romans], xi, 28 (Ficker, 232).

consummans et abbrevians."[401] Saint Augustine had said it well in his response to Faustus, and all those who say it with him are right: the Christian neither adds anything to Scripture nor takes a bit of it away. He extracts the substance of it. He abridges it, he condenses it, he unifies it without letting any of it be lost, he holds it all in Jesus Christ: "*for he is book enough for all*".[402] He accepts from the chosen people all the books of the Old Testament; he venerates them, he does not cease to explore them and to meditate upon them, he marvels at the ways of God within them—but this is always to culminate in Christ. All that he discovers in them—and his discoveries are endless—he sees finally transfigured in Christ. Always, in some manner, whatever the knowledge that he uncovers and whatever the processes of his exegesis over the centuries, after many detours perhaps, he recognizes Christ in them. A ray has come to him from the inner light with which the soul of Jesus was illuminated when, in the days of his mortal life, he took the Bible in hand:

> Jesus discovers himself, he recognizes himself in reading the Old Testament. He sees himself as the end-point of that whole History "of which the Law and the Prophets prophesied right up to the present moment." In it he sees the anticipation of his coming. From all the [p. 146] scattered features mentioned by the prophecies—the Messianic Prince of Peace, Isaiah's Emmanuel, Daniel's Son of Man, the Servant, the Judge, the Shepherd—he does not through some constructive labor perform an induction of what he ought to be, he just recognizes himself. . . . He allows the "wrapping" to fall into the shadow. . . . From all these features he divinely makes the synthesis: not from without, but from within. He casts his inner light upon the prophecies: then they are united, they lose any trace of the circumstances where they had been proclaimed, they harmonize and are fulfilled.
>
> In uncovering the Bible, Jesus recognized the reflection of the Light that shines in him; he hears a feeble echo of the Word [Parole] that rings within his human consciousness.[403]

---

[401] The origin of this theme is in Origen, *In Rom.* [On Romans], l. 7, c. 19. . . .

[402] . . . Absalon, *s.* 25 (PL, CCXI, 149 A).

[403] . . . Louis Richard, PSS [Priest of Saint Sulpice]. . . .

Rejoining the theologians and linking up the old tradition with them, some modern exegetes recognize it as well: in all that the apostles and the evangelists relate to us about Jesus, one rediscovers "the ore of the Old Testament melted down and purified," and "that entirely Christological orientation has not for good or ill been imposed" on the Old Testament, "but it is interior to it and penetrates all its parts."[404] The two forms of the Word, abridged and dilated, are inseparable. The Book remains, therefore, but at the same time it passes over entirely into Jesus,[405] and the believer's meditation upon it consists precisely in contemplating this passage. Mani and Mohammed have written books. For his part, Jesus has written nothing[406]—it is Moses and the other prophets who "have written about him." The relation of the Book to its Person is therefore the reverse of the relation that one observes elsewhere. The evangelical Law is thus not at all a "lex scripta," a "written law." Christianity is properly speaking not a "religion of the Book" at all: it is the religion of the Word [la Parole], but not only or principally of the Word under its written form. It is the religion of the Word [du Verbe], "not of a mute, written word, but of an incarnate, living Word."[407] The Word [Parole] of God is now present among us "in such a way that one can see it and touch it."[408] It is a "living and efficacious"[409] Word, unique and personal, unifying and sublimating all the words that give witness to it. Christianity is not "the biblical religion": it is the religion of Jesus Christ.

---

[404] . . . Hoskyns, *Mysterium Christi*, cited by Hebert, 118.

[405] Absalon, *s.* 25 . . . (PL, CCXI, 148 D).

[406] [Except on the ground (Jn 8:6).—Ed.]

[407] . . . Bernard, *Sup. Missus est*, h. 4, n. 11, making Mary say: "let it not be for me a written, mute word, but one incarnate and alive." . . .

[408] . . . John 1; 1 John 1:1–3. . . .

[409] Martin of Leon, *s. de Jo. Bapt.* [Sermon on Saint John the Baptist] . . . (PL, CCIX, 18 B).

# 6

# Buddhism

*This text was produced for a meeting of the Roman Catholic Church's Secretariat for Non-Christian Religions, of which de Lubac was a member, in Paris in 1971. It is his final assessment of Pure Land* (Jōdo Shū) *Buddhism. Also known, now archaically, as Amidism, this sect was founded by Hōnen Shōnin (1133–1212) and is dominant in Japan. In Pure Land Buddhism, the person of Amida Buddha is the focus of contemplation, by which the believer may enter into his compassionate heart. Similarly, Christian prayer is focused on Jesus Christ, and Sacred Heart devotion is strong in Roman Catholicism.*

*However, de Lubac's interest is more particularly in the True Pure Land* (Jōdo Shinshū) *or Shin sect, which was founded by Shinran Shōnin (1173–1262) as a continuation of the Pure Land sect. In Shin Buddhism, emphasis is placed on the feeling of absolute dependence on the other power* (tariki) *of Amida Buddha's infinite compassion for existence and salvation. This has parallels with de Lubac's theology of the supernatural, which presents people as primordially dependent on grace and refutes the notion that purely natural actions are possible independently of grace. Moreover, whereas political and social turmoil led Hōnen to view corruption as societal, Shinran regarded it as rooted in the individual. In his later years, de Lubac also saw the need to restate this introspective dimension of theology, in the face of sociological analyses that he regarded as attributing evil to social factors rather than to misuse of free will.*

*Although de Lubac identified some parallels between the place of Amida Buddha in Pure Land Buddhism and of Jesus Christ in Roman Catholicism, he was alert to important doctrinal differences. Above all, whereas Jesus Christ became incarnate so that he might enter into the material world and redeem it, Amida Buddha, on attaining enlightenment, transcended the world. These doctrinal differences have implications for anthropology. In Christian theological anthropology, Christ in his relation to the Godhead provides the model for selfhood relation to God, and bodily resurrection. In contrast, even in Shin Buddhism, individual selfhood is ultimately transcended. Moreover, whereas Christ founded and sustains his Church, Amida Buddha neither established nor remained in any earthly community.*

[p. 355] As a beginning, let us read some words that are already familiar to many of you.

O Amitabha [Amida], incomparable light,
O Amitabha, infinite splendor,
so pure, so serene,
so tender and so consoling . . .
How we long to be reborn where thou art!

Thou whose power is boundless,
Thou toward whom the beings of all worlds turn,
How beautiful is thy kingdom,
Where the breeze sows flowers under the feet of the blessed!
How we long to be reborn where thou art!

How beautiful is thy kingdom,
Where the most magnificent music resounds,
Where the most precious perfumes are wafted,
Where all beings are holy!
How we long to be reborn where thou art!

Desperately, during numberless existences,
We have renewed the karma that bound us to earth.
O protect us, kindly light, from now on!
So that we no longer lose the wisdom of the heart!
We exalt thy knowledge and thy works,
We desire that everyone turn toward thee!

Let no obstacle prevent anyone
From being reborn in peace and happiness where thou art!
We offer thee all that we have, all that we are:
In exchange, let us be reborn where thou art.
Hail to thee, O inscrutable splendor!
With all our hearts and in all trust we bow down before thee.[1]

---

Excerpted from "Faith and Piety in Amidism", in *Theological Fragments*, trans. Rebecca Howell Balinski (San Francisco: Ignatius Press, 1989), 355–69.

[1] [The poem is attributed to T'an-luan (476–542), who founded Pure Land Buddhism in China and was the third patriarch of Japanese Shin Buddhism.—Ed.]

[p. 356] And here is the teaching of Honen (1133–1212), Japanese monk and founder of the Jodo sect:

> Do not bother asking yourself if your heart is good or bad, if your sins are serious or light. Have only one thought, that of being reborn in the Pure Land [Amida's paradise], and repeat without ceasing, "*Namu Amida Butsu*" (Save me, O Thou, Buddha Amida!), and let a total confidence accompany the sound of your voice. Your salvation depends on this simple act of absolute and decisive confidence. As long as you vacillate, nothing will be done. But, from the moment that you conceive this act of unwavering confidence, your fate will be assured.
>
> The *nembutsu*[2] is superior to all other practices because all virtue is eminently contained in the sacred name alone.
>
> Even if a Buddha encircled with a halo of light were to come to you and say: It is absurd to believe that a man full of passions and sins can obtain paradise by doing nothing more than repeating the *nembutsu*, do not believe him. Never let the least doubt enter your head.

Finally, this beautiful legendary account in the Japanese epic *Heike Monogatari* (beginning of the thirteenth century):[3] After the naval disaster at Dan-no-ura, the elderly empress prepares to commit suicide with the young emperor, her grandson:

> She moved slowly toward the gunwale of the ship. With an expression of surprise and anguish, the little emperor asked her, "Where do you want to take me, Amazé?" Turning her tear-stained face to the young sovereign, she replied, "This world is a place of suffering; it is remote and unimportant and no bigger than a millet seed. But, under the ocean's waves, there is another country, the Pure Land of perfect bliss. In its capital, there is no sorrow, and it is there that I want to take you, my lord." And, all the while comforting him, she gathered his long hair in her hands and attached it to her robe, which was the color of mountain doves. At her bidding, the sovereign child,

---

[2] [The repeated recitation of the name of Amida.—ED.]

[3] [The *Tale of the Heike* is a chanted epic poem that narrates the Genpei War (1180–1185) between the ruling Taira clan and the Minamoto clan, from whom it had previously seized power, for political control of Japan. The passage that de Lubac quotes is from chap. 11. Following the Minamoto victory, the Taira clan was annihilated.—ED.]

blinded by tears, clasped his little hands, turned first toward the east to take leave of the goddess of Isé, and then toward the west to repeat the *nembutsu* several times. This done, he turned to the empress, who held him tight in her arms; to console him she repeated, "We have a capital in the depths of the ocean." And then she threw herself with him into the sea.

It is not our intention to comment on these texts. It has sufficed to cite them as examples, in order to place ourselves from the start in the *climate* of Amidism.[4]

It is known that Amidism—which has its roots in several ancient [p. 357] Buddhist texts, whose physiognomy is traced in northwest India within the Mahayana and which owes a great deal to Iran—came into being in the regions of central Asia before invading all of China and then, from there, Japan. Although as it developed it split into a series of branches that we call sects, it never severed its connection with the trunk of Buddhism.

What is its present situation? What is its importance? We shall leave those questions to be answered by others more competent in this field than we are. Some rare data are found in the second volume of our secretariat's work, *A la rencontre de bouddhisme*. It is practically impossible to say anything precise about its situation in mainland China. "In spite of a real revival before the Second World War, Buddhism has not been able to resist the Communist impact." This must be equally true for its Amidist form.[5] In Taiwan (Formosa), where the revival goes on in a small way, "the piety of most Buddhists is directed primarily toward the Buddha Amida" (Yves Raguin). In Japan, where more than half of the inhabitants claim to be Buddhists (but most often not exclusively) and where Buddhism ceased to be the national religion only at the end of the nineteenth century,[6] Amidism is at present only one of three forms in favor,

[4] [In the present day, this is usually termed Pure Land Buddhism. Amida, or Amitābha, meaning "infinite light", is the name of the Buddha on whom its teachings are focused. —Ed.]

[5] [Since the 1970s, Pure Land Buddhism has, along with other forms of Buddhism, undergone a revival in China.—Ed.]

[6] [At the 1868 Meiji Restoration, Shinto became Japan's official religion. Its doctrines and rituals were formally separated from those of Buddhism, which was regarded by its

the two others being Zen and the nationalist group that is inspired by the Nichiren sect.

Is Amidism in a stage of progress or of decline? Does it have any part in the revival that is currently taking place in Buddhism, whose extreme elasticity makes it astonishingly indestructible? I do not know.

And to what extent is Amidism marginal in its relationship to Buddhism? It is certainly as far away as possible from primitive Buddhism. But there is no lack of features in the Mahayana[7] to give it support. Asvaghosa[8] (first century) tells the story of a poor wretch who had little chance of being received in *samgha* (paradise). But, in a previous life, when he had been attacked by a tiger, he had shouted confidently, "Praised be Buddha!" By this invocation, says Asvaghosa, "the man brought an end to his troubles because, by it, he had shown his virtue. Having wholeheartedly taken refuge in Buddha, he will obtain deliverance." This is also the meaning of the famous fable of the boat carrying large stones, explained by the old Nagasena[9] to King Milinda (Menander). The transfer from Sakyamuni[10] to Amida presents no difficulty for the one who sees, in Amida, the Buddha of whom Sakyamuni was the earthly emanation.

As it developed, however, Amidism took on a character that is very different from classical Buddhism, even the Mahayanist branch. Ordinarily, historians insist on its popular and elementary character, which can be justified to a point, but perhaps their assessment is excessive, because several Amidist sects, notably in Japan, bear witness to a highly refined [p. 358] culture and profound spirituality. What interests us here is something else.

---

opponents as a foreign religion. However, the separation rapidly stalled and remains incomplete.—Ed.]

[7] [Meaning "Great Vehicle" in Sanskrit, this is the largest branch of Buddhism existing today.—Ed.]

[8] [An Indian ascetic poet.—Ed.]

[9] [A second-century Buddhist teacher who composed the *Questions of Milinda*. In chap. 7, 1, the boat is associated with good actions, and the stones, by implication, with the self. Whereas even a single small stone will sink in water, a boat is able to float while carrying a whole cartload of stones.—Ed.]

[10] [Also known as Siddhārtha Gautama, the ascetic on whose teachings Buddhism is founded.—Ed.]

How can one compare Amidism and the Christian faith? What major resemblances is it possible to observe? What solid bases are there for dialogue? What lessons might Christians learn from an examination of Amidism?

Paul Claudel, who could never be suspected of an excessively accommodating attitude, wrote: "The Amida of China and Japan is almost Christian." His opinion was not based on books but on numerous observations.[11] What are the grounds for such a judgment?

Let us first take a look at the simplest, most popular Amidism. For many of its followers, it is practically, as has been written, "a true theism". Amida is the Divinity; he is God. The thought hardly goes any farther. "But what God?" it will be asked. We must not insist that theories or definitions be too precise. It is certain, on the one hand, that Amida's power is acquired. It originated in a "vow" that he pronounced long ago in a previous existence. On the other hand, it is no less certain that he is only one Buddha among others within universal Buddhism. The average Amidist is surely aware of this. But it hardly matters as far as his concrete comportment is concerned. For him, Amida has no history at all; he has no rival. He reigns in the center of his paradise, which is the place of salvation. He certainly seems to be the equivalent of a unique God, a savior God. He is a God to whom one prays and who inspires a pure existence. Let us say that Amida's religion is a kind of moral theism. Judging not only from the texts but also from a long and keen observation, we find it unquestionable that many Amidists perform acts of contrition and love that are very beautiful; that no other prayer has ever resembled Christian prayer as closely as theirs, since they pray so humbly, fervently, and with such deep sincerity. "I shall never forget", wrote Fr. Léon Wieger, "my feelings while contemplating an Amidist, who was a young mother, worshiping before the illuminated and empty throne. First she closed her eyes and withdrew into herself. Then her lips began to murmur words of repentance and petition that obviously came from deep within her. She then placed before the throne her two little children—

[11] [Claudel served as French consul in China (1895–1909) and as the French ambassador to Tokyo (1922–1928). See his *Knowing the East*, trans. James Lawler (Princeton, N.J.: Princeton University Press, 2004).—Ed.]

the second could only just walk—and they, with perfectly stylized gestures, repeated with the greatest solemnity what their mother had just done. Then the mother lifted from her lap a third child, a newborn, took his head delicately between her thumb and forefinger and had it bow toward the throne."

Dostoyevski[12] describes a similar scene, which he has one of his heroes, Prince Myshkin, recount. In a Catholic Church in Rome, he saw a young mother, a humble woman, deeply recollected in prayer, and her little [p. 359] child was praying with her. The scene was so beautiful that he could not evoke it without emotion. But let us listen to Dostoyevski:

> The woman was still young and the child was about six weeks old. He had just smiled at her for the first time since his birth, she said. I saw her suddenly sign herself with inexpressible devotion. "Why are you doing that, dear lady?" I asked her. I had a mania then for asking questions. "Because each time that God sees from on high a sinner praying with all his heart, he must feel the same joy that a mother experiences in seeing the first smile of her child." That is almost literally what this simple woman said to me; she was able to express this thought, which is so profound, so subtle, so purely religious, and which synthesizes the essence of Christianity, a religion recognizing in God a heavenly Father who rejoices at the sight of man like a father at the sight of his child. A simple woman of the people! It is true, of course, that she was a mother.

We shall not go beyond this analogy. But let us say at least that, in certain Amidist prayers, there is an expression of religious feeling whose value could remain unacknowledged only by a theology that is excessively severe and hardly in conformity with Catholic Tradition. It is a religious feeling that Christian education, far from destroying, must deepen and lead to its perfection.

As we know, the Buddha Amida has a kind of "spiritual son", the bodhisattva Avalokitesvara, who in China has become Kuan-yin and is known in Japan as Kannon. He is full of compassion, and

[12] [Fyodor Dostoyevski (1821–1881) was a Russian novelist. The episode described is from *The Idiot* (1874), which was composed in an era when there was deep animosity between the Roman Catholic and Russian Orthodox Churches.—Ed.]

he rescues men from all dangers and conducts them to Amida's paradise. Let us listen to one of the hymns addressed to him:

> O thou whose eyes are beautiful, full of kindness, compassion and purity, thou whose face is so lovable!
>
> O thou who are spotless, who spread the splendor of a sun of knowledge cleared from all obscurity, thou whose light no cloud ever obstructs, your majesty shines above the worlds.
>
> Like a great cloud of mercy, you put out the fire of adversity that consumes us, by causing the ambrosia of the law to rain down on us. . . .
>
> Remember, remember Avalokita, that pure Being! In times of misery and death, he is the protector, the refuge, the sanctuary.
>
> Having reached the perfection of all virtues, expressing by his regard benevolence for all beings, this vast Ocean of virtues is worthy of all praise.

Whereas Amida's presence is often invoked by an empty throne which implies an elevated idea of the divinity—Kuan-yin is most often endowed with feminine traits, although he is neither a woman nor in [p. 360] any other manner a sexual divinity. But from these traits comes the comparison that has been made between him and the Virgin Mary, a comparison that can be based on still stronger resemblances. Often the object of "the purest and most gentle" worship "that pagan China has known", the images of Kuan-yin are assuredly the keenest expressions of the Amidist doctrine of salvation through intercession from on high. "Through him the severity of Buddhism was softened. An immense tenderness began to stream from the folds of Kuan-yin's robe. His eyes were no longer fixed in a stare of solitary contemplation: they were lowered on the world's suffering and are serenely searching for all those who invoke him in their distress." Because of this we should not be surprised that the image of the Virgin brought by the first Jesuit missionaries to China toward the end of the sixteenth century and placed in their "Temple to the Flower of the Saints" at Shinking was thought by the people to represent their beloved Kuan-yin. One even understands why, later, the Japanese Christians of Nagasaki and its environs "during 250 years of fierce persecution were able to pray to the Holy Virgin before a statue of Kannon. In the eyes of the Japanese police, he was only a Buddhist divinity: but the faithful had transformed him into an image of the Queen of Mercy." And the hymn that we cited earlier is not without a certain resemblance, considering the differences in spiritual climates, to the invocations of St. Bernard in his homilies on the Annunciation.

The disciple of Amida hopes to be reborn, after his death, in Amida's paradise, the "Pure Land", the "Western Paradise", the *Sukhavati*. It is a place of light and peace. The numerous written descriptions, which are full of imagery, and the paintings of this paradise resemble those found in many mythologies. But one must look a little farther. Are not the descriptions of Christian paradise also full of imagery? Take, for example, the celebrated hymns of St. Ephraem. Those of the Amidists are more exuberant and childlike, but some of them have a symbolic depth. Their *Sukhavati* is completely different from the vulgar heaven in which Buddhist mythology shows us men who have become gods and, amid their always ephemeral pleasures, are using up the fruit of their good karma,[13] without making any progress along the path to deliverance. The high terrace on which Amida's kingdom is established is a transcendent universe: from the pure water of its lakes, all levels of the universe of samsara[14] are flooded. . . . It is beyond our space and our miserable duration. "O plenitude of warmth and light, where shadow, aridity and all blemish are banned! Eternal solstice, where the day never ends and always has the brilliance of noon, the temperature of springtime, the charm of summer, the abundance of autumn and—so as not to leave anything out—the [p. 361] tranquillity and leisure of winter, but not its rigors! A place of total light, peace and plenitude! A place where one worships the unlimited light!" Those are St. Bernard's words,[15] but they could have come from an Amidist: "Unlimited Light" is one of Amida's most common names.

Actually, with the "simple people of Amidism", ignorant of doctri-

[13] [A person's accumulated past actions, especially as these determine his future.—Ed.]

[14] [The material world in its unending cycle of death and rebirth.—Ed.]

[15] [Sermon 33 on the *Song of Songs*, on the mystical noontide.—Ed.]

nal subtleties, who pray and hope humbly and sincerely, the Christian can have the impression, as Fr. Léon Wieger remarked, "that he is quite at home". And, even though, as we said earlier, Amidism, especially in Japan, has reached a more cultivated milieu where minds are more keen on doctrine, we can still feel something of a kinship with it. Contrary to what appears to be the most universal and solid foundation of Buddhism, the Amidists base their religious life on faith. This difference had been observed by St. Francis Xavier[16] and, since his time, has been pointed out frequently. Along with Francis Xavier, we can even agree that their faith presents a singular resemblance to Luther's. Pessimism regarding the world, disgust with doctrinal complications accumulated over the centuries, the impossibility of finding peace by traditional means, the need for simplification, fervor: all these attitudes are expressed by Honen, who "finds the assurance of salvation and a deep religious life in his faith in Amida".

It is true that all the subsequent explanations given by the Amidist doctors immediately lead us to a point a thousand leagues away not only from Luther but from all the Christian faith: if "Buddha's law is a vast sea", faith can be an "access", but "knowledge is the boatman": these words of Nagarjuna[17] are not contradicted by the Amidists. And they do not fail to recognize that their faith, which is only an entrance to the path of deliverance, is itself the fruit of merits previously acquired. It must only be kept in mind that, for ardent Amidists, these doctrinal backgrounds seem to remain in obscurity, having little influence on their practices or feelings. Also, many texts by Honen, Shinran and others have a resonance that one might even call Christian, evangelical. When their spiritual life overflows the bounds of simple piety, it is deepened less by learned reflections that would lead them back to Buddhist orthodoxy than by a mystical enlightenment. And one is justified in thinking that this concrete mysticism that they experience does not clash with the departure that it took in first invoking the Buddha Amida, which itself was an act of *faith*, corresponding to a certain *grace*.

---

[16] [Francis Xavier (1506–1552) was a Basque companion of Ignatius Loyola who led Jesuit missions to India and Japan.—Ed.]

[17] [A Buddhist philosopher who lived in the second and third centuries and was one of the founders of the Mahāyāna school.—Ed.]

It is this mysticism that is suggested by one of the Amidists' favorite pictorial representations entitled *Amida's Descent* (or, more precisely, his "coming for the meeting"). It seems to be a creation of Japanese art. The first "descents" were done by Genshin (tenth century), a well-read monk who was a painter as well as the head of an important monastery. His [p. 362] paintings are of several types. Let us consider the most original one (in which one still sees the influence of the Buddhist art at Tun-huang):[18] *Amida Rushing Forward from Behind the Mountains.* Genshin had contemplated him in a miraculous vision, at the end of a long night spent entirely in invoking Amida. For him the dawn became confused with this vision. In this kind of descent, Amida is most often accompanied by his two habitual acolytes; the three gigantic figures are delineated with half their bodies showing behind the extended ridge of mountains while, in the foreground, the countryside is still immersed in the night, or else the luminous cloud that carries them is already beginning to descend into the valleys, which are filled with a golden light. The arms of the Buddha are sometimes stretched out as a sign of the power and willingness with which he is coming to gather up his disciples. Whatever the variations, an essential characteristic consists in the marked contrast between the two parts of the painting. There are two zones: one, terrestrial, plunged in obscurity; the other, heavenly, completely luminous with a light that one feels to be all pervading. On the one hand, there is the glorious radiance emanating from the three supernatural figures, and, on the other, there is the shadowy green freshness of the wooded hills. Nevertheless, one senses a profound, although secret, harmony between this approach of the world on high and the serenity of nature. Amida shines forth on human misery like a pitying morning sun. A mysterious and calm force is preparing to seize the wretched realities here below and absorb them in its joy.

The impression that a Westerner has before the most beautiful of these descents will be, we believe, less a reminder of the Lutheran faith than of Catholic mysticism. It reminds one of that eruption

[18] [A city in northern China on the Silk Road close to the Mogao Caves. During the early twentieth century, the murals, statues, silk banners, and manuscripts in the Caves were excavated by archaeologists from several Western countries. The Frenchman Paul Pelliot (1878–1945) exported a selection of these to the Musée Guimet in Paris.—ED.]

of divine peace described by Surin[19] in his *Traité de l'amour de Dieu* [*Treatise on the Love of God*]: It is a "peace that descends on the soul, not violently, but impetuously, like water that has broken through its dykes. It comes in majesty, like an element of the other life, with the sound of celestial harmony. It spreads itself in plenitude, carrying with it God's blessings and the riches of his Kingdom." And, just as Amida is announced by his two messengers, this peace has its forerunners in the angels who precede it, like halcyons who mark the arrival of the waters. And Fénelon, in a more succinct style, wrote: "The world flees like a deceitful shadow, and already eternity comes forward to receive us."

Before we look for the best attitude for the Catholic Christian to adopt in regard to the important religious occurrence known as Amidism, perhaps it will be useful to voice a preliminary reflection.

St. Paul asked every disciple of Christ to receive all that is offered of the true, the just, and the good, whatever their origin or the place where [p. 363] they are found.[20] Today, similarly, a spirit of dialogue, indeed—if the occasion arises—a resolution for common action regarding a task of social interest, is very much recommended. It is necessary to understand, however, just what such an eminently Catholic open-mindedness requires in order to remain honest and to have the chance, as far as we are concerned, of being effective. At the base of all action, as its first condition, a critical regard is indispensable. By this I do not mean, of course, a critical regard in the abusive sense that, albeit unavowed, is too frequent: it is myopic and belittling, negative and destructive, because it stems from either narrow-mindedness or an a priori opposition, ill will or rejection. It must be critical in the only true sense of the word; that is, it must be an effort of true discernment that is as intent on setting aside the distortions coming from negative prejudices as the illusions provoked by generous inclinations.

This kind of healthy basic realism obliges us, it seems to me, to make the following observations:

In looking at Amidism, if we consider not only the elementary sentiments and practices of Amida's disciples but also their object, that is, the Buddha himself, we shall not be able to ignore either its

[19] [Jean-Joseph Surin (1600–1665) was a Jesuit mystic, ascetic, and exorcist.—Ed.]

[20] [Phil 4:8.—Ed.]

entirely mythological character or its doctrinal background, which is nothing other than the whole of Buddhism, taken in its essential categories that are Mahayanist in form. Although it may appear possible to make a value judgment on the prayer of the typical Amidist —who has no true intellectual culture—after the simple observation of his act and the vital context that surrounds it, without going any farther, a dialogue entailing an objective consideration of Amidism appears unworkable without a meeting with its doctors for an examination of the essential categories that make up Buddhism's doctrinal background. But it is plain to see that such an encounter, such an examination would quickly lead to the antipodes of our Faith, since the doctrinal framework of Buddhism differs so much on every point from that of Christianity. Moreover, if we observed that one of the most striking of the contrasts between the two religions consists in the phantasmagoric nature of a vast Buddhism seen from the perspective of the historical and sober character of our faith in Jesus Christ, our interlocutors would no doubt hasten to concede that we were right—but not without an indulgent smile for our unrefined ideas, if it is true that the final enlightenment that they profess to be seeking leads, they think, to the discovery that all the stages that lead up to it, with all the representations that those stages comprise, are nothing more than an immense system of illusions, as temporary as it is necessary.

[p. 364] It will be wise, then, to limit ourselves to the subjective aspect of things. In the first place, we shall have to ask ourselves if Amidism as it is lived, in what it offers to our simplest and best observation, does not have something to teach us. Could it not remind us of a certain number of features that should have their analogue in everyday Christianity but that are in danger of becoming blurred today? Then we shall have to find out, conversely, if the observation of a notorious insufficiency in Amidism in the present situation of the world where, to put it in the best light possible, it does little more than survive,[21] should not help us to become more keenly aware of the compelling necessity of our living in a Christian manner, as much because of Christianity's essence as be-

[21] [Only in Japan has Pure Land Buddhism been promoted by organized sects. Elsewhere, its teachings have tended to merge with those of other sects.—Ed.]

cause of present circumstances. Finally, we shall concentrate our regard on a completely central point, where we shall see both resemblance and contrast arise, in view of improving our understanding of the radical newness introduced into our history by Christian revelation.

1. Let us finish reading the page from Dostoyevski, which, as we have seen, applies so well to Fr. Wieger's description of Amidist piety: "the essence of religious sentiment eludes all reasoning; no fault, crime or form of atheism can control it. There is and there will be eternally something in this feeling that is imperceptible and inaccessible to the atheistic argument."

We shall not confuse the religious sentiment or, more simply, religion, as an essential human category, or, if you prefer, the religious instinct, with faith such as the Word of God incarnate created in the heart of his disciples and those who followed him. But neither shall we scorn it. We shall not consider it as an inevitable source of idolatry or an illusory phenomenon, illustrating a childlike aspect of humanity, destined to vanish in the grown-up man. Along with Dostoyevski, whose sounding lines dropped into our subterranean obscurities are far more illuminating than so many superficial sociohistorical or psychosocial analyses (even when they speak of "depths"), we shall recognize this instinct as springing from the deepest part of human nature and emerging everywhere in spite of all that, for a time, might succeed in stifling it. The Amidist religious instinct, frequently mixed with all sorts of slag, is also sometimes very pure, and it offers this similarity with the Faith of the Gospel: it is often in the simplest hearts, among the "small" and humble, that this faith blossoms in all of its beauty. For appreciating it, we have no need to ask [p. 365] ourselves right away if it is from nature or grace or in what proportion grace has been able to come, to complete and transform nature.[22] It is the Catholic spirit—and not some kind of doctrinal liberalism or some relativization of our Faith—the esteem for human nature that it inculcates in us, that leads us to sympathize and admire occurrences such as Amidist prayer.

In the Amidist prayer, however, especially as we encounter it in

---

[22] [De Lubac used his studies of Pure Land Buddhism to explore themes in Christian theology, such as the supernatural.—Ed.]

the texts of the founders and theoreticians of several sects, there is more than this simple religious sentiment, more than this surge of confidence toward a superior Being who can be the substitute for a true God in the popular imagination. There is, in addition, the sentiment of a need for salvation based on a sense of sin increased by the recourse to Amida's grace, without which it is impossible for man to be delivered from his sin. It is true that, to the extent that even this double sentiment becomes objective in theory, the idea of sin and, consequently, the idea of grace, which is its correlative, lose their correspondence to the notions of sin and grace that result from the biblical and Christian experience. We cannot forget this doctrinal background of Buddhism that more or less colors nature and grace or reduces them, and that can go so far as to take away all resemblance with what we understand by these two words. If it were possible to see in the Japanese Amidist sects of Honen or Shinran an equivalent to Lutheran Christianity, a keener regard could see, no less plausibly, the very opposite of Lutheranism.

If we leave aside all the more or less conditioned doctrinal subtleties, thanks to which every act of Amidist piety is perpetually reintegrated into the vast bosom of Buddhism, it is nevertheless permissible to find for ourselves, this very day, a valuable lesson in the humble recourse to Amida, savior of the man who knows that he is a sinner and judges himself incapable of liberating himself from his sin. We see him, for example, in the follower of the Shin sect, the founder of Judo-Shin, who, rejecting all pretension of "personal power", embarks on his confident prayer "on the raft of love steered by Amida". It is a very timely lesson for us, in this age when the sense of sin is rejected by a certain number of Christians as being an aftermath of Jansenism or as a depressing illusion from which the science of the psychologists and sociologists should free us; in an age when the call to divine grace is sometimes considered the effect of an outdated "Augustinism", whereas it is, like the meaning of sin, at the very heart of the Gospel; in an age when many people seem to be ashamed to allude to this call to divine grace, intimidated by others who violently rebuff it as unworthy of an adult who knows himself to be master of his destiny. Through Amida's disciples, we could relearn, if need be, the fundamental role of humility, something the modern [p. 366] world has unlearned and ancient paganism hardly knew, but that is and will always remain the basis for all of Christian life. And perhaps it was the great Augustine who better than anyone else gave divine grace its rightful place, by showing that it is the necessary foundation of the edifice that charity crowns, but in doing so he was only interpreting the purest Christianity, only commenting on the lesson he learned from his Master and ours, the Word of God born in the flesh.

2. But here we reach one of the fundamental gaps that our subject obliges us to note. In the invocation of Amida, faith blossoms in hope, the hope of being reborn in Sukhavati, the Pure Land. Amidism is a religion of individual salvation. It has no vision of any "salvation of the world". Each of its followers dreams only of an escape from this evil world. We should not say that his dream is "egoistic". Whether he envisages the Pure Land as a simple stage on the path to deliverance (as orthodox Buddhism would have it), or whether, in the simplicity of his heart, his aim stops there, the Pure Land is already the mysterious place where one is delivered from the limitations and servitudes of the *ego*. Neither should we misunderstand the simple word "escape", which has too readily become in all paratheological literature a kind of blemish. After all, Christian hope also does not aim at a salvation [that] would be obtained in this world, this spatial-temporal universe within which all of our individual and collective experiences take place. In this respect, there is no possible difference among Christians. Teilhard de Chardin, for example, whose thought is readily characterized by the terms "optimistic" and "cosmic", is as definite about this as his most outspoken adversaries. There is nothing more horrible in his eyes than the perspective of humanity's remaining "enclosed in the cosmic bubble" forever. The profound desire of every human, he declares, is to "escape" from it. Groping along, more or less in the dark, as much today as long ago, man is looking for the liberating "exit". Christ provides this exit, his revelation reveals it to us, his grace propels us toward it, his Church never ceases to hold it up before our eyes. She reminds us incessantly of the transcendent end for which we are destined, an end beyond and above the cosmos.

The radical difference between Christianity and Amidism is not found in the idea of escape, but in the nature and conditions of the escape.

First of all, its nature: the new heaven and new earth for which we hope are not completely alien to our earth and our heaven: they are their transformation, their transfiguration, and this will come to pass "at the end of time". It would be futile and contradictory to try to represent it other than "in images" or *per speculum* [in a mirror]. . . . What we believe is that our earth and heaven are the work of a Creator who never permits the loss of any of his creation. As disfigured as our world is by sin, it is not simply [p. 367] doomed to death. It is neither illusory nor essentially evil. It is already a germ—albeit paltry—of final reality. It will pass "through fire" to become what the Apostle Paul calls "the plenitude of Christ". It is a realistic conception that is in sharp contrast to the cosmic illusionism and pessimism that characterize most expressions of Buddhism.

Next, its conditions: our earth is the place where salvation is *prepared*. Man was created for cultivating and "subduing" it. He has the possibility, and, correspondingly, the duty, to exploit nature and, through it, to contribute to the development of all humanity. Across successive generations, the world spins toward its end. The phase of development that we have reached today allows us a better understanding of the teaching of Genesis that suggests the idea—which our ancestors could not have had—of the construction of a future. It is true that it presents a double temptation: one is a Promethean temptation, with man forgetting his condition as creature and usurping the position of the Creator; the other, apparently more modest, is the temptation of renouncing all metaphysical aims and forgetting every transcendent end, so as henceforth to envisage in a utopian way only an earthly future that becomes more or less confused with salvation. But it remains true that man, through a personal and collective work carried out in history, has to prepare the conditions for the end to which God destines him. This is not the place to expand on the character of these conditions, on the union and distinction of the natural and supernatural conditions. It suffices for our purpose to observe that there is a whole dimension of human activity, related to a total conception of the world, that the presuppositions of Amidism rule out.

3. In the end, we are concerned with much more than the presuppositions of Amidism, which represents only a province in the immense spiritual empire of Buddhism, itself a part of a vast unity. Contrary to what many historians seem to believe, the frontiers of

this domain are less geographical than temporal. We shall refer to it as the pre-Christian universe. It is by the Christian revelation, prepared in ancient Israel, that man finally became fully cognizant of the necessary universalism of his horizon and of its metaphysical personality. These two features are correlated. The awareness of them is maintained by the Church, and it is in the Christian Faith that this awareness, upheld by dogma, can realize its effectiveness. Whether in its highest speculations or its most profound spiritual intuitions, the pre-Christian mental world—in the East as in the West—is still a twilight world. Nevertheless, some patches of light glimmer in this twilight. The early Christians, imbued as they were with the newness of Christ, never stopped looking for precursory symbols in the imaginary creations of the ancient world, or even trying to save them by incorporating them into the Christian synthesis. Many human values [p. 368] ripened in the sun of Athens and Rome. As was pointed out by Fr. Pierre Charles and many others in the generation directly preceding ours, however, the spiritual fruits of oriental religions, equally pre-Christian, often have much less need of purification than the realities with which the Church Fathers were confronted. Certainly, Amidism is one of the most beautiful of these fruits.

It is undeniable, however, that the personalism found in it is still entirely relative. It is closer to a natural instinct of individuality than to the reflection that grows out of the mystery of the Trinity. Consequently, and precisely because of the spiritual deepening, it becomes diluted rather than becoming stronger. From that difference in the analogy, Amida's paradise will provide us with a symbol with which to conclude. For the Christian, as for the Amidist, there is a kind of mystical identification between "paradise" and its ruler—between the Kingdom and its King. But the resemblance is far from being perfect because, depending on the direction, the thought is just the opposite. Christ, as Origen says, is himself his Kingdom (*autobasileia*); he is himself, as Ruysbroeck says, the "living Paradise". Thus, the Christian heaven is, so to speak, absorbed in God; "God's paradise" disappears, in a final theophany, before the "God of paradise" (Nicetas Stethatos). The personalism of the Christian Faith asserts itself all the way to the final climax of mystical ardor and thought: Eternity, like Truth and Justice, is one of God's names. God is a mystery of supreme density; he is the inviolable Nucleus;

he is the hidden Being par excellence, because he is the personal Being par excellence—and, for the one who approaches him, he is the personalizing Being. However, in the Amidist religion—to the extent that reflection intervenes—Amida, who to begin with is a distinct and personal being, is reabsorbed in an Absolute transcending all knowledge that can be described only in the most minimal terms of void and space. When Amida shows his individual aspect to his followers, he does not even claim to be divine: by his origin and role, he is still a being essentially similar to all of us, and, in recalling the story of his "original vow"—the basis for the confidence placed in him—it was possible to speak of the "euhemerism"[23] that delights the sutras of the Pure Land, as it does so many of the Mahayanist sutras. But, when Amida takes on vaster proportions, becomes a supernatural being and seems to begin to take on a divine dignity, it is to inaugurate the process at the completion of which he vanishes like a phantom. In the cosmic or supracosmic principle that receives him, his personality is not sublimated but abolished. This [p. 369] principle is surely, like the Zeus of Orphic verse,[24] "the beginning, the middle and the end" of everything, but it is so empty, so evanescent, that one is not surprised that early Christian missionaries, looking for an analogy that would allow them to grasp it, designated it by a very imperfect approximation as the *materia prima* [prime matter] of their own philosophy. Aristotle himself had translated the *apeiron* [infinite] of Anaximander[25] in this way. Thus, he did not render full justice to his predecessor's thought, and neither did Catholic missionaries render full justice to the effort of Buddhist thought. What is certain, however, is that the more one relies on Buddhist texts, the recitations they contain—like the analyses, justifications and theoretical constructions that scholars offer us in abundance—the more removed Amida appears to be from our God. But if, afterward, one again envisages Amida as he seems to

---

[23] Euhemerism is a philosophical term meaning a system in which pagan gods were regarded not as divine persons but as human persons divinized by the gratitude or folly of man.

[24] [Orphism was a Greek mystical religion. Zeus, who was the highest of the Greek gods, featured prominently in its texts.—Ed.]

[25] [Anaximander (ca. 610–ca. 546) was a pre-Socratic Greek philosopher. The concepts of infinity and origin are traced to him.—Ed.]

be invoked in the concrete religious act of the best of his followers, then once again he comes closer. Before engaging in a dialogue with one of his followers that circumstances might bring about, we should address ourselves in the secret of our hearts to Jesus Christ, who is the only "true Amida".

# 7

# Renewing Theology

*This excerpt is taken from the third part of* Catholicism, *which de Lubac describes as more spiritual and personal than the preceding two parts, in order to show the interior character of Christianity alongside its social and historical dimensions.*[1] *Outlining the contribution of theology, and thereby of the theologian, to Church renewal, it speaks for itself.*

[p. 319] When the causes of an evil have been seen, it becomes easier to remedy it. The hoped-for cure has already begun. The disappointment caused by the bitter fruits of individualism in all branches of theology, as well as the widely felt need of avoiding minor controversies so as to achieve a synthesis, creates the right atmosphere. A better but still too imperfect knowledge of the patristic period, as well as of the golden age [p. 320] of medieval theology, studied in conjunction with the former, is a considerable guarantee of success. Theologians have set to work. One of them not long since summoned his fellows to this work in no uncertain terms: "Our academic teaching", he said,

> must be saved from the individualism with which for the sake of clarity and the needs of controversy we seem to have allowed it to be associated since the sixteenth century. Our treatises on Grace and the Sacraments, on the Eucharist, even on the Church, are fashioned so as to give the impression that God the Redeemer is never faced with anything but an untold number of individuals, every one of them regulating on his own account the measure of his personal relationships

---

Excerpted from *Catholicism: Christ and the Common Destiny of Man*, trans. Lancelot C. Sheppard and Sister Elizabeth Englund, O.C.D. (San Francisco: Ignatius Press, 1988), 319–25.

[1] *At the Service of the Church: Henri de Lubac Reflects on the Circumstances that Occasioned his Writings*, trans. Anne Elizabeth Englund (San Francisco: Ignatius Press, 1993), 27.

with God, just like the taxpayers, the travelers and the employees who pass successively, with no organic connection with each other, before the pay-desks and turnstiles of this world. In place of this conception we must bring back to the foreground the dogma of the Mystical Body in which the Church consists, where there are jointed limbs, a single nervous system, a single circulation of the blood and a single head, for the mystery of the Word incarnate is first and foremost the mystery of the New Adam and of the Head of Humanity.[2]

The task may appear heavy. But the preparation has been going forward for some time. An endeavor like that of the Catholic school of theology at Tübingen, begun upward of a century ago, not to mention other, more isolated or less ambitious efforts, still shows that the sap is strongly rising. In 1819 in the prospectus of its official organ, the *Theologische Quartalschrift*, could be read an attempted definition of the Spirit and Essence of Catholicism: "The central fact is the revelation of the plan realized by God in humanity: this plan is an organic whole, with a progressive development in history." Drey, Möhler and their disciples commented on this [p. 321] definition in magnificent fashion,[3] and the recent work of their successors has remained faithful to the first inspiration of the school.[4] Other publications, coming from all points of the theological horizon, are like so many little streams which promise well for the mighty river that our century needs. But why speak of books and schools? For what gives ground for the greatest confidence is that this is no mere surface agitation, that the theologians themselves, the interpreters of the living tradition, are urged forward by a revival which is reflected primarily in events because it springs from the very depths of the Catholic conscience. Take, for example, the success from a religious point of view of such authors as

---

[2] E. Masure, *Semaine sociale de Nice* (1934), pp. 230–31.

[3] See the studies on Möhler by Frs. Congar and Rouzet, O.P., in *Irénikon* (1935); and Pierre Chaillet, S.J., "L'Esprit du Christianisme et du Catholicisme" [The spirit of Christianity and of Catholicism], *Revue des [sciences philosophiques et théologiques]* (1937).

[4] The French public at least knows the name of Karl Adam, thanks to several translations. The ecclesiology owing to the work and teaching of Fr. Pierre Charles is also well known. See esp. *La Robe sans couture* (Museum Lessianum, 1923), and such articles as "Le pouvoir absolu dans l'Église" [Absolute power in the Church] [1925] or "Christi Vicarius" [The vicar of Christ] [1929], *Nouvelle revue théologique*. . . .

Péguy[5] or Claudel. Is it not extremely significant? But principally we should realize all the doctrinal implications of those great movements which in our day show so plainly the vitality of the Church: the missionary movement, the liturgical movement—so very different from that archeological sectarian spirit that at one time merely kept it in check—social movements like the J.O.C.[6] in Belgium or in France. But we realize, too, the need in which they stand, if they are to fulfill their promise, of fully enlightened support and guidance. Again, we see the urgent necessity of strictly theological doctrinal elaboration.

Just to imitate primitive Christianity or the Middle Ages will not be enough. We can revive the Fathers' all-embracing humanism and recover the spirit of their mystical exegesis only by an assimilation which is at the same time a transformation. For although the Church rests on eternal foundations, [p. 322] it is in a continual state of rebuilding, and since the Fathers' time it has undergone many changes in style; and without in any way considering ourselves better than our Fathers, what we in turn have to build for our own use must be built in our own style, that is, one that is adapted to our own needs and problems. We should gain nothing at all by breaking with an unhealthy individualism if in its place we dreamed of an impossible return to the past, for that is either an illusion which breeds schisms or a childish fancy which dulls the mind. Two conditions must govern our contemplation of the past. We must recognize, in the first place, the great diversity of the theories which have been professed in the course of Christian history on those innumerable subjects where religious truth comes in contact with our human preoccupations. Secondly, we must realize to how great an extent these theories depend on social, intellectual, or cultural conditions in a state of constant development. Only so can we contemplate and admire in all security the imposing unity of the great current of tradition, bearing in its ever-changing waves free from all contamination the same indefectible belief. It is only when we have

[5] [Charles Péguy (1873–1914) was a French socialist essayist and poet who became a philosophical Roman Catholic during the decade leading up to his death, which occurred while he was fighting in the First World War.—Ed.]

[6] [The Jeunesse ouvrière chrétienne (Young Christian Workers) is an international association for young Roman Catholics founded in Brussels in 1925.—Ed.]

realized very keenly how different we necessarily are in our human reactions, even toward revelation, and in our human methods of thought, even about dogma—from St. Paul or Origen, St. Thomas Aquinas or Bossuet, a monk of the Thebaid,[7] a medieval craftsman or a Chinese neophyte [convert]—that we shall be conscious of the full intimacy of our profound union with them all in this same dogma by which they lived as we live today: *in eadem doctrina eademque sententia* [having the same mind in the same doctrine]. Then a return to the sources of antiquity will be the very opposite of an escape into a dead past. We shall understand how disastrous it would be if we were to forego the great heritage which comes to us from the centuries of analysis and scientific research as well as from the definitive results, the clarifications, which emerge from the controversies. We shall not condemn [p. 323] self-examination or spiritual experience as if they derived from a merely individualist psychology or narcissist introspection, any more than, by an analogous method of misinterpretation, we shall confuse transcendental speculation with an abstract discarnate idealism. Even in our criticism of individualism we shall recognize that much of human progress has been bound up with its expansion, and that it is a question not so much of repudiating it as of rising above it. So too shall we reject the notion that the modern age has experienced outside the Church only error and decadence. That is an illusion, a temptation to which we have yielded only too often. The epoch of a "separated" philosophy was providential, like all others, and the fruits of the immense effort of thought which was undertaken in its name, and is still being undertaken, ought not, through our fault, to be left outside Catholicism. Certainly it requires a far more generous perspicacity to give a favorable reception to what has arisen outside our own body than to gather up what had at one time flourished within it and give it new life.

A much keener discernment too is necessary if mistakes are to be avoided.[8] So the work that is called for at the present day is in many respects far more delicate than that required in the patristic age, in

[7] [The desert region of the upper Nile in Egypt, where many Christian hermits settled.—Ed.]

[8] See on that Marcel Légaut, *La condition chrétienne* [The Christian condition], 19: "When you come, Lord, . . . hidden under the immense fermentation of this generation

St. Thomas Aquinas' time or even at the "humanist" epoch. It demands a comprehensive combination of opposing qualities, each of them brought to a high degree of excellence, one buttressed, so to say, on another, and braced with the greatest tension.[9] Who would not feel overwhelmed and disheartened at the very outset in face of such requirements, however unassuming the part which he [p. 324] hopes to play in the great common task? But once again it is faith that wins the victory, and he who realizes his helplessness retires within himself and with the whole Church begs for the grace of the Holy Spirit.

For it is indeed to this grace, in our opinion, that must be ascribed the present fervent propagation and the vigorous life of the traditional doctrine of the Mystical Body. But such a doctrine will produce the results that we have a right to expect from it only if it is established on solid foundations. Great care must be taken lest it should give the impression of being merely a passing craze. Many are already growing impatient with the new scholasticism, the mixture of abstractions and metaphors in which it tends to be entangled. Others are anxious, not perhaps without some semblance at least of reason, at the vague mysticism and the unsystematic speculation that are in some instances the price of its success. But there would be a much more serious danger if the very magnificence of the Pauline definitions and the commentaries on them were to dazzle certain minds, and cause in them the recrudescence of a kind of false gnosis, and if the consequent mental intoxication [p. 325] were to dissipate, as being something too humble, the charm of the Gospel itself. Paul is but a servant, an interpreter. His inspired teaching is not sufficient of itself, and it can never dispense with a continual reference to the only Master, the only Son in whom God has given us all, having expressed himself completely by him. But such a danger, which is entirely hypothetical, may be averted

---

which is going to give the world a new wine, there are few Christians who will be able to recognize you, for there are few who are awaiting you. Many, alas, think of the Church only as being in a majestic and timeless immobility. That assurance is a refuge for them against all uncertainties but also the obstacle that protects them from all your encounters. . . ."

[9] [De Lubac here deploys an architectural metaphor from the construction of medieval abbeys and cathedrals.—Ed.]

by prudent guidance. In any case, there are many problems to be probed, many applications and careful adjustments to be made if the movement which we are witnessing is not to be compromised. A doctrinal effort is imperative. For although dogma is essentially unchanging, the work of the theologian is never ended.

# Concluding Interpretive Postscript

On September 4, 1991, Henri Cardinal de Lubac died peacefully in Paris, aged ninety-five. Thus ended the life of one of the twentieth century's most remarkable theologians, and the task of posthumous reception and interpretation began. In 1973, almost twenty years earlier, de Lubac had bequeathed his papers to the Belgian Jesuit Georges Chantraine (1932–2010).[1] This decision was precipitated by health problems and the prospect of relocation to Paris following confirmation of the forthcoming closure of the Jesuit house at Fourvière in Lyon. Chantraine had long admired de Lubac's work, especially on scriptural exegesis, and the two had become friends in 1961, when they began an ongoing correspondence. In 1964, de Lubac visited the Jesuit house at Egenhoven, at Chantraine's invitation, to present an academic paper and, in 1971, wrote the foreword to Chantraine's study of Erasmus.[2]

At the time of de Lubac's death, Chantraine was working at the theological institute he had established at Lugano in Switzerland. However, in 1995, he returned to Namur and was asked by his provincial to produce a detailed intellectual biography of de Lubac and to direct the production of his collected works. These works include many articles and chapters that have been difficult to obtain in their original place of publication as well as previously unpublished essays and so are of the highest importance for de Lubac

[1] Georges Chantraine and Marie-Gabrielle Lemaire, *Henri de Lubac*, 4 vols. (Paris: Cerf, 2007–), 4:13, 355, 513; Jean-Marie Hennaux, "In Memoriam: Georges Chantraine, SJ (1932–2010)", *Bulletin de l'Association Internationale Cardinal Henri de Lubac* 12 (2010): 27–31.

[2] *Theology in History*, trans. Anne Englund Nash (San Francisco: Ignatius Press, 1996), 44–48.

research.[3] Following Chantraine's death, Marie-Gabrielle Lemaire, of the Jesuit Theological Faculty, Brussels, and the University of Namur, has continued his work as de Lubac's biographer and the director of his archive.

Several studies provide an overview of de Lubac's life and theology and set these in their wider contexts. The clear and informative biography by Rudolf Voderholzer gives admirably even coverage to the different periods of de Lubac's life.[4] Voderholzer also offers a balanced presentation of de Lubac's theology structured around synopses of key works.[5] I have produced my own, more synthetic, overview.[6] Jürgen Mettepenningen has compiled an excellent study of the wider *nouvelle théologie*, examining the movement's antecedents, history, and diversity and, thereby, setting out de Lubac's intellectual context. Especially noteworthy is Mettepenningen's attention to Dominicans and to developments in Belgium and the Netherlands.[7] The large *Ressourcement* volume, edited by Gabriel Flynn and Paul D. Murray, achieves something similar, with its thirty-four contributors offering a diverse range of perspectives.[8] The *T&T Clark Companion to Henri de Lubac*, edited by Jordan Hillebert, includes nineteen useful chapters on different aspects of theology and context.[9]

I shall now review de Lubac's interpreters under the headings used for the presentation of his texts. Due to space limitations, it will not be possible to include all available interpretive work. Priority will be given to monographs, to material in English, and to studies that advance a coherent critical or original perspective.

---

[3] *Oeuvres complètes*, 50 vols. (Paris: Cerf, 1999–).

[4] Rudolf Voderholzer, *Meet Henri de Lubac: His Life and Work*, trans. Michael J. Miller (San Francisco: Ignatius Press, 2008), 19–103.

[5] Ibid., 105–217.

[6] David Grumett, *De Lubac: A Guide for the Perplexed* (London: T&T Clark, 2007).

[7] Jürgen Mettepenningen, *Nouvelle Théologie—New Theology: Inheritor of Modernism, Precursor of Vatican II* (London: T&T Clark, 2010).

[8] *Ressourcement: A Movement for Renewal in Twentieth-Century Catholic Theology*, ed. Gabriel Flynn and Paul D. Murray with Patricia Kelly (Oxford: Oxford University Press, 2011).

[9] *T&T Clark Companion to Henri de Lubac*, ed. Jordan Hillebert (London: T&T Clark, 2017).

In 2012, Rowan Williams became the first archbishop of Canterbury to address the synod of bishops in Rome. He opened with de Lubac's theological anthropology. De Lubac, he says, "reminded us of what it meant for early and mediaeval Christianity to speak of humanity as made in God's image and of grace as perfecting and transfiguring that image so long overlaid by our habitual 'inhumanity'."[10] The Gospel message, Williams continues, is that it is "at last possible to be properly human". Several major studies have examined the theological anthropology that Williams outlines. Michel Sales presents the soul's relation to God in successive stages, beginning with the primary affirmation of God as absolute and progressing on to the spirit of God in humans as their natural response to the divine initiative. He then shows how the idea of God is rooted in the reality both of this spirit and of the divine object of its natural desire, notwithstanding the infinite qualitative difference between desire and its end. The most distinctive element of Sales' discussion is negative theology.[11] There is, he suggests, a necessary labor of the intelligence in which reason is negated and the spirit is affirmed by revelation. Indeed, negation is at the heart of divinizing union. In a study published in the same year, Eric de Moulins-Beaufort, who is now an auxiliary bishop in Paris, examines how de Lubac views human originality and uniqueness in the terms of mystery and image, but primarily of spirit. Human existence, this suggests, is spiritually dynamic, with tripartite anthropology at the heart of de Lubac's theology.[12] Moreover, spirit is as much collective as individual, being rooted and encountered in history. Jean-Pierre

[10] "The Archbishop of Canterbury's address to the Thirteenth Ordinary General Assembly of the Synod of Bishops on the New Evangelization for the Transmission of the Christian Faith", 3, at http://rowanwilliams.archbishopofcanterbury.org/articles.php/2645/archbishops-address-to-the-synod-of-bishops-in-rome.

[11] Michel Sales, *L'Être humain et la connaissance naturelle qu'il a de Dieu: essai sur la structure anthropo-théologique fondamentale de la Révélation chrétienne dans la pensée du P. Henri de Lubac* (Paris: Parole et silence, 2003), 59–88.

[12] Eric de Moulins-Beaufort, *Anthropologie et mystique selon Henri de Lubac: "l'esprit de l'homme", ou la présence de Dieu en l'homme*, Études lubaciennes 3 (Paris: Cerf, 2003); with themes in de Moulins-Beaufort, "The Spiritual Man in the Thought of Henri de Lubac", trans. David L. Schindler, *Communio* 25 (1998): 287–302.

Wagner's very clear earlier study endorses de Lubac's synthetic method, which shows the unity of the Christian mystery as well as his dialogical engagement with other disciplines.[13] However, Wagner contends that de Lubac gives insufficient recognition to the autonomy of contemporary philosophy and that his theology fails to account for sin, human finitude, and soteriology. Juvénal Ilunga Muya has argued, from an African theological perspective, that de Lubac's centering of faith on mystery has important implications for inculturation. Moreover, because the mystery must always be interiorized, *all* theology is contextual.[14]

Bertrand Dumas has argued that, in the 1960s, de Lubac changed his view of the relation of mysticism and theology. Before then, he states, de Lubac saw the Christian mystery as provoking and producing thought. On this reading, theology and dogma depend on the mystery and are oriented by it.[15] Later, however, de Lubac is said to regard mysticism and theology as co-original, promoting the "double progress" of faith and its dogmatic profession, with mysticism and theology conjoined in spiritual intelligence, whose object is Christ. Mysticism is thereby grounded in ordinary scriptural reading, worship, and experience, rather than being the intense self-consciousness of internalized spirit.

There is renewed interest in de Lubac's "Christian humanism", as the Vietnamese Assumptionist theologian François-Xavier Nguyen Tien Dung terms it. Dung shows how de Lubac presents this as a clear alternative to atheist humanism, grounding anthropology in Christ, who restores the image of God in humanity, in the Church, and in the beatific vision. Noteworthy is his comparison of *The Drama of Atheist Humanism*, which de Lubac produced in wartime and in which he took a combative stance, with the later and as yet untranslated *Athéisme et sens de l'homme*, in which de Lubac demonstrates a greater willingness to enter into dialogue with

---

[13] Jean-Pierre Wagner, *La Théologie fondamentale selon Henri de Lubac* (Paris: Cerf, 1997).

[14] Juvénal Ilunga Muya, "Henri de Lubac et le devenir de la théologie africaine", in *Henri de Lubac: La Rencontre au cœur de l'Église*, ed. Jean-Dominique Durand (Paris: Cerf, 2006), 211–37.

[15] Bertrand Dumas, *Mystique et théologie d'après Henri de Lubac*, Études lubaciennes 8 (Paris: Cerf, 2013).

atheism.[16] Combining anthropology with doctrine, Philippe Geneste reaches similar conclusions about de Lubac's anthropology, suggesting that he articulates a "Christology of accomplishment" in which humanism is converted in Christ, who is the true source of personalization and spiritualization.[17] This notion of conversion enables de Lubac's theological anthropology to be related to his theology of religion. As Ilaria Morali has argued, religion, even in its non-Christian forms, serves as testimony to the naturally Christian soul striving for a higher truth beyond the purely natural.[18] However, she concurs with de Lubac that a clear distinction must be drawn between religion as a generic spiritual capacity, founded on a shared humanity, and specific religious systems. Roman Catholicism, for instance, has a theology of collective salvation through grace that is different from the doctrine of other systems.

## The Christian Faith

In his foreword to *Catholicism*, Pope Benedict XVI—writing before his election—described the study as an "essential milestone on my theological journey", commending its articulation of the "fundamental intuition of Christian Faith" by re-presenting patristic and early medieval texts and by combining community and universality in trinitarian doctrine.[19] In a speech delivered in the same period, he praised de Lubac as himself a "true Father of the Church for our day and an exemplary European".[20] Focusing on texts such as

---

[16] François-Xavier Nguyen Tien Dung, *La foi au Dieu des chrétiens, gage d'un authentique humanisme: Henri de Lubac face à l'humanisme athée* (Paris: Desclée, 2010), 153–204.

[17] Philippe Geneste, *Humanisme et lumière du Christ chez Henri de Lubac*, Études lubaciennes 11 (Paris: Cerf, 2016).

[18] Ilaria Morali, *La salvezza dei non cristiani. L'influsso di Henri De Lubac sulla dottrina del Vaticano II* (EMI, 1999).

[19] Joseph Cardinal Ratzinger, "Foreword", in *Catholicism: Christ and the Common Destiny of Man*, trans. Lancelot C. Sheppard and Sister Elizabeth Englund, O.C.D. (San Francisco: Ignatius Press, 1988), 11–12 (11).

[20] "Le futur Benoît XVI et Henri de Lubac", *Bulletin de l'Association Internationale Cardinal Henri de Lubac* 7 (2005): 4–9; also Marie-Gabrielle Lemaire, "Joseph Ratzinger et Henri de Lubac", *Bulletin de l'Association Internationale Cardinal Henri de Lubac* 15 (2013): 45–62.

*The Splendor of the Church*, Alberto De Vita has also highlighted de Lubac's trinitarian doctrine, arguing for its importance in understanding the movement by which believers are incorporated into the Church and into Christ.[21]

De Lubac's exposition of the nature of faith has received some attention. Reflecting on the rapid Christian expansion in Korea, Germain Jin-Sang Kwak praises his clear distinction of the act of faith from the content of faith, on the grounds that this guards against misinterpretations of faith, whether as sentimental or as propositional, which hinder its basic apprehension.[22] Indeed, for de Lubac, the content of faith is inseparable from the act of faith, being communicated life, which itself draws the believer to the point of assent. Appraising his embrace of inwardness, as well as his abiding acknowledgment of paradox and his expository style, Joshua Furnal presents a powerful case that de Lubac was significantly indebted to Kierkegaard.[23] This suggests that his readers should not expect ordered sets of propositions but indirect communication.

Three significant books address de Lubac's Christology. Donath Hercsik emphasizes the importance of Christ's newness, then delineates three substantive elements: the Incarnation as paradox and as mystery, including Christ as the universal human and the new man; the Word of God, with Christ as the source of revelation, the abbreviated word, and the New Testament in person; and light, with Christ as both the revealing light and the enlightening light.[24] Christ, Hercsik persuasively argues, is the center of de Lubac's theology, and it is on Christ that his epistemology, anthropology, and ecclesiology converge. The second assessment of de Lubac's Christology is by Étienne Guibert, who describes this as "dispersed", with the light of Christ manifesting different dimensions of the mystery of Christ and opening four "christological senses" or

---

[21] Alberto De Vita, *La svolta ecclesiologica di Henri de Lubac. L'inserimento della dimensione ecclesiale nella teologia trinitaria* (Rome: Viverein, 2008).

[22] Germain Jin-Sang Kwak, *La foi comme vie communiquée: fides qua et fides quae chez Henri de Lubac* (Paris: Desclée, 2011).

[23] Joshua Furnal, *Catholic Theology after Kierkegaard* (Oxford: Oxford University Press, 2015), 104–33.

[24] Donath Hercsik, *Jesus Christus als Mitte der Theologie von Henri de Lubac* (Frankfurt am Main: Knecht, 2001).

"ways".[25] First, because of the economy, or simple fact, of Christ, revelation is necessarily historical. Second, intelligence of the fact of Christ, which is theology, is incarnational and includes paradox. Third comes the interiorization of the mystery of Christ, which Guibert identifies with soteriology, which is focused in the Cross and the gift of Christ as redeemer. Fourth is eschatology, which is given in the mystery of the hiatus between Christ's first and second comings. The whole forms an "integral Christology" that preserves the mystery of Christ. Indeed, de Lubac's doctrinal method, which converges on a topic from several different starting points and seeks neither exhaustive definition nor closure, promotes a high valuation of the mystery. The third study of de Lubac's doctrine of Christ is by Noel O'Sullivan, who examines what he terms de Lubac's "descending christology, with a marked emphasis on the Incarnation, understood as the definitive revelation of Trinitarian love, resplendent in all its transcendent newness".[26] Christ as savior "irrupts into human history" in accordance with God's original plan for the world, which finds its ultimate expression in the Cross and Resurrection. This objectivity needs to be safeguarded against subjective understandings of Christ's mission as being to save individuals: the passage from image to likeness is collective and is completed only in the eschaton.

De Lubac's theology is usually thought to be focused on Christology rather than on pneumatology. However, the Congolese priest and theologian Félicien Boduka N'glandey argues that these are complementary foci. The Spirit is part of the economy of Christ's revelation, preparing the human heart to receive this and continuing to deepen the intellectual apperception of the content of revelation. The Spirit founds, transmits, and communicates Christian revelation, especially through Scripture. The Spirit is active, creative, and absolute over human life, rather than merely immanent within it. The Spirit is from Christ and of Christ and inseparable from him. The Spirit makes possible the motherhood of Mary. The Spirit is intrinsic to Christ's sacramental action, and through its gift, nature is

[25] Étienne Guibert, *Le Mystère du Christ d'après Henri de Lubac* (Paris: Cerf, 2006).

[26] Noel O'Sullivan, *Christ and Creation: Christology as the Key to Interpreting the Theology of Creation in the Works of Henri de Lubac* (New York: Lang, 2008), 452.

graced. While generally praising de Lubac, N'glandey suggests that he places excessive reliance on the natural knowledge of God, rather than viewing knowledge as a gift of the Spirit. Moreover, N'glandey contends that greater attention should be given to the role of the Spirit in the Church and in constructing the Church as a family.[27] His study complements christological approaches to de Lubac.

## Church

In *Theology and Social Theory*, which was first published a year before de Lubac's death, John Milbank praises his high valuations of paradox and desire. Nevertheless, notwithstanding de Lubac's strong emphasis on the social and historical dimensions of salvation, Milbank critiques his "marked tendency to prescind from the political, and to insulate the Church from wider social processes". De Lubac, Milbank protests, regards salvation as nothing other than "incorporation into *ecclesia*" and tellingly concludes *Catholicism* with a chapter on transcendence.[28] Ultimately, it seems, de Lubac remains haunted by the fear of Marx' dissolution of human being into social being. However, to associate Christian belief with atemporal spirituality is to posit a social realm that the believer might stand outside of, which, relative to the Church, is autonomous. Viewing de Lubac's stance as representative of a wider pathology, Milbank perceptively writes that it was "difficult for thinkers of this era to define a field of autonomy and free action for the *laity*, without also placing self-denying ordinances on the Church, which they still automatically identified with the clerical hierarchy".[29] Yet in Latin America, Milbank argues, this distinction of the ecclesial plane from the secular plane collapses, because the Church "often provides the only social

---

[27] Félicien Boduka N'glandey, *Le Mystère de l'Esprit saint dans l'oeuvre du père Henri de Lubac: eléments de pneumatologie* (Paris: L'Harmattan, 2011). For the critiques, 140–41, 170–74.

[28] John Milbank, *Theology and Social Theory: Beyond Secular Reason*, 2nd ed. (1990; Oxford: Blackwell, 2006), 220–30. Although Milbank states in the new preface (xxxi) that he has "slightly modified" his account of de Lubac, the relevant portions of text are unchanged from the first edition.

[29] Ibid., 229–30.

space in which political resistance (especially peaceful political resistance) can be pursued".

Before his election, Pope Benedict XVI described the "special profit" that he derived from *Corpus Mysticum* and the "new understanding of the unity of Church and Eucharist" that the study opened to him.[30] Writing from a liturgical standpoint, Laurence Hemming lauds this text's contestation of the subordination of prayer to reason. Nevertheless, focusing (unlike Milbank) on *Corpus Mysticum*, he notes that the principal danger in worship is no longer fetishizing the host but idolizing the community. De Lubac, Hemming suggests, provides a beginning rather than an ending, with an "interior account . . . drawn from *within* the texts he reads" that "ignores the enormous pressure from without, from the wider context of the dramatic changes enacted in Europe by the ending of the Middle Ages and the beginnings of modernity".[31] Like Milbank and Hemming, Yik-Pui Au asserts that de Lubac is more intent on countering an individualistic culture of piety within the Church than individualism outside of her, and that this focus is due to an "inadequate cultural exegesis of the phenomenon of individualism."[32]

In a major study, which includes a similar, although more detailed, critique to Milbank's, Paul McPartlan endorses de Lubac's notion that the Eucharist makes the Church. At the heart of the Eucharist are anticipation, with a spiritual reality announced that will be made real only in the eschaton, and participation, by which the whole Church shares in the life of Christ to a degree appropriate to earthly life.[33] However, McPartlan goes on to argue that, in his later work, de Lubac retreats to exactly the kind of bureaucratic and hierarchic ecclesiology that, in earlier work, he sought

[30] Joseph Ratzinger, *Milestones: Memoirs 1927–1977*, trans. Erasmo Leiva-Merikakis (San Francisco: Ignatius Press, 1998), 98.

[31] Laurence Paul Hemming, "Henri de Lubac: Reading *Corpus Mysticum*", *New Blackfriars* 90 (2009): 519–34 (532–33).

[32] Yik-Pui Au, *The Eucharist as a Countercultural Liturgy: An Examination of the Theologies of Henri de Lubac, John Zizioulas, and Miroslav Volf* (Eugene, Ore.: Pickwick, 2017), 24–46 (43).

[33] Paul McPartlan, *The Eucharist Makes the Church: Henri de Lubac and John Zizioulas in Dialogue*, 2nd ed. (1993; Fairfax, Va.: Eastern Christian Publications, 2005), 75–97.

to overturn. This includes a strong doctrine of papal primacy, with bishops' jurisdiction viewed as deriving from the pope, and the suggestion that sacramentality is embodied in individual bishops, via their apostolic succession.[34] McPartlan contends that de Lubac is not well served by his view of Christ as an individual, whereas the Greek Orthodox theologian John Zizioulas, in contrast, understands Christ corporately. McPartlan suggests that a eucharistic ecclesiology entails that Christ and the Church be identified only momentarily, during worship, rather than on an ongoing basis. Indeed, there is distance between the Church and Christ: the Church is not a divinely endorsed institution and is sinful. Moreover, McPartlan critically suggests that, for de Lubac, Church members form a unity in identity, with the same Christ in each, and notes that little attention is given to how Church members relate to one other.[35] Catherine Pickstock offers a similar, if briefer, critique of de Lubac, stressing the mutuality of the Church and the Eucharist and emphasizing that the Eucharist is essentially a corporate act opposed to "clerical . . . aggrandizement".[36] Eugene Schlesinger advances a parallel case from the starting point of spiritual exegesis, arguing that, if the Church's eschatological identity is taken seriously, present structures must be regarded as contingent.[37] Gemma Simmonds gives a balanced presentation of these matters, which takes account both of *Corpus Mysticum* and of de Lubac's postconciliar writings.[38]

The Anglican theologian John Webster pursues a similar critique, opposing what he sees as the recent inflation of ecclesiology within his own tradition, which can obscure the miraculous quality of grace. Citing Milbank as an example, he argues that commitment to the "ontological union between Christ and the body of the church" makes the theologian "insecure (even casual) about

[34] Ibid., 98–120, 265–88.

[35] Ibid., 279–80.

[36] Catherine Pickstock, *After Writing: On the Liturgical Consummation of Philosophy* (Oxford: Blackwell, 1998), 158–65.

[37] Eugene R. Schlesinger, "The Threefold Body in Eschatological Perspective: With and Beyond Henri de Lubac on the Church", *Ecclesiology* 10 (2014): 186–204.

[38] Gemma Simmonds, "The Mystical Body: Ecclesiology and Sacramental Theology", in Hillebert, *T&T Clark Companion*, 159–79.

identifying Christological boundaries".[39] Webster recognizes the need for human cooperation with salvation, which is no mere salvage operation but a movement in which people are enabled to raise themselves, through the power that comes from Christ, to God. Yet the effects of this power are undermined if agency is transferred to the Church, especially when the sufficiency of Christ's sacrifice, his work of external pardon, and the theology of the Cross receive little attention. Rather, Webster argues, a dogmatics of "mutuality between God and creatures" is needed that recognizes that grace is truly a miracle. He writes: "Christ's perfection is not integrative or inclusive, but complete in itself, and only so extended to the saints in the work of the Spirit."[40]

Focusing on *Corpus Mysticum* and *Medieval Exegesis*, Susan Wood emphasizes the importance of de Lubac's view of the Church as Christ's mystical body. Working with these large, demanding, and then untranslated texts, she demonstrates that, for de Lubac, the ultimate head of the Church is Christ and that he sees a qualitative difference between the head and its human members. Christomorphic texts, she suggests, may be corrected by others.[41] Also, Wood affirms, on exegetical grounds, de Lubac's use of the traditionalist Roman Catholic image of the Church as Christ's spouse and endorses his notion that, through the communication of idioms and a union in distinction, the whole Church is the sacrament of Christ.[42] This is an intensely incarnational ecclesiology, with the Church viewed as continuing the hypostatic union of the divine and human natures in Jesus Christ. Writing from an African theological context, Édouard Adé underscores the importance, for de Lubac, of the Church as a social and familial body, although, in common with Wood, he does not examine his extensive imagery of motherhood.[43]

---

[39] John Webster, *Confessing God: Essays in Christian Dogmatics II*, 2nd ed. (London: Bloomsbury, 2016), 161–203 (170).

[40] Ibid., 180.

[41] Susan Wood, *Spiritual Exegesis and the Church in the Theology of Henri de Lubac* (Edinburgh: T&T Clark, 1998), 72–92.

[42] Ibid., 93–107.

[43] Édouard Adé, "Église-familiale et catholicité: une réception africaine de 'Méditation sur l'Église'", in Durand, *Henri de Lubac: La Rencontre*, 201–10.

McPartlan identifies the importance, in ecumenical agreements between the Roman Catholic Church and the Anglican and Orthodox Churches, of the idea that the Church is Christ's body.[44] Moreover, in the foreword to the second edition of his earlier study, Metropolitan John Zizioulas describes de Lubac's notion that the Eucharist makes the Church as "one of the most significant developments in the ecumenical dialogue of our time".[45] Several theologians of other denominations endorse elements of de Lubac's ecclesiology. Embracing a wider understanding of Catholicism, the Lutheran Mark E. Chapman praises de Lubac for identifying the new situation of social and spiritual crisis and for formulating, in response, a theology that values institutional unity, structure, and authority, but that grounds the Christian faith in creation, the divine image in humans, sacramental sociality, and human unity.[46] Writing from a Reformed perspective, Glenn Butner endorses de Lubac's intergenerational view of sociality as well as his rooting of ecclesial unity in theological anthropology, which suggests a doctrine of election as historical and thus as collective.[47] Scott Bullard suggests that de Lubac's notion that the Eucharist produces the Church effectively counters excessively individualized conceptions of Christian belonging and piety, which have sometimes been prominent in the Baptist tradition.[48] Finally, de Lubac's own generous although fragmentary approach to Protestantism is usefully surveyed by Kenneth Oakes.[49]

---

[44] Paul McPartlan, "The Body of Christ and the Ecumenical Potential of Eucharistic Ecclesiology", *Ecclesiology* 6 (2010): 148–65.

[45] Metropolitan John of Pergamon, Foreword to the second edition, in McPartlan, *The Eucharist*, xiii–iv.

[46] Mark E. Chapman, "De Lubac's Catholicism through Lutheran Eyes: Appreciation, Application, Convergence", *One in Christ* 29 (1993): 286–301.

[47] D. Glenn Butner, Jr., "Reformed Theology and the Question of Protestant Individualism: A Dialogue with Henri de Lubac", *Journal of Reformed Theology* 10 (2016): 234–56.

[48] Scott W. Bullard, *Re-membering the Body: The Lord's Supper and Ecclesial Unity in the Free Church Traditions* (Eugene, Ore.: Cascade, 2013), 59–97.

[49] Kenneth Oakes, "Henri de Lubac and Protestantism", in Hillebert, *T&T Clark Companion*, 373–92.

Rowan Williams affirms de Lubac's recognition that at the "heart of the theological enterprise" is the intuition that there is "no alien, hostile, or external relationship between God and God's creation", but that creation is "itself oriented to communion with and joy in its Creator".[50] Alfred Vanneste, the Belgian Jesuit who taught for thirty years at the Catholic Theological Faculty at Kinshasa in the Congo and who promoted a universalist theology above particularist expressions such as African theology, offers a series of careful historical expositions of de Lubac's doctrine.[51] However, setting de Lubac alongside other theologians of nature and grace, Stephen Duffy identifies, also some time ago, a lack of clarity about what precisely "natural desire" is. Possibilities include grace, appetite, some third entity, or a divine moral exigency. Moreover, Duffy asks, how may natural desire be constitutive of human nature yet gratuitous?[52]

De Lubac's work set a trajectory that several major continental philosophers have followed. Jean-Luc Marion describes his own essay on the ego and divinization as a "marginal note" to de Lubac's "magisterial and fundamental work" on the supernatural, tracing in Descartes the "semantic drift" of the language of "capacity" from receptive passivity to active power. In Augustinian theology, Marion contends, capacity "not only implies the possibility of a gift generally, but also indicates to humans that their own nature originates with a gift, evidenced by their very constitution", with the result that humans are "tied to the giving" that provides their only possible subsistence.[53] This suggests that participation is the

---

[50] Rowan Williams, "Christ, Creator and Creature: Reflections on Christology and the Nature of Created Being", De Lubac lecture, Saint Louis University, March 7, 2017, at https://www.youtube.com/watch?v=CsEbWMsaYm4 [accessed October 15, 2019].

[51] Alfred Vanneste, *Nature et grâce dans la théologie occidentale: dialogue avec H. de Lubac* (Leuven: Peeters, 1996). For background, Gordon Molyneux, "The Contribution to African Theology of the Faculté de Théologie Catholique in Kinshasa, Zaire", *Africa Journal of Evangelical Theology* 11, no. 2 (1992): 58–89.

[52] Stephen J. Duffy, *The Graced Horizon: Nature and Grace in Modern Catholic Thought* (Collegeville, Minn.: Liturgical Press, 1992), 66–84.

[53] Jean-Luc Marion, *Cartesian Questions: Method and Metaphysics*, 2nd ed. (1991; Chicago,

"constant opening up of capacity toward God" and the "stretching of the inner space . . . accomplished by desire". In contrast, within modern metaphysics, progress is construed, not as the extension of the capacity for participation, but as the enhancement of a dominating power. Daniel Rober brings de Lubac back into dialogue with Marion, as well as with Paul Ricoeur, setting the discussion of the supernatural within the context of Europe's descent into the Second World War. Affirming de Lubac's "continuing vitality" and concurring that "human desires exist in a state of originary and constant openness to the divine", Rober urges his readers to follow liberation theologians in developing a fuller understanding of the political implications of his doctrine.[54]

Olivier Boulnois shows that, for Aquinas, desire was associated with the whole intellect. He argues that the notion that man possesses two distinct ends, one natural and the other supernatural, was a product of the intellectual rupture of the later thirteenth century that spawned theology and philosophy as separate disciplines.[55] Only then did it become necessary to account for the relation between natural and supernatural ends in terms of both linkage and opposition. Moreover, only when philosophy broke away from theology to form a separate discipline did it come to define man exhaustively by his natural end. For Boulnois, de Lubac's achievement was to grasp the significance of these shifts for both philosophy and theology and to recognize the importance of paradox for understanding desire today. Jean-François Courtine makes de Lubac's analysis of the pure nature concept central to his analysis of Suárez' legal theory, which posits a laicized common good separated from beatitude, which contrasts with Aquinas' prolongation of Aristotelian nature into the supernatural so that the two remain unified.[56] Jean-Yves

Ill.: University of Chicago Press, 1999), 67–95 (86–87). The acknowledgment is at 180n24, with another at 199n26.

[54] Daniel A. Rober, *Recognizing the Gift: Toward a Renewed Theology of Nature and Grace* (Minneapolis, Minn.: Fortress Press, 2016), 14–28, 36–38, 215–20.

[55] Olivier Boulnois, "Les deux fins de l'homme: l'impossible anthropologie et le repli de la théologie", *Les Études philosophiques* 2 (1995): 205–22.

[56] Jean-François Courtine, *Nature et empire de la loi: études suaréziennes* (Paris: Vrin, 1999), 45–67.

Lacoste also focuses on pure nature, seeking deeper understanding of the issues at stake.[57] Although the concept appears remote from the present day, Lacoste writes, it in fact diagnoses the modern construction of the natural in terms of ends that are achievable by a subject's own power: I know and will what I want, I obtain it, and I am satisfied. A logic of satiety thereby extinguishes the possibility of transcendence that is brought by true desire, which is ambiguous and felt as a power that takes hold of the subject. While celebrating de Lubac's privileging of actuality and experience, Lacoste suggests that natural desire may now need to be conceived in more embodied terms. Adam Cooper also emphasizes that people are assimilated into God as the result of a non-natural grace, or call, taking hold of them.[58] Randall Rosenberg recognizes that de Lubac goes some way toward providing what Lacoste demands, presenting man as an anthropological unity with a concrete nature, although he draws on Lonergan to develop the idea of an "erotic-agapic subjectivity".[59]

The approaches of Marion, Boulnois, and Lacoste to gift, capacity, and desire are developed by John Milbank: the person who naturally desires God is "suspended between nature and grace", with the gift of grace constituting its recipient holistically, rather than as a natural being in contrast with grace.[60] Regarding de Lubac, Milbank makes three small but significant insertions in his work's second edition.[61] First, he discusses the late *Brief Catechesis on Nature and Grace* and strengthens his contestation of the notion that de Lubac later retreated to a more Neo-Scholastic view of the supernatural. Second, Milbank relates de Lubac's understanding of the development of dogma to the supernatural: revelation is not extrinsically given by grace and then confirmed by a preexisting natural reason, but,

---

[57] Jean-Yves Lacoste, "Henri de Lubac and a Desire beyond Claim" (1995), trans. Oliver O'Donovan, in Hillebert, *T&T Clark Companion*, 351–71.

[58] Adam G. Cooper, *Naturally Human, Supernaturally God: Deification in Pre-Conciliar Catholicism* (Minneapolis, Minn.: Fortress Press, 2014), 151–215.

[59] Randall S. Rosenberg, *The Givenness of Desire: Concrete Subjectivity and the Natural Desire to See God* (Toronto, Buffalo, London: University of Toronto Press, 2017).

[60] John Milbank, *The Suspended Middle: Henri de Lubac and the Debate concerning the Supernatural* (Grand Rapids, Mich.: Eerdmans, 2005), 47.

[61] John Milbank, *The Suspended Middle: Henri de Lubac and the Renewed Split in Modern Catholic Theology* (Grand Rapids, Mich.: Eerdmans, 2014), 53–54, 67–68, 112–13.

in an almost reverse movement, revelation is first given in Christ's restoration of human nature, then unfolded by the continuing gift of grace through the Spirit in the Church. Third, when picturing gender difference, male giving and female receptivity make natural and cultural sense, but real reciprocity is not extinguished, because giving entails receiving, and receiving implies giving.

Vitor Franco Gomes has highlighted the centrality of paradox in de Lubac's theology of natural desire for God, demonstrating the importance of the non-necessity of the man–God relation, the gratuity of grace, and the role of grace as the divine gift converting desire.[62] This shows that de Lubac does not deny the usefulness of pure nature as a hypothesis to account for the biblical affirmation that man is created in God's image. Brigitte Cholvy calls for a "theological renaissance" of de Lubac's doctrine of the supernatural grounded, not in theological minutiae, but in desire: a metaphysics of love rather than a doctrine of being, with the human spirit as the site of desire and encounter. For Cholvy, the desire for knowledge transmutes into a desire for vision, with reason both defeated and enlarged. She thereby envisions love as the "intrastructure of the created in its openness to the divine", with the mystery of Christ accomplished in humanity.[63]

Other positive appraisals of de Lubac's doctrine of grace and nature have been offered. Hans Boersma promotes what he terms the "sacramental ontology" of de Lubac and other *nouveaux théologiens*, tracing this from de Lubac's theology of grace and nature into his scriptural exegesis and ecclesiology.[64] However, such language might concern Milbank, for whom, in the Christian context of reconciliation, being is the gift of a contingent event rather than an enduring stable order. Although Boersma recognizes de Lubac's own wish to safeguard the freedom of grace in the face of Neoplatonic emanationism, the notion that de Lubac has an "ontology" that he applies to different topics might lead to the role of grace being un-

[62] Vitor Franco Gomes, *Le Paradoxe du désir de Dieu: étude sur le rapport de l'homme à Dieu selon Henri de Lubac*, Études lubaciennes 4 (Paris: Cerf, 2005).

[63] Brigitte Cholvy, *Le surnaturel incarné dans la création: une lecture de la théologie du surnaturel d'Henri de Lubac*, Études lubaciennes 10 (Paris: Cerf, 2016), 440.

[64] Hans Boersma, *Nouvelle Théologie and Sacramental Ontology: A Return to Mystery* (Oxford: Oxford University Press, 2009), 88–99, 151–68, 244–65.

derstated. Indeed, Christiane Alpers suggests that the "term non-ontology better captures de Lubac's theological program" by emphasizing "the real as the creative activity which constantly reveals the supernatural through nature in an ever renewing movement".[65] Christ, she adds, indwells as subject, not as object.

A strand of Dominican-inspired scholarship has vigorously contested the growing acceptance of de Lubac's doctrine of the supernatural. Lawrence Feingold contends that de Lubac, by positing an innate and unfrustratable natural desire for God, remained in thrall to the Jansenism that he purported to refute.[66] However, a difficulty with this assessment is that, whereas Jansenius viewed grace mastering the desire of the elect, desire, for de Lubac, is internalized and free. Also critiquing de Lubac, Ralph McInerny defends Cajetan's understanding of obediential potency as a passive capacity activated by an external agent through infused grace on the grounds both that it is internally coherent and that it is consistent with Thomas Aquinas. Moreover, he contends that de Lubac's discomfort with distinguishing supernatural ends from natural ends may be due to his suspicion of philosophy as an autonomous discipline.[67] Steven Long censures de Lubac for preferring those texts of Aquinas that address supernatural ends to those concerned with proximate ends.[68] In contrast with Feingold and Long, Bernard Mulcahy recognizes de Lubac's Augustinian heritage but also traces the pure nature theory back to Augustine and to Paul's letter to the Romans.[69] There, it was pertinent in the presentation of the nascent Christian faith to Jews living under the law, as well as to Gentiles, who acknowledged no law but nature, as well as in debates about whether outward observance may renew inner nature. Andrew Swafford reviews the pure nature debate and introduces Matthias Scheeben (1835–1888),

[65] Christiane Alpers, "The Essence of a Christian in Henri de Lubac: Sacramental Ontology or Non-Ontology", *New Blackfriars* 95 (2014): 430–42 (441).

[66] Lawrence Feingold, *The Natural Desire to See God according to St. Thomas Aquinas and His Interpreters*, 2nd ed. (2001; Ave Maria, Fla.: Sapientia, 2010).

[67] Ralph McInerny, *Praeambula Fidei: Thomism and the God of the Philosophers* (Washington, D.C.: Catholic University of America Press, 2006), 69–90.

[68] Steven A. Long, *Natura Pura: On the Recovery of Nature in the Doctrine of Grace* (New York: Fordham University Press, 2010).

[69] Bernard Mulcahy, *Aquinas's Notion of Pure Nature and the Christian Integralism of Henri de Lubac: Not Everything Is Grace* (New York: Lang, 2011).

demonstrating that de Lubac's doctrine is by no means antithetical to Thomism.[70] Nicholas J. Healy has sought to advance the debate, although by rooting human relationality with God in external, institutional sacramentality, rather than in graced natural desire, he appears to side with Suárez and de Lubac's detractors.[71]

A recurring question is whether de Lubac's theology, in which grace permeates the whole of nature, respects natural human dignity more than a neo-Thomist theology that allows nature greater autonomy. In particular, the tone in which Feingold exalts the capacities of human reason and knowledge is discordant with de Lubac's Augustinian grounding of dignity in graced relation. This Augustinian context, which is frequently ignored as de Lubac is presented and critiqued within the context of Thomist debates, is usefully delineated by Chad Pecknold and Jacob Wood.[72] De Lubac's concern that the strictly neutral, purely natural order constructed by medieval theologians, and earlier imagined by Paul, is vulnerable to colonization by a hostile modern secularism is well founded.

## Eucharist and Scripture

In a chapter on the Eucharist in *God without Being*, Jean-Luc Marion draws heavily on de Lubac. Eucharistic presence, he argues, is gifted, inaugurating a Christic temporality that is framed by memorial and anticipation and is consummated by the assimilation of the communicant into Christ's mystical body the Church.[73] Nathan Halloran follows this trajectory, suggesting that the Church is therefore not simply body but flesh.[74]

---

[70] Andrew Swafford, *Nature and Grace: A New Approach to Thomistic Ressourcement* (Eugene, Ore.: Pickwick, 2014).

[71] Nicholas J. Healy, Jr., "The Christian Mystery of Nature and Grace", in Hillebert, *T&T Clark Companion*, 181–203.

[72] C. C. Pecknold and Jacob Wood, "Augustine and Henri de Lubac", in *T&T Clark Companion to Augustine and Modern Theology*, ed. C. C. Pecknold and Tarmo Toom (London: T&T Clark, 2013), 196–222.

[73] Jean-Luc Marion, *God without Being. Hors-Texte*, trans. Thomas A. Carlson (1982; Chicago: University of Chicago Press, 1991), 161–82.

[74] Nathan Halloran, "Flesh of the Church: De Lubac, Marion, and the Site of the Phenomenality of Givenness", *Irish Theological Quarterly* 75 (2010): 29–44.

David Williams provides a lucid synopsis of de Lubac's scriptural exegesis, addressing Christ, the newness of the New Testament, and the four senses.[75] The fact that awareness of reception history is now commonplace in theological deployments of Scripture is partly due, Williams suggests, to de Lubac. However, he also avers that, being a theologian rather than a biblical scholar, de Lubac excessively emphasizes Scripture's spiritual unity while giving insufficient attention to the plurality of authorial intentions. Thomas Harmon highlights de Lubac's debt to Origen for the notion that Scripture's spiritual meaning is contained in history rather than in abstract inward reflection. Moreover, Origen shows de Lubac that, when Scripture is read, the critical mind is purified or converted. Yet de Lubac is himself by no means uncritical of Origen, questioning in places his lack of a concrete historical sense and his haste to offer spiritual readings of passages that are sometimes based on purportedly "profound intentions beneath miniscule particularities".[76] Another significant account sets de Lubac's spiritual exegesis alongside possible alternatives. Bryan Hollon presents de Lubac's refusal of scientific exegesis as a corollary of his denial of pure nature: just as the end of nature is supernatural, so the meaning and end of Scripture is spiritual. Like the postliberal exegetes Hans Frei and George Lindbeck, de Lubac is open to intratextual and interstitial engagement, but is more accommodating of allegory as a path from text to doctrine. Furthermore, de Lubac's exegesis, like that of radical orthodoxy, is based on an acceptance that Scripture in its literal sense does not define Jesus exhaustively. For de Lubac, the Church is the place where the spiritual exegesis and ongoing re-narration of the life of Christ take place. By closely attending to Scripture and the Church, he goes farther than radical orthodoxy in "extending a fully Christianized ontology".[77]

Three readers demonstrate the relevance of spiritual exegesis for

[75] David Williams, *Receiving the Bible in Faith: Historical and Theological Exegesis* (Washington, D.C.: Catholic University of America Press, 2004), 130–73.

[76] Thomas P. Harmon, "Historicism versus History and Spirit: What We Can Learn from Studying Origen", *Logos: A Journal of Catholic Thought and Culture* 19, no. 3 (2016): 29–58 (36).

[77] Bryan C. Hollon, *Everything Is Sacred: Spiritual Exegesis in the Political Theology of Henri de Lubac* (Eugene, Ore.: Cascade, 2009), 134.

practical spirituality. Ranging across the different senses, Robert Faricy expounds the significance of de Lubac's method for prayer: Scripture has a spiritual meaning, the Holy Spirit is the inner source of spiritual understanding, and the unity of Scripture is given by Christ.[78] Indeed, the senses may be successively deployed in prayer. Christopher Ruddy shows how, in general, de Lubac's Ignatian sensibility makes him open to discern the action of good and bad spirits on individuals, the Church, and the wider world and attunes him to the dispossession and suffering that are part of the individual and corporate spiritual life.[79] Focusing on the collection *Scripture in the Tradition*, Angela Lou Harvey accessibly shows how spiritual exegesis might bear fruits in the Church today, because its aim is not the accumulation of knowledge but the ever-deeper entering into the knowledge and love of Christ.[80]

Other accounts assess de Lubac's treatment of one or other of the senses. From an evangelical perspective, Kevin Storer praises de Lubac's sacramental model of communication but calls for greater clarity on aspects of the literal sense. This includes the role of human authors and the structuring of the understanding of mystery, which, Storer contends, needs to be rooted more closely in Christ than de Lubac and the wider Roman Catholic theory of ecclesial doctrinal development allow.[81] William Wright argues that de Lubac needed to distinguish more clearly between the literal and historical senses, in view of the incarnational analogy for the relation between the literal and spiritual senses.[82]

Andrew Louth provides an important early endorsement of the doctrinal function of allegory, which grasps the newness of the Christian mystery by emerging from it, rather than being arbitrar-

---

[78] Robert Faricy, *Praying* (London: SCM, 1983), 85–98.

[79] Christopher Ruddy, "The Ignatian Matrix of Henri de Lubac's Thought on Temptation, Ascesis, and the *Homo Ecclesiasticus*", *The Heythrop Journal* 58 (2017): 789–805.

[80] Angela Lou Harvey, *Spiritual Reading: A Study of the Christian Practice of Reading Scripture* (Eugene, Ore.: Cascade 2015), 108–39.

[81] Kevin Storer, *Reading Scripture to Hear God: Kevin Vanhoozer and Henri de Lubac on God's Use of Scripture in the Economy of Redemption* (Eugene, Ore.: Pickwick, 2014), 50–53, 95–98, 139–43.

[82] William Wright, "The Literal Senses of Scripture according to Henri de Lubac: Insights from Patristic Exegesis of the Transfiguration", *Modern Theology* 28 (2012): 252–77.

ily derived. The placement of allegory before the moral sense is significant, he argues, with allegory being the movement from the perception of the dogmatic dimensions of the mystery to the response called for by the believer to the final mystery of Christ, which will be eschatologically fulfilled.[83] Furthermore, in the New Testament, the literal meaning may itself be doctrinal and, hence, spiritual. Turning to the moral sense, this brings the interiorization of the mystery in experience. William Murphy shows how mystery thus provides an internal principle of action, harmonizing Scripture, spirituality, and morals.[84] In a later article, Lewis Ayres also advocates for a robust notion of the soul in scriptural exegesis. The moral sense should be highly prized, he argues, within the broad understanding of the shaping of the life of the soul by scriptural reading.[85]

The anagogical sense has received considerable attention. Rudolf Voderholzer presents de Lubac as contesting the Modernist equation of historicizing with relativizing, which privileges "plurality without essential identity" and a "mutability without substantial continuity", as well as opposing the Scholastic neglect of historical contingency.[86] Instead, Christ saves through history, and the Spirit comes exegetically from history. The Argentinian theologian Omar César Albado collates the diverse elements of a theology of history in de Lubac's oeuvre, which include not only his critique of Joachim of Flora, but his engagements with atheism and Buddhism, too.[87] It is clear, as Alain Rauwel highlights, that de Lubac uses Joachim partly as a foil to critique his own contemporary

[83] Andrew Louth, *Discerning the Mystery: An Essay on the Nature of Theology* (Oxford: Clarendon Press, 1983), 114–26.

[84] William Murphy, "Henri de Lubac's Mystical Tropology", *Communio* 27 (2000): 171–201.

[85] Lewis Ayres, "The Soul and the Reading of Scripture: A Note on Henri de Lubac", *Scottish Journal of Theology* 61 (2008): 173–90.

[86] Rudolf Voderholzer, "Dogma and History: Henri de Lubac and the Retrieval of Historicity as a Key to Theological Renewal", trans. Adrian Walker, *Communio* 28 (2001): 648–68 (649); also Voderholzer, *Die Einheit der Schrift und ihr geistiger Sinn: der Beitrag Henri de Lubacs zur Erforschung von Geschichte und Systematik christlicher Bibelhermeneutik* (Freiburg: Johannes, 1998).

[87] Omar César Albado, *El sentido teológico de la historia: elementos para una teología de la historia en la obra de Henri de Lubac* (Saarbrücken: Credo, 2013).

context.[88] Nevertheless, this critique is motivated by deep theological commitments. Significantly, Joseph Flipper identifies de Lubac's eschatology as the "organizing principle and guiding intuition of his diverse theological projects".[89] Relating de Lubac's contribution to the wider renewal of apocalyptic thinking in response to Nazism, Flipper views eschatology as governing history, from which, in turn, derives ontology. Noteworthy is his case that de Lubac contends as much with the Neoplatonism of Dionysius as with the eschatological immanentism of Joachim. "Though opposed," Flipper writes, both "shared the same dissociation between the future and the invisible": Dionysius "viewed the historical figures and realities of the Bible as figures for the unthematizable transcendent", whereas Joachim "projected a form of eschatological fulfillment into the historical future".[90]

Charles Kannengiesser, while commending the value of de Lubac's "prodigiously rich analysis" for patristics, avers that it is grounded in a "patristic faith" that lacks "*critical space in which a hermeneutical theory would have blossomed in its own right*".[91] Today it is simplistic, he argues, to view Scripture as straightforwardly mirroring inner and corporate identities. Although, Kannengiesser affirms, de Lubac offers a new openness to divine transcendence in history and to a "nondogmatistic form of faith", his work now requires critical retrieval. Robin Darling Young has forcefully made this case, contending that, following the tumult of the First World War, de Lubac and his confreres sought refuge in an idealized, romanticized, and fictional antiquity, with their image of "patristic" unity preventing them from recognizing the conflicts, polemics, anti-Semitism, and deprecation of women and sexuality that, in reality, characterized the early Church. At the time of the Second Vatican Council, she

---

[88] Alain Rauwel, "Henri de Lubac et le xix$^{e}$ siècle comme symptôme", *Archives de sciences sociales des religions* 172 (2015): 193–200.

[89] Joseph S. Flipper, *Between Apocalypse and Eschaton: History and Eternity in Henri de Lubac* (Minneapolis, Minn.: Fortress Press, 2015), 14.

[90] Ibid., 190, 200.

[91] Charles Kannengiesser, "A Key for the Future of Patristics: The 'Senses' of Scripture", in *In Dominico Eloquio = In Lordly Eloquence: Essays on Patristic Exegesis in Honor of Robert Louis Wilken*, ed. Paul Blowers, Angela Russell Christman, David G. Hunter, and Robin Darling Young (Grand Rapids, Mich.: Eerdmans, 2002), 90–106 (103–4), original italics.

writes, this "failed to prepare de Lubac . . . for the rancorous conflict that followed. It was a premodern theology", she continues, "that has not, at least so far, contained and shaped the changes that it helped to inspire."[92] Although the notion of a patristic unity might have energized the Church during the interwar period, and might even have contributed to the "combative asceticism" of spiritual resistance to Nazism, Young argues that it has ultimately impeded real engagement with modernity. From this perspective, de Lubac was *more* reactionary than his neo-Thomist opponents, who at least saw the need to distinguish the order of nature from the order of revelation and thereby to open a hermeneutical space between the two.

Nonetheless, the case has also been persuasively made for the radically transformative role of spiritual resistance in shaping de Lubac's theology. Noting that perhaps just fifty of the two thousand Jesuits then in France followed this path, James Bernauer identifies its six key elements: critical self-reflection, a grasp of the moment, a critique of the purported Vichy return to Christian values, a communal and ecumenical approach, opposition to racism and anti-Semitism, and an orientation to action.[93] Lucia Scherzberg praises the fact that the core of de Lubac's theological reform program—the supernatural, the fight against anti-Semitism, and the social conception of mankind—stems from this experience.[94]

From a hermeneutical perspective, Young's critique prompts a return to the development of de Lubac's exegesis pursued by his former mentee and executor Michel de Certeau (1925–1986). In an early article, de Lubac's fellow Jesuit praises him for following "everywhere the mobility of spirit under the fixity of words", recognizing the internal movement and shifting signification of language to be a conversion of sense. With de Lubac, de Certeau continues, the

---

[92] Robin Darling Young, "A Soldier of the Great War: Henri de Lubac and the Patristic Sources for a Premodern Theology", in *After Vatican II: Trajectories and Hermeneutics*, ed. James L. Heft with John O'Malley (Grand Rapids, Mich.: Eerdmans, 2012), 134–63.

[93] James Bernauer, "A Jesuit Spiritual Insurrection: Resistance to Vichy", in *"The Tragic Couple": Encounters between Jews and Jesuits*, ed. Bernauer and Robert A. Maryks (Leiden: Brill, 2014), 203–15.

[94] Lucia Scherzberg, "Katholische Reformtheologen in Deutschland und Frankreich", in *Vergangenheitsbewältigung im französischen Katholizismus und deutschen Protestantismus*, ed. Scherzberg (Paderborn: Schöningh, 2008), 41–56.

spiritual sense is "not only the subject of his study, but the principle of his reflection and the origin of his language".[95] De Lubac sees that the newness of Christ changes human reality from the inside, appearing first in the "conversion" of language and of nature. De Certeau's study of mysticism may be viewed as a prolongation of de Lubac's own research on exegetical method into the modern period. However, de Lubac's commitment to a hermeneutic of continuity between the past and present led to his estrangement from de Certeau, who increasingly celebrated strangeness, difference, otherness, and heterodoxy, as biographically related by Brenna Moore.[96] Despite this, Graham Ward stresses the continuity from de Lubac to de Certeau, such as in shared views of history as both archaeology and genealogy and of paradox as entailing both presence and absence, through the mediating sacramental cosmology of Teilhard de Chardin.[97] However, Johannes Hoff justly contrasts de Certeau's notion of desire as an amoral and undirected movement of transgressive exploration with de Lubac's natural desire for the true end of human life, who is God.[98] Moreover, Hoff argues, de Certeau's poststructuralist celebration of the absent body of Christ above allegedly corrupt religious institutions now appears to express the polarities of modernity rather than to overcome them. Finally, whereas de Certeau's exegesis allowed for the potentially indefinite substitution of terms, de Lubac's nonidentical repetition was predicated on the ultimately christological unity of text and rite.

---

[95] Michel de Certeau, "Exégèse, théologie et spiritualité", *Revue d'ascétique et de mystique* 36 (1960): 357–71 (368).

[96] Brenna Moore, "How to Awaken the Dead: Michel de Certeau, Henri de Lubac, and the Instabilities between the Past and the Present", *Spiritus: A Journal of Christian Spirituality* 12 (2012): 172–79.

[97] Graham Ward, "Certeaus Geschichtschreibung in ihrem jesuitischen Kontext", in *Michel de Certeau: Geschichte, Kultur, Religion*, ed. Marian Füssel (Konstanz: UVK, 2007), 343–63.

[98] Johannes Hoff, "Mysticism, Ecclesiology and the Body of Christ—Certeau's (Mis-) reading of *Corpus Mysticum* and the Legacy of Henri de Lubac", in *Spiritual Spaces: History and Mysticism in Michel De Certeau*, ed. Inigo Bocken (Leuven: Peeters, 2013), 87–110.

## Conclusion

Some areas of de Lubac's oeuvre have attracted more criticism than others. In general, discussions of his theological anthropology and of his doctrine have been largely expository. Engagements with other topics have been more critical. Regarding ecclesiology, McPartlan, Milbank, Schlesinger, and Webster have all called into question de Lubac's apparently high valuation of the Church as an earthly institution, with Au, Hemming, and Pickstock deploying liturgical perspectives to suggest that this reveals internal tensions in his theology. Turning to the supernatural, Cholvy, Halloran, Lacoste, and Rosenberg have all sought to flesh out de Lubac's categories into a more embodied or erotic theology of graced, desiring nature for the present day. From a quite different standpoint, however, Feingold, Long, McInerny, and Mulcahy have critiqued the very idea of natural desire. Regarding hermeneutics, Storer and Wright, while commending aspects of de Lubac's project, wish for a clearer presentation of the literal sense, while Kannengiesser and Young have sounded cautionary warnings to those who might become captivated by the patristic synthesis that de Lubac promotes. There is much to keep students and researchers interested, and, in order to advance understanding farther, greater engagement between Anglophone scholars and those working in French and other languages is needed.

# Patristic and Medieval Authors Cited

*References are included to English translations of works cited by de Lubac. If none are available, references to related works by the same author are sometimes given. Figures about whom very little is known are omitted.*

Absalon of Springiersbach (d. 1203)

The abbot of Springiersbach in the Rhineland, then of Saint Victor in Paris, where he had previously been a canon.

Adam of Perseigne (ca. 1145–1221)

A canon, then a Benedictine, who became the Cistercian abbot of Perseigne in the Loire. Born a peasant, he nevertheless became the confessor and counselor of kings and nobles and met Joachim of Flora.

Adam of Saint Victor (d. 1146)

A Parisian poet and composer at Notre-Dame cathedral, then, due to his commitment to the Augustinian rule, at the abbey of Saint Victor. His *Sequences* were sung during the Mass, before the Gospel, and following the other readings.

Text: *Sequences*, trans. Juliet Mousseau (Leuven: Peeters, 2011).

Aelred of Rievaulx (1110–1167)

A courtier who joined the Abbey of Rievaulx in Yorkshire, England, rising to become its abbot and occupying this post for twenty years. Cistercian abbots were required to preach to their community on seventeen specified occasions each year and to travel to the motherhouse of Cîteaux for their order's annual general chapter. Because of his writings and administration, he has been called the "Bernard of the north".

Texts: *On Jesus at Twelve Years Old*, trans. Geoffrey Webb and Adrian Walker (London: Mowbray, 1956); *The Liturgical Sermons: The First Clairvaux Collection, Advent—All Saints*, trans. Theodore Berkeley (Collegeville, Minn.: Cistercian, 2001); *The Liturgical Sermons: The Second Clairvaux Collection, Christmas—All Saints*, trans. Marie Anne Mayeski (Collegeville, Minn.: Cistercian, 2016).

Albert the Great (ca. 1200–1280)

A Dominican who studied and taught in several Frankish centers, rising to hold a theology chair at the University of Paris. While there, he taught Thomas Aquinas, whom he ultimately outlived. As prior of his order's German province (1254–1256), he was instrumental in establishing its curriculum, promoting the study of philosophy and the natural sciences. He was briefly bishop of Regensburg (1260–1263), then lived in Würzburg and Cologne.

Alcuin of York (ca. 735–804)

A deacon who studied at York and came to head the school there, he joined the court of Charlemagne at Aachen, where he raised academic standards and personally taught the royal family. He combatted adoptionism and became abbot of Marmoutier near Tours.

Text: *Early Medieval Theology*, ed. George E. McCracken (London: SCM, 1957), 192–210.

Alexander of Hales (ca. 1185–1245)

A native of Shropshire, England, who studied at the University of Paris, then taught there. When aged about fifty, he became a Franciscan and was thereby the first member of his order to hold a university chair. He developed a systematic theological method that did not rely on scriptural sources alone, promoting the *Sentences* of Peter Lombard (ca. 1100–1160).

Amalar of Metz (ca. 775–ca. 850)

A courtier of Charlemagne who was briefly bishop of Trier and of Lyon and ambassador to the Byzantine emperor. He reformed the Frankish liturgy and was a renowned liturgical commentator, notably promoting tropological (moral) exegesis.

Text: *On the Liturgy*, trans. Eric Knibbs, 2 vols. (Cambridge, Mass.: Harvard University Press, 2014).

Ambrose Autpert (ca. 730–784)

A Frankish courtier who tutored the young Charlemagne, then became a Benedictine and abbot of San Vincenzo in southern Italy.

Ambrose of Milan (ca. 340–397)

An unmarried Roman governor stationed in Milan who became the city's bishop (374) by popular acclaim. He combatted Arianism, promoted antiphonal chant, and was a charismatic and politically powerful Christian leader.

Texts: *Commentary of Saint Ambrose on Twelve Psalms*, trans. Íde M. Ní Riain (Dublin: Halcyon, 2000); *Exposition of the Holy Gospel according to Saint Luke*, trans. Theodosia Tomkinson, 2nd ed. (Etna, Calif.: Center for Traditionalist Orthodox Studies, 2003); *Seven Exegetical Works*, trans. Michael P. McHugh (Washington, D.C.: Catholic University of America Press, 1972).

Athanasius of Alexandria (ca. 296–373)

Patriarch of his city from 328, he spent several periods in exile due to imperial persecution. He developed strong pastoral links with the desert hermits and monks of upper Egypt and lived with them during his third exile. He defined the New Testament canon accepted today and strongly opposed Arianism, promoting the doctrine of the Council of Nicaea that Christ and the Father are consubstantial, sharing a single nature.

Text: *Nicene and Post-Nicene Fathers*, second Series, ed. Philip Schaff and Henry Wace, vol. 4 (1892; Peabody, Mass.: Hendrickson, 1995).

## Augustine of Hippo (354–430)

An ethnic Berber who studied in Carthage, then taught there as well as briefly in Rome and Milan. While an auditor in the Manichean sect, he had a long-term lover, whose name is unknown. They had a son, Adeodatus, who died in early adulthood. In 385, Augustine ended the relationship to prepare to marry a very young heiress, but was instead baptized by Ambrose (387). He returned home to Hippo, where he was ordained a priest (391) and bishop (395), remaining in the city for the rest of his life and dying during the Vandal siege.

Texts: *Answer to Faustus, a Manichean*, trans. Roland J. Teske (New York: New City Press, 2007); *On Christian Belief*, trans. Edmund Hill, Ray Kearney, Michael G. Campbell, and Bruce Harbert (New York: New City Press, 2005); *The Christian Combat*, trans. Robert P. Russell (Washington, D.C.: Catholic University of America Press, 1950); *The City of God against the Pagans*, trans. R.W. Dyson (Cambridge; New York: Cambridge University Press, 1998); *Confessions*, trans. Henry Chadwick (Oxford; New York: Oxford University Press, 1991); *Expositions of the Psalms*, trans. Maria Boulding, 6 vols. (New York: New City Press, 2000–2004); *On Genesis*, trans. Edmund Hill (New York: New City Press, 2002); *Homilies on the First Epistle of John*, trans. Boniface Ramsey (New York: New City Press, 2008); *Homilies on the Gospel of John 1–40*, trans. Edmund Hill (New York: New City Press, 2009); *Instructing Beginners in Faith*, trans. Raymond Canning (New York: New City Press, 2006); *Letters*, trans. Roland J. Teske, 4 vols. (New York: New City Press, 2001–2005); *The Manichean Debate*, trans. Roland J. Teske (New York: New City Press, 2008); *Nicene and Post-Nicene Fathers*, first series, ed. Philip Schaff, vols. 1–8 (Peabody, Mass.: Hendrickson, 1995); *Sermons*, trans. Edmund Hill, 11 vols. (New York: New City Press, 1990–1997); *Teaching Christianity*, trans. Edmund Hill (New York: New City Press, 1996); *The Trinity*, trans. Edmund Hill (New York: New City Press, 1991); *Writings on the Old Testament*, trans. Joseph T. Lienhard, Sean Doyle, and Joseph T. Kelley (New York: New City Press, 2017).

Basil (the Great) of Caesarea (329/330–379)

Born into a wealthy Christian family, he studied in Constantinople and Athens and traveled in Egypt and Syria, where he became a monk. Eusebius persuaded him to move to Caesarea in Cappadocia, where he became the city's administrator and then bishop (370). He composed a liturgy and a monastic rule and was well known for his care of the poor. Gregory of Nyssa was his younger brother.

Text: *On the Holy Spirit*, trans. Stephen M. Hildebrand (Crestwood, N.Y.: St. Vladimir's Seminary Press, 2011).

Beatus of Liébana (ca. 730–ca. 800)

A cleric and later abbot of Saint Martin (Saint Toribio) in northern Spain. He is best known for his apocalypse commentary and combated adoptionism. Alcuin admired his work.

Bede (672/673–735)

Schooled in childhood at the abbey of Jarrow in northeast England, he helped reestablish it after a plague, being ordained a deacon and later a priest. Excepting occasional visits to other British monasteries, he spent his whole life there.

Text: *On the Song of Songs and Selected Writings*, trans. Arthur Holder (New York: Paulist Press, 2011).

Berengaud [also Berengar, Berengard] of Tours (840–892)

A Benedictine monk of the abbey of Ferrières, south of Paris, who produced an apocalypse commentary.

Bernard of Clairvaux (1090–1153)

A Burgundian nobleman who joined the reforming Benedictine monastery at Cîteaux (1113). He became abbot of a new house at Clairvaux (1115), which had a strict rule, and was a key figure in the founding of the Cistercian Order.

Texts: *Five Books on Consideration: Advice to a Pope*, trans. John Anderson and Elizabeth T. Kennan (Collegeville, Minn.: Cistercian, 1976); *On the Song of Songs*, trans. Kilian Walsh and Irene Edmonds,

4 vols. (Kalamazoo, Mich.: Cistercian, 1971–1980); *Selected Works*, trans. Gillian Evans (Mahwah, N.J.: Paulist Press, 1987); *Sermons for Advent and the Christmas Season*, trans. Irene Edmonds, Wendy Mary Beckett, and Conrad Greenia (Kalamazoo, Mich.: Cistercian, 2007); *Sermons for Lent and the Easter Season*, trans. Irene Edmonds with John Leinenweber and Mark A. Scott (Kalamazoo, Mich.: Cistercian, 2013); *Sermons for the Autumn Season*, trans. Irene M. Edmonds and Mark Scott (Collegeville, Minn.: Liturgical Press, 2016); *Sermons for the Summer Season: Liturgical Sermons from Rogationtide and Pentecost*, trans. Beverly Kienzle with James Jarzembowski (Kalamazoo, Mich.: Cistercian, 1991).

Bonaventure (1221–1274)

A Franciscan who studied and then taught at the University of Paris, lecturing on Peter Lombard's *Sentences*. He became his order's minister general (1257) and later a cardinal (1273), but died suddenly at the Second Council of Lyon, possibly due to poisoning.

Text: *Commentaries on the Four Books of Sentences* (Mansfield, Mass.: Franciscan Archive, 2014–).

Bonizo of Sutri (ca. 1045–ca. 1094)

An Italian bishop who promoted the Gregorian Reform, including the political supremacy of the papacy above secular rulers and the moral reform of the Church. Although already a bishop, he was elected to the See of Piacenza but was blinded and maimed by opponents.

Bruno of Segni (ca. 1047–1123)

A bishop who entered the Benedictine abbey of Monte Cassino and was elected its abbot. He was later forced to resign this office due to objections to his holding both roles at once.

Candidus of Fulda (d. 845)

A monk and administrator at the leading Benedictine abbey in central Germany during the abbacy of Rabanus Maurus.

Cassiodorus (ca. 485–ca. 585)

A court lawyer, administrator, and diplomat who in retirement founded a monastery at Vivarium in Calabria. He saw reading as key to educational formation and was committed to classical pedagogical ideals.

Text: *Explanation of the Psalms*, trans. Patrick G. Walsh, 3 vols. (New York: Paulist Press, 1990–1991).

Claudius of Turin (ca. 780–827)

A scholar at the imperial court of Aachen under Louis the Pious, who was Charlemagne's son. He was made bishop of Turin (817), where he opposed the veneration of relics and images. He authored some of the works previously attributed to Pseudo-Eucherius.

Text: *Early Medieval Theology*, ed. George E. McCracken (London: SCM, 1957), 211–48.

Clement of Alexandria (ca. 150–ca. 215)

A Christian convert from a pagan family who traveled widely to build up his knowledge of the Christian faith. In the period 180–202, he taught in the metropolis of Alexandria, was ordained a priest, and possibly married. However, he departed during the Severian persecutions. Origen was his pupil.

Texts: *Ante-Nicene Fathers*, ed. Alexander Roberts and James Donaldson, vol. 2 (1885; Peabody, Mass.: Hendrickson, 1995), 163–629; *Christ the Educator*, trans. Simon P. Wood (Washington, D.C.: Catholic University of America Press, 2008).

Cyprian of Carthage (ca. 200–258)

An ethnic Berber lawyer who converted to Christianity aged 35, was ordained, shared his wealth with the poor, and was elected his city's bishop (248/249). During the Decian persecution, he went into hiding and afterward defended the readmission of lapsed Christians into the Church, following repentance. He was executed in the Valerian persecution.

Texts: *Ante-Nicene Fathers*, ed. Alexander Roberts and James Donaldson, vol. 5 (1886; Peabody, Mass.: Hendrickson, 1995), 261–600.

Cyril of Alexandria (ca. 376–444)

A Christian scholar who became patriarch of Alexandria (412), succeeding his uncle. His tenure was marked by civil unrest and doctrinal controversy. He presided at the Council of Ephesus (431), at which Nestorianism was condemned.

Texts: *Commentary on the Book of Exodus: First Discourse*, trans. Evie Zachariades-Holmberg (Rollinsford, N.H.: Orthodox Research Institute, 2010).

Cyril of Jerusalem (ca. 313–386)

A deacon, then priest, in Jerusalem, before being elected his city's bishop (350). He was twice banished amid political and moral turmoil. In his *Mystagogical Lectures*, he explained the sacraments to baptismal candidates and to the newly baptized.

Text: *Works*, trans. Leo P. McCauley and Anthony A. Stephenson, 2 vols. (Washington, D.C.: Catholic University of America Press, 1970).

Ephraem the Syrian (ca. 306–373)

A poet, hymn-writer, and exegete, who for most of his life was a deacon in Nisibis but, after the city was surrendered to the Persians (363), settled in Edessa.

Text: *Hymns on Paradise*, trans. Sebastian Brock (Crestwood, N.Y.: St. Vladimir's Seminary Press, 1990).

Eusebius of Caesarea (d. ca. 340)

A Greek historian and bishop (from ca. 313) of the large port city of Caesarea. He admired Origen, who had bequeathed his library to the Christian community there, and was opposed by Athanasius.

Text: *The Proof of the Gospel*, trans. W. J. Ferrar, 2 vols. (London: SPCK, 1920).

Faustus of Riez (d. ca. 490)

A Briton who entered the monastery of Lérins, where he was elected abbot (432). He later became bishop of Riez, although he maintained close monastic links. Along with other theologians in the region around Marseille (Massalia), he argued that people may cooperate with grace, as well as defending the corporeality of the soul.

Florus of Lyon (d. ca. 860)

A deacon who directed the Lyon scriptorium, where many ancient texts were copied and distributed. He opposed Amalarius' allegorical interpretation of the Mass and suggested his understanding of the fraction destroyed the unity of Christ's body. De Lubac first gained knowledge of him when examining a thesis.

Garnier of Rochefort (ca. 1140–ca. 1225)

A Cistercian of northeastern France who became successively abbot of Auberive, abbot of Clairvaux, and bishop of Langres. He produced an early dictionary.

Gaudentius of Brescia (d. 410)

Unwillingly elected bishop of his hometown in northern Italy while away on pilgrimage, he was consecrated by Ambrose and defended John Chrysostom.

Text: *Sermons and Letters*, trans. Stephen L. Boehrer (Washington, D.C.: Catholic University of America Press, 1965).

Gerhoh of Reichersberg (1093–1169)

A canon of Augsburg who sought a stricter rule of life in the Augustinian house at Raitenbuch and was later appointed provost of Reichersberg (1132). He promoted the Gregorian reform of the clergy and saw communal living as the best means of achieving this.

Gilbert Foliot (ca. 1110–1187)

An Englishman who joined the Benedictine abbey at Cluny in France and became its prior but returned home to be successively abbot of Gloucester (1139), bishop of Hereford (1148), and bishop of London (1163). He supported King Henry II in his conflict with Thomas Becket, the archbishop of Canterbury.

Godfrey of Admont (d. 1165)

The elder brother of Irimbert. He became abbot of the Benedictine abbey of Admont (1137) in Austria. He improved the library, which is now the largest monastic collection in the world.

Gregory Nazianzen (ca. 329–390)

From a wealthy Cappadocian family, he studied in several intellectual centers and briefly taught rhetoric in Athens, before returning home and being ordained a priest (361) by his father. His friend Basil of Caesarea ordained him bishop of Sasima (372), but he preferred to remain in Nazianzus, assisting his father but also pursuing the monastic life. Invited to Constantinople to combat Arianism, he was made patriarch (380), but resigned the following year and went back home again.

Text: *On God and Christ: The Five Theological Orations and Two Letters to Cledonius*, trans. Frederick Williams and Lionel Wickham (Crestwood, N.Y.: St. Vladimir's Seminary Press, 2002).

Gregory of Bergamo (d. 1146)

A Benedictine who became bishop of Bergamo (1133) and established the Cistercian Order in his diocese. In his eucharistic teaching, he opposed Berengar of Tours' rejection of transubstantiation.

Gregory of Elvira (d. ca. 392)

A bishop in southern Spain who was a vigorous opponent of Arianism.

Gregory the Great (ca. 540–604)

Born into a privileged Roman family and well educated, he was elected his city's prefect, but then became a monk and turned his family estates into monasteries. Nevertheless, he was appointed ambassador to the Byzantine court (579), then elected pope (590), launching the first major Christian mission, to Britain.

Texts: *Homilies on the Book of the Prophet Ezekiel*, trans. Theodosia Tomkinson, 2nd ed. (Etna, Calif.: Center for Traditionalist Orthodox Studies, 2008); *Moral Reflections on the Book of Job*, trans. Brian Kerns, 3 vols. (Collegeville, Minn.: Cistercian, 2016).

Gregory of Nyssa (ca. 335–ca. 395)

The younger brother of Basil, he studied in Caesarea and was elected bishop of the new see of Nyssa (372), traveling to mediate several ecclesiastical disputes. He promoted divine infinity and, hence, incomprehensibility.

Texts: *Christology of the Later Fathers*, trans. Cyril C. Richardson (Louisville, Ky.: Westminster John Knox Press, 1995), 233–325; *Nicene and Post-Nicene Fathers*, second Series, ed. Philip Schaff and Henry Wace, vol. (1893; Peabody, Mass.: Hendrickson, 1995).

Guerric of Igny (d. 1157)

A member of the Tournai cathedral school community who became the Cistercian abbot of Igny (1138) in the Champagne under the patronage of Bernard of Clairvaux.

Text: *Liturgical Sermons*, 2 vols. (Kalamazoo, Mich.: Cistercian, 1970–1999).

Guibert of Nogent (ca. 1055–1124)

Privately tutored as a child, he became the Benedictine abbot of Nogent-sous-Coucy. His memoirs are the first Latin autobiography after Augustine's *Confessions*.

Texts: *A Monk's Confession: The Memoirs of Guibert of Nogent*, trans. Paul J. Archambault (University Park, Pa.: Pennsylvania State University Press, 1995); *Early Medieval Theology*, ed. George E. McCracken (London: SCM, 1957), 285–99.

Haymo [also Aimo, Aimon] of Halberstadt (d. ca. 853)

A Benedictine monk who studied with Rabanus Maurus at Tours under Alcuin, became chancellor of the abbey of Fulda, then bishop of Halberstadt (840).

Helinand of Froidmont (ca. 1160–ca. 1237)

A Cistercian monk at Froidmont (ca. 1190) in northern France, who preached and compiled a chronicle of world history that influenced Vincent of Beauvais.

Henry of Marcy (ca. 1136–1189)

The Cistercian abbot of Hautecombe (1160) and Clairvaux (1177) and a cardinal (1179). He led the suppression of Catharism in the Languedoc and later declined the papacy.

Hervaeus of Bourg-Dieu (ca. 1080–1150)

A French Benedictine exegete at the abbey of Déols in the Loire.

Hilary of Poitiers (ca. 310–ca. 367)

A pagan convert to Christianity who was elected bishop of Poitiers (350) and later spent four years in exile in Anatolia. He is known as the "hammer of the Arians" and the "Athanasius of the West".

Texts: *Commentary on Matthew*, trans. D. H. Williams (Washington, D.C.: Catholic University of America Press, 2012); *Nicene and Post-Nicene Fathers*, second series, ed. Philip Schaff and Henry Wace, vol. 9 (1899; Peabody, Mass.: Hendrickson, 1995); *On the Trinity*, trans. Stephen McKenna (Washington, D.C.: Catholic University of America Press, 1968).

Hildegard of Bingen (ca. 1098–1179)

A Rhineland Benedictine of Disibodenberg who founded women's abbeys at Rubertsberg (1150) and Eibingen (1165). Her theology was based on mystical visions rather than on traditional learning, and she was also a composer, botanist, and medical writer.

Text: *Scivias*, trans. Columba Hart (New York: Paulist Press, 1990).

Hippolytus of Rome (170–235)

A Greek priest and theologian in Rome who opposed the popes and died in exile in Sardinia.

Texts: *Ante-Nicene Fathers*, ed. Alexander Roberts and James Donaldson, vol. 5 (1886; Peabody, Mass.: Hendrickson, 1995) 1–259.

Honorius of Autun (1080–1154)

A monk who spent time in England and Bavaria and produced popular expositions of a wide range of theological topics.

Text: *The Old Norse Elucidarius*, trans. Evelyn Scherabon Firchow (Columbia, S.C.: Camden, 1992).

Hugh of Rouen (d. 1164)

A Norman nobleman who studied at Laon and became a Benedictine at Cluny. He was appointed the first abbot of Reading (1125) before his election as archbishop of Rouen (1130).

Hugh of Saint Cher (ca. 1200–1263)

A native of southeastern France, he studied at the University of Paris, where he taught law, then joined the new Dominican Order (1225). He became prior provincial (1230) and later a cardinal (1244). He combatted the teachings of Joachim of Flora, defended the mendicant orders, and produced the first biblical concordance.

Hugh of Saint Victor (ca. 1096–1141)

He joined the Augustinian order at Hamerleve in central Germany, relocating to the more secure abbey of Saint Victor in Paris. Following the murder of Thomas of Saint Victor [Thomas à Becket], he became its head (1133). He combined mysticism and scientific learning, commenting on *The Celestial Hierarchy* of Pseudo-Dionysius.

Texts: *Selected Spiritual Writings* (London: Faber, 1962).

Ildephonsus of Toledo (ca. 607–667)

A Benedictine monk who spent his life in his home city, founding a convent, of which he became abbot, and succeeding his uncle as archbishop (657).

Irenaeus of Lyon (d. ca. 202)

A Greek Christian from Anatolia who became the second bishop of Lyon following the martyrdom of Pothinus. He combatted Gnosticism and is the earliest witness to the canonicity of all four Gospels.

Texts: *Against the Heresies* 1–3, trans. Dominic J. Unger with John J. Dillon and Irenaeus M. C. Steenberg (New York: Paulist Press, 1992–); *Ante-Nicene Fathers*, ed. Alexander Roberts and James Donaldson, vol. 1 (1885; Peabody, Mass.: Hendrickson, 1995) 309–602;

*Demonstration of the Apostolic Preaching*, ed. Iain M. MacKenzie, trans. J. Armitage Robinson (Aldershot: Ashgate, 2002).

Irimbert of Admont (ca. 1104–1176)

The Benedictine abbot of Seeon (1147) and of Michelsberg (1160) in Bavaria and, finally, of Admont (1172) in Austria, where he succeeded his elder brother, Godfrey.

Isidore of Seville (ca. 560–636)

Educated in the cathedral school founded by his much elder brother, Leander, he succeeded him as archbishop (ca. 600) and promoted the school model for other Spanish dioceses. His *Etymologies* advanced an encyclopedic expository style, and he has been considered the last of the Latin Church Fathers.

Texts: *De Ecclesiasticis Officiis*, trans. Thomas L. Knoebel (Mahwah, N.J.: Newman, 2008); *The Etymologies of Isidore of Seville*, trans. Stephen A. Barney, W. J. Lewis, J. A. Beach, and Oliver Berghof (Cambridge: Cambridge University Press, 2006).

Jerome (ca. 347–420)

Baptized while a student in Rome, he traveled widely with companions to learn about the Christian faith. He lived as a desert hermit, and was ordained. After studying Scripture under Gregory Nazianzen in Constantinople, he returned to Rome, where he produced a Latin translation of the Bible, known as the Vulgate. He also translated many of Origen's homilies from Greek into Latin. His promotion of asceticism led to conflicts with the Roman clergy, and he left the city, visiting Alexandria and Palestine and settling in Bethlehem.

Texts: *The Commentaries of Origen and Jerome on St. Paul's Epistle to the Ephesians*, trans. Ronald E. Heine (Oxford: Oxford University Press, 2002); *Commentary on Isaiah*, trans. Thomas P. Scheck (New York: Paulist Press, 2015); *Commentary on Matthew*, trans. Thomas P. Scheck (Washington, D.C.: Catholic University of America Press, 2008); *Commentary on Jeremiah*, trans. Michael Graves (Downers Grove, Ill.: IVP, 2012); *Homilies*, trans. Marie Liguori Ewald, 2 vols. (Washington, D.C.: Catholic University of America Press, 1964–1966); *Nicene and Post-Nicene Fathers*, second series, ed. Philip Schaff and Henry Wace, vol. 6 (1893; Peabody, Mass.: Hendrickson, 1995); *St. Jerome's Commentaries on Galatians, Titus, and Philemon*, trans. Thomas P. Scheck (Washington, D.C.: Catholic University of America Press, 2010).

Joachim of Flora (ca. 1135–1202)

A Calabrian legal clerk who converted to the Christian faith while in Jerusalem on pilgrimage (ca. 1159), then lived as a hermit before joining the Cistercian abbey of Sambucina, then the Benedictine abbey of Corazzo, where he was ordained priest and later elected abbot (ca. 1177). After spending time in Rome, he founded his own monastery at Flora in Calabria (1188), under a strict interpretation of the Cistercian rule. After his death, his theology of history was condemned.

John Cassian (ca. 360–435)

A wealthy and educated Scythian, he toured monasteries in Palestine and Egypt. He was made a deacon in Constantinople and spent several years in the patriarchal court. While on a diplomatic mission to Rome, he accepted an invitation to found an abbey near Marseilles (ca. 415), which became a model for subsequent Western communities. Benedict of Nursia commended his works.

Text: *The Collations*, trans. Jerome Bertram (Leominster: Gracewing, 2015).

John Chrysostom (ca. 349–407)

Born in Antioch and baptized in early adulthood, he studied rhetoric but turned to theology and asceticism. He was made a deacon (381), ordained a priest (386), and was a popular and eloquent preacher. As patriarch of Constantinople (from 397) he was twice exiled to the Black Sea. The most widely used Orthodox liturgy bears his name.

Texts: *Homilies on Genesis*, trans. Robert C. Hill, 3 vols. (Washington, D.C.: Catholic University of America Press, 1986–1992); *On the Incomprehensible Nature of God*, trans. Paul W. Harkins (Washington, D.C.: Catholic University of America Press, 2000); *Nicene and Post-Nicene Fathers*, first series, ed. Philip Schaff, vols. 9–14 (1889; Peabody, Mass.: Hendrickson, 1995).

John of Damascus (ca. 675–749)

The son of a Syrian Christian civil servant in the Damascus Caliphate, who became a monk and strongly opposed iconoclasm. He is regarded as the last of the Greek Fathers.

John of Ruusbroec (1293/1294–1381)

A Flemish mystic who wrote in Dutch. He became a prebendary at the Church of Saint Gudula in Brussels (1318), but later retired to a hermitage at Groenendaal (1343), which developed into a community of canons with him as its prior (1349).

Texts: *The Complete Ruusbroec*, eds. Guido de Baere and Thom Mertens, 2 vols. (Turnhout: Brepols, 2014).

John of Salisbury (ca. 1120–1180)

Born in Salisbury, he studied in Paris under Peter Abelard and others, and in Chartres. He became secretary (1148) to Archbishop Theobald of Canterbury and to his successor, Thomas Becket, whose infamous murder he witnessed, then Bishop of Chartres (1176).

Text: *Policraticus*, trans. Cary J. Nederman (Cambridge: Cambridge University Press, 1990).

John of the Cross (1542–1591)

A Spaniard who joined the Carmelite Order (1564) and was ordained a priest (1567). With Teresa of Ávila, and amidst great controversy, he founded the Discalced Carmelites.

John Scotus Eriugena [also Erigena] (ca. 815–ca. 877)

An Irish theologian influenced by Neoplatonism who moved to Aachen (ca. 845) to teach in the imperial court. His competence in

Greek was rare in the West at that time, and he translated Pseudo-Dionysius, Gregory of Nyssa, and Maximus the Confessor.

Text: *Periphyseon*, trans. I. P. Sheldon-Williams and John J. O' Meara (Montreal: Bellarmin, 1987).

Jonas of Orleans (ca. 760–843)

A courtier to the imperial kings of Aquitaine, he became bishop of Orleans (817) and opposed the iconoclasm of Claudius of Turin.

Julian of Toledo (642–690)

Born in Toledo of Jewish parents but educated as a Christian in the cathedral school, he became a monk, then abbot of Agali, and later his city's archbishop (680). He asserted the primacy of his see over the whole Iberian peninsula and revised the Mozarabic liturgy.

Justin Martyr (100–165)

In the course of his education, he sampled the teachings of several schools, but subsequently embraced the Christian faith and was eventually martyred.

Text: *Dialogue with Trypho*, trans. Thomas B. Falls with Thomas P. Halton (Washington, D.C.: Catholic University of America Press, 2003).

Leo the Great (400–461)

A deacon in the papal court, he became pope (440) and with imperial support established papal authority over Gaul. His credal *Tome* was accepted by the Council of Chalcedon (451).

Text: *Nicene and Post-Nicene Fathers*, second series, ed. Philip Schaff and Henry Wace, vol. 12 (1895; Peabody, Mass.: Hendrickson, 1995).

Martin of Léon (ca. 1130–1203)

An Augustinian canon at the church of Saint Isidore in the royal capital of Léon in the northwest of the Iberian peninsula.

Maximus of Turin (ca. 380–ca. 465)

A bishop in northern Italy. Many of his sermons survive.
Text: *Sermons*, trans. Boniface Ramsey (Mahwah, N.J.: Newman Press, 1989).

Maximus the Confessor (ca. 580–662)

A senior Byzantine civil servant who became a monk and then abbot at Chrysopolis near Constantinople. When the Persians invaded (626), he fled to Carthage, where he accrued further political and spiritual authority. He promoted the doctrine that Christ had two wills, and he was present at the Lateran Council (649), where the opposing position of Monothelitism was condemned. However, he was arrested (658) on the orders of the emperor, taken to Constantinople, put on trial, and exiled. Four years later, he was placed on trial again, mutilated, and exiled to the eastern Black Sea, dying soon after.

Melito of Sardis (d. ca. 180)

A Jew by birth, he nevertheless embraced Greek culture and promoted Johannine theology. He became the bishop of his city in western Anatolia and compiled the first known Old Testament canon.

Methodius of Olympus (d. ca. 311)

Bishop of his city in southern Anatolia. Against Origen, he promoted bodily resurrection, although, in common with him, he deployed allegorical scriptural exegesis.
Texts: *Ante-Nicene Fathers*, ed. Alexander Roberts and James Donaldson, vol. 6 (1886; Peabody, Mass.: Hendrickson, 1995), 305–402.

Nicetas Stethatos (ca. 1005–ca. 1090)

A Byzantine monk, theologian, and later abbot of the famed Stoudios Monastery in Constantinople.
Text: *The Philokalia*, trans. G. E. H. Palmer, Philip Sherrard, and Kallistos Ware, vol. 4 (London: Faber & Faber, 1995), 76–174.

Nicholas Cabasilas (d. 1392)

Born in Thessalonica, he moved to Constantinople soon after the accession of John VI Kantakouzenos, with whom he was on good terms, as Byzantine emperor. He was a mystic and a liturgical commentator.

Texts: Nicholas Cabasilas, *A Commentary on the Divine Liturgy*, trans. J. M. Hussey and P. A. McNulty (Crestwood, N.Y.: Saint Vladimir's Seminary Press, 1960); *The Life in Christ*, trans. Carmino J. Decatanzaro (Crestwood, N.Y.: Saint Vladimir's Seminary Press, 1974).

Nicholas of Cusa (1401–1464)

Born in Cusa in the Rhineland, he studied at Heidelberg, Padua, Cologne, and Paris. A papal envoy with extensive experience in mediating Church disputes and relations with the state, he was created a cardinal (1448), prince-bishop of Brixen (1450), and vicar-general of the papal states (1459).

Texts: *The Catholic Concordance*, trans. Paul E. Sigmund (Cambridge: Cambridge University Press, 1996); *Selected Spiritual Writings*, ed. Lawrence H. Bond (New York: Paulist Press, 1997).

Odo of Cluny (ca. 878–942)

A young nobleman who became a canon at the wealthy abbey of Saint Martin at Tours but withdrew to lead a more ascetic life. He joined the Benedictine abbey at Baume in Burgundy, where Berno was abbot, and was ordained priest there. Berno founded the abbey of Cluny, and Odo succeeded him as abbot (927), leading the reform of discipline and asserting independence from secular influences.

Odo of Ourscamp (or Soissons) (d. 1171/1172)

As chancellor of Notre Dame cathedral, he taught at the University of Paris, where he introduced the question format that came to characterize Scholastic teaching. He became the Cistercian abbot of Ourscamp (1167), near Soissons in northeastern France, then a cardinal.

Origen (184/185–253/254)

A Greek Christian ascetic who studied under Clement in Alexandria, then taught there, founding the city's school of theology. He visited Rome, Arabia, and Caesarea in Palestine, where he was later ordained, in order that he might preach without controversy, and settled there (232). During the Maximinian persecution (235–238), he fled to Caesarea in Cappadocia and later visited Athens. He was imprisoned and tortured in the Decian persecution (250), dying shortly after from his injuries. Eusebius admired him.

Texts: *Ante-Nicene Fathers*, vol. 4, ed. Alexander Roberts and James Donaldson (1885; Peabody, Mass.: Hendrickson, 1995), 237–669; *Commentary on the Epistle to the Romans*, trans. Thomas P. Scheck (Washington, D.C.: Catholic University of America Press, 2001–2002); *Commentary on the Gospel according to John*, trans. Ronald E. Heine, 2 vols. (Washington, D.C.: Catholic University of America Press, 1989–1993); *Contra Celsum* [*Against Celsus*], trans. Henry Chadwick (Cambridge: Cambridge University Press, 1964); *On First Principles*, trans. G.W. Butterworth (London: SPCK, 1936); *Homilies 1–14 on Ezekiel*, trans. Thomas P. Scheck (New York: Paulist Press, 2010); *Homilies on Genesis and Exodus*, trans. Ronald E. Heine (Washington, D.C.: Catholic University of America Press, 1982); *Homilies on Jeremiah and 1 Kings 28*, trans. John Clark Smith (Washington, D.C.: Catholic University of America Press, 1998); *Homilies on Joshua*, trans. Barbara Bruce (Washington, D.C.: Catholic University of America Press, 2002); *Homilies on Judges*, trans. Elizabeth Ann Dively Lauro (Washington, D.C.: Catholic University of America Press, 2010); *Homilies on Leviticus, 1–16*, trans. Gary Wayne Barkley (Washington, D.C.: Catholic University of America Press, 1990); *Homilies on Luke. Fragments on Luke*, trans. Joseph T. Lienhard (Washington, D.C.: Catholic University of America Press, 1996); *Homilies on Numbers*, trans. Thomas P. Scheck (Westmont, Ill.: IVP, 2009); *The Song of Songs: Commentary and Homilies*, trans. R. P. Lawson (London: Newman Press, 1957).

Othloh of Saint Emmeram (ca. 1010–ca. 1072)

A Bavarian cleric who became a monk (1032), then dean (1055), at the abbey of Saint Emmeram in Regensburg. Owing to conflicts with his abbot and his bishop, he later spent time in the abbeys of Fulda and Amorbach.

Papias of Hierapolis (ca. 60–130)

A disciple of the apostle John and the first known figure to discuss the authorship of the Gospels.

Paschasius Radbertus (786–865)

An orphan raised by nuns, he became a monk at the renowned abbey of Corbie in northern France. He disputed eucharistic theology with his abbot Ratramnus (836), but then became abbot himself (844), although he later resigned (854) to devote more time to his studies.

Text: *Early Medieval Theology*, ed. George E. McCracken (London: SCM, 1957), 94–108.

Paulinus of Nola (ca. 354–431)

Raised in Bordeaux, he became a Roman consul and the governor of Campania (ca. 380), within which was Nola, where the shrine of Saint Felix was located. On a return visit to Bordeaux, he married Theresia and was baptized, then was ordained a priest in Barcelona (ca. 393). He returned to Nola with his wife (395) and was elected the city's bishop soon after her death (410).

Text: *Letters of St. Paulinus of Nola*, trans. P. G. Walsh, 2 vols. (Westminster, Md.: Newman Press, 1966–1967).

Peter Abelard (1079–1142)

A Breton who began studies at the cathedral school of Paris (1100) but clashed with his teacher, William of Champeaux, and established his own schools near the city, becoming famous. He courted the learned Héloïse d'Argenteuil (ca. 1115) and had a son with her. He then became a monk at the royal abbey of Saint Denis, while she entered a convent. Amid conflicts with his fellow monks, he left and established a hermitage in the Champagne. He was then abbot of Saint Gildas, back in Brittany (ca. 1127), but left there, too, becoming abbot of the new convent of the Paraclete, north of Paris (ca. 1130), where Héloïse was abbess. He recommenced teaching in the metropolis, but his logic was opposed by William of Saint Thierry and Bernard of Clairvaux. He was condemned at a council in Sens (1141) and finished his life at a priory in Burgundy.

Peter Cantor (d. 1197)

A Scholastic theologian who studied at Reims and Paris, where he became the cathedral chanter.

Peter Cellensis (b. ca. 1115–1183)

An aristocrat who became a Benedictine monk and was successively abbot of La Celle near Troyes (1150), abbot of Saint Rémy (1162), and bishop of Chartres (1181).

Text: *Selected Works*, trans. Hugh Feiss (Kalamazoo, Mich.: Cistercian, 1987).

Peter of Cornwall (1139/1140–1221)

A Cornishman who studied in London and became an Augustinian canon at the Holy Trinity priory, Aldgate, and later prior (1197).

Rabanus Maurus (ca. 780–856)

A native of Mainz, he became a Benedictine monk at Fulda and was made a deacon. With Haymo of Halberstadt, he studied diligently under Alcuin at Tours. He returned to Fulda (803) to build up the abbey's school, was ordained a priest (814), and elected abbot (822). Close to the end of his life (847), he was appointed his city's archbishop. His hymns include "Come, Holy Ghost, Our Souls Inspire" and "Christ, the Fair Glory of the Holy Angels".

Text: *Early Medieval Theology*, ed. George E. McCracken (London: SCM, 1957), 300–13.

Remi of Auxerre (ca. 841–908)

A Burgundian Benedictine monk of the late Carolingian Renaissance who taught at the abbey of Saint Germain in Auxerre, then at the cathedral school in Reims (883), then in Paris. He combined classical and Christian thought, partly under the influence of the Irish theologian John Scotus Eriugena.

Richard of Saint Victor (d. 1173)

A Scot who studied at the abbey of Saint Victor and rose through its ranks to become prior (1162).

Texts: *Interpretation of Scripture: Theory*, trans. Hugh Feiss and A. B. Kraebel (New York: New City Press, 2011), 287–370; *Trinity and Creation*, trans. Christopher P. Evans (New York: New City Press, 2011), 195–352.

Rupert of Deutz (d. ca. 1129)

A Benedictine monk of the abbey of Saint Lawrence in Liège, he became abbot (1120) of Deutz near Cologne. He strongly believed in Christ's physical presence in the Eucharist.

Text: *Early Medieval Theology*, ed. George E. McCracken (London: SCM, 1957), 249–82.

Severus of Antioch (d. ca. 540)

An Anatolian Greek who studied in Alexandria and became patriarch of Antioch (511). He led and unified the opposition to the two-natures Christology of the Council of Chalcedon, although when a new emperor took office he fled to Alexandria (518), where he spent the rest of his life.

Text: Pauline Allen and C. T. R. Hayward, *Severus of Antioch* (London: Routledge, 2004).

Sylvester of Ferrara (ca. 1474–1528)

A Dominican who was prior of houses in his native Ferrara and then in Bologna, before election as his order's master general (1525).

Tertullian (ca. 155–ca. 225)

A Berber layman of Carthage who converted to the Christian faith (ca. 197) and is regarded as the founder of Western theology. His moralism and rejection of pagan philosophy influenced Cyprian and Augustine.

Texts: *Adversus Marcionem*, trans. Ernest Evans (Oxford: Oxford University Press, 1972); *Ante-Nicene Fathers*, vols. 3–4, ed. Alexander Roberts and James Donaldson (1885; Peabody, Mass.: Hendrickson, 1995) *Early Latin Theology*, trans. S. L. Greenslade (London: SCM, 1956); *Homily on Baptism*, trans. Ernest Evans (London: SPCK, 1964); *On the Testimony of the Soul and on the "Prescription" of Heretics*, trans. Herbert Brindley (London: SPCK, 1914); *Tertullian*, trans. Geoffrey D. Dunn (London: Routledge, 2004); *Treatise against Praxeas*, trans. Ernest Evans (London: SPCK, 1948).

Theodore of Mopsuestia (ca. 350–428)

Born into a wealthy family in Antioch, where he was a friend of John Chrysostom, he considered marriage but instead pursued the monastic life. He became bishop of Mopsuestia (392) in Anatolia and was widely respected.

Text: *Commentary on the Twelve Prophets*, trans. Robert C. Hill (Washington, D.C.: Catholic University of America Press, 2004).

Theodoret of Cyrus (ca. 393–ca. 460)

A native of Antioch who became the bishop of Cyrus in Syria (423), he defended Nestorius against the charge of promoting a two-person Christology and opposed Cyril of Alexandria.

Text: *Eranistes*, trans. Gerard H. Ettlinger (Washington, D.C.: Catholic University of America Press, 2003).

Thomas Aquinas (1225–1274)

From the Aquino region of central Italy, he was schooled as a child at the Benedictine abbey of Monte Cassino, then relocated to the University of Naples (1239). Against the wishes of his family, he became a Dominican, studying in Paris (1245) and following his teacher Albert the Great to teach in Cologne (1248). He returned to Paris (1252), then taught in Orvieto (1261), Rome (1265), and Paris again (1268), where Bonaventure and other Franciscans charged him with promoting the philosophy of Averroes. He returned to Naples (1272), where he established a house of studies.

Texts: *Commentary on the Sentences*, trans. Jason Mitchell, Beth Mortensen, and Dylan Schrader, 10 vols. (Lander, Wyo.: Aquinas Institute, 2017–); *On the Power of God* (London: Burns, Oates & Washbourne, 1932); *Summa contra gentiles*, trans. Anton C. Pegis, James F. Anderson, Vernon J. Bourke, and Charles J. O'Neil, 4 vols. (Notre Dame, Ind.: University of Notre Dame Press, 1975); *Summa theologiae*, 61 vols. (London: Blackfriars, 1964–81).

Walafrid Strabo (ca. 808–849)

A Benedictine monk who studied at the abbey of Reichenau on Lake Constance, then under Rabanus Maurus at Fulda. He tutored the emperor's son, then returned to Reichenau as abbot (838).

Text: Alice L. Harting-Correa, *Walahfrid Strabo's Libellus de exordiis et incrementis quarundam in observationibus ecclesiasticis rerum. A Translation and Liturgical Commentary* (Leiden: Brill, 1996).

Walter of Châtillon (1135–1180)

A French poet and theologian who studied at the University of Paris.

Text: *The Shorter Poems: Christmas Hymns, Love Lyrics, and Moral-Satirical Verse*, trans. David A. Traill (Oxford: Clarendon Press, 2013).

William of Auvergne (d. 1249)

From a rural French family, he studied and taught at the University of Paris, promoting an Aristotelian theology. He became a cathedral canon, then was made bishop of Paris (1228). Later, he formally condemned ten theological propositions (1241).

William of Ockham (ca. 1287–1347)

A Franciscan Scholastic theologian born in southern England, who studied in Oxford before working in Avignon and then in exile in

Munich. He composed a controversial commentary on the *Sentences* of Peter Lombard.

William of Saint Thierry (d. 1148)

A nobleman from Liège who became a Benedictine monk at the abbey of Saint Nicaise in Reims, then abbot of the nearby abbey of Saint Thierry (1119). He was a close friend of Bernard of Clairvaux, resigning his position (1135) to move to the new Cistercian abbey at Signy.

Text: *The Golden Epistle: A Letter to the Brethren at Mont-Dieu* (Kalamazoo, Mich.: Cistercian, 1980).

# Index